Praise for *The Story of Tibet:*

"This book presents a much wider range of material than we are accustomed to hearing discussed by His Holiness the Dalai Lama. . . . It is the Dalai Lama's mastery of a wealth of historical information that makes this captivating reading. He candidly discusses topics such as the early history of Buddhism in Tibet, the first incarnate Lama, his memories of Chairman Mao, and his favorite image of the Buddha." —*Tricycle*

"Laird uncovers a history of Tibet not found in other books about the country." —*Phayul*

"A thoughtful dialogue . . . about Tibet's past not simply as a sequence of events, but as seen through the perspectives of myth, spirituality, morality, human frailty, and fate. . . . Will deepen general readers' knowledge of Tibet, its religion, and its engaging leader." —*Kirkus Reviews*

"The Fourteenth Dalai Lama's fresh account of Tibetan myth and history, as shared at Dharamsala over a three year period with Thomas Laird, is wonderful instruction and a great true pleasure, not less so because of the small informal moments that clarify these encounters with that delightful Buddha being who manifests in the beleaguered public figure of His Holiness." —Peter Matthiessen

"Thomas Laird's lively conversations with His Holiness the Dalai Lama about the history and mythology of Tibet couldn't come at a better moment, as China stubbornly persists in negating the distinctive Tibetan identity. The honestly, subtlety, and complexity of His Holiness's thoughts on these crucial matters comes through in these fascinating dialogues. Everyone who cares about Tibet, or about a stable peace in Asia, should read this amazing account."
—Robert Thurman, author of *Inner Revolution*, Professor of Buddhist studies, Columbia University

"Thomas Laird captures the beauty, the magnificence, and the humor of this world spiritual leader, the Dalai Lama."
—James Lilley, former U.S. Ambassador to China and South Korea, and author of *China Hands: Nine Decades of Adventure, Espionage, and Diplomacy in Asia*

"Throughout, Laird's colorful and lively writing brings to life thousands of years of Tibetan history, inviting the reader on his journey to a strange and wonderful land." —*Publishers Weekly*

"Laird teaches a memorable and vivid history lesson about a remote mysterious place that, in terms of its sheer survival, has implications for our own lives." —*New Orleans Times Picayune*

"*The Story of Tibet* . . . is a work of real value . . . a narrative that is readable, instructive, and at times touching." —Straight.com

"A fascinating journey to a strange and wonderful country. . . An amazing account." —*Derby Evening Telegraph*

"The Dalai Lama's input is invaluable in the telling of a story that has been the victim of disinformation and revisionist history. The result is an authoritative guide to Tibet's turbulent past (and present)."
—*Western Daily Press (UK)*

"The research and academic weight of this study is breathtaking. . . . The cut-and-thrust debate between Laird and the Dalai Lama . . . brings the history alive. Laird reveals much about the personality and human frailties of the Tibetan leader, what rattles him and when he felt acutely betrayed." —*The Age (Australia)*

"A significant contribution to the outpouring of recent writings on Tibet." —*Library Journal*

THE STORY OF TIBET

Conversations with the Dalai Lama

Also by Thomas Laird

Into Tibet: The CIA's First Atomic Spy and His Secret
Expedition to Lhasa

The Dalai Lama's Secret Temple: Tantric Wall Paintings from Tibet
(with Ian Baker)

East of Lo Monthang: In the Land of Mustang
(with Peter Matthiessen)

THE
STORY OF TIBET

Conversations with the Dalai Lama

THOMAS LAIRD

Grove Press
New York

Published simultaneously in Canada
Printed in the United States of America

FIRST PAPERBACK EDITION

Library of Congress Cataloging-in-Publication Data

Laird, Thomas, 1953-
    The story of Tibet : conversations with His Holiness the Dalai Lama / by Thomas Laird.
      p. cm
    Includes bibliographical references and index.
    ISBN-13: 978-0-8021-4327-3
    ISBN-10: 0-8021-4327-x
    1. Tibet (China)—History. 2. Bstan-'dzin-rgya-mtsho, Dalai Lama XIV, 1935- —Interviews.
I. Bstan-'dzin-rgya-mtsho, Dalai Lama XIV, 1935- . II. Title.
DS786.L25 2006
951'.5—dc22
                                                     2006041700

Grove Press
an imprint of Grove/Atlantic, Inc.
841 Broadway
New York, NY 10003

Distributed by Publishers Group West

www.groveatlantic.com

07 08 09 10 11 10 9 8 7 6 5 4 3 2 1

If it is reasonable action which is by nature beneficial to truth and justice, then by abandoning procrastination and discouragement the more you encounter obstruction the more you should strengthen your courage and make effort. That is the conduct of a wise and good person.

Tibetan Shakya Bhikshu
Dalai Lama, Tenzin Gyatso

To Tenzin Gyatso, the Fourteenth Dalai Lama of Tibet
For the people of China and Tibet

CONTENTS

LIST OF MAPS

Maps drawn by Haisam Hussein (www.haisam.com). The borders for all maps, with the exception of the modern maps, should not be considered definitive.

LIST OF ILLUSTRATIONS

INSERT ONE

p. 1. *Left,* mural, Drepung Monastery. *Top right,* mural, Bhutan. *Bottom right,* rock painting, shores of Lake Namtso. All photographs © Thomas Laird.

p. 2. *Top and bottom left,* mural, Norbulingka, Lhasa, circa *1956. Bottom right,* statue in collection of Tenzin Gyatso, Fourteenth Dalai Lama of Tibet, Dharamsala, India. All photographs © Thomas Laird.

p. 3. *Top right,* the Jo, in the Jokhang, Lhasa. *Top left,* Ramoche Buddha, in Ramoche Temple, Lhasa. *Left middle,* mural fragment, second floor, Jokhang, Lhasa. *Left bottom,* wooden carving, ground floor, near the Jo, in the Jokhang, Lhasa. All photographs ©Thomas Laird.

p. 4. Photograph of armored Tibetan cavalryman © 2006, Metropolitan Museum of Art. Bequest of George C. Stone, 1935; Bequest of Joseph V. McMullan, 1973; Gift of Mrs. Faïe J. Joyce, 1970. Objects are Tibetan, and possibly Bhutanese and Nepalese, eighteenth-nineteenth century, iron, gold, silver, copper allow, wood, leather, and textile.

p. 5. *Top left,* The Dalai Lama's favorite image of the Buddha, now in the Lahore National Museum, Pakistan. Carved in the Kingdom of Ghandara. Parts of the territory of this kingdom are now within the modern borders of both India and Pakistan. Statue is circa 200 A.D. *Top right,* mural of the Buddha from Drathang, Tibet, circa eleventh century. The style for this mural of the Buddha originated in India (drawing on Greek influences

c4a 1954, China. The Norbulingka Institute, Sidhpur, India. *Bottom,* photograph, of (left to right) Panchen Lama, the Fourteenth Dalai Lama, and Prime Minister Nehru. The Norbulingka Institute, Sidhpur, India.

p. 12.   Top, the Fourteenth Dalai Lama (on horse) and entourage during their escape from Lhasa to India, 1950. The Norbulingka Institute, Sidhpur, India. *Bottom,* the Fourteenth Dalai Lama and entourage arriving at the Indian border, 1950. DIIR/Tibet Museum, CIA.

p. 13.   *Top left,* Mao mural painted over Buddhist murals in Lhasa, Tibet. *Top right,* Mao banner above singing women, western Tibet. *Bottom,* statue of Yamantaka, in Lhasa, is just one of many statues and monasteries destroyed in Lhasa during the Cultural Revolution. All photographs © Thomas Laird.

p. 14.   Drepung Monastery and ruins of parts of Drepung destroyed during the Cultural Revolution, photographed, 1997, during a ritual display of a large appliqué thangkha of the Buddha, Lhasa, © Thomas Laird.

p. 15.   *Top left,* the Fourteenth Dalai Lama and Pope John Paul: DllR/Tibet Museum, CTA. *Top middle,* Choekyi Gyaltsen, the Tenth Dalai Lama shortly before his death in 1989: DIIR/Tibet Museum, CTA. *Top right,* Gedhun Choekyi Nyima, the Eleventh Dalai Lama, recognized by the Fourteenth Dalai Larna. He is now the world's youngest political prisoner, and China has recognized another boy as 'the Eleventh Panchen Lama': DIIR/Tibet Museum, CTA. *Bottom,* Photograph of photographs showing the Fourteenth Dalai Lama with Bill Clinton and Tony Blair, Barkhor, Lhasa, photographed 1992. Photograph © Thomas Laird.

p. 16.   *Top left,* Tibetan nomad in western Tibet. Barka Plain in front of Lake Manosovar and Mt. Gurlamandhata, western Tibet: many nomads live on the plain. *Bottom left,* the seventeenth Karmapa, was reborn in Tibet (after the Sixteenth Karmapa died in Chicago), and was ultimately recognized by both the fourteenth Dalai Lama and the Chinese Government. He was raised in Tibet until his mysterious, and secretive, journey to India in 1999——where he lives now in exile as he pursues his religious education. *Bottom right,* young boy prostrating in front of the Jokhang, Lhasa, Tibet. All photographs © Thomas Laird.

FOREWORD

This book draws on several decades of primary research and on eighteen personal audiences with His Holiness the Dalai Lama in India between November 1997 and July 2000. All fifty hours of our conversation were in English, recorded with either video or audio equipment, or both. Michael Victor, our secretary, spent months transcribing the tapes, a heroic job that I gratefully acknowledge here. The scholar Tenzin Tinley kindly checked the draft transcript against the tapes. The final transcript, which runs more than 320 single-spaced pages, is the most important primary source for this book, which is in essence a series of conversations with His Holiness about the story of Tibet.

I've made it clear when the Dalai Lama is speaking, and when I am speaking. My opinions about Tibetan history, along with those of many others who contributed to this project, are clearly delineated from those of His Holiness, and no endorsement of these different viewpoints by him should be inferred by their appearance in this book. His Holiness encouraged me to edit his English when required, which I did only when necessary to clarify meaning; words that have been added are *(in italicized parentheses)*. He also gave me permission to combine sentences, if they were about the same subject but from different interviews—for instance, when he would recall later something he wanted to add to a particular subject. His Holiness selected three scholars to double-check all of his quotations in this book to ensure accuracy: my thanks to these gentlemen.

Before my first conversation with His Holiness the Dalai Lama, I spent several months immersed in preparatory research to create the series of questions that would form the backbone of our discussions. That research continued throughout the interviews, and then during the six years spent writing the book. The Library of Tibetan Works and Archives in Dharamsala, India, was an invaluable resource, and I thank the librarian Pema Yeshi for his assistance. Likewise, State Department files at the National Archives in College Park, Maryland, helped inform my understanding of the period from 1942 to 1960. The books and other sources that I read or consulted are listed in the bibliography. Readers curious about the facts behind certain passages will find unnumbered notes citing source material in the endnotes section.

There is no universally accepted transliteration standard for Tibetan, and the most precise transliteration methods create what is gibberish to the uninitiated. Though experts know that "Srong-brtsan-sgam-po" is an exact transliteration of the name of Tibet's first great emperor, the average reader will prefer "Songzen Gampo." Ease of reading and common usage have guided all transliteration. My apologies to specialists who might object to the resulting lack of consistency.

This book would not exist save for the generosity and patience of His Holiness the Dalai Lama. I also gratefully acknowledge the assistance of Tenzin Choegyal, Tenzin Geyche Tethong, and Tenzin Taklha, who contributed immensely to the dialogue in many ways, and to Venerable Lhakdor, who aided the Dalai Lama during our talks. Sincere thanks to Lodi Gyari, Tashi Wangdi, and Lesley Friedell for their assistance in seeing this book published. I also acknowledge His Holiness the Sixteenth Karmapa and Anne Thondup, who both shaped my initial interest in Tibet. Western scholars of Tibet have kindly engaged me in hours of conversation, offering a crucial education about Tibet, its culture and its history. In particular, I acknowledge Warren Smith, Melvyn Goldstein, Robert Thurman, Thupton Jinpa, Tom Grunfeld, and Eliot Sperling, though I am sure each of them will find things to disagree with in these pages. This list fails to mention the many scholars and friends who enhanced my understanding of Tibet over the past thirty years. Jann Fenner supported me unstintingly every step of the way, no matter the cost: thank you. Brando Skyhorse, editor, and Morgan Entrekin, publisher, both devoted so much more to this book than is normally called for that I remain in their debt. I extend my sincere thanks also to Kay Murray, Jan Constantine, and the Author's Guild, as well as to Donald David, Scott Kessler, and Brian Bloom at Cozen O'Connor for their generous support in my time of need. I alone bear responsibility for any error of fact or interpretation that follows.

A number of Tibetans generously granted on-the-record interviews, including Gyalo Thondup, the Dalai Lama's elder brother, along with the nuns Pasang Lhamo and Chuying Kunsang. Additionally, I interviewed Tibetans and Chinese across Tibet and have concealed their identities to protect them. Some Tibetans in both India and Nepal preferred to remain as unacknowledged background sources.

Besides formal interviews, I've gained a sense of Tibet and its people from living alongside exiled Tibetans in Nepal during the past thirty years and while traveling in Tibet during the past twenty years. Hundreds of Tibetans and Nepalese of Tibetan ethnic descent—yak herders, writers, monks, farmers, scholars, telephone operators, carpet knotters, shoemakers, yogis, business executives, painters, taxi drivers, village priests, and others—graciously offered their friendship, wisdom, songs, myths, and hospitality, for which I am forever in their debt. My heartfelt thanks to you all.

Thomas Laird
New Orleans
August 14, 2006
StoryofTibet@yahoo.com

INTRODUCTION

The Dalai Lama had just answered the last question on my list. We were coming to the end of my fourth interview with him for a magazine story. Like most who talk to him, I felt I'd met an exceptional human being and was inspired as much as awed. It was hard to pinpoint why. He answered my questions in a businesslike manner, but he did so in a way that made me wonder at the untapped possibility inside each of us.

Outside in the sunshine, a loud flock of mynah birds swooped through the forest that surrounds his small bungalow on a hilltop above the plains of India. He has purposely not re-created the pomp and splendor of the Potala in Lhasa since he fled his homeland in 1959 after the Chinese invasion. He calls himself a simple Buddhist monk, and there is a Zen-like sparseness to the rooms he inhabits in exile.

He adjusted his wine-red robe, and his rich brown eyes calmly stared at me, waiting for my next question. I brushed my sweaty palms across my jacket and looked at the blank half of the page, below my prepared questions. I summoned my courage and explained that although I am not a historian, I wanted to write a history of Tibet.

He looked at me quizzically. "There are excellent academic histories of Tibet," I explained, "but what is lacking is a popular history of Tibet—aimed at modern Westerners and Chinese—that is accurate, concise, and easy to read. You told me two years ago, in our first meeting, that Tibetan history is complex. You sounded despondent, as if it was impossible to explain Tibet's history to the average person. The way you said that haunted me, and since then I found myself reading everything available about Tibetan history. It is not impossible. I want to strip away the complexity and reveal the heart of the matter. I think that by focusing on your viewpoint of Tibetan history, this could be achieved. Most people will not read an academic history about Tibet, and they don't care what I think about Tibetan history, but they do want to know what you think about this history."

He continued to look at me, waiting.

"Would you work with me so I can write a popular history of Tibet?" I asked. "You know that no Dalai Lama has written a history of Tibet since the 1600s."

I had interviewed him four times previously over several years, so he knew that I was passionate and often frank enough to be rude. He seemed to find my impertinence refreshing or amusing, if only because so many others are formal and reverential with him. He also knew that I was an American writer and photographer who had lived in Nepal for the past twenty-seven years. What else did he see as he looked at me in silence for the next ten seconds? Whatever summation he made, it was made quickly.

"Yes, that would be a very important work. I will do that with you. Though I do not have the time to write such a history myself."

"I could interview you, as you have time," I replied eagerly, "and then write a book that presented your viewpoint. I would also present summaries from the historic consensus and the viewpoints of others who may agree with you or contradict what you say. It would require many hours of interviews."

A secretary was sitting in on the interview. He made a sudden disapproving noise—sucking his breath in through his nearly closed lips—and interjected, "Your Holiness, your schedule is so full I do not see how we could find the time for . . ."

Still looking directly at me, the Dalai Lama said, "It is important work. We will find the time. He is living in Nepal. It is close. He can come here as we have time. Yes?"

"Yes sir. I am happy to come here as you have time," I said.

"It should be easy to read, but it must also be true," he replied.

"Yes, that is my goal," I said.

"It is easy to talk about, but it will be hard work for you," the Dalai Lama said.

Over the course of the next seventeen months, I traveled to Dharamsala whenever the Dalai Lama had time to see me. He is a monk and has spent his life studying Buddhism, not history.

"Actually, I am not very interested in history," the Dalai Lama told me initially, "mainly because I don't know too much. When I was young, my teachers did not make any special effort to teach me about Tibetan history. I was trained as any ordinary monk at that time; my curriculum was devoted to Buddhist philosophy. As a boy, I learned about history from paintings and people talking, from world events. But it was not a subject I studied. After the Chinese invasion, after I left Tibet in 1959, I grew more interested in history. But I want to make it clear I am not a historian. In some cases I don't even know the details."

He laughs at the absurdity of the situation. The Dalai Lama's laughter is infectious, one of the first things I learned from working with him. It rumbles up from deep in his belly, beginning as a low note that shakes his whole body. By the time it reaches his face—and he takes off his glasses to wipe the tears away—high-pitched laughter, mine included, fills the room.

When we are both composed again, he continues.

"My teachers did not spend the time to teach me about history. But if someone asks my interpretation, then of course I have my own opinion. Sometimes I think my opinion could be sharper than others'." The frustration that crossed my face at his apparent contradiction amused him and he laughed again.

It was impossible not to join in, but even as I did so, I began to realize there would be obstacles to overcome in trying to bridge the gap between his beliefs as a Tibetan monk and my own beliefs as a Western journalist. He is, after all, a monk first.

The Dalai Lama spends four or five hours every day doing Buddhist meditation. One of the ideals—he would say practical attitudes—he cultivates through meditation is lack of attachment. Thus he is not easily angered or startled in most situations, and he does not blame others or outside events for his own reactions, as most of us would do.

One day during an interview, the Dalai Lama had just raised one arm straight above his head to make a point (he can be very animated when he speaks)—suddenly the windows in the room rattled with a distant loud explosion. Everyone in the room except the Dalai Lama was startled, and we all jumped in our seats and laughed nervously.

The Dalai Lama smiled at us. At the sound of the explosion, he had paused with his arm raised, his finger pointed straight. Neither arm nor finger wavered as he waited patiently for us to settle down; then he continued as though nothing had happened. He appeared to have no involuntary reaction at all. His utter stillness when everyone else flinched is the physical aspect of the lack of attachment he has developed through meditation.

Experimentation by Western researchers has confirmed that meditation masters can control such involuntary physiological responses and that most of us do not have this control. While detachment developed through mental training may seem abstract, or spiritual, it is fundamental to who the Dalai Lama is. A lifetime of meditation has changed not just how he physically responds to situations; it has changed how he sees the world and how he behaves within it. It would take several years for me to appreciate how his lack of attachment, born of intense meditation practice, has shaped his view of history.

During blocks of interviews scattered over the year, we outlined the essence of thousands of years of Tibetan history and myth. We began with distant Tibetan myths concerning the origins of the first Tibetans and then moved through the development of the Tibetan Empire in the eighth century, when Tibet stretched from what is now southwestern China to northern India. We discovered, at length, Tibet's greatest yogis, meditation masters, and ordinary Tibetans and covered the foundation of the institution of the Dalai Lama and the nation's giant monasteries. Next were the years of Mongol and Manchu domination and finally the Chinese invasion of 1950 and the Dalai Lama's meetings with Mao Tse-tung, just before the Dalai Lama fled the country in 1959. It was the entirety of Tibetan history, from the origins of Tibetans to the present day. As the scope of the project emerged, I was alternately terrified at the responsibility of such an undertaking and immensely happy for the opportunity to spend so much time with the Dalai Lama.

During our initial meetings, I first experienced the Dalai Lama's underlying Buddhist beliefs that give structure to his knowledge of Tibetan history. Buddhism, along with ancient Indian concepts that came with it to Tibet, such as reincarnation, has shaped how the Dalai Lama sees Tibetan history. Some, like the Dalai Lama's belief in reincarnation, were predictable; others, such as miracles or visions that non-Tibetans would call mythology, are spiritual events in Tibetan history that the Dalai Lama kept returning to and clearly felt were historically important. The Dalai Lama was quick to call some but not all of these events myth.

For example, he described an event that took place around 1920, in which a respected Buddhist teacher, Serkhong Rinpoche, was among a group of six people who had an audience with the Thirteenth Dalai Lama. The teacher had spent five hours a day, or more, meditating, over many years. For Tibetans he had "purified his mind." Five of the six who met the Dalai Lama that day had a normal meeting with him. The sixth man, Serkhong Rinpoche, though in the same room at the same time, did not see the Thirteenth as an ordinary man at all. He saw the Buddhist Bodhisattva Chenrizi instead; rather than conversing with the Thirteenth Dalai Lama, he heard Chenrizi give secret teachings on a meditation practice. This happened while everyone else—men who had not purified their minds—saw just a man with a mustache dressed in red robes talking about affairs of state. Which event took place?

"There can be two visions of the same thing," the Dalai Lama said, "one of people who have a pure insight developed through spiritual practice and one that is purely conventional. In these special cases—and these events are rare, but important—both are true, both are reality. So there are two viewpoints, one common and one uncommon. The uncommon viewpoint is not considered history, because historians cannot record these things. But we cannot say that all such things are just the imagination of the Buddhist faithful. They can also be true."

Two people looking at the same event might see two entirely different things because of who they are, what they have experienced in life, what they believe, or how they have trained their minds. It took a long time, and many examples, for me to understand how important this is to him and what a central place it has in his vision of Tibet and Tibetan history.

"We cannot discuss Tibetan history without an understanding of this," the Dalai Lama said.

As a journalist, I sometimes found his inclination to speak about the world from the uncommon viewpoint frustrating. This inclination shaped his thoughts, even about simple things. On one occasion, I asked him to talk about the importance of the Potala, which I saw as one of the most significant symbols of the Tibetan nation.

He looked at me blankly. "It's just a building," he shrugged with a small laugh.

It was as if he was being too literal, or that he resisted all metaphor. This was not the first time he had frustrated the journalist in me with this kind of response. Unlike Tibetans who meet the Dalai Lama—so reverential that they cannot contradict him or have an open dialogue with him—I could not restrain the anger in my voice. "What do you mean, it's just a building? It has been the symbol of the Tibetan nation for three hundred years. Was it 'just a building' to the young Tibetan who was arrested and beaten after he strapped explosives to his body in 1999 and tried to pull down the Chinese flag in front of the Potala?"

He looked at me gravely. "No, you are right. It was not just a building to him."

The Dalai Lama then proceeded to describe the construction of the Potala in detail. As he talked for half an hour, it became an amazing display of his trained memory. Historic eras and temple names flew off his lips without any hesitation, from a man who had told me he didn't know much about history.

When he was finished, he looked at me and said, "But still, for someone who has trained his mind, the Potala is still just a building. Meditation is not a philosophy; it is a technique to develop that type of attitude, detachment."

He had answered the question as I thought it should be, yet I could not let go entirely of my annoyance with his detachment.

"But you also understand that for the common man the Potala is much more than just another building?" I asked.

"Yes, as I said earlier, there are common and uncommon views of history, and of everything we see. We cannot understand the Potala or Tibet unless we understand this. We must approach Tibetan history from a holistic viewpoint. The Western academics just pick one viewpoint—say, political—and then draw their conclusions from that viewpoint alone. That is a mistake."

My face flushed in embarrassment as I realized I had made the same mistake. Though I was writing a popular history of Tibet, the work would also have to reflect the Dalai Lama's vision, his purity, complexity, and holistic viewpoint. I had to listen to him very carefully yet at the same time, unlike Tibetans, I needed to challenge the Dalai Lama to peel the layers of meaning within his words. Thankfully, the Dalai Lama welcomed the thrust and parry of such open debate. On a practical level, this encounter taught me to preface some questions by asking him for either the common or the uncommon view of history; I could not discuss history with him unless I distinguished between the two. According to his own beliefs, his ultimate truth at the "uncommon level" is that Tibet is no different from India, the United States, or anywhere else, and that ultimately all people are the same.

On the other hand, the history of Tibet, as the Dalai Lama understands it, does not describe an otherworldly Shangri-la, as some Westerners imagine Tibet was before the Chinese invasion of 1950. The Dalai Lama's detachment gives him a razor-sharp objectivity about Tibetan society before 1950. He acknowledged that Tibet was a deeply flawed nation—though I would point out that so are all countries—as he talked about "the Dharma," or the teachings of the Buddha.

"There was a negative aspect to Tibetans' devotion to Buddhism," the Dalai Lama said. "They had too much devotion. The religious leaders thought of religion and their monastery or order first and then thought of the Tibetan nation second, if at all. Their first concern was the Dharma. Worse, it was not even the true Dharma that they thought about. They were concerned with making things big and grand. They thought of big monasteries and big statues, as though this was the true Dharma. . . . This was foolish. This was one of the seeds in Tibetan history that led to today's Tibetan tragedy," he concluded. "This one-sided concentration on Dharma."

Only one other factor has influenced Tibetan history and the way the Dalai Lama understands it as much as Buddhism, and that is Tibet's relations with China and Mongolia during the past fourteen hundred years.

The Chinese government calls its 1950 invasion of Tibet a "peaceful liberation" in spite of the fact that Tibet had its own government, currency, and army and was largely devoid of Chinese inhabitants prior to 1950. Today Beijing says that an uninterrupted series of Chinese governments has ruled Tibet and China since Genghis Khan and his successors conquered both countries and the rest of Eurasia in the thirteenth century. Chinese president Hu Jintao asserted in 2005 that Tibet has been an "inalienable part of Chinese territory" from the time of the Mongol conquest onward.

Since 1912, schools have taught generations of Chinese students this very history. Yet over fifty years after China's invasion of Tibet, with the Dalai Lama and more than 135,000 other Tibetans living in exile, the two nations remain locked in battle about Tibet's status. As the Dalai Lama became a world figure, particularly after he received the Nobel Peace Prize in 1989, questions about the legitimacy of China's role in Tibet continue to mount.

Knowing all of this, the Dalai Lama chooses his words about China's view of Tibetan history carefully. "Modern Tibetan history is very delicate because the Chinese government always accuses me of trying to 'split' Tibet from the 'Motherland,'" he said. "Whether I keep silent or not, there is a lot of criticism. Maybe it's now best to present my viewpoint."

"Why is this so delicate for China?" I asked.

"An explanation of the past always has implications for the present," the Dalai Lama said. "This is why China is always insisting that Tibet is part of China now, and has always been part of China. They want to use the past to explain their actions in Tibet today. The past is not as simple as the Chinese government would make it. Most Chinese consider Tibet as a part of China. And most believe that history proves that. It is a fact for them. This is what they have been taught to believe," he concluded with a deep sigh.

The Dalai Lama's sigh, alive with the tragedies of humanity, echoed in my mind for days. But his amazing ability to reach out across any divide, to see the shared human heart in every situation, gave me hope and inspiration. As I embarked on a journey through fourteen hundred years of Tibetan history, I was moved by the Dalai Lama's willingness to frankly discuss history that has divided so many, in search of a shared vision of the future. He has a remarkable faith in the power of the truth.

1

THE FIRST TIBETANS

It was a sunny day in February when we sat down to talk about Tibetan myths of origin, and the Indian sky was cloudless blue: like spring in Europe or North America. The bougainvillea that hangs off the bungalow, where the Dalai Lama meets visitors, was in riotous pink bloom. He was dressed in the same wine-red robes he always wears, with one shoulder bare to the air, as the Buddhist regulations, or *Vinaya*, which govern the behavior of a monk, require, even though it was chilly enough inside the bungalow for me to wear a sweater. Three Buddhist statues, each clothed in glittering gold brocade, sit on a small altar above a shuttered fireplace. There is a relief map of Tibet on one wall, and a Tibetan religious painting on another. Otherwise, the white walls and cement floor are unadorned.

The Dalai Lama's understanding of the earliest myths opens the door to Tibetan history, so I was excited to discuss them with him. Like any Tibetan child, he learned the myths first, then the history. Yet unlike any other child, he quickly comprehended that the nation's earliest myths are in part also about his own life, his past lives, and the heart of Tibet. He has never stopped examining these myths. His grasp of them has changed as his vision of the world has evolved.

Buddhists, like Christians, Hindus, and Muslims, cherish ancient religious myths, which explain human origins for the faithful. Jews, Christians, and Muslims share a myth in which God blows spirit into clay to create Adam. In one of several Hindu creation myths, the primeval creature Purusha was dismembered and people emerged from its parts. A Chinese myth tells of warring mythical emperors who hammer a primeval creature with bolts of lightning. Tibetans learn about a monkey who mated with a rock-dwelling demoness.

Tenzin Gyatso, the Fourteenth Dalai Lama, first heard this myth when he was four and a half years old, shortly after he was recognized as the next Dalai Lama and enthroned in Lhasa in 1940. Despite his unusual circumstances, he discovered the creation myth just as many Tibetans have during the past five hundred years. He saw a painting of the monkey in a temple, and a monk used it to illustrate the story. "There were some paintings there, and I saw that monkey for the first time," the Dalai Lama recalled. "I thought 'nice monkey.' And a monkey who has a sense of responsibility. That's beautiful.

"The myth shows a sense of responsibility and compassion and service, rather than fighting or killing," the Dalai Lama continued. "It's a beautiful story. Very positive and creative. The story is teaching us Buddhist values."

The Great Fifth Dalai Lama summarized Tibet's creation myth when he wrote his history of the nation in 1643.

It is said that the flesh eating red-faced race of Tibetans were the descendants of the union between a monkey and a rock-dwelling demoness. Through the compassion of the Holy One, who had changed his form to that of a monkey, who united with a rock-dwelling demoness—six children came into being. Growing from these in course of time, Tibet became a kingdom of human beings.

The Holy One mentioned here is the Bodhisattva Chenrizi. Tibetans believe that the Great Fifth Dalai Lama was a manifestation of Chenrizi, just as they believe that the Fourteenth Dalai Lama is. After helping the Tibetan people evolve from animal life, Chenrizi has manifested himself in a human form repeatedly to guide them. Tibetans do not believe that the Dalai Lama is the fourteenth incarnation of the human being who was the First Dalai Lama; rather, he is considered to be the fourteenth manifestation of Chenrizi, or the Holy One. But what is a Bodhisattva, and who is the Bodhisattva Chenrizi?

Bodhisattva is a Sanskrit word: *bodhi* means "enlightenment" and *sattva* means "being." Bodhisattvas are "beings aspiring for enlightenment"; they are on the path to enlightenment, though they have not yet reached it. Bodhisattvas vow to devote their life's work to the enlightenment of others, rather than to work for their personal enlightenment. Bodhisattvas are Buddhist saviors who work during the course of thousands of lifetimes for the benefit of others trapped in the prison of cyclic existence. They will not pass over into final enlightenment, and escape from the wheel of birth, death, and rebirth, until all other beings do so.

Chenrizi is the Tibetan name for the Bodhisattva Avalokiteshvara (pronounced Ah-va-low-key-tesh-va-ra) in Sanskrit; Chenrizi works specifically for the salvation of Tibetans. The Dalai Lama says that Chenrizi is also "the embodiment of the Buddha's compassion." Tibetans believe that this Bodhisattva intervened in Tibet out of compassion, and because he was told to do so by the Buddha. A scripture records the moment when the Buddha told Avalokiteshvara to devote himself to the guidance of the Tibetans.

As the Buddha lay on his deathbed in northern India in the year 483 B.C., Avalokiteshvara bent down beside him and urged him not to die, because he had not visited Tibet. The Fifth Dalai Lama recorded the scene in his history of Tibet. Tibetans are "unprotected by your words. Remain for the sake of these," the Bodhisattva said.

> "The kingdom of snows in the north is, at present, a kingdom of animals only," the Buddha replied. "There is not even the name of human beings there . . . in the future O Bodhisattva, it will be converted by you. At first, having been reincarnated as a Bodhisattva, protect the human world of your disciples . . . then gather them together by religion."

The Dalai Lama looked out a window toward some distant trees as he referred to this text and said, "This explains how the Buddha foretold that Avalokiteshvara, whom we call Chenrizi, will have some special connection with Tibet. So these are the words. These are the basis of our people."

Tibetans have repeated their creation myth about Chenrizi and the monkey for more than a thousand years. In different parts of Tibet, communities tell different versions of the myth. Villagers in one part of the country swear that Tibetan infants sport a vestigial tail at the tip of their spine that withers as the children grow. Some say that Chenrizi merely gave the monkey the vows of a Buddhist layman before he sent him to mate with the demoness; others, like the Great Fifth, say that Chenrizi "took the form of a monkey" and mated with the demoness. There is no single standardized version. The Great Fifth Dalai Lama said in his history, "As far as the appearance of human beings in this land of Tibet, the assertions of learned men are endless." Worn by a millennium of retelling, each variation of the myth still reveals the essential themes.

In one of the myth's persistent threads, the monkey-demoness children refused to eat either monkey food or demon food. It was Chenrizi who caused self-sprouting barley to grow in a sacred field. Only after they ate this sacred food did the children evolve into the first Tibetans.

The Dalai Lama chuckled benignly about this. "That monkey looked after all his children even though it was frustrating when they would not eat what monkeys eat. So he approached Chenrizi and asked him how he should look after them. Nice. Very responsible."

As the monkey-demons with a Bodhisattva's spirit in their heart ate the sacred barley over seven generations, they slowly lost their fur and their tails. These monkey-demons evolved into the first Tibetans.

The Dalai Lama and I examined a photograph of a mural in Tibet that illustrates the myth. He pointed to a rainbow flowing from the heart of the Bodhisattva to the heart of the monkey, just before he mates with the demoness.

"This rainbow is a symbol of the energy from Chenrizi. A blessing," the Dalai Lama said. The rainbow is a metaphor for the unbreakable bond between every Tibetan and Chenrizi. The Dalai Lama said the rainbow in the mural is a symbol for the "positive karmic connection" that exists between Tibetans and their patron savior. Whether Chenrizi took the form of the monkey, or whether he sent his energy into the monkey, the myth symbolizes the most fundamental of Tibetan beliefs. Chenrizi is the spiritual father of all Tibetans, and he continues to be manifest in human form to guide his people.

When Tibetans approach the Dalai Lama after waiting in long lines for an audience of only a few seconds to receive his blessing, their faces are radiant with a reverence that non-Tibetans find both amazing and mysterious. The root of their faith is a link between the heart of the Bodhisattva and the heart of the monkey, represented by the rainbow in the mural. Tibetans believe that this connection is alive today and that it flows from each incarnation of the Dalai Lama, who they see as a living manifestation of Chenrizi, to each one of them.

Devout Tibetans accept as fact the Great Fifth's belief, recorded in venerated Buddhist texts even before his time, that there were no people in Tibet before the time of the creation myth, or sometime after the death of the Buddha, in 483 B.C. According to the Dalai Lama, the first Buddhist teachers in Tibet grafted existing myths onto Buddhist beliefs arriving from India to create the monkey myth.

The Dalai Lama does not concur with every belief held by the most traditional and devout Tibetan Buddhists. For example, he accepts Darwin's theory about the origin of species through natural selection as the most logical explanation regarding the origins of humanity.

"When science clearly contradicts Buddhist beliefs, and it is proven, then we must reject the earlier beliefs," the Dalai Lama said. "We will accept the evidence of science, not early beliefs. The Buddha himself made it clear that the final decision for every person must come through investigation and experiment, not by relying solely on religious texts. The Buddha gave us each that freedom. I am following this line."

Thus it was no surprise, after I asked the Dalai Lama about the first Tibetans, that, the next day, he pulled a clipping out of the folds of his red robe. He follows news from recent archaeological digs in Tibet with great interest.

"The Tibetan population has been living in Tibet for more than ten thousand years," he said as he pointed at the clipping. "We were there." The Indian archaeologist V. N. Misra has shown that early humans inhabited the Tibetan Plateau from at least twenty thousand years ago and that there is reason to believe that early humans passed through Tibet at the time India was first inhabited, half a million years ago.

"During the prehistoric period we can deduce a few things about these first Tibetans from archaeological evidence," the Dalai Lama said. "It seems that the first Tibetans were in Western Tibet and then slowly they moved eastward. According to archaeological findings, Tibetan civilization started much earlier than the time of the Buddha: perhaps six thousand to ten thousand years ago. So the story of the demon and the monkey, which is said to have happened after the death of the Buddha, seems to be a myth. This myth is connected with Buddhism. When Buddhism arrived in Tibet *(in about A.D. 600)* there were older traditions, and Buddhist scholars tried to make some connection with those traditions. They did not rewrite, but they sought to link Buddhism to the old stories that already existed."

Exactly when Tibetans developed a culture, a language, and a shared set of beliefs that are identifiably "Tibetan" is debated among the few scholars who study Tibetan history seriously. The first Chinese references to proto-Tibetans, four thousand years ago, describe a non-Chinese people who herded sheep. Scientific findings about the emergence of Tibetan culture remain sketchy, but the earliest Tibetan documents depict a society with a culture very different from that of China. Two ancient poems, one Chinese and one Tibetan, reveal a marked contrast between the two cultures.

Water and a wet fertile valley are the metaphors Lao Tsu used in the *Tao Te Ching* to describe a spiritual path, in one of the world's earliest religious books, but his metaphors also define China's earliest self-image. Lao Tsu saw China as a fertile low-lying valley.

> A great country is like low land.
> It is the meeting ground of the universe,
> The mother of the universe.
> The female overcomes the male with stillness,
> Lying low in stillness

Why is the sea king of a hundred streams?
Because it lies below them.

. . . .

Be the valley of the universe!

. . . .

The highest good is like water.
Water gives life to the ten thousand things and does not strive,
It flows in places men reject and is like the Tao.

Compare these Chinese images of a low-lying "great country" with the following stanzas from two ninth-century Tibetan poems.

Land so high, made so pure,
Without equal, without peer,
Land indeed! Best of All

. . . .

And when he first came to this world,
He came as lord of all under heaven
This center of the earth
This heart of the world
Fenced round by snow,
The headland of all rivers,
Where the mountains are high and the land is pure.
Oh country so good
Where men are born as sages and heroes,
To this land of horses ever more speedy
Choosing it for its qualities, he came here.

Tibetans are a mountain people, and the Chinese are a valley people. A glance at a map, where the Tibetan Plateau soars two, three, even four miles above the plains of China, makes this obvious. The first Tibetans herded flocks in high treeless meadows, while the first Chinese farmed in low-lying valleys. The first Tibetans had more similarities with the people of Mongolia and other nomads of Inner Asia than with Chinese farmers. Though agriculture later made its advent in Tibet, the society's deep bond with nomadic cultures has never been broken, while Chinese farmers' adversarial relations with the nomads of Inner Asia is just as deeply rooted.

"The first Tibetans were not farmers," the Dalai Lama said. "They lived as nomads, following herds of animals. Then slowly in some valleys in Western Tibet, they began to farm crops. According to some modern scholars, as early as two or three thousand years ago they were in contact with the Indus River Valley civilization and they developed an early script in the Shang Shung kingdom, the *mar yig* script. They could not have developed that script themselves. It must have been influenced from somewhere else, perhaps the Indus or even farther west. Perhaps they borrowed farming techniques as well."

The Dalai Lama grew excited talking about scholarship regarding the Shang Shung kingdom and its achievements.

"Recently I saw one short report in a Chinese newspaper," he said. "Chinese archaeologists found *(and carbon-dated)* inscriptions in *mar yig* script *(proving that it was at least)* three thousand years old. So there was a civilization . . . several thousand years ago in the western part *(of Tibet with)* a large population, and then because of changes, *(declining rainfall, desertification)*, the population moved toward the east, toward the lower valleys."

Speculating about this era, the Dalai Lama noted that these first Tibetans received more than farming and script from the West. "Even now in Ladakh there are some Tibetan people with features very similar to those of the Europeans," he said. "They may have come from Greece in ancient times. And one small community there has facial features like modern Arabs."

The first tiny bands of humans to arrive in Tibet fought a harsh battle to survive on a high plateau so vast it still inspires anyone who sees it. The entire Tibetan Plateau, 14 percent larger than Alaska and Texas combined and 62 percent the size of the European Union, was the Tibetan homeland in ancient times. During the course of history, and particularly after the Chinese invasion of 1950, boundaries were redrawn while Chinese and others migrated slowly to the edge of the plateau. The Tibetan Autonomous Region (the TAR, or Xizang) on modern Chinese maps is less than half of the Tibetan Plateau and the territory that was historically Tibet. Nor does the TAR include all ethnic Tibetan areas. Tibetans still live across the plateau, not just in the TAR, so that the province of Qinghai (Ambo) and the Chinese provinces of Gansu, Sichuan, and Yunnan have substantial Tibetan populations. Only about one third of the Tibetan population lives inside the TAR. The geographic area we call the Tibetan Plateau and the region of historic Tibet are virtually the same (except for Ladakh and Sikkim); therefore, when the Dalai Lama speaks about Tibet, he is referring to those parts of the plateau that were historically Tibetan, and are primarily populated by Tibetans. On the other hand, to the Chinese, Tibet is simply the TAR. These issues remain matters of substantial debate.

The Tibetan Plateau (2.5 million square kilometers, or 965,000 square miles) ranges over the highest mountains on earth, sandy deserts, immense gorges, two-mile-high fertile plains, densely forested valleys, and vast treeless plateau. Tibet juts up like a high-altitude island rising from the lowlands around it. It is the highest, largest plateau in the world. The Himalayas line the southern edge of the plateau, the Pamirs and the Hindu Kush guard the western edge, while the Kunlun parade along the northern ramparts. Five of the planet's greatest rivers drain off the plateau to the east: the Mekong, Salween, Tsangpo/Bhramaputra, the Yellow, and the Yangtze. It has historically been sparsely populated, and remains so today. Chinese sources say the Tibetan Plateau's entire population was only six million in 1990: four and a half million Tibetans; the rest Chinese and others. The Dalai Lama's exile government disagrees, saying that there are six million Tibetans and a much larger number of Chinese in Tibet. In comparison, the European Union—which is only about 40 percent larger than the Tibetan Plateau—has a population of 455 million. Tibet remains the sparsely inhabited heart of Asia, while to the south a billion people live on the Indian plains and to the east a billion people live on the Chinese plains.

India and China were far more hospitable for early humans, and civilization emerged there first along fertile low-lying rivers, where it was possible to grow large grain surpluses. Tibet was a little-populated highland, surrounded by a ring of glacier-carved peaks. Many ethnic groups found their way onto the Tibetan Plateau during the prehistoric period—Mongolian, Turkic, and others—as the Tibetan people and culture coalesced over thousands of years. For many centuries, Tibetans remained a nomadic people with no large towns. A critical event was the establishment of settled farming in the comparatively low-lying valleys of Central Tibet, where the largest cities are. "Low-lying" is used loosely: the average altitude of these valleys is 12,000 feet, but hardy forms of barley grow there, when irrigated. Farmers maintained strong links with nomads in the highlands, and the culture remained mobile.

While the Dalai Lama relies on archaeological findings when discussing his country's origins, he believes that a particular group might have appeared, under mysterious circumstances, in Eastern Tibet about two thousand years ago, after the birth of the Buddha, and that their arrival may have helped to spark the creation myth of the monkey and the demoness. We spoke about his beliefs on two occasions, in February and May 1998.

"I believe that some children emerged without a father in one valley in Eastern Tibet," the Dalai Lama said. "A special group emerged; not the entire Tibetan population, but some group came from that valley from some sort of semigod. I do not mean a 'creator god'—since Buddhists do not believe in that—but according to Buddhism, there can be a specially blessed person, a manifestation of Chenrizi: that I believe."

"So you are saying that the compassion that came from Chenrizi, as a special gift to the Tibetan people, that this is real?" I asked.

"Yes, that's right. This is real. It's not necessary to believe that the entire Tibetan population came from this small group that the myth talks about, though that special group I believe is real. . . . The Tibetan population has been here for more than ten thousand years. But then after Buddha's time, I think about two thousand years ago, more, in some valley, a special people emerged. So there is a middle way. I am not denying that *(humans have been in Tibet for much longer than that)*, but I am finding a middle way with the scientific evidence."

In the second interview, several months later, I followed up on this line of discussion with His Holiness, as I found it too fascinating a line of inquiry to ignore.

"The Tibetan race was already there in other areas," the Dalai Lama said. "But then, it *(happens)* even in our generation, some Tibetan women have been heard to give birth to children without a human father, through some special dreams or through some strange experience. . . . So *(these are)* usually called *Lha Trug*. A God child. Some of these children, these human beings, *(are)* physically very, very powerful. So even *(though this has)* not yet *(been proven)* scientifically, from the Buddhist viewpoint I feel that there *are* different forms of life, or different forms of beings. . . . So perhaps some special small lineage comes from there."

For the Dalai Lama, the theory of evolution is compatible with the belief that Tibetans are, as he said, "some sort of chosen people of Chenrizi. And the Chinese again are a chosen people, by the Bodhisattva Manjushri. That I believe." According to him, Manjushri, the embodiment of the Buddha's Wisdom, has incarnated in different human forms to guide the Chinese, just as Chenrizi has incarnated in human births to guide the Tibetans.

Talking with the Dalai Lama about Bodhisattvas who "guide their children," even at the time of their inception, it was clear that he never confused this concept with the idea of a "creator god." Bodhisattvas influence the stream of events and the millions of factors that interdependently cooriginate life, but they do not create life.

"Buddhism does not accept the existence of a god-creator," the Dalai Lama said bluntly. "Yet a creator, god, the concept of god—this is the ultimate truth to Christians *(and other theists)*. There is of course a big difference between Christian *(and other theistic)* religious beliefs and Buddhist beliefs. The self or the consciousness, or mind, is beginning-less. For each different form of life, for each different experience, there are different causes and conditions for each life, but basically everything comes and goes and comes and goes according to the law of causality. That is the Buddhist concept. There is no absolute creator. This law of causality," he concluded, "is very similar to the scientific theory of evolution. Causes and conditions cause changes or evolution."

His attitude astounded me. I said, "This is a dramatically different approach to the conflict between scientific evidence and scriptural dogma than the path taken by traditional Jews, Christians, and Muslims."

"That's okay," he replied. "But at the same time I am not saying that only the Buddhist concept is the truth."

The Dalai Lama is eager not to offend other religions and worries that some of what he has said might do so.

"My view," he continues, treading carefully, "is that for each individual there is one truth, one religion which is true. This is very important. So I am Buddhist. For me Buddhism is the only religion, the only truth. For Christian practitioners, Christianity is the only truth, the only religion. From this situation the concept of pluralism arises, the concept of several truths, several religions which must coexist peacefully. That is my fundamental belief. I don't want to do anything to contribute to conflict, and I respect all religions."

"And do all the religions take us to the same place?" I asked.

"Having the same potential does not mean that through Christianity you can achieve nirvana, or Buddhahood, as Buddha described; that is different. And the Buddhist, to achieve or reach heaven according to Christianity, that is also different."

"And what about Christians who would consign all Buddhists to hell?" I asked.

"I think, fortunately, Buddhists may not go to hell," the Dalai Lama said. "At least not the one of the Christian concept. There is Buddhist hell, but afterwards if you want to remain there, you can, and if you want to leave there, you can leave from there. So, you see, it's a very different concept of hell." For Buddhists it is the merit, or demerit, one earns in life, which sends you to heaven, hell, or a new birth in one of the realms of life. Once that accumulated karma is spent, then one's stay in heaven or hell is over. The cycle of death and rebirth, the cycle of existence, can be eternally broken only when one achieves enlightenment. The perspective is completely different from Western concepts about eternal hell or salvation.

"What do you think of Westerners converting to Buddhism?" I asked.

"My fundamental belief," the Dalai Lama answered, "is that for some people the concept of a creator is much more effective than the Buddhist law of causality and the theory of dependent origination. So for them, Christianity (or other religions) is much more effective, much more beneficial. But for those people who accept the law of causality and the theory of dependent origination, it really does make a deep impact on them. That causes transformation or improvement of oneself; it makes it easier. So for such people, then, Buddhism is much more suitable. That is my fundamental belief. And yes, frankly, from my viewpoint the Buddha has given us the freedom to follow our own perceptions, and in a way, this path is closer to modern science."

"Why is it closer to science?" I asked.

"Fundamentally, the Buddha gave us the liberty to investigate and come to our own judgment. Even with a classical Buddhist cosmological theory—where it says, for example, that Mount Meru is in the center of the earth and the sun goes around the earth. Now the scripture that describes such cosmos is very ancient, but we have the liberty to reject this concept if we prove that it is contrary to empirical evidence. This is good. This is closer to modern scientific approach."

As much as he rejects pairing fundamentalism with religion, the Dalai Lama also refuses to seek absolute answers in science. "There is a limitation with scientific thinking. They only accept things proven by the methods that exist up to now. Buddhism as a philosophy explains things beyond. Scientists, unless they can prove something they can neither accept nor deny it."

Because of his strong scientific-humanist streak, the Dalai Lama has sought what he calls "a middle way" between Tibetan myth and modern science. He tries to incorporate scientific theory while retaining the essence of Buddhist thought when he constructs his own explanation of Chenrizi's link to Tibetans, and to himself.

"We believe that Chenrizi took this special sort of role in Tibet, and through his special blessings a special group of people develops," the Dalai Lama said. "That's our belief. Tibetans are specially descended with this energy from Chenrizi. Energy, blessing, positive karmic connection—Tibetans are all linked directly with Chenrizi in this way. Tibetans believe that. Actually, I am myself sometimes surprised at the strength of the spiritual connection."

Tibetans frequently remind the Dalai Lama of the strength of this link between them and the Dalai Lama. He says that often they tell him that they received precise instructions from the Dalai Lama in a dream. Bemused, he related one example in which "I told them to escape from Tibet on a certain day . . . or to go to such and such a place and do this or that . . . and they believed it, and did it, and all went well."

The Dalai Lama has heard of such experiences so often that he is convinced that there is a connection between himself and ordinary Tibetans. He said that it exists "in a spiritual way" and that because of this "positive karmic connection, certain things happen. I myself also believe," he said. "I have had certain proof."

He hesitated, fearing that if he said more, it might sound as if he was proud of these incidents. However, there was no pride, only conviction, when he continued.

"If someone asks me whether I am the reincarnation of the Dalai Lama," he said, "then I answer, without hesitation, *yes*. This does not mean I am the same being as the previous Dalai Lama. Some Dalai Lamas are a manifestation of Manjushri. Some are a manifestation of Chenrizi. Chenrizi is the manifestation of compassion. Manjushri is the manifestation of wisdom. I have a special connection with the Thirteenth Dalai Lama and the Fifth Dalai Lama. I have felt some kind of karmic relations or connections even with the Buddha. I feel I can say I have *some kind* of connection with the previous Dalai Lamas, some of the previous masters, with Chenrizi, even with the Buddha."

"This English word *connection* you keep using," I said. "It doesn't give a true explanation of everything that you mean when you use it."

"It has a number of meanings," the Dalai Lama said. "It can mean that there was a personal connection; we might have been born in the same time during a past life; a teacher and student; or a ruler and a subject or we might even have been spiritual friends. There could have been a personal life connection. Also, there can be other factors. In my own case, from my previous lives, there is some connection to virtues. So on the basis of these virtues, a connection is formed. From the devotion, faith, or belief in the Fifth Dalai Lama or some of these other masters, these connections can cause a birth or human life where the work of the Fifth Dalai Lama can be carried on. Though we may never have met, even in a prior life, never met personally, but spiritually because of strong faith, it is possible that you are carrying out his work."

Pointing at himself, the Dalai Lama said, "This person's connection with the Fifth Dalai Lama, this person now has the power or merit to carry out some work or duty in such and such a period. So all these forces are connected and then a birth is caused."

As I listened carefully to the Dalai Lama, an image took shape in my mind of how reincarnation shaped the history the Dalai Lama spoke of. I thought of different human "souls" as strands braided together, down through time, forming one rope. The lineage of fourteen Dalai Lamas has not been a reincarnation of one human soul. Several human souls have been the vessel for Chenrizi in their own time, and a few of these have reincarnated several times. At the same time, they all interact with one another, as humans, during different incarnations. This was completely different from the idea I had previously had that the Dalai Lama was the fourteenth reincarnation of a single human soul, who was also a manifestation of the compassion of the Buddha.

"Is it possible," I asked, "for the human being who is today Tenzin Gyatso to have been reincarnated earlier? Not as the Dalai Lama, but as a person who was a friend of, or worked with, the Fifth Dalai Lama?"

"Yes, that is possible," the Dalai Lama said. "Yes. When someone asks me if I am the Dalai Lama, or reincarnation of the Dalai Lama, then without hesitation I say yes. If they ask me if I am the reincarnation of the Thirteenth Dalai Lama, then I say I don't know."

Surprised at the turn of conversation, I carried on. "So the Thirteenth Dalai Lama as a human being is separate from the Thirteenth Dalai Lama as a manifestation of Chenrizi?"

"Yes," he answered, "although there are a lot of interpretations of the word *soul*." Buddhists do not believe in the existence of a "soul" that migrates from one body to the next. Reincarnation is more complex than that. When the Dalai Lama or I used that word, we both knew it had quotations marks around it. "Still, speaking simply, my soul may not be the same soul as the soul of the Thirteenth Dalai Lama."

"But the Chenrizi in you," I asked, "is the same Chenrizi that was in the Thirteenth Dalai Lama?"

"No, not Chenrizi," he said, gently correcting me. "It's some kind of special connection or special blessing from Chenrizi in the Thirteenth Dalai

Lama. Or in my case, yes, perhaps a special blessing from Chenrizi. Whereas with the Thirteenth Dalai Lama, maybe he was a true reincarnation of Chenrizi. But these things are very mysterious."

"Yes, mysterious," I added, "but at a simple level there are two distinct things happening simultaneously. There is the Chenrizi connection, and there is a human connection. These two braiding together through time, going forward. It is difficult to understand."

"Yes," he said, nodding his head, "mysterious. But some people can understand this, if they have developed certain power of mind. It is very rare. But several masters have had visions that indicate I have some connection. . . . I feel strongly that I have some connection—that word again—with the Buddha."

His use of the word *connection* allowed me to make a leap that I had previously been unable to imagine.

"Do you mean," I asked, "that perhaps you were an incarnated human being at the time of the Buddha?"

"Yes, that is possible," the Dalai Lama said. "Sometimes, I wish . . . and some of these masters, I don't know. Maybe it is just wishful thinking." I knew as he said this that he was turning away from a public discussion of ideas he preferred not to discuss. Buddhist texts specifically forbid a teacher, except under certain circumstances, from discussing his past incarnations if he is aware of them. "The practical thing is that, yes, I made some contribution to the Dharma. This simple little boy born in Amdo *(a Tibetan province)*. Of course in the scientific way all of this is very mysterious, unproven. But at a spiritual level there must be some forces. So in a very remote area one child was found"—as he said this, he pointed a finger at his chest. "Then peculiar names also appeared in the vision lake—Lhamo Latso—and the exact shape of my house also appeared in the lake, to the regent himself," he said as he described the visions seen by his regent in the sacred vision lake used to find him as a boy. He seemed bemused that these visions about his rebirth could have come to his regent but also convinced that they did. "So you see at the spiritual level there is connection, a lot of connection, a lot of karmic forces or spiritual forces."

My head was reeling. "This is vast and complex," I said.

"Yes, very difficult," the Dalai Lama said, "but I think from a Buddhist standpoint it's very easy to understand. But you cannot really pinpoint it and say it is this, or it is that."

"Of course none of this is scientific," I said. I felt my Western beliefs rearing up in protest, as they would many times during our conversations. It's a wonderful Buddhist explanation, but it's not a scientific one.

The Dalai Lama smiled at me confidently. For a moment, he seemed to glance backward toward the rainbow from Chenrizi, and then beyond our moment in time, into the future.

"Yes," he said, "up to now."

2

THE FIRST TIBETAN EMPEROR, 600–650

It had been six months since the Dalai Lama and I had last met. It was July—the wet heart of the monsoon, when you never see the blue sky and black clouds come right down to the treetops. Giant stands of bamboo, heavy and dripping with rain, bend over the pathway up the hillside to the audience hall, where he meets all visitors. It was a wet slog, and the lights from the audience hall gleamed brightly as I came in from the dark rainy day. As soon as the Dalai Lama entered and sat down, we picked up the thread of our conversation as though no time had passed, without any comment about the weather. As the rain fell, we talked about the earliest Tibetan records, when mythology gave way to history for the first time.

Between A.D. 575 and 600, battles between competing monarchs flared across the Tibetan Plateau. The plateau was not a single state. Petty princes and kings ruled their own states. Nomadic herders on the mountain ridges and farmers in the valleys looked to local rulers for protection. The first written history began when the royal house of Yarlung struggled to unify the kingdoms. In the war for national unification, defeated troops joined the Yarlung dynasty's army, which soon became the greatest military force ever assembled in Tibet. After unifying the entire plateau, the army marched off to do battle with foreign kingdoms and empires in parts of what is now India, China, Pakistan, and Afghanistan. When Tibet emerged from the fog of mythology, it was an imperial power fighting for an empire the size of Rome's.

Initially the ancient kings of Shang Shung, in Western Tibet, fought off the armies of the emerging Yarlung kings of southern Tibet. It took two generations for the house of Yarlung, based in its stone castle on a cliff above the Yarlung tributary of the Tsangpo River, to emerge as lords over the largest farming district in Tibet. One petty lord after another was defeated in battle or submitted without a fight. Within two decades, the Yarlung dynasty unified all the farmers and nomads of southern and central Tibet. Yet the rivalry, resentment, and infighting were so fierce that before the Yarlung king could extend his authority over the Shang Shung kingdom, he was poisoned and died. His son was the first real historic Tibetan figure.

In about 618, Songzen Gampo ascended the Yarlung throne at age thirteen. Though he is perhaps the first Tibetan to emerge from myth, such is his stature that parts of his life remain shrouded in mystery. For Tibetans, Songzen Gampo is the great emperor who unified and created Tibet.

The young Fourteenth Dalai Lama first heard about Songzen Gampo before he learned to read. Installed in the Potala from the age of six, the young boy had as his closest friends the adults who cared for that vast fortress. They were celibate monks in red robes with shaved heads who swept the chapels or helped to clean his quarters. I soon learned that the Dalai Lama calls them all "sweepers" and that his first teachings on many subjects often came from them, rather than from his regent or his tutors. They became the voice of the common man, in his very uncommon childhood.

"I don't remember when I first learned about Songzen Gampo explicitly," the Dalai Lama said. "Everyone knows about Songzen Gampo. The sweepers, of course, they told me stories, how Songzen Gampo waged war against the Chinese and so on."

Slowly he picked up the basics of Songzen Gampo's history. According to the Dalai Lama, the emperor "started the unification of Shang Shung and Central Tibet. He founded an empire that increased in size after his death; the borders expanded *(throughout the eighth century)*."

The Fourteenth Dalai Lama learned how the Yarlung dynasty's empire reached its greatest size under the heirs of Songzen Gampo. "But Songzen Gampo began the imperial period of Tibetan history," the Dalai

Lama said. "He brought about unification of Tibet and then began the imperial expansion."

During the childhood of the Fourteenth Dalai Lama, in 1942 and 1943, just after he arrived in Lhasa, he saw several ancient festivals which brought Songzen Gampo to life for him even though the first emperor had been dead more than a thousand years.

In August 1943, during Lhasa's Yogurt Festival, an opera company erected a Tibetan awning, white with swirling indigo patterns stitched into it, in the garden that enclosed the Norbulingka, the Dalai Lama's summer palace. Opera singers performed all day in the shade, warbling archaic couplets about the life of Songzen Gampo. Athletic dancers turned cartwheels. Hundreds of Tibetans gathered for the performance, setting up their tents for a week of picnics. As the public watched the opera, mothers told stories about the emperor to their children. The Dalai Lama remembers the opera singers in their gaudy costumes dancing and singing underneath the canvas. He had a fine view of the opera from his pavilion, built into the walls of the Norbulingka just so he could see the annual performance.

These celebrations in Lhasa, prior to the Chinese invasion, kept Tibet's past alive. The Dalai Lama also recalls an annual "elaborate pilgrimage" around the temples in the Potala and Lhasa that housed statues of Songzen Gampo.

"Even at five or six," the Dalai Lama said, "I had some idea about Songzen Gampo because every year when I went to these chapels, people talked about him."

The Dalai Lama firmly accepts the fundamental Tibetan belief about Songzen Gampo. The Bodhisattva Chenrizi had promised the Buddha that he would unify and protect the Tibetans and then guide them with Buddhism.

"There is no doubt that Songzen Gampo was a manifestation of Chenrizi," the Dalai Lama said. "There is no doubt about this. I am Buddhist. I believe in reincarnation, believe in the manifestation of a higher being, like the manifestation of Chenrizi in Tibet. I believe in this. Songzen Gampo was a special person with a connection to Chenrizi."

Songzen Gampo's first task, when he became the thirteen-year-old emperor, was to quell the rebellion that accompanied the broader plot to

poison his father. After he won the succession battle, his vassals swore allegiance to the young ruler in prose that illuminates much about early Tibet.

> Never will we be faithless to Emperor Songzen Gampo, to his
> sons and his descendants. . . . whatever they do!
> Never will we seek other overlords among other men!
> Never will we be at ease with others who are faithless!
> Never will we interfere with food and mix poison with it!
> Never will we address the first word to the Emperor!
> Never shall there be . . . envy towards our comrades!
> Never will we act unfairly towards those who are subject to us!
> Never will we be disobedient to whatever command the Emperor
> may give!

Once firmly seated on the Yarlung dynasty's throne, Songzen Gampo
resumed his family's march toward empire with the help of elder, more
powerful ministers. He turned his armies on a kingdom in the northeast
and sent his sister Sadmakar off to marry the king of Shang Shung in the
west. Shortly after her marriage, she led her husband into an ambush set
by Songzen Gampo; such was her allegiance to the house of Yarlung. Once
the king of Shang Shung was dead, young Songzen Gampo became the
first Tibetan emperor of a united Tibetan Plateau.

In the same year that Songzen Gampo ascended the throne in Tibet,
China was also in chaos. The Sui dynasty fell, and the Tang dynasty
emerged. The Tang ruled China from 618 to 907 from their capital,
Chang'an (modern Xi'an), which became the largest city on earth.

After he unified Tibet, Songzen Gampo decided that he would have a
Chinese princess as a bride. He sent an envoy to China to demand one.
The Fourteenth Dalai Lama first heard about this story from a strange
old physician who had been the Thirteenth Dalai Lama's personal doctor
until he was fired.

The Dalai Lama was still living in Lhasa after the Chinese invasion of
1950. He estimates he was about nineteen and had just made a visit to a
medical college, which once covered Chagpori, a hill that faces the Potala.
The People's Liberation Army destroyed every building in the college in

1959, and today tourists standing on the roof of the Potala looking south at Chagpori see a rocky peak ringed with barbed wire to defend the giant television and radio tower that crowns the hilltop.

The Dalai Lama and his entourage made their way down the steep hill and stopped at a small complex of temples and houses at the base of Chagpori, where Songzen Gampo had once lived. The Thirteenth Dalai Lama's physician was staying there.

"In one way, I had great respect for this learned man," the Dalai Lama recollected. "But he was filled with great pride and was dismissed by the Thirteenth Dalai Lama as his personal physician. Still he was a learned person. He had very good connections with many lamas and ministers and powerful people. So he was living there. And he spoke very fast, 'shi, shi, shi.'" The Dalai Lama imitated the old man's lisp. "Many people could not understand him or get a word in when he spoke. When he explained Songzen Gampo's story in his own style, he started accidentally spitting at me."

"What did he tell you?" I interjected.

The Dalai Lama continued. "He said Songzen Gampo lived there, in that small place, and while there he got the idea that he wanted to bring a Chinese princess to Tibet. The next day he called a meeting of all the ministers. Tibetan lifestyle was more nomadic then, and so, according to tradition, each minister brought his own lunch. One minister brought a leg of mutton, and one brought a head, and so on. They all came together and by chance all the meat brought together represented a whole sheep. They considered this very auspicious. After lunch, he gave them the instructions that he wanted to have a Chinese princess as his wife."

The Dalai Lama laughed as he recalled the disgraced physician of his predecessor hissing so quickly at him. "'Shi, shi, shim,' he said. It was a good way for me to remember the story."

Songzen Gampo's decision to take a Chinese bride was emblematic of a larger transformation brought on by Tibetan unification. "As Tibet became more powerful," the Dalai Lama said, "the attitude toward the eastern neighbor, China, changed."

As an independent empire that was never part of the Tang dynasty, Tibet was the most serious foreign threat to the dynasty's existence for two hundred years, from 620 to 820. The Tibetans were the only conquerors who sacked the Tang capital and installed a puppet ruler during this period. The internally fractured Tang was never able to defeat the military power of the Tibetans resoundingly. A counteroffensive against Tibet's capital was unthinkable no matter how often the Tibetans attacked the Tang. China dealt with the militarily stronger "barbarian tribes" that surrounded it—and Tibet was only one of several—first with bribery or appeasement and then, if that failed, with a military response.

The Chinese were in constant conflict with nomadic people from the beginning of their recorded history. Nomads, who own only what they can carry as they move about with their herds, are the natural enemies of sedentary farmers who thrive by accumulating agricultural surpluses. This was the most important factor in the history of China, Russia, Tibet, and all of Inner Asia, for millennia. Every fall and summer Mongol, Turkic, and other nomads from the surrounding plateau and steppes raided farmers in the valleys of China for grain, silk, or other pillage. In a good year, Chinese troops prevented the cities from burning. The Great Wall, built to prevent the nomads from plundering the cities, divided Asia into two distinct categories. Those within the wall were farmers who spoke some form of Chinese; those beyond the wall were mostly nomadic herders who did not speak Chinese and did not share the Chinese worldview.

Built along a natural divide, the Great Wall was abutted to the north by treeless steppes that swept off northward and westward to Russia, where nomadic animal husbandry was the preferred lifestyle. Just south of the wall, trees and fertile fields made farming the best choice. The wall marked two distinct environments and the two different livelihoods people had adopted in each of them. The nomadic empires of Inner Asia did not conquer the lands of the farmers because they did not have the administration to govern an agricultural society. Similarly, the Chinese found it impossible to prevent the annual attacks on their settlements, nor could they administer or conquer the nomads. The Great Wall was the line of stalemate, the point of demarcation between two worlds.

The nomadic tribes that threatened the Tang and earlier dynasties relied on the Chinese far more than the Tibetans did. Captured Chinese farmers performed most of the agriculture in the nomadic empires. The nomads accrued wealth by siphoning from the Chinese economy through trade or raids, not by taxing their own people. Nomads relied on captured Chinese craftspeople for certain luxuries, or they took them on raids. Conversely, the Tibetans were independent of the Chinese, though the former regularly traded with and pillaged the latter. Even in the seventh century, Tibetan culture was more cosmopolitan than that of the nomads who regularly attacked the Tang: most of the nomads had contact only with China. From the beginning, Tibet was in contact not only with China but with Indian and Inner Asian empires, drawing from all of them both culturally and economically. Overall, the Tibetan economy was more balanced than that of its nomadic counterparts: if heavy snows killed off animals, the Tibetan stores of grain were sufficient to feed the population. When times were hard, Tibetans did not need to move close to the Chinese border, because their farmers had more arable land than the nomads who occupied the steppes and they traded with Tibetan nomads. Additionally, Tibetan farmers were a source of troops for early emperors who had already developed an administration that governed both farmers and nomads. Uniquely poised between the nomadic and the agricultural worlds of Inner Asia, Tibet drew on the strengths of both. Rather than demand subsidies from the Tang, as the nomadic powers that attacked China often did, Tibet would compete with China for domination and territory. When Tibet and China first met, Tibet presented a unique challenge for China.

The two empires first came into contact during the time of Songzen Gampo's father, in about 600, as their armies fought to dominate the tribes along their shared border. Chinese troops had never before penetrated the Tibetan Plateau, nor had Tibet attacked Chinese cities at the foot of the plateau. Only when a unified Tibet began to expand off the plateau during Songzen Gampo's reign did the Chinese take detailed note of the Tibetans.

The Tang dynastic histories—the history of the dynasty written from period documents—describes battles in July 634 with a nomadic group they call the Aza. The Aza, who lived between Tibet and China, along the eastern edge of the plateau, had thrown off Chinese rule, as tribes along the border were constantly doing. A Tang war with the Aza prompted a Tibetan diplomatic mission to the first Tang ruler, Emperor Taizong, which arrived in Chang'an in the fall of 634. A Tang ambassador sent to Songzen Gampo's court the following winter continued the dialogue.

In the summer of 635, the Chinese-Aza skirmishes ended with a resounding defeat of the Aza. Now Tibetan and Chinese armies faced one another directly.

That summer a Tibetan delegation again went to the Tang capital at Chang'an. The message from Songzen Gampo to Taizong was simple: he wanted a Chinese princess as a consort. In his letter to the Tang emperor, he warned that if he did not get his wish, he would lead fifty thousand troops to kill the emperor and take his bride, personally. Songzen Gampo already had several princesses as wives. One was from the defeated Shang Shung king, and he had just demanded a bride from a king in Nepal as a form of tribute. Taizong did not view China as a subordinate power, and turned down Songzen Gampo's request in a way that insulted the Tibetan. When he refused to furnish the bride, he rejected peace with Tibet. During the next two summers, Songzen Gampo conquered two powerful border tribes, and then in 638 looted the Chinese town of Sung Chou. The message was clear. The army would raid deeper into Chinese territory until Tibet received a princess. A Chinese force sent to fight the Tibetans was defeated, while the Tibetans urged border tribes, loyal to China, to revolt. It is impossible to say precisely what prompted Taizong to accede to Songzen Gampo's demands for a wife, but a minor skirmish, which ended in a rare Tibetan defeat, gave the emperor a face-saving pretext to end the conflict. Even at this early stage of Sino-Tibetan relations, Tibetan and Tang sources contradict each another completely about the nature of their relationship. Both sides say the other came to their court to pay tribute.

In December 640, a Tibetan minister, Gar Tongzen, arrived in Chang'an with a princess's dowry: five thousand ounces of gold and other treasure. A Tibetan opera written long after the event, which the Dalai Lama saw as a boy, lingers over the protracted negotiations between the clever Tibetan minister and the Chinese emperor. In the spring of 641, a Chinese prince escorted Princess Wencheng as far as the Tibetan border, where Songzen Gampo met his newest bride. The princess's arrival in Tibet marked the start of a period of peaceful communication and cooperation between the two states. In 648, when a Tang envoy was attacked in northern India, Tibet sent troops to India to rescue the envoy and defeat those who had attacked him. Diplomatic envoys from both nations made numerous trips between Chang'an and Lhasa.

The Chinese consort was one of Songzen Gampo's five wives. Tibet's crown prince was born to the Tibetan queen. The Nepalese and Chinese consorts are not famous because of their children but because of the statues of the Buddha they brought to Lhasa. Songzen Gampo built two temples, Ramoche and the Jokhang, to house them—the first two Buddhist temples in Tibet: Nepalese and Tibetan artisans built them in a Tibeto-Indian style, and even today, the Jokhang remains the most revered temple in Tibet. It houses fragments from the statue brought by Princess Wencheng. Red guards destroyed the original in the 1960s. Tibetans tell this history of Songzen Gampo, his wives, and the statues to explain how the first Buddhist temples were built in their country.

Behind the Great Wall, a different vision of this history is told. On several Chinese Web sites, Songzen Gampo is portrayed as a famous Chinese who made "outstanding contributions to the unification of the Chinese nation." To Chinese who would like to prove that there has been a continuous Chinese state from the time of the Tang up to the present, the Tang dynasty was the "civilizational [*sic*] center of East Asia. Neighboring nations and tribes fell under the influence of the Tang dynasty, and earnestly sought ties with the dynasty. They either claimed allegiance to the Tang or paid tributes to the imperial court."

This view of Tibetan history posits Songzen Gampo as a love-struck warrior who became a loyal vassal of the Tang emperor. He supposedly built the Potala for his Chinese wife. There is a clear implication from the Tang records, and on Chinese Web sites, that the civilized Chinese educated these ignorant barbarians.

"Princess Wencheng," according to one Chinese Web site, "was touched by her husband's love for her and gradually came to care for him and her borderland home. She summoned Han *(Chinese)* artisans to Tufan *(Tibet)* to pass on their skills in metallurgy, farming, weaving, construction, milling, brewing and the manufacture of paper and ink. The local farmers were taught new agricultural techniques to raise different varieties of grain. Han astronomy and the Chinese calendar were also introduced to the region. Perhaps the most important innovation was the writing system developed by Princess Wencheng and the king, for before her arrival Tufan was without a written language."

Ironically, Tibet had already mastered many of the skills allegedly introduced by Princess Wencheng. Even the Tang dynastic histories extol the Tibetans' mastery of metallurgy. "The men and horses all wear chain mail armor. Its workmanship is extremely fine. It envelops them completely, leaving openings only for the two eyes. Thus strong bows and sharp swords cannot injure them."

There is no evidence that China was the source of Tibet's iron technology. Tibetans probably mastered the production of fine mail coats for men and horses after learning the rudiments of that skill from the Sasanian dynasty, which ruled extensive territory to the west of Tibet (including what is now modern Iran) from the third to the seventh centuries. By the eighth century, the production of iron weapons, as well as armor and mail coats, were all quite mature in Tibet. Tibetans did not acquire their mastery of such technology from Princess Wencheng, but sometime several centuries before that.

China did share paper with the Tibetans, possibly at the time of Princess Wencheng's journey to Lhasa, but Europe received paper technology from China two centuries after that. While a Tibetan developed his country's alphabet during the reign of Songzen Gampo, Princess Wencheng was not involved. Songzen Gampo sent the scholar Thomi-sambhota abroad, where he worked with foreign scholars to create the alphabet. Tibetans and Western historians believe he went to India, but at least one source indicates that Thomi-sambhota may have gone to Khotan, a Central Asian kingdom north of Tibet, where Indian scripts were also used, and based the Tibetan script on the Khotanese one. In any case, the Tibetan alphabet bears no relation to Chinese ideograms, and an Indian script was used as a model when it was created. Traditionally Buddhist scholars in Tibet piously asserted that the main impetus for the invention of this script was to facilitate the translation of Buddhist texts. However, the rulers of the Yarlung dynasty needed a means to administer their far-flung empire, and recent studies assert that this was the driving force behind the creation of Tibet's modern script. The Dalai Lama understands this debate.

During Songzen Gampo's reign, the Dalai Lama said, "laws were codified and one code covered all of Tibet for the first time." He agreed that Songzen Gampo built the Jokhang in Lhasa and patronized scholars who translated Buddhist texts into a new form of Tibetan.

To study Buddhism, the Dalai Lama said, Tibetans across the vast land "had to study one Tibetan language. They still spoke in their local dialect, but when they studied Dharma, it was in one language, literally a new standardized Tibetan. As Buddhism spread all over Tibet, it also spread one script. So this helped to create a sense of national identity, perhaps for the first time."

"So the nation is emerging then?" I asked.

"Yes. All of these factors contributed to this sense of national unification," the Dalai Lama explained. "Language, Buddhism, and a national set of laws. All this caused Tibetan identity to grow stronger. People might affiliate with their region as they had in the past, but they also identified themselves as Tibetan."

Songzen Gampo has earned universal acclaim among Tibetans as one of the greatest figures in their nation's history because of all that he and his descendants accomplished. Tibetan and foreign records show that these achievements are neither exaggerated nor mythologized.

Songzen Gampo is one of the key figures in Tibetan history about whom the Dalai Lama believes there are several levels of understanding. "People who have a pure insight from spiritual practice," he said, hold one view of the first emperor, while people who have not achieved that insight maintain what he calls the "purely conventional" view. "The uncommon viewpoint is not considered as history, and as I said before, historians cannot record these things. But we should not say that all such things are just the imagination of the Buddhist faithful. They can also be true."

According to the Dalai Lama, some of Songzen Gampo's actions were part of "Chenrizi's master plan for Tibet" to "govern and nourish" the country and to allow Buddhism to spread within it.

At the same time, he says, Songzen Gampo's fight for "unification and his kingly duties, those were at the human level." He believes that

Tibetans over the course of several centuries have "mixed the conventional level and the uncommon level. I think ordinary people might not know the distinction."

For the Dalai Lama, Songzen Gampo's motivation was "guided by Chenrizi"; he wanted Buddhism to flourish in Tibet. Therefore, Songzen Gampo's use of an army to unify Tibet was acceptable, even though Buddhism forbids all killing.

Although Songzen Gampo was guided by the Bodhisattva, as an embodiment of Chenrizi's positive karmic connection with the Tibetan people, he also had feet of clay, a fact not lost on the Dalai Lama.

He notes that Gar Tongzen, the minister Songzen Gampo sent to the Tang court to obtain his Chinese consort, suffered a horrible fate at the hands of his emperor. Songzen Gampo suspected him of involvement in plots against him and had him blinded, as the Fourteenth Dalai Lama says, "because he created some dissension with others."

Twelve hundred years later, according to this traditional account, Gar Tongzen was reincarnated as a Buddhist Lama in a monastery in Tibet, during the time of the Thirteenth Dalai Lama. Again, the two personalities clashed. The reincarnated Lama sided with the Chinese army that invaded Tibet in 1910; after the war the Thirteenth Dalai Lama had his monastery closed. For the Fourteenth Dalai Lama, Songzen Gampo and his minister acted out their conflict, again, in another life.

Conversations with His Holiness the Fourteenth Dalai Lama are strange for a Westerner who does not believe in reincarnation. He points out such linkages, nodding his head with pity at how human behaviors continue to spin the web of lives, one after the other, through connections—actions, motivations, associations in past lives—that are impossible for most of us to see. For the Dalai Lama, this is a story of a connection, as he defines it, between two humans, played out over a thousand years, demonstrating a mixture of the divine and the human as manifested in corporeal lives. Speaking of the humans in Songzen Gampo's court, the Fourteenth Dalai Lama says, "Yes, some have reincarnated again, some have not. Others I do not know."

Though convinced of Songzen Gampo's reincarnation and his link to Chenrizi, Tibetans tell so many myths about the first emperor's life that the Dalai Lama seems to grow weary of them. When I ask about the story of rainbows flaring into the sky while Songzen Gampo and his Chinese and Nepalese wives supervised construction of the first temple in Tibet, the Dalai Lama is dismissive.

"To me as a Buddhist monk," the Dalai Lama observed, "a possibility is there that such miracles happened. But at the same time, when there are too many possibilities, then some miracles seem impossible. When there is too much of this, we begin to doubt."

I pointed out that, according to a Tibetan myth, the temple was built over a lake and that geological research confirms that there was indeed a lake in ancient Lhasa Valley. Tibetan myths say that the Jokhang was built on top of that lake at the insistence of the Chinese and Nepalese princesses. The Dalai Lama laughed and, as always, found his own way to explain this. "Songzen Gampo was very stubborn. He could have built the Jokhang anywhere else, where it was more stable! There must have been some spiritual reason for building it exactly in that place."

Workers laid beams over the water, to form an intricate web, and built the temple atop the boarded-up lake. "I was in the Jokhang courtyard," the Dalai Lama recalled, "and there is a well that is supposed to go down to the lake. That's what I was told. I remember when I was a child some people told me that if you listened in the well, you could hear the ducks in the lake. But then later the sweepers wanted me to come away from the well. They told me the ducks will come out and snatch small boys!"

During 1966, the Cultural Revolution swept through Lhasa. Young Chinese intent on teaching barbarian Tibetans a lesson turned the Jokhang, Tibet's first and most sacred Buddhist temple, into a slaughterhouse for pigs. The ancient Chinese Buddha that Princess Wencheng brought to Lhasa was shattered; and in an act of utter desecration, blood spattered the walls of the inner shrine. Across Tibet, in the eight monasteries that were not destroyed during the Cultural Revolution, fewer than one thousand monks remained. For a decade, Tibetans were forbidden to worship in the Jokhang. In 1972, restoration began in the Jokhang, and the work was largely finished by 1980. In the following years, Tibetans began slowly to return to the temple after the worst of the religious persecution faded. Songzen Gampo's temple was reconsecrated, and now thousands of pilgrims throng to it every day. Some pieces of the ancient statue of the Buddha from China were found, and Tibetan faith has wrought a miracle. The inner shrine of the Jokhang is again a place of flickering butter lamps, where apparently whole and miraculous statues gaze out benignly at the tens of thousands of pilgrims who come to prostrate there.

One afternoon during a visit I made to the Jokhang in 1985, an old monk stood over the well in the courtyard, frightening a squealing boy with tales of ducks that stole young boys. I listened as he told the boy to look down to try to see the lake. "Listen carefully," the monk said, "and you can hear the ducks." The real history of the Jokhang, as well as the myths about it and the statues within it, give Tibetans a way to share their past and to create a future. The Red Guard attacked the Jokhang in 1966 for many reasons; one was to stop that transmission of identity. History is never dead in Tibet, not even when you destroy it.

There are hundreds of statues in the Jokhang, but two in particular play a part in the final act of Songzen Gampo's life. Once again, the ancient stories, although based on history, convey more than just events from the past. During Songzen Gampo's reign, a wooden statue of the Buddha was famous in Nepal. It seemed to grow out of wood on its own. Songzen Gampo sent men to bring it to Lhasa.

The Dalai Lama said, "A large clay statue of Chenrizi was made in the Jokhang, and that wood statue of the Buddha from Nepal was put inside the bigger one." These two statues, a tiny wooden one nested inside the larger clay one, sat in the Jokhang undisturbed for thirteen hundred years.

Historians say that Songzen Gampo died at the age of thirty-seven in 649, when a plague swept through his camp, killing him and his Nepalese wife. Tibetans tell many versions of his death and do not seem confused at the differences between them. "Some say he lived to eighty years," the Dalai Lama explained. "At the time of his death, he dissolved as light rays into that statue in the main cathedral of the Jokhang"—into the small wooden statue inside the large clay Chenrizi statue in the Jokhang. "The large clay statue, like nearly all of those in the Jokhang, was destroyed during the Cultural Revolution. When they destroyed the larger clay statue, they found the small wooden statue at its center. Some Tibetan kept it after the large one was destroyed and then sent it to me, which is very good."

"And you still have the tiny wooden statue with the spirit of Songzen Gampo?" I asked.

"Yes, I will show you one day," he replied.

An hour later, I had left the audience room and was next door preparing to leave the building. One of the elderly monks who is always with the Dalai Lama rushed up with a beatific smile on his face.

"Come back!" he said and then hurried to return to the Dalai Lama.

I ran after the monk, back into the audience hall. Entering the room, I saw the Dalai Lama standing by a window reverently clutching something tiny, swaddled in silk.

The Dalai Lama looked up at me and said, "Come see the statue from Songzen Gampo." It was the wooden statue saved from the Jokhang, into which the spirit of Songzen Gampo had vanished. Up close, it seemed to be made of sandalwood. There was a very happy smile on Chenrizi's wooden face.

"I really think this is the original one which came from India or Nepal," he said in amazement. In the sixth century, it was a long journey from Nepal across the Himalayas to Lhasa. Then it sat, immured inside a larger clay image, for thirteen hundred years. After the desecration of the Jokhang during the 1960s, the statue traveled back over the Himalayas, through Nepal to India, until it reached the reverent protection of the Dalai Lama's hands. "When I saw this small wooden statue the first time," he said, "I felt such great *ningje*, compassion."

Tears rimmed his eyes as he showed me the statue, and his face lit up like a child's. The statue is so sacred to him that he put a cloth over his mouth and nose to protect it from his breath. The elderly attendant to the Dalai Lama bowed low and the Dalai Lama tapped the statue against the monk's head, giving him a blessing from Songzen Gampo and the Buddha. As the monk stepped back, the Dalai Lama motioned me forward. I bowed and then he tapped it lightly on my head.

3

THE TIBETAN EMPIRE AND THE SPREAD OF BUDDHISM IN TIBET, 650–820

Growing up in the Potala, the Dalai Lama heard about the might of the Tibetan Empire founded by Songzen Gampo. In dozens of stories, mostly told by the Potala's sweepers, he heard how it expanded dramatically after the first emperor's death. Yet Buddhism was the focus of the young Dalai Lama's education, not Tibet's political and military history. His vision of imperial Tibet from the seventh to the ninth centuries became more concrete only during another stage of his life, while he stood on the ancient walls that still surround the ruins of the Tang Empire's capital city of Chang'an. In 1954, at age nineteen, he was in the middle of a two-year tour of the People's Republic of China, as a state guest of Mao Tse-tung. How did the boy who grew up in the Potala arrive there?

When Tibet was invaded in 1950, its military lacked modern equipment and training, whereas China was armed with the latest American weapons, seized from the defeated Nationalist leader Chiang Kai-shek. Since the United States and all other nations refused to offer useful military assistance to Tibet or to provide useful support in the United Nations, despite Tibet's pleas for help, the Dalai Lama saw no alternative but to try to work directly with Chinese commanders in Lhasa and ultimately with Chairman Mao.

"There was no choice," he remembered wistfully. For a second, there is a glimpse of the lonely, frail teenage boy, thrust onto the throne of Tibet to take absolute responsibility for the fate of his country.

When the tiny Tibetan army was overwhelmed, in a matter of days, and the Chinese army began their march on Lhasa, the Dalai Lama urged Tibetans not to fight. Since it was impossible to defeat China, he wanted to spare his people from pointless slaughter, so he returned to Lhasa and, after trying to work with the Chinese for several years, he subsequently accepted an invitation to visit China. He quotes a Tibetan saying when describing why he walked into a fire—alone—that had just burnt his nation: "What is burnt by fire should be healed by using fire. Tibet's trouble came from the East, from China, and so the only way to deal with it was to go there, to have dialogue with them."

Eager to educate the Dalai Lama about the wonders of modern China, his hosts escorted him, relentlessly, through factories and communes. Yet one day in Xi'an (ancient Changàn), the program ran out of steam.

"There was no official program in the afternoon and a free evening," the Dalai Lama remembered. "The mayor of Xi'an and the deputy minister of Gansu Province suggested that we go outside the city. Outside there are walls from the Tang dynasty more than one thousand years old. We were on the walls, which are quite high and thick, and the sun was about to set. Sitting there, the mayor told me that the Tibetan army reached up to these walls and the emperor of China, living then in Xi'an, had to run away. I thought that in an airplane I could have flown from there to Lhasa in a one-hour flight. And I thought, 'Oh, the Tibetan army, in order to create such a panic in the capital of the Tang . . . at least tens of thousands of soldiers must have been there, must have come to China on foot.'"

His eyes glaze over as he recalls this memory. "The Tibetan army traveled such a far distance into inner China, not just to the border, with no modern logistics and no technology. Still they were able to take this city."

The young Dalai Lama, who had recently witnessed the Chinese invasion of Tibet, had never dreamed of a Tibet so mighty. His understanding of ancient Tibet changed while he sat on the Tang walls of Xi'an, watching the sunset. The tales he had heard as a boy from the sweepers in the Potala about Songzen Gampo's fierce army were as real as Xi'an's massive walls. Tibetans had conquered the capital of China and installed their own emperor.

"Tibet was large and powerful at that time," the Dalai Lama said. "Otherwise it would be difficult to invade China. I know that army came there to the walls of Xi'an, and I have heard they conquered the city and installed an emperor. But I do not know the full details. You should investigate what the historians have written."

The Tang dynastic histories, along with the Arabic, Turkic, and Tibetan historical records, provide a reliable history of the wars between imperial Tibet and China. At its height, when Xi'an was the Tang capital, its name was Chang'an, or the City of Enduring Peace, and was the largest metropolis in the world. The city had a population of over one million people, within adobe walls that were forty feet high and sixty feet wide and ran for thirty-six kilometers surrounding an area of eighty-four square kilometers. No other city in history would exceed a population of one million until London surpassed that number in the twentieth century.

Chang'an was one of the first planned cities. From north to south there were fourteen avenues, which intersected the eleven east-west streets to form an urban grid lined with shade trees and water channels. Elevated, enclosed highways linked the emperor's hunting parks and palaces so he could shuttle between them out of sight of his subjects. Jews, Nestorian Christians, Zoroastrians, Hindus, Manichaeans, Buddhists—members of nearly every religion in the Old World—had priests or temples in the city. Foreign foods, goods, and music, brought along the Silk Road, were popular with the cosmopolitan Chinese residents of Chang'an. Imperial officials assigned several quarters of the city to foreign trade (an imperial monopoly) and foreign residences, since Chang'an served as the eastern terminus of the Silk Road. The Tang rulers commanded the production of hundreds of thousands of silk weavers throughout their empire, and much of the silk passed through the warehouses of Chang'an and out on the backs of camels, headed as far as Europe in exchange for silver. The Inner Asian nomadic empires bordering the Tang also received silk payments not to loot Chinese cities or the caravans on which the Tang depended.

Representatives from conquered states—what are now Korea and northern Vietnam, for example—who paid annual tribute to the Tang emperors made regular journeys to Chang'an. There they rubbed shoulders with trade missions from India, Tibet, Persia, and dozens of nomadic groups from Inner Asia. The Chinese insisted that all these visitors accept official positions as "vassals" bearing tribute. Visitors from independent states accepted this interpretation of their status as long as they could continue to trade for Tang silk. What did it matter that the Chinese insisted on calling them vassals of the Son of Heaven?

The Sino-centrism that shaped Chang'an's dealings with foreigners had deep roots. China was the only literate "civilized" society to emerge in relative isolation. Civilizations as diverse as the Indus, the Euphrates, and those of ancient Egypt, Rome, and Greece developed in the company of at least one literate sibling. Chinese civilization was in a sense an only child, without a literate equal, and this indelibly marked the Chinese. All non-Chinese were considered "barbarian." Even today, travelers to China are sometimes heckled as "barbarians" while they walk down the street. China's isolation ended in 128 B.C. By then, Emperor Hadrian ruled a Roman Empire in regular trade contact with India, Afghanistan, Persia, Spain, central Africa, even Russia; representatives from dozens of societies thronged Rome. Yet no literate Chinese of the day read any other language. Even though Chinese silks were on the backs of Roman emperors, the two civilizations never read reliable reports of the other's existence—such were the distances separating China from the rest of the world. China's certainty of its supremacy was, to a degree, the terrified overcompensation of a people who had been routinely defeated by their "inferior barbarian" neighbors, people the Chinese referred to as maggots and slaves. Its overcompensation is the root of China's sense of aggrieved nationalism, which continues to dominate its foreign relations to this day. The historian Pan Yihong summarized the Tang dynasty's outlook on international relations when she writes that, for the Chinese, the emperor was "the only legitimate ruler, of not only China, but the world."

One of the rare written exceptions to this long-standing policy of supremacy is the treaty the Tang rulers signed with Tibet, recognizing it as an equal. The informal treaty between the two states that was symbolized by the marriage of Songzen Gampo and Princess Wencheng preserved the peace as long as both Songzen Gampo and the Tang emperor Taizong were alive. In 649, Taizong and Songzen Gampo died within a few months of each other. The succeeding Chinese emperor, Kao-Tsung, attacked Tibet. During the next two hundred years, Tibet and China concluded six written treaties. China broke the first two. Despite efforts at peace, the two empires were constantly at war with each other and with the three other major powers in Central Asia: the Arabs, the Turks, and the Uighurs. The five empires fought for supremacy in Central Asia, amid ever-changing alliances, loyalties, and betrayals. A Tibetan princess was married off to a Turkic khan. Chinese princesses went to Uighur and Turkic khans. In 677, Tibet controlled the entire Tarim Basin. Tibetans joined forces with Turkic princes against the Tang, and vice versa. It was a history of continual war and shifting alliances.

The oasis city-states in the Inner Asian deserts of the Tarim and Dzungarian Basins, that vast land along Tibet's northern border, were the trade depots of the Silk Road. Whoever controlled the isolated city-states—founded and largely inhabited by Buddhist Indo-Europeans and Turks, not Chinese or Tibetans—controlled the trade along the Silk Road. During the two-hundred-year Great Game, the Tibetans controlled the Silk Road for two periods, totaling fifty years; however, there was no final victor during the two centuries of competing colonialism and imperialism.

No Chinese army ever penetrated deeply onto the Tibetan Plateau, certainly not to Lhasa; thus Tibet was never a part of China at this time, though some of the border regions were occupied for brief periods. On the contrary, Tibetans repeatedly sacked and occupied dozens of Chinese cities deep inside China, sometimes for decades. Tibet ruled not just the Tibetan Plateau; large armies swept down and occupied most of western China in the eighth and ninth centuries. Nor did Tang China ever occupy large swathes of Tibet. The Tang dynastic histories offer conclusive evidence that Tibet and China were equal, independent states, fighting with each other, along with the Arabs and the Turks, to control the wealth of the Silk Road, and that Tibet occasionally ruled large parts of China, not the contrary.

The Tang rulers eventually withdrew from Inner Asia, unable to invest their military power in securing the Silk Road—which had brought the empire such great profits—because of threats to stability within China. In 755, a rebellion broke out among foreign mercenaries led by the Turkic or Sogdian general An Lu-Shan, employed to guard China's northern border. While Tang China was preoccupied with this rebellion, from 760 to 800, Tibet held off the Arabs and the Turks and seized most of the Silk Road cities from China, for the second time in two hundred years. Tibet controlled all routes leading from China to the West and deprived China of tributary treasure, horses, taxes, and one third of Tang territory.

Tibet had become the most serious threat to Tang China's existence. In 763, Trisong Detsen, one of Songzen Gampo's great-great-grandsons, sent an army composed of Tibetans and troops from allied and vassal

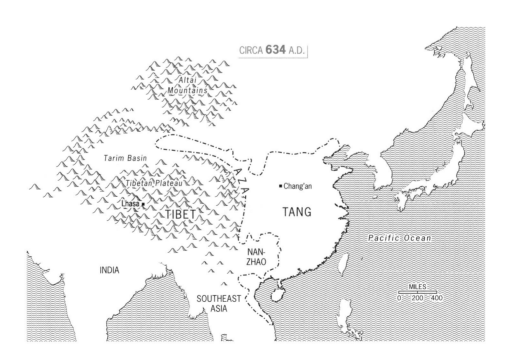

kingdoms to attack Chang'an. The chief eunuch of the imperial court hid the news of the approaching army from the emporor, Daizong, and had General Guo Ziyi, who was desperately preparing for war with the Tibetans without the support he required, sacked. When the emperor at last learned of the attack, he fled the capital just after he restored General Guo, who was able to summon only twenty cavalrymen to defend the city. Estimates of the size of the Tibetan army vary from 200,000 to 100,000, but the battle was lopsided as Tibetans poured across the vast walls surrounding Chang'an and easily engulfed the city. These were the walls that the Fourteenth Dalai Lama would one day stand upon.

Because of this comedy of errors, the Tang dynastic histories say, the Tibetans held Chang'an for fifteen days. Tibetan sources say that the army from Lhasa attacked Chang'an as punishment for Emperor Daizong's refusal to honor an agreement made by his father, swearing that China would pay Tibet fifty thousand bolts of silk a year in tribute. Once they took Chang'an, the Tibetans installed a puppet Chinese prince of imperial blood, who proclaimed the start of a dynasty and signed a document guaranteeing that he would pay an annual tribute to Tibet. Chinese sources concur on these details and add that the usurper appointed chief ministers and other court officials, while the Tibetans plundered the city and burned down many of it houses. In the end, Tibet retreated, Daizong recovered his capital, and the Tibetans' usurper, one of the emperor's sons, was soon dead. The Tang dynasty survived until 906, but the rebellions of 750 and the Tibetan sacking of Chang'an in 763 marked the end of Chinese conquest in Inner Asia. Tibet occupied the Silk Road cities it had seized from the Tang for about fifty years, from approximately the 760s until the local Uighurs recovered their independence by 820. No Chinese empire would retake the oasis states (what China now calls Xinjiang) until the eighteenth century. The Tibetan Empire reached its pinnacle during these campaigns: never again would Tibetans rule the Silk Road cities or sack China's capital.

After the sack of Chang'an, Tibetans and Chinese continued to fight for another sixty years. The two empires repeatedly negotiated and verbally swore to peace treaties, though the two sides did not create bilingual agreements. The historian Pan Yihong writes that the six treaties before the final Tibeto-Tang pact in 822 meant "different things to the two sides and were not very effective. While the Tibetans demanded an equal footing and reciprocity with Tang, the Chinese insisted on acceptance of their claims of superiority." Tibetan and Chinese troops thus guarded both sides of the border between the two states, which were never unified into a single state.

When the Tang dynasty felt that its existence was at stake because of Tibetan attacks, it finally signed a written treaty with Tibet, which was also eager for peace as China had succeeded in luring former Tibetan allies into joint assaults on its borders.

The Chinese emperor had refused to sign the preceding six treaties, but in 822, for the first time, a bilingual Chinese and Tibetan text was drafted. As the two nations signed and then broke one treaty after another, Tibetans

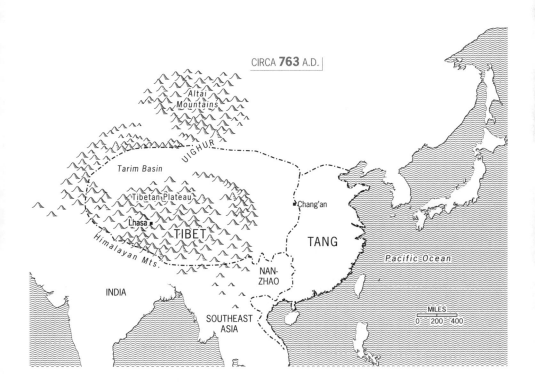

grew wary of China's practice, in the documents, of belittling their rivals from Lhasa. During negotiations in 781, according to the Tang dynastic histories, the Chinese again tried to insert demeaning language. Tibet's emperor, Trisong Detsen, quickly pointed out, "Our great Tibetan and Tang nations are allied by marriages, and how is that we are treated with the rites due to a subject?" At Detsen's insistence, the wording was changed.

During the rites to formalize the final treaty, in 822, China—grudgingly agreeing to follow "barbaric" Tibetan customs—swore to uphold the treaty, in front of a Buddhist statue, while burning incense as an offering. Tibet negotiators agreed, after much pressure, to affirm the pact in the "civilized" Chinese fashion: spreading the blood from animals, butchered as offerings to the treaty, on their lips. The language of the document is unequivocal.

> The great king of Tibet . . . and the great king of China . . . have made a great treaty and ratified the agreement. In order that it may never be changed . . . the terms of the agreement have been inscribed on a stone pillar. . . . Both Tibet and China shall keep the country and frontiers of which they are now in possession. . . . From either side of that frontier there shall be no warfare, no invasions, and no seizure of territory. . . . And in order that this agreement establishing a great era when Tibetans shall be happy in Tibet and Chinese shall be happy in China shall never be changed, the Three Jewels, the body of saints, the sun and moon, planets and stars have been invoked as witnesses.

Though the Dalai Lama learned a great deal about Emperor Trisong Detsen in his childhood, he knew almost nothing about the emperor's sacking of Chang'an until he went to China. Trisong Detsen's role in the First Spreading of the Dharma in Tibet, on the other hand, is celebrated in Tibetan literature, architecture, folk songs, opera, painting, and dozens of myths. Oddly, the outline of his life told by Tibetans mentions Chang'an only in passing.

After Trisong Detsen sent his army to sack Chang'an, in 763, he invited two great Indian Buddhist masters, Padmasambhava and Santaraksita, to propagate Buddhism in Tibet. With their help, Trisong Detsen founded Tibet's first monastery, at Samye, and supported the first Tibetans who took the vows of Buddhist monks. In 792, the emperor called for a debate between conflicting Indian and Chinese Buddhist schools of thought, which were both taught at Samye. The Indian masters defeated the Chinese in a two-year public debate, and Indian Buddhist philosophy, rather than Chinese Buddhist philosophy, became the dominant influence on the development of Tibetan Buddhism.

For the Dalai Lama, as for most Tibetans, the sack of Chang'an is a minor event. Tibetans have never portrayed their victory over the Tang as evidence of the superiority of Tibetan civilization. It was Trisong Detsen's support for Buddhism in Tibet—the invitation of two great Buddhist masters to Tibet and the founding of Samye—that Tibetans hold in greatest regard. One of the two masters invited to Tibet, Padmasambhava *(pad-ma-sam-ba-va)*, also called Guru Rinpoche (Precious Teacher), played a unique role in Tibetan history, comparable perhaps only to that of the Bodhisattva Chenrizi.

He stands at the door of the reception hall, waiting for me with a beaming smile on his face. When I walk toward him, his twinkling eyes remain locked on mine. "How are you, Mr. Laird?" the Dalai Lama says in a happy, booming voice.

He shakes my hand and guides me toward my seat. He has just spent three hours talking with delegations from five countries. Formalities can dominate such meetings, which he detests, and he is eager to get to work. He slips his feet out of his made-in-India Bata sandals and folds his legs underneath his body, Asian style, up in his chair, the equivalent of rolling up his shirtsleeves. With his ever-present *mala* of prayer beads in his hands, he is ready. One part of his mind will be on his prayer beads throughout our conversation.

"Let's work," he said, peering over my shoulder curiously at the long list of questions I have prepared. He shifts the beads through his fingers and a mantra slips quietly from his lips as a whisper.

"When did you first hear of Padmasambhava?" I asked.

"I was always very familiar with him for several reasons. There were statues and paintings of him everywhere. In the Potala, in the Jokhang cathedral in Lhasa, everywhere there was an image of Padmasambhava. Also there was a monthly ritual for a statue of Padmasambhava that had been there since the time of the Fifth Dalai Lama. So every month on the tenth day, in the morning, I had to send an offering to one particular image of Padmasambhava. I remember that one of my monk bodyguards, the senior one, would come with this special *khata* to be taken to Guru Rinpoche's statue in the Jokhang. He always asked me to make a wish or prayer because he was going to offer it to the statue." A *khata* is a white scarf of silk or cotton that Tibetans offer to one another, like flower garlands offered elsewhere. Tibetans also present these ritual greeting scarves to statues in the temples.

"How was the bodyguard dressed?" I asked, because I was curious who these bodyguards were.

"Monks," he replied, shrugging his shoulders. Their dress was the same as his, with a shaved head and the body wrapped in woolen burgundy robes. "These monks had large pads on their shoulders under their robes, like an American football player. Padded like the *Dhob Dhobs*. There were four monk bodyguards with me, and it was always the senior monk who brought the *khata* to me, for me to make a prayer over it." *Dhob Dhobs*, a class of monastic police officers, were large men who wore padded clothing to enhance that appearance.

"I remember this very clearly," the Dalai Lama continued, "even though I was only six or seven then, because I used to be playing in the dirt or playing with some water, and this large senior monk bodyguard would come find me with a pure white *khata*. Sometimes my little hands were very dirty. Then I wouldn't be able to touch it, so I would bless the *khata* with my head by touching my head to it. Even in the middle of playing, I would have to do this, so I remember it very clearly. I have such a clear picture of this also because I was so small and the bodyguards were quite big. I had to touch my forehead to the *khata*, so this giant bodyguard would have to kneel down on his knees, because I was so small."

"Did you know at first who it was for?" I asked.

"No, at first I did not know which statue it was for," the Dalai Lama replied, "but every month I heard the name of the statue, 'The Great Liberator'; I didn't even know where it was. 'The Precious Liberator,' people said. So therefore, I had a very early and perhaps very funny familiarity with Padmasambhava. While I was playing, my prayer would come from my mouth. Anything I could think of, like: 'May there be no war'; 'May I have a long life.' I think these two were the ones I always said. He would put the scarf on my head and I would automatically think of these prayers in the middle of playing. I think my main mind was still concentrated on my playing, but my mouth automatically repeated one of these two prayers." He paused to make sure I was listening closely, and as he looked me in the eyes, he exclaimed, "Serious prayer!" and laughed uproariously at his joke. Once again, his laughter is self-deprecating.

Padmasambhava was invited only after Santaraksita *(San-ta-rak-see-ta)*, who was teaching in Nepal, arrived in Tibet.

"It was Emperor Trisong Detsen who invited Santaraksita to come and help spread, help propagate Buddha Dharma," the Dalai Lama said. "When he came and started to teach the Dharma, there were some hindrances, some obstacles he faced."

The Tibetan historian Tsepon Shakabpa writes that after Santaraksita began to preach the pre-Buddhist animistic spirits of Tibet, the gods of the Bon religion "were so resentful and displeased that they caused storms, lightning, and floods. The people interpreted these omens as a sign that the new religion was not acceptable."

Sherpas in Nepal, who practice Tibetan Buddhism, tell stories of the challenges Trisong Detsen faced when he started building the first monastery, at Samye. Stonemasons worked all day on walls, but at night, angry spirits came and tore them down. Folk Buddhists believe that the wrathful protector deities and spirits of mountaintop, spring, hearth, and cemetery resisted the new religion.

The Dalai Lama said, "Santaraksita advised the emperor, 'Now we need one who has power to control physical reality.'" They needed a miracle worker.

"Then Padmasambhava was invited to come to Tibet," the Dalai Lama continued. "After Padmasambhava arrived, Santaraksita advised the emperor that he would only be giving ordination to monks, and spiritual advice, teachings, and discussion of philosophical works. He carried that responsibility. These two Indian masters had different work in Tibet. The emperor founded the temples. Santaraksita ordained monks. Padmasambhava was brought to overcome obstacles, to tame the spirits of the land. Padmasambhava gave some very secret, high teachings to Trisong Detsen himself and twenty-five other close disciples, but he also visited many places as he did this, all over Tibet."

"You say that Guru Rinpoche had to tame the spirits of Tibet," I observed to the Dalai Lama. "Over the years I have heard folk stories from all over Tibet about how Guru Rinpoche defeated the local spirits in a certain valley, during some magical combat, and then instead of killing them, he made them swear to be 'Protectors of the Dharma.' Many times Padmasambhava marks the earth—he presses his handprint into solid stone—to signify the victory of Buddhism in that valley. Buddha also touched the earth, at the moment of his enlightenment, so the earth would testify, swear to, his enlightenment."

"That is right," the Dalai Lama said. "Again, it appears as a miracle. I know one monk, Ketsang Rinpoche. I heard that once he was playing with some other children, when he was very young, seven or eight. He was running in the marshy land and he jumped on a stone and he slipped and fell and he somehow made this foot imprint in stone without any intention."

"Yes," I said. "Tibetans say that a number of reincarnate lamas have done such things. Padmasambhava is the beginning of this tradition, I believe."

"Yes, I think so, probably," the Dalai Lama answered.

"Is that associated with taming the protector deities of the earth?" I asked.

"Perhaps, I don't know," he said. "With such a young Rinpoche, it happened unintentionally. With others we hear they intentionally do such things. In some cases, I think they are trying to lessen negative forces. In Milarepa's case, he was in a magical competition with someone else, showing his spiritual power."

"But this is not the case of Padmasambhava," I said, "unless he was trying to convert the Tibetans and show that the power of Buddhism is real, greater than that of the protector deities?"

"This is possible," the Dalai Lama said. "The main task of Guru Padmasambhava was at the mysterious level. He established the Tantric level of the teaching in Tibet."

We were straying from history into myth, but Padmasambhava was so important and so mysterious that it was essential to continue. In ninth-century India, Tantric Buddhist yogis, using sexual yoga and other radical means, claimed to acquire magical powers, and enlightenment. Padmasambhava was one of the greatest of all Tantric yogis. I knew that Padmasambhava was a central figure in the propagation of Buddhism in Tibet, but getting the Dalai Lama to elucidate the idea was difficult. "So Trisong Detsen worked with Santaraksita and Padmasambhava to propagate Buddhism. That much seems solidly grounded in history. One of the things they did was to build the first monastery, at Samye in Central Tibet, and then to ordain the first monks there, right?"

"Correct," the Dalai Lama replied.

Samye is only a few hours' drive southeast of Lhasa, on a highway paved by the Chinese in the 1990s. Seen from the air, the original would have looked like a Buddhist mandala, with a circular outer wall enclosing the main temple at the center and half a dozen minor temples arranged around it. The adobe walls of the ground floor tower forty feet high, though the restored temple today is only a shadow of the original. The original survived almost intact right up to the twentieth century, until its destruction during China's Cultural Revolution in the 1960s.

"Unfortunately, I never went to Samye," the Dalai Lama said. "Traditionally I should have gone after my final examination. But as soon as my final examination was over, it was 1959 and then things changed. So when I crossed the river and was fleeing Tibet, people told me, 'That is the road to Samye,' but then there was no time to visit because I was escaping."

The Dalai Lama said that there were Indian and Chinese monks at the monastery in Samye in Trisong Detsen's time and that each had his own quarters. There were also separate quarters for a team of translators who rendered Indian Buddhist texts into Tibetan.

"Santaraksita, as an experiment, gave ordination to see whether Tibetans could practice and follow *Vinaya* or no," the Dalai Lama said. In the centuries after the death of the Buddha, the community of Buddhist monks codified the rules of discipline for monks, first established by the Buddha, in a Sanskrit text called the *Vinayasutra*. The Dalai Lama refers to the discipline, or vows, of a monk as *Vinaya*. These rules start with vows of celibacy, nonviolence, and honesty but include many others as well, somewhat similar to the rules of Saint Benedict in the Christian tradition.

"After these seven young boys were ordained and trained," the Dalai Lama said, "they became successful monks. From this, we can see that before Santaraksita, there was no ordination of Tibetans as Buddhist monks. So at Samye at this time you had Santaraksita teaching the Indian tradition, Chinese teaching Chan, and Tibetans, and Tantric practitioners. After Trisong Detsen passed away and Santaraksita passed away, then one unqualified Chinese master named Mohoyen was teaching a version of Chan at Samye, and this caused a lot of misunderstanding. He defended the 'instantaneous system,' saying enlightenment could be had at once." The Chan school of Chinese Buddhism spread to Japan, where it developed further and became Zen Buddhism, which still seeks the thunderclap of enlightenment in this life.

"And what happened when the Chinese master spread this teaching in Tibet?" I asked.

"Other monks disagreed," the Dalai Lama said. "Then a student of Santaraksita in India, an Indian monk called Kamalasila, was invited from India. Santaraksita had passed away, but he left a testament for Kamalasila. So Kamalasila came to Samye and debated the Chinese master who spread the misunderstanding *(about Chan)*. Kamalasila debated the Chinese for two years, and made clear the interpretation of the texts and the authenticity of the Indian view that was first established by Santaraksita."

"And this was important for the establishment of Buddhism in Tibet, wasn't it?" I asked.

"Yes," the Dalai Lama replied. "The Chinese master Mohoyen made the wrong interpretation of Buddha's words. Tibetan Buddhism, while accepting instantaneous enlightenment, says that there are many things that come before that instant. It requires meditation on impermanence and gaining insight into the nature of suffering, without which one cannot achieve deeper nonconceptual states. My point is that the Chinese master also followed Buddha. It was a problem because of one person's misunderstanding, not the tradition."

"So those were the most important things achieved by Trisong Detsen," I summarized for the Dalai Lama. "The first Tibetan monks, the founding of Samye, and then the debate. How did Emperor Trisong Detsen and Padmasambhava relate to one another? Did they share power?"

"Basically," the Dalai Lama said, "the religious king—and we say that Trisong Detsen was a Dharma Raja—he had his own domain. Then the spiritual teacher had his own domain. There is a special relationship between Trisong Detsen and Padmasambhava, and in fact Tibetans believe that any ruler of Tibet must have some special relationship with Padmasambhava."

Listening to the Dalai Lama, I could not help but recall all the miracles I had heard attributed to Padmasambhava by folk Buddhist believers throughout the Himalayas. Sometimes it seems as if Padmasambhava visited every village and left some miraculous mark in stone in every one of them. I said to the Dalai Lama, "There are so many stories told in Tibet about the miracles of Padmasambhava. He will seem mythical to many Westerners. Do you believe that Padmasambhava was a real human being?"

"Yes, I think so. He was an Indian from Udiyana," the Dalai Lama said. "But then no one knows where exactly Udiyana is *(although some modern scholars identify it with the Swat Valley in modern Pakistan)*. So yes, he is a very mysterious figure and it is controversial. In ancient Indian literature we can read about the great masters of Buddhism a thousand years ago. They are well known. Even if the teachings they wrote have vanished, still we have their names in other texts from the time. Padmasambhava is not known or written about by any of the ancient Indian masters in their texts from the period. He seems not to be there. But in Tibet he came and worked, and then later, many great Buddhist masters have had clear visions of Padmasambhava, calling him Lopon, Guru Rinpoche, calling him by so many names in Tibetan. I also had some dreams of Padmasambhava. There is a real effect here in Tibet. So he must be a historic person. Then there is the question of whether he lives today: we believe that he is still alive *(in some manner)*."

"All of this sounds a bit mythical," I told the Dalai Lama.

"Yes, you are right," he said. "Guru Rinpoche is not like other historic figures, like Songzen Gampo or Milarepa. He had a very strange, sort of mysterious personality. Some say he lived many years in Tibet. Some say he lived in Tibet for a very short period. But in any case, there is definitely Guru Rinpoche. Irrespective of how long he lived in Tibet, something happened. This person, Padmasambhava, is a special person with a connection to Chenrizi. He is one of the highest. He was a Buddha, a fully enlightened one."

"What were his motivations for coming to Tibet?" I asked.

The Dalai Lama numbered three names on his fingers as he said, "Trisong Detsen, Padmasambhava, Santaraksita, these three in previous lives had some special, unique relations. There was karmic history." Because of past lives in which these three encountered one another, they were fated to work together again in Tibet.

"Did Padmasambhava achieve enlightenment in that life?" I asked.

"No, I think long before," the Dalai Lama said. "Guru Rinpoche had magical powers, or *siddha*. Since he is a manifestation of Amitabha (*The Buddha of Boundless Light*), he is regarded as the sublime activities of all the Buddhas. These emanations *(of Amitabha)* come in different forms at different times, but they all come mainly to save *(the sentient beings)* of Tibet."

"In what other ways did Padmasambhava work to save Tibet?" I asked.

"You have heard about what we call the revealed treasure texts that were found much later?" the Dalai Lama responded.

"Yes, I know that he left Tantric books or teachings all over Tibet, to be found at a later time," I said.

"All these revealed texts or treasures are related to Guru Padmasambhava, and in this way he also made a contribution," the Dalai Lama explained. "They were all hidden by Guru Padmasambhava, at the time of Trisong Detsen."

"These hidden texts, sometimes, they can be hidden in the mind?" I asked.

"There are different categories," the Dalai Lama said. "But yes, they can be, as you say, hidden in the mind. Someone may have received a particular teaching from Guru Padmasambhava at a particular time, in the past. Then later on, in another life, the grosser-level mind is manifesting or dominating the person, so then that person is unable to recall what he or she has been taught. In a future life, through one's own spiritual meditation or practice, then one is able to activate the subtle mind and one is suddenly able to recall these teachings."

"I have heard," I said, "that he did not die when his work was finished in Tibet—that he flew away with his Tibetan consort Yeshi Chogyal?"

"Yes, that's right," the Dalai Lama replied. "From Tibet, according to this account, he flew away on the rays of the sun."

"So he never died?" I asked.

"We believe that he is still living," the Dalai Lama said, "and some people have had special visions where they reach Padmasambhava's land, even now. For example, with the Fifth Dalai Lama it is well known that he reached Padmasambhava's place. There he received some instructions, and then it is said he returned to Tibet. There are two levels of interpretation about these events, depending on one's realization. I also believe these events happened. But even at the first level, though there might not have been Indian sources written about him, still there is the construction of the Samye monastery. That is something very real. There are the great deeds of Padmasambhava, and Santaraksita and the Tibetan king Trisong Detsen."

I had a hard time accepting this as history. "But then he seemed to visit almost every town in Tibet, if we look at all the local myths?"

"Perhaps it was through miraculous forms that he actually visited," the Dalai Lama replied.

"But there are so many mentions in Tibet about his miraculous visits and actions," I said. "It seems that maybe there were more miraculous visits than there were conventional visits."

"Possibly," the Dalai Lama said, unperturbed as I peppered him with my doubts.

"Why?" I asked.

"Because of his special powers," the Dalai Lama said patiently, "he could reach more places than could be reached by his actual presence. So he might have reached a place by some miraculous means, but once he was there, people could see him."

"This is very difficult for non-Tibetans to understand," I insisted.

"Yes," the Dalai Lama said, "but the point is that based on different realizations or experiences, Padmasambhava could reach many places a normal person could not. Perhaps even if he reached a place in an out-of-body experience, still the ordinary people there would have seen him as normal."

"And when Padmasambhava reached these places, all over Tibet, he . . ." I began.

"Guru Rinpoche's special task," the Dalai Lama interjected, "was to pacify or eliminate all destructive or negative forces. Among the human beings, at another level there were also the negative forces, which means some opposed the Buddha Dharma, but those the emperor can handle. At the mysterious level, there were also forces opposing the Buddha Dharma. To counter such forces, that was Guru Rinpoche's task. So the opposition was on the mysterious level, and his method to combat it too was on a mysterious level. The main task of Guru Padmasambhava, at the mysterious level or otherwise, was to make the Tantric level of the teaching flourish."

"And when he finished his work in Tibet, at that time, Padmasambhava did not die?" I questioned with obvious disbelief. "He disappeared on the rays of the sun, to his own land, somewhere that people without realization cannot go. None of this is like with Songzen Gampo and other figures, where we have a second level in Tibetan history. It seems almost everything Padmasambhava did was at the second level. At least at the conventional level, Songzen Gampo died, even if at a higher level he did not. But with Padmasambhava . . ."

"Yes," the Dalai Lama interjected. "Padmasambhava, even his body might not have disappeared. This is very complicated. For the Buddha there is no conventional level. For some people, even now they can receive teachings from the Buddha and the Buddha can manifest through people. Chenrizi, for example, is a manifestation of Buddha."

"You are not saying," I asked combatively, "that when we talk about Tibetan history, there are always two levels?"

"No, that's not what I mean," the Dalai Lama said with a hint of annoyance. "There are historically important people in Tibetan history, whether lama or king or others for whom there is no second level of understanding. There is no uncommon level; they are ordinary people. However, in some few cases, there are extraordinary people in the history of Tibet. For these people there are two levels of meaning, of understanding, two different levels of reality, about their lives. But that does not mean for the whole history there are two levels. But at any rate, today the conventional is more important." He laughed loudly at my attitude and then continued, looking for some other way to reach me.

"Look," he said. "I understand that it is difficult to accept for Americans. However, for us as Buddhists, depending on our level of experience and belief, there are no difficulties for us to explain the resurrection of Jesus Christ. We can easily accept this because of the fact that we accept that there are these two levels. From a Buddhist viewpoint there are no difficulties to accept the resurrection of Jesus Christ at the second level."

Suddenly much of what I had been arguing with him about, the fact that Padmasambhava did not seem like a historical figure to me, changed. I was stunned.

"But few modern Christians would give you the same latitude," I said, "when they look at the miraculous events surrounding Padmasambhava, which you say happened mostly at the second level."

"Yes, that is true," the Dalai Lama replied. "But that is a matter of opinion. The underlying belief is the same."

Discussing Tibetan history with the Dalai Lama, I began to think that the belief structures of all human societies are remarkably similar. It's only the beliefs that vary.

4

LANG DARMA: DECLINE, REVOLT, AND A PERIOD OF CHAOS, 797–977

The rain had not stopped once during the previous three days or nights. The roads of the Indian hill town of Dharamsala were always potholed and rutted, but the constant rain had caused more damage and some were now small streams. Every afternoon I took a taxi up to the Dalai Lama's compound at the top of the hill, above the rest of the town, made my way through security, and then, walking under an umbrella, made my way to the audience hall. We had spoken the previous day about Songzen Gampo and the beginning of the Tibetan Empire, and so it was natural to move on to the reign of his descendants.

The reign of Trisong Detsen, and the propagation of Buddhism in Tibet during his reign, marks the height of the Tibetan Empire. Trisong Detsen's two sons and two grandsons presided over the empire's glory days before collapse and a period of chaos. The reign of Trisong Detsen's son Muni Tsenpo, in the 790s, is renowned among Tibetans because of a strange episode in which the emperor tried to redistribute wealth throughout his empire. The Tibetan historian Tsepon Shakabpa writes:

Muni Tsenpo, in an effort to reduce the great disparity between the rich and the poor, introduced land reform and appointed ministers to supervise the equitable distribution of land and property. When the emperor later inquired as to the fate of his reforms he discovered that "the rich had become richer and the poor, poorer." He is said to have tried this reform twice more—with no success. Padmasambhava was questioned on these events and told the emperor, "Our condition in this life is entirely dependent upon the actions of our previous life and nothing can be done to alter the scheme of things."

The Dalai Lama and I had settled into a working routine, so as soon as we took our seats, I read the extract from Shakabpa. Padmasambhava's attitude is so different from modern political attitudes, and reflects such a dominant ethos within Tibetan culture, that I was curious how the Dalai Lama viewed this.

"This is important," he said, "because it shows how much influence Buddhism had on Muni Tsenpo. He developed a serious understanding about the unequal distribution of wealth and wanted to make it equal. He tried to do this three times. I do not know how exactly he attempted to do it." His voice broke into skeptical laughter as he added, "But what is very clear is that he did not kill the rich people! The records about these events are not clear, but the concept is there and I was very impressed by this ideal as soon as I first heard it as a boy."

The Dalai Lama's laughter grew from history he had lived through. In the twentieth century, Marxism tried to solve the same problem recognized by Muni Tsenpo in the eighth century, by killing the rich. In the early 1950s the Chinese Communist Party executed several million landowners after its victory in the Chinese Civil War, and there was a massive redistribution of wealth in China. China eventually carried out a similar policy in Tibet. Yet today China's government has abandoned its earlier experiment, without ever saying the death of millions was unjustified, and now, throughout China, the rich are even richer. The Dalai Lama's laugh alluded to these tragic chapters of history. Despite this, the Dalai Lama has what I saw as a curious respect for the ideals of Marxism. I asked, "Do you see some link between Buddhist and Marxist ideals?"

"Yes," the Dalai Lama said. "I think that there is a similarity between Buddhist and Marxist thought. But Muni Tsenpo didn't do this because of Marxist thought. Clearly he attempted this because of the influence of Buddhism. But there is a connection between the two *(the ideals of*

Marxism and those of Buddhism)." To continue with Tibetan history in the eighth and ninth centuries, I put aside this line of questioning, vowing to return to the Dalai Lama's appreciation of Marxist ideals when we came to the history of the twentieth century.

Records about the reign of Muni Tsenpo are incomplete. Still, the quality and the quantity of Tibetan historical documents from the late eighth and early ninth centuries are comparable to the skimpy sources about the reign of Charlemagne, who ruled in Europe during the same period. Muni Tsenpo's reign was brief; and because he produced no heir, his brother, Trisong Detsen's other son, inherited the throne by 804. The new emperor, Tride Songzen, continued the policies of his father. He invited Indian Buddhist masters to teach in Tibet, founded temples, and defended the heartland as well as distant conquests of the empire, in battles with both the Arabs and the Chinese. Tibetan troops occupied large swathes of the plains in northern China, which was repeated cause for alarm in Chang'an. The Tang capital was nearly encircled for a decade as the Tibetans pushed eastward, beyond Chang'an, deep into China.

Tride Songzen sired only two male heirs, Tri-Ralpachen and Lang Darma. Their battle for the throne is the final chapter of imperial Tibet. When Tride Songzen died in 815, a year after the death of Charlemagne, the elder of the two sons, Darma, did not become emperor. Tride Songzen's powerful chief ministers passed him over because he was anti-Buddhist and a hothead. The younger son, Tri-Ralpachen, became emperor instead and, like his predecessors, continued to support the propagation of Buddhism in Tibet by inviting Indian masters to teach and by overseeing the translation of texts into Tibetan.

It was Emperor Tri-Ralpachen who signed the treaty with Tang China, in 822, in which Tibet and China recognized each other as equals. It was the final diplomatic exchange between the two countries for centuries. The size and unity of both the Tibetan and the Chinese states were about to shrink dramatically during a period of chaos in the ninth and tenth centuries. When the successor to the Tang, the Song dynasty, emerged it governed a much smaller Chinese state. Border states sprang up separating Tibet and Song China, and diplomatic relations were virtually nonexistent.

In Tibet, the decline into chaos began with Lang Darma's bitterness at losing his throne, which was inflamed by an anti-Buddhist sentiment spreading throughout Tibet and China. The two factors doomed both imperial Tibet and Darma's brother, the emperor Ralpachen. In 836, two anti-Buddhist ministers plotted with Darma to remove the most pro-Buddhist ministers from Ralpachen's court. The two then crept up on Ralpachen, who lay drowsy in the sun after a few glasses of Tibetan beer, or *chang,* and broke his neck with their bare hands.

As soon as Lang Darma seized the throne, he issued edicts designed to destroy monastic Buddhism. Monasteries shut their doors and monks disrobed, under penalty of death. Lang Darma, "Bull" Darma or "the young ox," and his supporters never accepted Buddhism's rise to dominance over Tibet's aboriginal religion, Bon, and because of Darma's actions, the clock was turned back; monastic Buddhism died in Central Tibet for perhaps a century. No monks were ordained for about seventy years. Though some temples did not close, there were no celibate monks to lead the Buddhist community of Tibet and the Buddhism that survived was folk Buddhism. Darma's reign also marked the end of the Tibetan Empire. "The Tibetan military power was at its highest under Ralpachen, and then by the time of Lang Darma, it went down" the Dalai Lama told me.

The Dalai Lama sees the emperors Tri-Ralpachen, his father, Trisong Detsen, and their great-great-great-great-grandfather Songzen Gampo as "the three great forefathers, or three greatest kings and patrons of Buddhism. But the height of Tibetan military power came under Ralpachen. Then *(after that Tibet declined because)* there was a religious conflict between Buddhism and the local religion Bon, because of political reasons. And then Lang Darma." The very name is a symbol of collapse and chaos for Tibetans.

The Dalai Lama heard of Lang Darma from the sweepers who took care of the chapels in the Potala in the same way he first learned about many things. The workers in that vast establishment were his playmates and, through them, he learned Tibet's folklore. To them, Lang Darma was a devil with horns.

"Because he had these horns," the Dalai Lama said, "the girls were sent to comb his hair and after they finished, he would use his horns to kill them.

Actually, they saw his horns and he didn't want others to know that he had horns, so he would kill them with the horns." The Dalai Lama laughed as he told this tale. "So one girl went to do his hair and while she was combing his hair, she began to weep. This weeping surprised Lang Darma and he asked, 'Why are you weeping?' She replied that she knew that once she was done, she would be killed. Then he felt a bit concerned or guilty and he said, 'If you promise not to tell others that I have horns, then I will spare you.' She promised, and he spared her life. Then after a while she became restless and wanted to share the secret. But she had made a promise. So she went to a crevice in a rock and whispered into the crevice that Lang Darma has horns on his head. After this a bamboo shoot grew from the crevice. And then someone cut the bamboo and made a flute from this bamboo. And whenever he played the flute, it would sing, 'There are horns on the head of Lang Darma.'"

The Dalai Lama could not stop himself from laughing as he finished this tale he learned as a child. There was some essence of Tibetan belief in reincarnation embedded here: truth or human motivation can be enacted over many incarnations. It never dies.

"I don't know if this is important. Youth . . ." the Dalai Lama began, but again laughter overcame him. As I laughed with him, I caught a glimpse of how crucial this parable could be, to understand the spiritual evolution of the Dalai Lama's beliefs. Because he found it so funny, I almost missed the point.

After he'd caught his breath, the Dalai Lama continued. "The popular belief was that Songzen Gampo had this Buddha on his head. It is there in the paintings you see of him. And that Lang Darma had horns. I think that people were confusing the first and second levels of interpretation." When he said this, I took a deep breath, and he looked at me: it seemed he would say no more than this. The uncommon reality, as seen by wise men, may have been transformed into popular myth. If myths had some of their origin in such misinterpretation, I wondered how many myths, in how many societies, came from this sort of misunderstanding. It seemed to me that this might be how spiritual metaphor, and myth, become fundamentalist reality: as distortions of visions of reality that are so difficult to see they require great training. The persistent repetition of the Dalai Lama's stereo vision—seeing the "common" and "uncommon" view at the same time—had been difficult enough. Now he said that some aspects of Tibetan popular culture developed when the two levels were confused with each other.

As I pondered this in silence, the Dalai Lama continued. "Recently one of our Buddhist Christians told me that in Christianity, their hell beings have horns as well. In Tibetan history, bad people were supposed to have horns. Negative people had horns, to show they were fiercer. On the conventional level, Lang Darma might not have those horns and Songzen Gampo might not have the Buddha growing from his head. But at the spiritual level, Songzen Gampo had this Buddha head *in* him; he had the sign of the lineage of Chenrizi and Amitabha."

Though I wanted to linger, I moved on, asking the Dalai Lama, "What caused the conflict between Ralpachen and Lang Darma?"

"For a long time, I think, there was a religious conflict between Buddhism and the local religion Bon," the Dalai Lama said. "And then there were always purely political conflicts, locally, and then Lang Darma came. He sided with the Bon tradition, and he killed his brother. I can imagine that there were some people against Ralpachen even though he was very much respected. When he was killed by Lang Darma, that created jealously, division, and more problems. Because Ralpachen was killed, people might not have had the same respect for the new ruler. In those days great ministers or well-trusted persons were posted in outer areas, like Amdo and Kham *(in eastern Tibet along the Sino-Tibetan border)*. In fact, Songzen Gampo's descendants were posted in these border areas. So naturally, when they heard the emperor was assassinated, they went their own way, taking local power. And when Lang Darma himself was later killed, there were more divisions. And so the central power declined, and then there was a retreat from the border." Thus began a "period of chaos and demoralization, especially among those people who had responsibility in the border areas. By then, in the east, semi-independent ministates were created along the border with China."

"Tibetans often tell me," I said, "that the arrival of Buddhism tamed the Tibetan heart, and that this contributed to the collapse of Tibetan military power."

"I think there are many reasons," the Dalai Lama said, "and, yes, the arrival of Buddhism had something to do with it. Modern writers view this in a different way, though. They say there was too much devotion to monks and that a lot of land was provided to the monasteries, so that harmed national wealth and development. So from the viewpoint of national interests, Lang Darma took the action to destroy Buddhism. This is one possible way to view these events. There are many causes and conditions for every event. So one of the causes and conditions might be this. Often when we explain something, we look at one factor and say everything is caused by this one factor, but usually there are many factors."

Returning to the facts of Lang Darma's destruction of Buddhism, I asked, "Did he do that deliberately?"

"Yes. Deliberately. His motivation was to show disrespect. He was trying to destroy Buddhism."

"Why did he force the monks to become hunters, to marry, or to become soldiers?" I asked.

"Once a monk kills something, he is no longer a monk," the Dalai Lama responded. "His motivation was to destroy Buddhism. He deliberately made monks destroy life, to destroy their vows. Killing animals will not revoke ordination of a monk, but killing a human being will; Lang Darma's purpose was to destroy Dharma. Then I think for sixty to eighty years there were no monks in Tibet. The whole *Vinaya* community *(monks following the monastic rules of discipline)* was destroyed. However, there were some Tantric practitioners who remained in remote areas."

Two hundred years of Buddhist civilization was suppressed within a few years. By 836, the Indian masters had fled home to India. Worship in Songzen Gampo's Jokhang, founded with the help of his Nepalese and Chinese wives, and worship at Trisong Detsen's Samye, founded with the help of two Indian masters, ceased altogether, although, oddly enough, the temples were only locked, not destroyed. Darma's followers locked or destroyed the Buddhist libraries. Some faithful monks hid other Buddhist texts, along with statues, treasures, and Buddhist relics. Publicly, Tibet reverted to its native religion, Bon.

A similar persecution of Buddhism took place only a few years later in China, officially beginning in 845. The Tang ruler felt Buddhism had grown so powerful that it had become an economic and political challenge to the authority of the emperor. Perhaps Lang Darma felt similar pressures from the growing power of monks in Tibet, just as the Dalai Lama hinted to me.

In the ninth and tenth centuries, Buddhism in China slowly recovered, but ever after, it remained within the control of the emperor. In Tibet, after the power of the state collapsed, Buddhism emerged as the dominant force in the country. China and Tibet were competing imperialist powers when they first met, in the sixth century; but by the tenth century, when they encountered each other again, the souls of the two states had diverged in radically different ways.

Lang Darma's persecution angered Tibetan Buddhists, and eventually they rebelled. In 842, an ordinary monk named Lhalung Palgyi Dorje rode into Lhasa and shot Lang Darma between the eyes with an arrow, killing him.

Dorje knew that a monk who killed a human being breaks the most basic Buddhist vow and is no longer a monk. He found Lang Darma in front of the Jokhang, bending over to read an inscription on a stone pillar, the text from the 822 Sino-Tibetan treaty. Dressed in a black robe, the monk pretended to be a Bon dancer. He concealed his bow and arrow in his long robes, and this ruse allowed him to get close enough to make his shot. In the confusion after Dorje shot Lang Darma, the monk escaped to his black horse, waiting on the edge of town.

The murder of Lang Darma is familiar to the Dalai Lama because of the ethical issues it raises.

"In order to save the Buddha Dharma, the monk took that action," the Dalai Lama said. "The reason is very clear. His motivation was to save the Buddha Dharma. That is very clear. Then he went to the Amdo area where some monks remained and he joined them. Actually, this story is often told in Tibet. He had his horse painted black and then he had a robe, which was black on the outside and white on the inside. After he committed this murder, he reversed his robe and then he crossed the river—where the charcoal dust on the white horse washed away. When guards went to search for him, they asked if anyone had seen a man with a black dress on a black horse. And people said no, but we saw a man in white on a white horse." Dorje, who was never caught, spent most of the rest of his life in meditation retreats. Because his motivation was pure, Tibetans believe, he was able to atone for his sin. Even the Dalai Lama says it is "very possible" that he managed to have a positive rebirth in his next life. There is no eternal hell for Tibetans, so even the worst karma, earned from the worst sins, has an end. Even with the worst sins, such as murder, there are degrees. If one murders with the right motivation, it is not as evil as if one murders for personal gain or pleasure.

The murder of Lang Darma by the monk Dorje brings up a central tenet of Tibetan Buddhism and something close to the heart of Tibetan history. Tibetan Buddhism does not teach that nonviolence is the only possible response to injustice or evil. Tibetans, like all people, have not always been nonviolent. I cut to the heart of this issue when I asked the Dalai Lama a variation of an age-old philosophical question: "What if I had been able to kill Hitler before he began to kill millions of people?"

"Theoretically speaking," the Dalai Lama said with sudden gravity, "in order to achieve greater benefit for a greater number of people, you can use a violent method. This is true in Vajrayana and Mahayana Buddhism and is one of the things that separate these schools from Theravada Buddhism." Theravada Buddhism, the first form of Buddhism taught at the time of the Buddha, survives today in Southeast Asia and Sri Lanka. Mahayana and Vajrayana (or Tantric) Buddhism developed later in India and today are practiced in Tibet, China, Japan, and Central Asia.

"There is a famous Buddhist story," the Dalai Lama continued, "about the five hundred merchants crossing the sea and the leader of the merchants realized that one of them wanted to kill all the people on the boat. So in order not only to save the people on the boat but also to save this man from committing the sin, the lead merchant took on the sin of killing the murderer before that action took place."

"So Palgyi Dorje did take on the sin of killing Lang Darma to save the Dharma," I said.

"Yes," the Dalai Lama said. "It's a unique aspect of Mahayana Buddhism, even from ancient times. One reason that ancient Hinayana (*Theravada*) monks argued that Mahayana was not taught by Buddha was that in the Mahayana there are teachings that say that there could be occasions where even killing could be permitted."

After the murder of Lang Darma, in 842, his sons and wives competed for the throne in a climate of spreading chaos. Imperial Tibet eventually split into two kingdoms. By 866, the last descendants of Songzen Gampo migrated to Western Tibet *(Ngari)*, where they tried to preserve some semblance of control. In fact, the empire had already collapsed, and in the resulting chaos, Tibetan troops retreated from the borders. Along the former Sino-Tibetan border, mini–buffer states sprung up. Tibetan society contracted, and for almost a century, historical records are rare. Those that do survive are no longer composed by officials of a central state but by monks.

"When you read some of the Tibetan histories," the Dalai Lama said, "after the imperial period, the perspective and focus is on religious history. So there are more details about the great lamas. Unfortunately, there is no clear tradition of recording political events throughout all of Tibetan history. There is an overemphasis on religious history rather than on political history. Often you have to pick through all these religious histories, and there is no coherence."

"How do you summarize the end of empire and Lang Darma?" I asked.

"First," the Dalai Lama said, "Tibetan troops began to be withdrawn from the border from the start of his reign, and eventually Lang Darma's successors divided the empire, and Tibetan external power collapsed. Also, the central authority collapsed with Lang Darma as his two sons split power and divided Tibet. After Lang Darma's destruction of Buddhism, which was mainly the destruction of the monastic institution, there was sixty to eighty years of complete despair and destruction. Then Buddhism returned to Central Tibet (*divided into two areas Tibetans call* U *and* Tsang), moving in from all the border areas. Slowly it was reintroduced and grew, but there was no central political power."

"And what happened to the last inheritors of imperial power?" I asked.

"One supposed Tibetan king," the Dalai Lama said, "established his capital in Western Tibet. It was almost like changing the capital from Central Tibet to Western Tibet, and they had some of the feeling of imperial power, from earlier times. But there were other kings, and each king took interest only in his immediate area, not far away. This is a natural sort of process. Each was able to pay attention only to his immediate surroundings, rather than all the far-flung areas that Tibet covered in the imperial period. Then slowly areas gained independence. Like in the northern areas *(along the Silk Road),* the Muslims took over. In the south, the Nepalese took the land back. During this period the political area began to shrink."

"As we leave this imperial period from Songzen Gampo to Lang Darma," I asked the Dalai Lama, "as we leave this period—from about 600 to 850—tell me, do you see this as one unit?"

"Yes, this is one period of Tibetan history."

From Songzen Gampo to Lang Darma, a period of almost 250 years, Tibet was unified under a strong central government. Buddhism prospered, and tens of thousands of Tibetans were exposed to a much broader world of trade, expansion, and growth. Suddenly, with Lang Darma's death, the central government collapsed and, for close to a century, foreign relations ceased and international trade ground to a halt. We have no written record of this period; however, amid the chaos, the cosmopolitan ideas that had found their way into Tibet during the imperial era began to ferment in every region and village. The country that emerged was immensely rich both spiritually and culturally, yet the idea of a unified state was no longer a primary goal. In its place came an era of factionalism and regionalism that was to last over three hundred years.

5

THE DHARMA RETURNS, AND BUDDHIST ORDERS ARE BORN, 978–1204

The first ordained celibate Buddhist monks returned to Central Tibet in 978 from the eastern provinces of Kham and Amdo. At the same time, monks who had survived Lang Darma's purge in Western Tibet began to make pilgrimages to India to study. A few monks returned from India with new Buddhist texts for translation. By the start of the eleventh century, monastic Buddhism was spreading back into Central Tibet from both east and west, in what Tibetans call the Second Spreading of the Dharma. After nearly two centuries of disunity and disorder, the light of history returned to a changed land. The empire was gone, and the emerging monastic powers wrote little political history—they were concerned, as the Dalai Lama said, "not with Tibet as a whole but with monks and monasteries. The Tibetan nation was secondary to their school of Buddhism, and politics was secondary to the Dharma."

During the eleventh century, three of the four major modern schools, or orders, of Buddhism in Tibet started to emerge: Nyingma, Sakya, and Kagyu; a fourth order, Kadam, existed for a couple of hundred years, as an independent school, and then essentially dissolved. Gelug, which is the order of the Dalai Lama, is the main historical successor to Kadam. These religious orders grew to dominate Tibetan society as the country assumed the essential form that it would retain for a millennium: an inward-looking religious state.

In the late tenth century, the returning celibate monks found several forms of folk Buddhism—which they saw as debased and in need of reform—entrenched among the villagers of Central Tibet. Lang Darma had only to lock the monasteries and defrock the monks to destroy monasticism. It was harder to destroy folk Buddhism, based in the home rather than the monastery, where married priests, not celibate monks, celebrated rituals. In the tenth century, the returning monks called the worst of the surviving Buddhists "robber monks," or so says R. A Stein, a noted French historian of Tibet. According to Stein, they had perverted esoteric Tantric texts and "kidnapped and killed men and women, ate them, drank alcohol and indulged in sexual intercourse." Most Tibetans reject the possibility that such excesses occurred.

Even though few of the debased Tantric cults descended into murder during the chaos after Lang Darma's murder, the Dalai Lama pointed out that folk Buddhism strayed far from its original path.

"Before the reformed orders of Tibetan Buddhism were created," he said, "many Tibetans practiced Tantra literally. So there were rites with women, alcohol, and sometimes even drinking blood. Because Tantric practice was very popular, there were some very negative outcomes, excesses by people who did not have proper understanding. They practiced with no real understanding. They were pleasure seekers."

Although the celibate monks, who returned to Central Tibet from the fringes where monastic Buddhism had survived Lang Darma's persecution, also studied Tantric Buddhism, theirs was an orthodox form.

Tantric Buddhism evolved, according to modern scholars, in north India during the seventh to the eleventh centuries, from earlier schools of Buddhism. Tibetans insist that Tantric teachings were taught by the Buddha but were kept esoteric until they emerged publicly in later centuries. Tantra is a multifaceted aspect of Buddhism that defies easy definition. Even the origins of Tantra are debated. Modern Hinayana Buddhists, like Thais or Sri Lankans, say Tantra was created long after the death of the Buddha, whereas Mahayana Buddhists, like Tibetans and Mongolians, say that the Buddha gave Tantric teachings secretly and those teachings then remained secret for many years. Some people see Tantra as a corruption of Buddhism in which the search for magical powers overtook the search for enlightenment. Others view Tantra as a school of Mahayana that preserved the Buddha's most esoteric teachings about a rapid path to enlightenment.

Historically, Hinayana schools, including modern Theravadan Buddhists, were among the first orders of Buddhism. Dozens of different Hinayana orders thrived in India from the time of the Buddha until about the first or second century. By the tenth century, Tantric and other Mahayana schools largely supplanted the Hinayana orders in India. Mahayana, or the Greater Vehicle, was introduced to Tibet, China, and Japan in the fifth to eighth centuries. After the destruction of Buddhism in India, some three or four centuries later, Theravada survived in Sri Lanka and Thailand.

When Mahayana emerged in India, members of its orders pejoratively called the Theravada, and other early schools, Hinayana, or Lesser Vehicle. Mahayana Buddhists believe in the Bodhisattva vow: those who are able to enter enlightenment must defer doing so until all others achieve enlightenment. Thus the Mahayana were devoted to taking greater numbers of sentient beings toward enlightenment. Mahayana monks disparaged the Hinayana because they sought only personal enlightenment. By the eleventh century, Tantric forms—collectively called Vajrayana, or the Thunderbolt Vehicle, to indicate how quick results could be—grew out of Mahayana and became the dominant schools in India, with two trends emerging.

The orthodox Vajrayana monks lived a settled life in vast monasteries, some housing thousands of monks, supported by donations from rulers and the public. Although these celibate monks still followed the strict code of conduct for monks, they performed Tantric rites. The Buddha himself established the *Vinaya*, or code for the monks. It demanded celibacy and forbade drinking and the killing of any animal or human, among many other prohibitions. Both Mahayana and Vajrayana monks maintained *Vinaya*. In contrast, noncelibate, unorthodox Tantric yogis roamed the countryside practicing radical experiments in self-realization. Outside the monasteries, they flouted the *Vinaya* but insisted they were seeking instant enlightenment, through sex, drugs, and other radical methods in this life. According to their critics, they were depraved and were distorting the teachings of the Buddha.

Speaking of Tantra during the Second Spreading of the Dharma, the Dalai Lama said that there was a strong reaction against the excesses of Tantric Buddhists. "The reaction was very strong in Tibet. There was a movement to the *Vinaya*, and many of the early Tibetan masters never publicly practiced Tantra, as a reaction against the previous excesses. However, very secretly some of the masters practiced Tantra, even among the reformed sects." This esoteric religious dispute ultimately had immense consequences for the political life of Tibet. During the eleventh century, however, the impact of these differences was hundreds of years away.

It was a time of intense political and religious chaos. Charlatans and great Buddhist teachers alike espoused a rich array of religious thought and practice without any central control. Although dozens of Buddhist schools emerged in Tibet, and vanished, the four modern schools, or lineages, all began to sprout during the same century. The word *pa* means "man" or "person of," so members of the four great orders are the Nyingmapa, Kagyupa, Sakyapa, and Gelugpa.

The Nyingma, the first order, claims Padmasambhava as its founder. The Nyingmapa are called the Ancient Ones because they are the only school of Buddhism remaining in Tibet to have emerged from the First Spreading of the Dharma, under the emperors. Though many Nyingmapa originally followed married priests—following the precedent established by Padmasambhava—the Nyingma also developed a strong celibate monastic tradition, like all the later orders of Buddhism in Tibet. The other reform orders coalesced around the teachings of charismatic masters during the Second Spreading of the Dharma, beginning with the return of celibate monks to Central Tibet. As these orders developed, the Nyingmapa were those who did *not* follow the reforms, which drew most deeply on the traditions established by Padmasambhava. Although all Buddhists in Tibet before 978 were Nyingma, they did not use the term. Only as the reformed orders of Buddhism emerged did the Nyingma order become the Ancient Ones, and thus a distinct school.

The first prominent Indian invited to Tibet after the period of chaos was the great teacher Atisha. From Atisha's teachings, Drom Tonpa founded the first reform order of Tibetan Buddhism, the Kadam. The Dalai Lama's school of Buddhism, the Gelugpa, would eventually emerge from the Kadam. Atisha is important to the Dalai Lama because, until "the eleventh century, there was only the Nyingma tradition. It was only after Atisha arrived in Tibet that the other Buddhist orders developed."

I am fond of what the Dalai Lama calls the sweeper stories. So I asked if he remembered any of their stories about Atisha, from his childhood in the Norbulingka, his summer palace, and in the Potala.

He laughed at once and began to tell a story from his childhood. "There was a small bird like a thrush, a bit smaller than a pigeon, which lived in the gardens of the Norbulingka. The Tibetan name of the bird is Jolmo, and its tune is very special. They sing a very good sort of melody, and there are some stories about that bird and Atisha. The sweepers told me that I should listen carefully and I could hear that the bird sings 'Jowo Yong Ba, Jowo Yong Ba,' or 'Atisha is coming, Atisha is coming.' I remember listening for the bird. But it was sad also, because of another story they told me.

"They said that the Thirteenth Dalai Lama was very fond of Jolmo," the Dalai Lama continued. "In fact, it is nearly always seen around another monastery, beyond Lhasa. It usually resides there all year round. It only came sometime to the Norbulingka. The Thirteenth Dalai Lama was so fond of Jolmo that he showed less mercy to one bird that would attack it. So when I was a boy in the Norbulingka, because of that harassment, that other bird would land on a branch and then quickly disappear. So the sweepers told me. They also said that the Thirteenth Dalai Lama was so fond of Jolmo that once he sent some instructions to one of the protector deities to send this beautiful bird to the Norbulingka. So when I was there, some of the older sweepers who knew the Thirteenth Dalai Lama, they said that after he sent those instructions, a few more of the Jolmo came. But then the other birds attacked them and they disappeared. In any event, they always told me that the Jolmo's song sounded like 'Jowo Yong Ba,' or 'Atisha is coming.' That is one of the first stories I heard that came from the mouths of the sweepers. I was a very small child when they told me about this."

As he finished recounting this memory, he glanced at me and frowned. "You need to be careful when you write this, because we are talking about a serious subject," he said. "If you just rely on the sweeper stories, then it will sound very funny!" He ended his comment in booming laughter, imagining how others might view him.

As his laughter died away, I said, "I think such stories let people see into your childhood, and they also bring history to life. This is a book not just about history but about how you learned it." He nodded his head and seemed to agree. Then I asked him why he was afraid of laughing when talking about Atisha.

"Why is the story of Atisha so serious?" I asked.

"Because of the price that was paid to bring Atisha to Tibet," the Dalai Lama replied gravely. "I have never forgotten that."

Around the start of the tenth century, in Western Tibet, there was a king named Lha Lama Yeshe Od. He was a descendant of Songzen Gampo from the sons of Lang Darma, who had fled the chaos in Central Tibet when the empire collapsed. Yeshe Od was so concerned at the degeneration of Buddhism in Tibet that he sent twenty-one young men to study Buddhism and Sanskrit in India. All but two died from heat and the rigors of the journey. On their return, the two survivors became famous translators and brought the first word to Yeshe Od that Muslim invaders were starting to attack the Buddhist monasteries of India. In fact, over the coming century, Tibetans would inherit the final flowering of Buddhism in India, since invading Muslims destroyed Buddhism in India during the eleventh and twelfth centuries.

Yeshe Od also heard about the greatest Indian Buddhist master of the day living in the monastic city of Vikramashila. Hoping such a teacher could help reform Buddhism in Tibet, he sent an emotional plea, along with a large amount of gold, to Atisha, urging him to come to Tibet. Atisha, worried about the decline of Buddhism because of attacks from Muslims, returned the gold with the reply that it was important he stay in India.

Yeshe Od decided he had not sent enough gold, so he led an attack against some of the Muslim kings to the north, who now occupied the Silk Road in search of more. He was subsequently captured but was offered his freedom if he would renounce Buddhism. Battlefield conversion of "infidels" was a common Islamic practice of the day. When Yeshe Od refused, the Muslim king demanded his weight in gold as ransom. A young great-nephew raised a fortune to pay the ransom only to find, after traveling to the Muslim king's fortress, that he didn't have enough gold. He managed to speak with Yeshe Od briefly in his dungeon cell. The uncle had shrunk to a near-skeleton, and the Dalai Lama said it was an old man's voice that spoke to his great-nephew.

The Dalai Lama showed a great deal of emotion as he told this story. "Yeshe Od said, 'I never thought you had such strong determination or inner strength to come here with this much gold. Seeing you now, I am no longer worried, as you can carry out my task without me. So do not think of me. Even if I were to escape, I have only ten years of life remaining to me at most, so it is not important. Therefore, instead of looking for more gold as ransom, everything should be taken to India to invite Atisha. Tell Atisha, "I sacrificed my life to bring you to Tibet. And please remember that in my next life I will be near you and receive teachings from you."'"

The room was utterly silent as the Dalai Lama looked right in my eyes. This story seemed to express, for the Dalai Lama, not just Tibetan history but his underlying belief that reincarnation and human motivation create a tapestry of motivation played out over many generations.

"Very powerful. Deep belief," the Dalai Lama said. Then he began to speak as though he were Lha Lama Yeshe Od in his jail cell. "'It is very sad for this family. It is also sad that Buddhism has degenerated at this time. It is also sad that my life is in the hands of this king. At this moment, however, all we can do is keep our determination to bring Atisha. We must keep our determination.' Wonderful story. Such deep faith in Buddhism. It's very sad. Actually, Lha Lama Yeshe Od sacrificed his own life for Buddha Dharma. When I was a boy, his body, without the head, was still kept in salt in the Potala. The body was destroyed, but there is a small stupa still there."

The monks at Vikramashila did not want their teacher to leave, but the Dalai Lama believes that Lha Lama Yeshe Od's sacrifice moved Atisha so much that he agreed to travel to Tibet. He arrived in Western Tibet at the age of sixty yet was very active. He wrote books, gave public teachings, and supervised the editing of translations of Indian texts. As Lha Lama Yeshe Od had hoped, Atisha started and helped guide a Buddhist renaissance. Eventually the kings and Buddhist priests who ruled the many rival principalities in Central Tibet invited Atisha there.

"When he first arrived," the Dalai Lama said, "some Tibetan lamas wearing luxurious cloth with sleeves of brocade, riding on horses, rushed toward Atisha. When Atisha saw them, he covered his head and said, 'Now these Tibetan ghosts are coming.' He was being sarcastic. Their clothes offended him, since they were dressed as high officials rather than as monks should be. The Tibetan lamas were very embarrassed, and then they took off their luxurious clothes, put on a monk's yellow robe without sleeves, and gently approached Atisha. Atisha was then very happy and he received them."

The Dalai Lama pointed out many ways, both large and small, that Buddhism in Tibet had degenerated during the centuries after Lang Darma. For Atisha and the reformers who followed him, nothing was more important than the *Vinaya*, the code of conduct created by the Buddha. Atisha helped to reestablish the *Vinaya* in Tibet, after years of neglect— and included in the reintroduced code was the rule that monks must not wear fancy clothes.

"Even today," the Dalai Lama said, "some monks wear things that are forbidden by the *Vinaya*. That is very sad. We say one thing, very seriously, but then never think if this contradicts our daily practice or behavior. This is so sad."

After Atisha's death, in 1054, his chosen successor, Drom Tonpa, codified his teachings. Thus emerged the reform-minded Kadam order, whose adherents are called Those Who Uphold the Buddha's Words as Personal Instructions. For Kadampa, the Buddhist texts were not scripture to be worshipped so much as they are precepts intended as practical guides. The Dalai Lama's order, the Gelug, eventually grew out of the Kadam. Gelugpa today share many essential precepts with the early Kadampa.

"The Kadampas' uniqueness was their practice of *Vinaya*," the Dalai Lama said, "but at the same time they practiced Tantra in the proper way, secretly. 'Properly' means they visualized the different rituals in their meditation. They visualized, in meditation, drinking alcohol, women, whatever, but they never touched them. So if a Tantric ritual called for wine, they used tea. In place of blood they use red color, and so on." The Dalai Lama is careful never to say anything that could be misconstrued as sectarian criticism of any of the modern schools of Tibetan Buddhism.

For me to understand what the Dalai Lama said, I had to make simple generalizations and form my own opinions about the Tantras, which do seem to teach forms of sexual yoga, if only because the Tantras are a subject that has been so widely written about by many modern authors. Though the celibate monks of the Nyingma tradition share the Dalai Lama's certainty that Tantra is to be practiced as a metaphor, I discovered that some Nyingma and Kagyu teachers still follow a literal path. There are Tibetan practitioners today who still teach the yoga techniques of sexual Tantra because they believe that, if used properly, these methods can bring enlightenment quickly, in this life. These teachers assert that the ancient Tantric texts were not written as metaphors for rituals but as practical guides to using sex as yoga. One of the approaches these masters teach is a way for men to engage in intercourse with a female yoga partner for hours at a time without emission of semen. They believe, in fact, that men thus absorb their semen for spiritual purposes. Clearly, according to some practitioners, these techniques can lead to heightened levels of awareness for both partners, even to enlightenment. However, such techniques are not considered suitable for many people, and there is a persistent fear that the practices will be misused for pleasure, which is considered dangerous to health and sanity. Because of this, the Tibetan Buddhists who practice sexual yoga literally rather than as ritual metaphors do so in strict secrecy. It takes years of extensive meditation to find a true Tibetan master who might give a student esoteric instruction.

The distinction between celibate and noncelibate practitioners has become one of the chief divides within Tibetan Buddhism. Although there seem to be celibate and noncelibate Buddhist teachers of every sect, I found that the Nyingma and Kagyu sects are more famous for their noncelibate practitioners, while the Gelugpa are best known for their celibate ones. It's also important to remember that the practice of sexual yoga was, and still is, extremely rare.

All Tibetan schools of Buddhism agree that if you are a practitioner of yoga with a female consort, you must not claim to be celibate. This ideal is subject to abuse. There have been modern instances in which Buddhist teachers used talk about Tantra as a means to seduce students. A great majority of Tibetans believe, as the Dalai Lama does, that the only proper practice of the Tantric texts is metaphorically, in rituals and during meditation visualizations, not with women partners.

A thousand years ago Atisha taught, and the Dalai Lama still believes, that the *Vinaya* is essential to the practice of Buddhism. The name Kadampa was chosen to differentiate its adherents from Buddhists in Tibet who disparaged *Vinaya* practice as relevant only to the beginner's path. The debate over celibacy and the interpretation of certain Tantric texts is an important thread in Tibetan history, and it continues today.

While Indians like Atisha were teaching in Tibet, Tibetans went to India, studied there, and returned to teach Buddhism in their country. Perhaps the greatest of these was Marpa, guru of Tibet's most famous yogi, Milarepa. As Atisha's students institutionalized his teachings to form the Kadampa, so Milarepa's chief disciple, Gampopa, solidified the foundation of the Kagyu order, or Those of the Whispered Teaching. Milarepa is more than a father of the Kagyu school. A yogi who dedicated his life to meditating in Himalayan caves, Milarepa is esteemed for his spontaneous songs, unsurpassed devotion, spirituality, and wit. Only humble Milarepa could pull up his robes to expose his naked buttocks—and the thick calluses on them after years of immobile meditation—to a student and have the experience register as a deep Buddhist teaching. "This is the determination it takes," he was saying. Milarepa is a living presence even now, throughout the Himalayan region, because his pungent humanity and wisdom, preserved in his biography and a collection of songs, still inspire Buddhists, though he lived nearly a thousand years ago, from 1040 to 1123.

"When I first heard the story of Milarepa, I cried a lot," the Dalai Lama said. "When I tell the story of his life today I still cry a lot."

"Do you remember where you were when you first heard of Milarepa and his master, Marpa?" I asked.

"Yes, I remember clearly," the Dalai Lama said, "because I had such strong feelings when I first heard the story. There was a set of very beautiful paintings—*thangkha (painted scrolls)* not murals—that were stored away in the Potala. Every year when my winter retreat in the Potala started, they were hung on the walls of one temple and some offerings were made. These were very beautiful paintings of the lives of Tilopa, Naropa, Marpa, and Milarepa." Marpa studied in India with his teacher Naropa, whose teacher was Tilopa, so the *thangkhas* illustrated the fathers of the Kagyu lineage.

"It was almost like watching a show or entertainment to look at these paintings," the Dalai Lama continued. "I had such a strong reaction that I developed a special interest. In order to know the meaning of the stories in the paintings, I took out the biographies of all these masters, I hung the *thangkhas* in front, and then I read the biographies. So I would look at the painting and then read the biography, back and forth, for hours. Often I would cry when I read these stories, because they were so moving, especially Milarepa's story, which was very moving to me."

"Which part of his biography struck you the most powerfully?" I asked.

"When I was young," the Dalai Lama answered, "the story about how much suffering Milarepa endured, after his father died, when his aunt and uncle stole his inheritance, that made me cry in frustration." The death of his father, and his uncle's subsequent betrayal, turned Milarepa and his mother into beggars, hired field hands who worked like animals and were forced to eat maggot-infested scraps, wearing nothing but rags. The description of his youth stands as an accurate portrayal of many of the problems faced by the poorest people in Tibet at that time. Young Milarepa's father had been rich, and Milarepa spent his first years as a young lord. For Buddhists, there is a quirky resemblance in Milarepa's story to that of the young Buddha, in Nepal, who was also born a prince, and then voluntarily gave up his wealth to seek enlightenment. Milarepa's story differs because of the all-too-human search for vengeance that is the mainspring of the narrative. Milarepa's mother, enraged when her brother-in-law stole her inheritance, vowed to send her son away to study black magic, hoping to have revenge.

"His poor mother's departing advice when he left," the Dalai Lama continued, "was so very sad. She borrowed money to send her only son to study black magic." The Dalai Lama's haunting laughter at the world we live in ended suddenly as he went on with the story, speaking now as Milarepa's mother. "'My son, you should be very attentive in your studies, because we have encountered so much suffering and we have had to become beggars.' She described what a difficult position they were in and told him that 'you cannot study like the wealthier boys. You will have to put more effort in because of our terrible situation.'"

Milarepa recorded his mother's parting words to him in his biography:

Above all, remember our misfortune and let the signs of your magic be manifested in our village. Then come back. The magic of your companions and ours is not the same. Their magic is that of well-beloved children, who want it only for pleasure. Ours is that of people who have suffered tragedy. That is why an unyielding will is needed. If you return without having shown signs of your magic in our village, I, your old mother, will kill myself before your eyes.

The Dalai Lama laughed with tears in his eyes as he recalled this passage. "You see this is a very rich story. I felt so sad, when I was younger, particularly about the passage where the mother advised Milarepa about his study. I found this very sad."

It is no surprise that Milarepa, living under this threat, followed his mother's instructions precisely. He found the finest black magician in Tibet, devoted himself unswervingly to his teachings, and then used magic to cause his uncle's house to collapse during a grand wedding feast. The family of those who had persecuted his family were killed. Milarepa's mother's happiness was unrestrained. Her words are recorded in the biography: "Imagine what my happiness will be from today onwards!" she said while strutting around the ruins proudly, though a bystander muttered, "She may be right, but her vengeance is too brutal."

Milarepa himself soon regretted his act of mass murder, and Tibetans believe that the karmic retribution in his life was heavy. His mother died alone in the ruins of the family home. Her neighbors were so frightened of her son that they would not even cremate her corpse. Eventually her unburied bones shone in the moonlight that slanted in through the roof of the abandoned homestead. After Milarepa realized that his murders had created a mountain of negative karma, he devoted his life to atonement and meditation so single-mindedly that he had no time to return home until long after her death. Terrified of the fruit his sins would bear in future lives, he turned away from black magic and sought out Marpa, the greatest Buddhist yogi in Tibet.

As a child, the Dalai Lama had first reacted to Marpa in anger.

"When I was young," the Dalai Lama said, "I lost my temper toward Marpa because he was so mean to Milarepa."

Marpa knew that for Milarepa to achieve enlightenment in this life, his student would first have to atone, through suffering, for his evil deeds. Even to the Dalai Lama, though, Marpa seemed, at first glance, to be hard-hearted.

Marpa insisted that Milarepa build a stone tower for him before the master would provide any teachings to the student, to prove Milarepa's serious intent. When it was half finished, Marpa said, as recorded in Milarepa's biography, "I had not fully considered the matter. Tear down this tower and take the earth and stones back to their places."

On another occasion he told Milarepa to build the tower again, in a different location, and when it was half finished, Marpa said, "The other day I was drunk and did not give you good direction. Build a sturdy tower here." After a few days, he returned and berated Milarepa: "Who gave you the instructions? I do not remember having given you such orders!"

According to Marpa himself, he worked Milarepa like a horse or a donkey. Milarepa toiled so strenuously that his back was covered with sores, which ran with pus and blood, as he carried rock and mud for the Sisyphean towers of Marpa. Remarkably—and this was the point of the exercise—Milarepa never became angry with his tormenter. He grew frustrated because he wanted to receive the teachings, but his devotion was so intense that nothing Marpa did provoked anger.

When Marpa's wife insisted he look at the wounds on his student's back, Marpa told Milarepa, as recorded in the autobiography, that "my Master

Naropa underwent twenty-four mortifications . . . all of which surpass yours. As for me, without a thought for my life or my wealth, I gave both to my Master Naropa. So if you see the teaching, be humble and continue to work on the tower." Marpa used what Tibetans sometimes call "Crazy Wisdom," providing the instruction the student needed, though conventionally the lessons looked insane.

When Milarepa tried to attend Buddhist teachings, which Marpa was giving to others, the master grabbed Milarepa by the hair and threw him out, because the tower was not completed. On similar occasions, Milarepa said that Marpa "cursed me, kicked me and threw me out. . . . He hurled me to the ground on my face, and everything went black. He threw me on my back and I saw stars. . . . he came out and slapped me again and again."

These stories of Milarepa's treatment agitated the young Dalai Lama as he sat in the Potala staring furiously back and forth from the *thangkha* to the biography. "In the end," the Dalai Lama said, "Marpa took him as his dearest sort of disciple, and then I really felt consoled."

"Did you identify personally with this story? Were your teachers harsh with you?" I asked.

"My teachers were not so harsh," the Dalai Lama responded. "Stern sometimes, but not like Marpa. But they always had beside them two whips: one for my elder brother, and one for me. The distinction between these two whips was that the one for the Dalai Lama was yellow. It was saved for me. But the color difference did not make any difference in the pain. Both were very conventional in that way!

"My teacher," the Dalai Lama continued, "Ling Rinpoche, sometimes he would show his temper and anger to me and on a few occasions he used harsh words, but otherwise he was very gentle."

Sensing a link between his education and Milarepa's, I observed, "But Milarepa was not treated gently by his master, and at first that bothered you a great deal."

"Yes," the Dalai Lama said. "Milarepa was very gentle and very humble and so eager to receive Buddhist teachings from Marpa, but instead of giving him teachings, Marpa punished him and gave him more hard work. Of course, at the end you can see the meaning and purpose of this harsh treatment. Of course, Marpa was a great master."

"But your teachers still treated you harshly sometimes? Did they really use the whip on you?" I asked.

"No, my teachers were very gentle," he said. "Sometimes they would show the whip to me. On occasion, one teacher used some harsh words and more sarcastic remarks."

"What was the purpose of that? To get you to work harder?" I asked.

"Yes," he said.

I wondered if the Dalai Lama consciously connected such actions to those, inspired by wisdom, of a Bodhisattva who vows to lead all beings to enlightenment. That ethos does not spring to mind naturally for non-Tibetans, yet it is central to understanding the Dalai Lama's belief that the Bodhisattva Chenrizi, for example, guides the Tibetan people with Bodhisattva action. I said to the Dalai Lama, "So it was the same with Marpa and Milarepa. As you grew older, you realized that Marpa was a great teacher. He was treating Milarepa harshly, consciously. So this was Bodhisattva action."

"Yes, of course. Exactly," the Dalai Lama agreed. "Afterwards Marpa explained the real reasons why he treated Milarepa that way. Even Gautama Buddha went through six years of hardship before he reached enlightenment. So similarly, Milarepa required some hard penance to purify his negative deeds. So Marpa finally explained these things and then treated Milarepa as his own son."

Milarepa lived many years nearly naked in high mountain caves in search of enlightenment under Marpa's guidance. His life was one of penance. He wore only a thin white cotton robe even in the coldest weather. For years at a time, he ate only stinging nettles, plants so noxious that only the poorest farmers in the Himalayas today eat them. Even those so poor that they will eat nettles mix them with potato and wheat, using the nettles more as a spice. Milarepa ate only the prickly plant, for months at a time. He ate so many that his body turned a shade of green similar to that of nettles. It is Milarepa's extreme asceticism, based on unswerving determination, that the Dalai Lama seems most to admire.

"I really admire Milarepa's determination and his way of practice based on such a hard and unshakable determination," the Dalai Lama told me. "So when I tell other people about Milarepa, it is because they should copy his determination. I myself often think about him or read about him, because I too need that sort of determination. Milarepa was a great master. Enlightened in this very life, through determined meditation practice, of that there is no doubt."

"So you first heard of Milarepa when you were a boy, but your ideas about him and your respect for him are still continuing to grow?" I asked.

"Yes, I have always felt that." The Dalai Lama paused. "But I have never dreamt of him in my dreams up till now. I am expecting some dreams of him. I really admire him."

When the Dalai Lama spoke of Milarepa's death, the issue of levels of interpretation presented itself once again. When Marpa mistreated Milarepa, it was at the second level, the actions of a wise man and for Milarepa's own good. Similarly, when Milarepa died, his biography asserts that rainbows appeared in the sky, flowers fell from heaven, and the dead saint appeared to people, at the same time, in locations widely separated. He even appeared, alive and well, to one disciple hours after he had died, reminiscent of Christ's appearances to his disciples after his death. By now, I knew what the Dalai Lama would say about these miracles. He had no doubt, particularly with Milarepa, about the authenticity of these interpretations. They were real to people who had developed a higher consciousness, through meditation, though a person with what the Dalai Lama called a "common" mind would not have seen things the same way.

We had been talking for quite a while about Milarepa when the Dalai Lama looked at me curiously.

"But how are these things connected to Tibetan history?" he asked.

"Milarepa is one of the great heroes of Tibetan history," I replied. "What is Tibet? Is Milarepa a good example of who the Tibetans are?"

"Yes, true," he admitted.

"The things you tell us about Milarepa also tell us about the heart of Tibet, don't they?" I asked.

"Yes, that is right," he said.

Milarepa is Tibet. For outsiders, a monk meditating in a Himalayan cave is perhaps the most clichéd of metaphors of Tibet. At the same time,

Milarepa is one of Tibet's most revered saints. The ideals he lived for, the ideals that motivated him, his years in caves, the struggles he had under Marpa— these acts of Milarepa's life are definitions of Tibet as Tibetans themselves know the culture, and as outsiders would come to see Tibet.

To hear the Dalai Lama talk about Atisha and then Milarepa together was strange. Both are his heroes, yet they are, conventionally, very different. Atisha helped reestablish *Vinaya*, the code requiring monks to wear a prescribed maroon robe and to refrain from drinking alcohol and having sex, among other strictures. He was also a great scholar who wrote books and translated them. Only after long scholastic preparation, Atisha felt, could the "instant" methods—favored by Milarepa— lead to enlightenment. Yet Marpa, Milarepa's teacher, was renowned for drinking quantities of beer and engaging in sexual yoga with women. Though Milarepa was celibate, both he and his teacher, Marpa, are famous for reaching advanced states of consciousness—even those in which humans can perform miracles—through intense meditation. Milarepa rejected monastic debates and academia, saying rigorous meditation was the way to enlightenment.

"Milarepa captured the essence, the emptiness. He hit the real essence without much scholarly study," the Dalai Lama said. "So because of that the followers of Milarepa emphasize direct practice and meditation."

The Dalai Lama's praise for Milarepa and Atisha highlights the coexistence in Tibet between Buddhism's two, apparently contradictory paths to enlightenment: wild meditating yogis and formal scholastic monks. The seeming disagreement is about means, not the goal. Tibet is the only nation to preserve teachings from all the Buddhist schools of thought up to today. The Dalai Lama, like many Tibetans, has respect for many schools of Buddhist thought. Atisha and Milarepa took different paths to the same goal, and Tibetan history was shaped by a unique respect for, and synthesis of, both yogic and scholastic forms of Buddhism. Milarepa's primary disciple, Gampopa, codified Milarepa's teachings into a finely crafted scholastic text, still used today. *The Jewel Ornament of Liberation* helped to preserve the teachings of the yogi Milarepa in a book that is often compared to Atisha's guide to the stages on the path, *Lamp for the Path to Enlightenment*.

As Buddhism was reestablished, by different teachers, during the Second Spreading of the Dharma—the return of monastic Buddhism after the chaos that followed Lang Darma—many varieties of religious expression emerged. There were solitary monks in caves, some beyond *Vinaya* and some strictly following it. There were hundreds of celibate monks living in one monastery, whose lives were focused on translating Indian texts. There were a dozen students, all married, gathered around one charismatic teacher, who believed that sexual yoga could lead to enlightenment in one life. There was no central figure in Tibet to establish and enforce a strict set of religious guidelines. Monks and other Buddhists at first debated and celebrated the manifest differences among sects. This religious diversity and freedom created one of the richest spiritual chapters in human history, which Westerners became aware of only after the 1960s, when translations of basic Tibetan works like the *Hundred Thousand Songs of Milarepa* began to appear.

There were always different levels of meaning within Tibetan Buddhism, or what the Dalai Lama has described as "common" and "uncommon" perception, depending on one's level of mental training. Tibetan masters knew that true seekers must rely on meaning, not words, on the true doctrine, not men, and on gnosis (knowledge of spiritual mysteries), not perception. They left room for both levels, realizing that individuals differ in their level of spiritual capacity.

It was in this climate that Nyingma teachers discovered esoteric Buddhist texts, similar to Tantric works from India, that—or so it was said—had been hidden by Padmasambhava, during the imperial period. While historians know that these texts were later inventions, faithful Tibetans believe that *tertons*, or "treasure finders," found these texts. At the same time, Nyingma teachers preserved and transmitted one of the deepest of Tibet's meditation practices, Dzogchen, which incorporates aspects of ancient Chinese Chan practices, elements that were eventually transformed in Japan to Zen.

Every school in Tibet, new and old, preserved many forms of Buddhist practice, from thoroughly ritualistic to advanced meditation practices. Each monastery tended to be independent of central control, and there were many suborders and divisions. At one point, there were more than twelve Kagyu schools of Buddhism. Tibet is so large and the monasteries were so widely separated that there was little central administration. Every Nyingma monastery jealously guarded its independence, for example.

Along with the Nyingma, Atisha's Kadam (the Gelug order would not emerge from the Kadam until the fifteenth century), and Marpa and Milarepa's Kagyu, another major sect emerged during the eleventh century. The Sakya, Those of the Gray Earth, was named after the clay found around the main Sakya temple. Sakya devotees splash the adobe walls of their homes and temples with this color.

The Sakyapa, like the Kagyupa, trace their foundation to teachings of a charismatic Tibetan teacher for the Sakyapa it was, Drogmi, a mystical wonder worker who studied the Tantras in India. On his return to Tibet, he attracted a group of devotees, who codified his teachings after his death. Drogmi is famous for acquiring a secret teaching that made use of sexual practices for mystical realization. A disciple of Drogmi from a wealthy and powerful background, the Khon family of Sakya, founded the first Sakya monastery, in 1073. The Sakya eventually became the first of Tibet's Buddhist schools to achieve political power over the country, in the thirteenth century, with the backing of a Mongol patron, but during the late eleventh century, it was just one of many emerging orders.

By late in the century, the founders of the four sects were dead and their disciples had codified their teachings. All four sects attracted patrons from powerful regional lords. As the monasteries grew in size, wealth, and administrative complexity, there was a price: compromised ideals. To cite a typical example: a modest grass hut built by one of Milarepa's spiritual descendants was enshrined within a massive monastic city, built by a wealthy family who supported the Kagyu. Spiritual principles and austerity gave way to pomp and ritual.

From the monasteries, branch institutions were seeded, and within a few decades, hundreds of monks were living inside the walls of large compounds. The size and number of monasteries increased over the centuries. Statues and murals adorned these places of worship for the growing numbers of monks. Some of the early monasteries housed more than ten thousand monks. In valleys across Tibet, peasants and serfs who had once provided a portion of their harvest, or a son in time of war, to the lords or emperors who defended their valleys now paid tribute to the local monastery. The annual cycle of rituals, to figures like Padmasambhava and Chenrizi, grew in number, and the monasteries could not make the required offerings for these rituals without a constant flow of butter and barley from the surrounding farmers and nomads.

Though some of the monks and nuns (who were a distinct minority) undertook long retreats, or engaged in a life of academic study, others came to the monastery, took their vows, learned to read and write, then renounced their vows and left to take a spouse. Among monks who took degrees, some studied philosophy, psychology, and logic, while others translated and collated the Buddhist teachings from India. Still others studied medicine, painting, rituals, and astrology, or devoted themselves to carving the woodblocks to print the collected translations of the Buddha's teachings. Many monks earned a living by performing ceremonies for the dead in the homes of the faithful.

The walled monastic forts housed not only monks. They became primary schools and universities, hospitals, medical schools, drugstores, temples, museums, printing presses, libraries, crematoriums, banks, old age homes, orphanages, and even, on occasion, barracks for monk-warriors. Monasteries became the one public institution, replacing all others, just as they became one of the main political powers, curtailing the development of nationalism. By the twentieth century, experts believe, between 20 and 30 percent of the population were monks (though estimates vary), and most of them did not perform long meditation retreats. Speaking of one large monastery he knew of, the Dalai Lama said that it had, in his day, "about eight thousand monks, students, and scholars. And I think that out of the seven or eight thousand monks, if we count the true scholars, including teachers, only about three or four thousand were good monks. So half were rubbish." Monks still spent their lives engaged solely in meditation, but over the centuries their numbers declined.

Discussing the tendency, over the centuries for monks to spend more time focused on rituals, I noted, "It seems that all the sects developed rituals, and that more and more monks spent their time doing these rituals, rather than real meditation."

"Rituals!" he laughed. "All the sects have a lot of ritual. There is nothing wrong with ritual. Everyone can perform rituals, but not everyone can do the real practices. So for those who cannot meditate deeply, then their only way is through ritual. They stick to these easier sorts of things. Through ritual there can be contemplation. But without a proper understanding, yes, there can be excesses, which is sad."

Nevertheless, popular devotion increased, and as more devotees made offerings in temples and monasteries, the monks grew wealthier. This historic process began in the eleventh century with the foundation of the first sects by idealistic Buddhist teachers. As the monasteries became regional power centers, feuds and wars between the orders centered on politics and economics rather than on any religious differences. There were a few saints whose concerns transcended politics and money. Some addressed the problems caused by the lack of central state. One saint tried to protect travelers from the highwaymen who made Tibet's roads unsafe, while another founded hospices to tend to the sick. Such saints were the minority, however, and the monastic establishments cared more for their own power, despite the price the people of Tibet, and Tibetan nationalism, paid for the lack of a central government.

"After Lang Darma's destruction of Buddhism," the Dalai Lama said, "it was the monastic institutions and traditions and power that grew back. There was no central political power. All the attention of each regent or monk was focused on his own area and on his own school or tradition. So they did not look out for the whole of Tibet. Also, I think the geography had some impact. Tibet is a huge area. If it had been a small country, it would have been easy to control it from the center, but it is huge. In this situation, there was a negative impact from too much devotion to religion. The monks considered the Tibetan nation as secondary to their school, and political things were secondary to the Dharma.

"Then worst of all," the Dalai Lama continued, "as I said before, it was not true religion they were concerned with. They were concerned to make things big and grand: to make big monasteries, and big statues."

From about the year 1000 until about 1200, as Tibetans established the great monasteries of Tibet, they continued to travel to India to acquire new teachings. Tibetan monks translated thousands of Indian Buddhist texts, but as Buddhism evolved in Tibet, there was less reason to travel to India. The most important texts were in Tibetan, and teachers in Tibet were numerous. Yet it came as a shock, early in the thirteenth century, when the invading Muslims destroyed Atisha's monastery in eastern India.

The Muslims had led annual campaigns out of what are now Afghanistan and Pakistan, fighting their way across the Gangetic Plain from west to east for two hundred years. Muslim armies looted and then torched the monasteries: the Buddhist statues appalled the iconoclastic Muslims. Finally, the Muslims reached Vikramashila, the last great monastery left intact.

At Vikramashila, the Muslims slaughtered the monks. The libraries burned for days. The attackers shattered the statues and stole the gold and jewels that adorned them. The army demolished every building, down to the last stone in the foundations of the dozens of temples that once towered in the morning mists; they uprooted them and threw them into the Ganges River. The destruction of Vikramashila was complete: the site has never been identified.

This image of the destruction of Buddhism in India, the irony of its disappearance from the land of its birth, had haunted me for decades. I was eager to discuss with the Dalai Lama how Buddhism died in its homeland.

"How was Buddhism destroyed in India?" I asked. "Was it just the Muslim attacks?"

"Nothing is caused by one factor," the Dalai Lama began. "One good scholar, who has now passed away, sent me a book that he wrote where he discussed the three causes of the decline of Buddhism in India.

"First," the Dalai Lama continued, "the patrons of the monasteries developed more of an inclination toward non-Buddhist traditions. Second, external forces like the Muslim invasions and others—these forces tried to destroy Buddhism. Third, the monasteries and the monks themselves became very wealthy, and they accumulated a lot of gold in the name of Tantra. As we have discussed, there was drinking and sex. These things happened. So the public lost their respect for the monks, some despised the monks, or lost their trust. So I think that there was not one cause but many."

I was surprised to hear him blame Buddhists for these events; I had always held the Muslims responsible. "Really?" I inquired. "You do not blame the Muslims?"

"I think in the Tibetan case also, just as with the Indian case, there is a tendency to look at the external causes. The tendency to look at external forces first is deeply rooted in the human mind and difficult to eliminate. We cannot do so much about others, about external forces. But then ourselves, if we do not practice well, if we are not disciplined, then our religion becomes hypocritical. This is real. So this is the real history of Buddhism in India and Tibet."

I was shocked to see that, in every case, the Dalai Lama looked first for his own faults, before he would look for faults in others. He looked first for the faults of Buddhism before he looked for the faults of other religions. He looked first for the faults in Tibet and then for the faults in other countries. His inclinations shape the way he sees history, just as it does for all of us. But with him, his inclination was to see the faults of himself, his nation, and his religion, first. I had known, intellectually, that this is one of the vows of a Bodhisattva. Listening to him describe the destruction of Buddhism in India as the fault of the Buddhists—at least in part—brought that knowledge to life in a way that was acutely painful. I knew he was right, but I had never met anyone who gave more than lip service to this ideal.

"The tendency to look at external forces first is deeply rooted in the human mind and difficult to eliminate."

I should not have been surprised when a conversation with the Dalai Lama about the history of Tibet led to something more universal than just the study of one country. But I was. The more time I spent with him, the more he surprised me in ways I was not prepared for. There was nothing vague about his spirituality. It was practical advice.

Tibetan Buddhism as we know it today would not exist without one central figure in the monasteries, which Tibetans call a *Tulku*. Teachers who consciously choose to reincarnate as a human, out of compassion for the suffering of others, though they could have gone on to Nirvana at death, are Tulku, and the Dalai Lama is the best-known Tulku in the world. Tulku, like so many aspects of Tibetan culture, are an expression of the Bodhisattva ideals that Mahayana and Vajrayana Buddhism brought to Tibet. By 1950, many of the monasteries in Tibet were led by a Tulku, and throughout Tibetan history this institution played a unique and powerful role. The honorific *Rinpoche,* or Precious One, is added to the name to signify the teacher's position. Buddhist monasteries in India were never led by reincarnated teachers; that system first appeared in Tibet.

The first Tulku was the Kagyu teacher Dusum Khyenpa, in the twelfth century. Prior to his death he told his students where he would be reborn. He instructed them to find his new incarnation and then to educate him so that he could continue to guide them. Since Buddhist teachers in Tibet had long taught Bodhisattva action as the ideal for an enlightened person in the world, the message required only a small leap of faith. At the same time, it was an audacious extension of Buddhism's power. Explaining the significance of this development, the historian Melvyn Goldstein writes:

> In a world where religious sects constantly competed for lay patrons, the religious and political benefits of this form of rebirth were striking, and it quickly became a general part of the Tibetan religious landscape. Incarnate lamas developed lineages, which functioned like corporations in the sense that they came to own property and peasants and retained a legal identity across generations.

After reading this quotation to the Dalai Lama, I asked, "When did you first hear of Dusum Khyenpa, the first Tulku?"

"By reading his biography," the Dalai Lama said. "I don't remember how old I was. In fact, he was a well-known figure in Tibet."

"Why did he decide to reincarnate?"

"There is no doubt that Lama Dusum Khyenpa was a great master," the Dalai Lama replied. "He very clearly mentioned, before his death, that he would be born at such and such a place and at a certain time. He did this in order to serve the Bodhisattva vow. What else can I say? I think the Tulku system helped. Still, I think that, as with every event, there are many different aspects.

"Now with the reincarnation system, one aspect is negative," he continued. "Wealth was being passed down in the name of the institution, and this included serfs who were held by the monastery, so there was a lot of suffering there. There is no doubt about this. And in the name of the institution, some conflicts happened *(fighting between orders and monasteries)*. So these are negative factors. But there are not only negative factors; there are also positive ones. The Tulku system, the system of successive abbots, helped to keep the Kagyu tradition alive. So we must ask why this happened. This tradition is not for just one generation but for many generations. So the abbot, the person, changed, but there was the same institution. The institution is useful for keeping the tradition alive. Instead of appointing another person, it was supposed to be the same person in a new body. I think this system worked and helped."

"Do you mean," I asked, "that it protected the institutional strength of Buddhism?"

"No, more than that," the Dalai Lama responded. "The Tulku system helped to protect the spiritual tradition, to preserve it." When I remained silent, he looked at me with exasperation, as if he were talking to someone who had missed his point entirely.

"Look," the Dalai Lama continued. "With the Buddha himself there were seven successive holders of his teachings. In a spiritual lineage, there is a qualified teacher, and he passes his spiritual traditions to his successor of the same or similar quality. In this way, the spiritual tradition, the teachings, can continue over many generations without degeneration. This is not about money or economy but about protecting and preserving a pure spiritual tradition. Then you have human nature, which is another thing. The original tradition with the Tulku system was purely spiritual, but then it gets corrupted. There is money and power and then dirty politics."

"Still," I replied, "Tulku help to preserve the institution, don't they?"

"Yes, but that is a by-product," the Dalai Lama insisted. "For me, the most important thing is the spiritual purity of the spiritual practice and the lineage. Many reincarnate teachers have been very pure, even within very big monastic institutions. The Seventh Dalai Lama, for example. He didn't possess any articles except the thirteen articles that monks are allowed to keep, as written in the *Vinaya*. When he went to a government ceremony or function, he had to wear special clothing. He actually had to hire or rent those, because he did not own them. He was a genuine practitioner. There were many like him. So, you see, we have inherited, we have been given, wonderful and beautiful teachings from our spiritual masters. These can all be corrupted because of evil influences and practices. In this way, false people can claim to be very good teachers, and this will pollute and corrupt the Buddhist teaching. The Tulku system helped to prevent that.

"In fact," the Dalai Lama continued, "the Gelug order, in terms of material things, might look very pompous and magnificent. But to the degree that it is devoid of content or spiritual practice, then, to that degree, it is worthless. When I think about this, I can't help but lament from the heart. We must remember that the main purpose," and here he paused for emphasis, "the main *purpose* of the Tulku tradition was to propagate and preserve the Buddha Dharma and one's own tradition. This was something positive and necessary and also welcome."

"It seems to me," I said, "from what you have told me, and what I have read, that all Tibetans now see you as a Tulku, who is also a manifestation of Chenrizi. But aren't other Tulku, from other sects, also seen as manifestations of Chenrizi by followers of those sects? Hasn't there been a change in how all this is seen over the years?"

"Well, yes, but that is complicated," the Dalai Lama replied. "For the Karma Kagyu, the Karmapa is considered an incarnation of Chenrizi, not only the Dalai Lama. Karmapa is also considered an incarnation of Chenrizi. My point is that different orders or different traditions, during the previous time they rarely used the name of Dalai Lama. In the Kagyu area, they refer to the Karmapa or Kamtsang. Those who live in the Drikhung, they followed the Kyabgon. The Taglung Kargyu, they identify with the Taglug Shabtrug Rinpoche. In each of the different areas, they were following one of the many different orders, each with its own Tulku, and each order had its main temple or monastery in Central Tibet. All of the leaders were stationed in Central Tibet. Their main monasteries were there. Each order had followers even out in the remote border areas, but they all followed the Tulku who was head of their order. But because of the recent situation with the Chinese, since 1950, my name now reaches everywhere," the Dalai Lama said finally. "Everyone considers that the Dalai Lama is the savior and protector of Tibet, and I carry the main responsibility."

I studied what the Dalai Lama had told me, and read many books about the emergence of Buddhist orders in Tibet. Between two trips to India to interview him, I traveled to Chinese-occupied Tibet. The fact that the Dalai Lama was willing to criticize the way Tibetans had focused too much on statues and monasteries was something I found laudable; yet despite his self-criticism, I considered the giant statues that have survived in Tibet awe-inspiring—in part because of their scarcity. China destroyed 90 percent of the temples after the invasion of 1950. The preservation of monumental statues, as well as ancient murals and books, is one of the many things that monastic Buddhism has achieved in Tibet during the past thousand years, in spite of many invasions. The beauty of the surviving murals and statues, along with the intense popular devotion they inspire, can be deeply moving.

One bright winter morning at Tashilunpo Monastery, in Shigatse, I followed a line of pilgrims, illiterate nomads who spend their lives on the high plains herding yaks, as they entered a dark temple and made their way around the largest statue in Tibet. The men and women were dressed in wool they had woven themselves. Their hair was uncut from birth, braided and wrapped around their heads, and they reeked of yak butter, popped barley, and yak-dung fires. The base of the statue was about thirty yards in diameter, and the image was freestanding in a pitch-black room. Occasionally I could make out the head of the Buddha glimmering four stories above, in the light from a tiny window.

In this enormous room, which housed one giant statue, I followed the nomads, people who had never owned a house and had lived in tents all their lives, and was impressed by what monasteries achieved in Tibet. These vast interior spaces with giant images seemed to create a feeling of spirituality for pilgrims. We held on to one another's shoulders in the darkness as we felt our way around the giant toe of the Buddha that towered above us, and I began to understand why monasticism succeeded so well in Tibet. The Dalai Lama spoke about how rituals were for people who could not meditate, and here I was, following a group of people who were not well enough educated to study the ancient teachings of the Buddha from India. Nevertheless, I could see that this room and this statue brought something vast, something I could only dimly perceive, into their lives. The Dalai Lama's laugh as he barked "Rituals!" came back to mind.

The nomads left the dark temple after circumambulating it, to gain merit in the type of ritual that Tibetan Buddhism has been so good at creating for the so-called uneducated masses. I followed them outdoors, and the light blinded me. As my eyes adjusted, I saw the dirt on the windburned faces and on the calloused hands of the nomads. I saw the prayer wheels that they were endlessly turning, and the prayer beads with which they counted the mantra of the Buddhist deities, which they were repeating.

Through these simple rituals they had focused their body, mind, and speech on the Buddha. They visualized the Buddha and spoke his mantra as they walked around the giant statue. During the past millennium, monasticism created, promoted, and sustained this spiritual experience. For these pilgrims, their moments in the temple were part of a lifelong experience. Indeed, the paintings and statues that fill the dozens of temples at Tashilunpo offered support for the pilgrims I saw that day, for all who have preceded them, and for all those who would follow them. The pilgrims seemed to become the Buddha. Scholars argue whether such practices come from ancient Buddhism, in India, or are rooted in the practices of Himalayan shamans who "become the gods" in trances. Yet such arguments were meaningless that morning in Shigatse. The power of the pilgrims' devotion was stunning.

Their devotion moved me so much that the image of a young Chinese woman I met briefly in an elevator in Canton sprang to mind. In 1989, after a trip to Lhasa, I had flown out to Guangzhou (Canton), en route to Hong Kong, to have some exit papers stamped. Both headed to her office, we stared politely at different corners of the elevator until she asked me a question. Thousands of foreigners were passing through Guangzhou to Lhasa on a newly initiated flight. She could not understand why. "Why do Westerners want to go to Tibet so much? I mean, the people stink, and it's so dirty and poor. What do they see there?"

Startled by her frankness, I said, "They want to see the monasteries, I think. At least that's what draws them to Tibet at first."

The statues, and the monasteries that preserve them, have become, over the past millennium, a support for an inner sanctuary that Tibetans have cultivated with tremendous determination. The nomads that I followed at Tashilunpo had only the Buddha in their hearts. For Tibetans, though Chinese and Westerners might not see it, the monasteries, with all their flaws, are partly judged by their usefulness in leading people to apply Buddhism to their lives. Through their own practice, individuals gain their own merit. The religious relics and rituals are only tools. As I followed the nomads out of that dark chapel in Tashilunpo, into the light, I decided to ask the Dalai Lama, the next time I saw him, which was his favorite statue of the Buddha. If statues were such significant religious tools in the lives of the nomads, then surely one image of the Buddha was an important religious tool for the Dalai Lama.

It was snowing in Dharamsala, India, when I arrived for my meeting. When I had last seen him, four months earlier, I spotted him emerging from a forest wrapped in thick monsoon clouds. He walked along a pathway beneath his maroon umbrella, through a dense stand of trees dripping with rain. Now he was bareheaded and bare-armed, as the *Vinaya* dictates for an ordinary Buddhist monk, walking along a path freshly shoveled through the snow. As always, there were a dozen people a day waiting to meet him, and so our session was strictly scheduled. As I waited, he was giving an audience to about one hundred refugees who had crossed the snowbound winter passes of the Himalayas to escape Tibet. The look in their eyes reminded me of the nomads walking around the giant statue in Tashilunpo. In our meeting the previous day there had been so many questions about the development of monastic Buddhism that I had forgotten to ask him about statues. The look in the eyes of the refugees, as they approached the Dalai Lama, reminded me to ask him about his favorite statue.

The Dalai Lama said that his favorite representation of the Buddha is a three-foot-high stone image carved in the ancient kingdom of Ghandara, about A.D. 100. Today, the statue is in a glass case in the Lahore Museum, Pakistan, famous as the Wonder House in the opening of Rudyard Kipling's novel *Kim*.

It is an image of the Buddha on the night of his enlightenment. He had just completed six years of extreme asceticism; he had starved himself and was nearly naked. His belly is obviously shrunken, along with his gaunt cheeks, and his blood vessels stand out clearly over his emaciated rib cage. The stone carving is remarkably detailed. The Buddha has only just broken an extended fast and eaten enough food to sustain the long nights of meditation that will lead to complete liberation, underneath the Bo tree at Bodh Gaya, on the Full Moon of May. The Dalai Lama has never seen the statue in person, only pictures of it.

"You say this is your favorite statue of the Buddha?" I asked. "What do you see?"

"It clearly conveys the message that is taught in the Buddhist texts," the Dalai Lama said. "It shows how we must undertake many hardships during spiritual practice for countless eons. This is clearly demonstrated in his life, and in this statue. When we compare the hardship that we have undergone to those of the Buddha, then we clearly see how spoiled we are. Especially, generally speaking, those who have the name of Tulku, they are much spoiled."

"And when you see this statue, what do you feel?" was my next question.

"What we really need," the Dalai Lama explained, "is the determination to work hard. Like Milarepa and many authentic lamas or masters, they all spent time in hardship and then they had high spiritual realizations. It is very difficult to achieve anything if we follow the easy way. For instance, Dilgo Khyentse Rinpoche also took hard practice by isolating himself in a cave for three years. Later in his life, he actually shed tears from happiness when he recalled that time in the cave. It was years of hard work and meditation, but it was the happiest period of his life. So that is the proper way. I think many of us, including myself, are hoping to achieve Buddhahood easily."

"So the Lahore Buddha," I said, "reminds you that without hard work, it is impossible to achieve enlightenment. But the statue is also a great artistic achievement, isn't it?"

"I don't have much sensitivity to the aesthetics," the Dalai Lama replied.

"Yes, you have given me that feeling," I said. "Why don't you appreciate the artistic achievement?"

"Strictly speaking," the Dalai Lama said, "from a Buddhist practitioner's point of view, if it is an image of the Buddha, then merely because of that fact you regard it with respect. Not because it is costly or beautiful-looking or made of gold or made of mud."

"But it does count if the artist has skillfully conveyed the determination of the Buddha, very powerfully, in a statue," I said. "It is preferred over an ugly image of the Buddha that does not convey his determination."

"Yes, that is true," the Dalai Lama conceded.

"So that counts," I said, "and this Lahore Buddha you like more than any other Buddha because it conveys this determination. This art is worthwhile because of that."

"Yes," he said.

"But generally speaking, if it is made of diamonds or mud, or beautiful or not, it doesn't matter," I said.

"That is so" was his answer.

6

MONGOL OVERLORDS AND
THE SEEDS OF A PROBLEM,
1207–1368

Monsoon had turned to winter. Another six months had passed and still the Dalai Lama and I continued to meet, when he had time between his many trips abroad. Bright blue skies had replaced the twilight of monsoon. Riding in the taxi up to the Dalai Lama's compound above Dharamsala was almost like being in a plane. The road wound in and out among pine trees; beyond them, I caught sudden glimpses of the Himalayas, glittering white with fresh snow. As I went up the hill to meet with him, my mind was full of the day's topic: the establishment of the largest empire in world history by Mongol nomads.

It was the Mongol conquest of Eurasia in the thirteenth century that accidentally brought Tibet and China into contact, after centuries of mutual isolation. Both became subject nations within the Mongolian Empire, which stretched from Korea to Hungary and from Moscow to Istanbul, controlled by an army of 125,000 "barbaric" nomads and their leader Genghis Khan.

Subjects paid tribute to the Mongols, if they were lucky, or Mongolia's mounted archers and swordsmen exterminated them. The illiterate Genghis believed that the Eternal Blue Heaven itself, out of the mouth of a Mongol shaman, gave him a divine right to rule the world. An unexpurgated translation of Genghis Khan's motto reads something like: The best life for a man is to hunt down and butcher your enemies, steal their wealth, listen to their families wail, gallop their best horses, and rape their women. Recent genetic research substantiates the facts behind this boast. Eight percent of all men in the lands conquered by Genghis Khan bear a marker on their Y chromosomes that scientists have traced to his family.

From the start of Genghis Khan's foreign invasions in 1206 until his death in 1227, he applied one law. Those who resisted conquest or reneged on a promise were butchered, be it man, woman, or child. He dealt with foreigners who opposed him, just as he had dealt with Mongol tribes who betrayed him in his youth, as recorded in the *Secret History of the Mongols*. As a youth, after one victory,

> Genghis then gathered his spoils from the . . . camp
> and executed the clan leaders
> their sons, and their grandsons,
> so that their seed blew away in the wind like the ashes.

Extermination awaited those who did not surrender as soon as the Mongol cavalrymen appeared at the city gates, and especially those who fought the Mongols. For Genghis all people were his subjects; they would surrender and pay tribute, or he would crush them. Sometimes nations that surrendered with little or no opposition were treated quite well.

China resisted the Mongols while Tibet did not.

Though no nation was prepared to meet the Mongols, Tibetans were utterly defenseless. After the death of Lang Darma, in 842, Tibet had disintegrated. From the collapse of the Tibetan Empire until Tibet became a Mongol subject in 1268, the state remained disunited. Regions fought with one another, while nobles and powerful monasteries battled for control of each region. At first the monasteries sought the protection of nobles, but by the thirteenth century, the monks were wealthy and the situation was reversed: some noble families sought the protection of the monasteries. The foreign policy was in disarray, because numerous princes had entered into a variety of alliances with the empires and tribes that surrounded the plateau. Ironically, Tibet's inability to defend itself against the invading Mongols turned out to be a strategic blessing in disguise, since the Mongols slaughtered those who resisted.

The Dalai Lama grew animated when we discussed this. "If Tibet had been a strong country at that time," he said, "it might have fought and suffered like so many others. But there was no strong state; nationalism was weak and the monasteries were strong. So there was little fighting."

"Chinese government publications," I said, "insist that Tibet became part of China because of the Mongol invasion. But historians I have read do not agree with that."

"I think actually the Mongol army came to Tibet, and controlled Tibet first, and then they went to China," the Dalai Lama observed. "I am not a person to judge; I am not a historian. So therefore, from my point of view, I want to make it very clear that this is very complicated and then leave it up to the historians and the experts."

"But when the Chinese government distorts this history," I replied, "to prove that Tibet has been part of China since the Mongol period. . . ." The Dalai Lama, however, had a more nuanced view and was not about to let me shape the conversation in such simplistic terms.

"I can publicly mention," he interjected, "without hesitation, that Tibet's historic relations with China are not as simple as the Chinese government has said. And this comes out when we look at how the Mongols controlled Tibet before they reached China. As I have said to you earlier, any explanation of the past always has implications for the present and the future. Therefore, the Chinese always insist, very strongly, that Tibet is part of China."

In the eyes of patriotic Chinese everywhere, Tibet has been part of a unified Chinese state since the Mongol subjugation of the two states. Wang Jiawei and Nyima Gyaincain present the government's viewpoint in *The Historical Status of China's Tibet*. Their argument involves one key assumption: the Mongol occupation of China, which Kublai Khan would call the Yuan dynasty, was a Chinese state. It underlies all they write.

"The Yuan dynasty emerged as the first national political power characterized by minority rule of China. . . . The Mongolian, Han *(Chinese)*, Tibetan, and various other nationalities joined hands to form a political entity featuring economic and cultural prosperity." According to Wang and Gyaincain, the Mongol conquest occurred during a period when Chinese of ethnic minority descent ruled the motherland.

This blind spot is not a recent development. Chinese writings about the Mongol conquest—from the first hundred years after China expelled the Mongols until today—fail to acknowledge that the state was absorbed into a larger, non-Chinese political unit. What's more, the Mongols never administered Tibet as part of China or even with China. Rather, they ruled these territories separately, as the British administered India and New Zealand in more recent times; the fact that Britain once colonized both does not make India part of New Zealand today.

If you accept that the Mongol Empire was actually a Chinese state, as the Chinese today are taught, then it takes only a short leap to argue, as Wang and Gyaincain do, that China has exercised "sovereignty over Tibet . . . since the Yuan dynasty . . . [and] the Tibetans are undoubtedly part of the Chinese. This fairly and accurately tells the historical reality that has existed for more than 700 years, since the Yuan dynasty. The historical status of China's Tibet is clear as clean water and the blue sky—a fact known to the world."

Later Tibetan and Mongolian accounts grew out of shared tenets of Buddhism, though they, like all non-Chinese historical narratives, never portray the Mongol subjugation of Tibet as a Chinese one. The root of this history can be traced back to one man, who reshaped the world by claiming most of Europe and Asia as part of the vast Mongol Empire.

Temujin was a Mongol who survived a youth of extreme poverty. After he and his hungry brother murdered a half brother over a fish, Temujin's mother screamed at the boys.

> Killers, both of you!
> When he came out screaming from the heat of my womb
> this one was born holding a clot of black blood in his hand.
> And now you have both destroyed without thinking . . .
> like the lion who can't control its own fury . . .
> like the wolf who hides himself in the blizzard to hunt down
>   his prey . . .
> like the jackal who fights with anyone who's touched him

After many bloody battles, Temujin emerged as the leader of a coalition of nomadic Mongol and Turkic tribes in what is today Mongolia. Temujin became Genghis Khan, a name that probably means "oceanic" or "world-embracing" ruler, in 1206, at the conclusion of a pantribal conference. Between 1207 and 1215, Genghis Khan's warriors subdued their closest southern neighbors and then set out to conqueror the world.

There were five major empires, or kingdoms, south of the Mongols in 1206: Uighur, Tangut, Jurchen, Tibetan, and Song China.

Southwest of Mongolia lay the Uighur *(we-gur)* kingdom of Qocho, in what is now the Chinese province of Xinjiang *(shin-jang)*. In 1205, Turkic kings of Uighur stock ruled the Indo-European natives. The brown, blond, and red-haired people of Qocho were not Chinese, nor did they speak the language. Chinese did not live in the region—none had lived there since the Tang were evicted centuries before. The Uighur

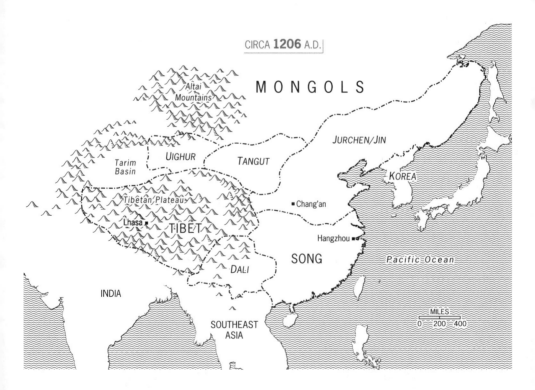

submitted voluntarily to the Mongols between 1207 and 1209, as soon as they were threatened, and became trusted vassals. Though Genghis was illiterate, Uighur scribes, who transliterated Mongolian into their script, schooled his sons. The scribes wrote the earliest Mongolian records with an alphabet, not Chinese characters. Uighur bureaucrats tallied the flood of tribute payments received by the Mongol Empire as it expanded, and loyal Uighur vassals helped administer it. Because they were useful to the Mongols, submitted readily, and displayed loyalty, the Uighur prospered under the Mongols.

Due south of Mongolia lay the Tangut Empire, in what is today the Chinese provinces of Gansu and Inner Mongolia. The Tangut were ruled by Tibetan-speaking nobles. The Tanguts had lived on the Tibetan Plateau in the seventh century, but by the thirteenth century they had migrated to the Gansu Corridor, a depression separating the Tibetan and Mongolian Plateaus. Although the Tangut were not Chinese, many of their subjects were. Their imperial armies invaded Song China frequently in search of wealth. From 1044 onward, the Chinese paid an annual tribute to the Tangut princes, as specified in a treaty, to avoid attack, and they accepted "inferior" status. Because the Tangut yielded to the Mongols without much fighting, Genghis spared them, at first. However, a later betrayal by the Tangut caused their extermination.

Between 1207 and 1209, the Uighur and the Tangut were the first two nations to submit to the Mongols; at the time of their subjugation, they were not part of China, nor were they Chinese states, though they governed territory that is today within the People's Republic of China.

To Genghis Khan's east and southeast lay the Tungusic-speaking Jurchen people. The Jurchen (or Jin) Empire encompassed both nomadic tribes in northern Manchuria and at least one hundred cities on the north China plain, where the majority of the people were Chinese farmers and artisans. As with the Uighur and Tangut kingdoms, part of the territory within the Jin Empire had been lost to non-Chinese-speaking nomads after the Tang dynasty collapsed in 906. Like the Tangut, the nomadic rulers of the Jin had learned how to siphon off the wealth of China's sedentary farmers and artisans. The nomads used several methods to extract the riches: they imposed taxes on the settled Chinese in the Jin and the Tangut realms, looted Chinese cities in Song China, and demanded that silver be paid by Song China to prevent the Jin and Tangut raids. They adopted Chinese administrative techniques when that was useful, just as Chinese corporations today have adopted Western methods of administration when it is profitable to do so. The Jurchen and the Tangut did not become Chinese, no more than modern Chinese become Westerners when they adopt their technology. The Mongols attacked the Jurchen in 1211, and did not subdue them until more than two decades later. Because the Jurchen and their Chinese subjects had resisted so fiercely during this long war, the Mongols reduced at least ninety walled cities on the north China plain to rubble.

In 1207, when Genghis Khan began his world conquest, he attacked the Uighur, the Tangut, and the Jurchen first. The Chinese and non-Chinese peoples of this era were not joined in a transethnic nation-state; the modern nation of China did not exist. It was only later Chinese historians, following the intellectual dictum that what could not be avoided had to be rationalized, who wrote about the conquest of the Chinese as an extension of the empire's borders. In fact, at the time, the alien Uighur, Tangut, and Jurchen rulers did not see themselves as Chinese and were not viewed as Chinese by the Chinese-speaking people.

In 1205 most Chinese-speaking people lived in the Chinese-ruled Song Empire, south of the Jin and the Tangut Empires. The Song's Tangut and Jurchen neighbors had pushed its northern border farther and farther south in the preceding centuries. While the Mongols incorporated the Uighur, the Tangut, and the Jin into their emerging empire, Genghis ignored Song China. The early Mongols' greatest strength was their highly mobile cavalry forces. The rice fields of Song China were a quagmire for such a force. While the nomadic rulers who preyed on Song China could have been a threat to Genghis's rear unless he subdued them first, Song China posed no such problem. Having subdued the threat, Genghis could turn his mounted forces westward into the treeless sea of grass that stretched from Mongolia toward Europe. He spent the rest of his life, from 1207 to 1227, conquering a vast stretch of territory to the west of China, encompassing the modern nations of Iran, Afghanistan, Kazakhstan, Turkmenistan;

parts of Turkey, Armenia, the Caucuses, Azerbaijan; and large areas of Russia and Europe.

In the midst of these conquests, Genghis Khan asked one of his first vassals, the Tangut, to supply him troops. They refused. After he had finished his western conquests, Genghis Khan marched part of his army home to Mongolia and, en route, sacked and burned all the Tangut cities. In 1227, from his deathbed, as his armies lay siege to the Tangut capital, he ordered every Tangut to be slaughtered. His troops carried out his orders, even though he was dead by the time of the final slaughter. So complete was the extermination that until recently the Tangut were a historical blur virtually erased from history by the Mongols.

Tibet became part of the Mongol Empire only after Genghis Khan's death, and by then the Tibetan princes and monastic leaders knew what happened to those, like the Tangut, who dared to oppose the Mongols. In 1240, Genghis's grandson, Prince Godan, sent a small army into Tibet, probably just as a reconnaissance party. The Mongols killed five hundred Tibetans in an attack on one monastery, and several other monasteries were looted. During this incursion, the Mongol commander developed an interest in Buddhism and heard about the spiritual powers of one monk, Sakya Pandita. A few years later, Prince Godan sent a letter to Sakya Pandita, the abbot of one of the largest and wealthiest monasteries in Tibet, and summoned the monk to his court.

> I, the most powerful and prosperous Prince Godan, wish to inform the Sakya Pandita, Kunga Gyaltsen, that we need a lama to advise my ignorant people on how to conduct themselves morally and spiritually. I need someone to pray for the welfare of my deceased parents. . . . I have decided that you are the only person suitable for the task. . . . I will not accept any excuse on account of your age or the rigors of the journey. . . . It would, of course, be easy for me to send a large body of troops to bring you here.

This ultimatum is typical of the Mongols, who did not see their empire as a single nation, or as a multiracial Chinese society. They did not seek legitimacy in the eyes of those they ruled, nor did they share the modern concept of a nation-state. The Mongols imposed their will solely by force; according to their beliefs, their rule was the will of heaven.

On receipt of this ultimatum from the Mongols, Sakya Pandita left Tibet with two of his young nephews, including ten-year-old Phagpa Gyaltsen, and a Mongol escort. En route to Godan's encampment, one thousand miles to the northeast, the party stopped in Lhasa, where young Phagpa took the first oaths of a Buddhist monk, in front of the image of the Buddha installed in the Jokhang by Songzen Gampo's Chinese bride, Princess Wencheng.

Sakya Pandita met Prince Godan in Lanzhou, in what is today the province of Gansu. When he arrived in 1247, Mongol troops were exterminating the Chinese population of the area. One of Sakya Pandita's first acts, on meeting the Mongols, was to convince Prince Godan to stop throwing thousands of Chinese into the river. The nomadic Mongols saw Chinese farmers as pests eating away at grasslands with their plows. It was only decades later that the Mongols were convinced that they could make more money by taxing Chinese farmers and craftsmen than by eliminating them and turning the fields back into grazing lands: such was the purpose of land so far as the early Mongol conquerors knew.

Sakya Pandita was horrified at the scene of mass murder he encountered when he met Prince Godan. He offered the prince religious teachings, including the idea that it is a sin to kill any living creature. After the Tibetan lama had been with Godan for some time, the Mongol prince appointed Sakya Pandita as the Mongol's viceroy for Central Tibet, though the eastern provinces of the old Tibetan Empire—Kham and Amdo—were under direct Mongol rule. After Sakya Pandita saw the power of the Mongols firsthand, he sent a letter to the Tibetans. He urged them to offer their submission and tribute payments at once. Sakya Pandita remained with the court of Prince Godan for four years; just before his death, in 1251, he sent a final letter to his homeland:

> The Prince has told me that if we Tibetans help the Mongols in matters of religion, they in turn will support us in temporal matters. In this way we will be able to spread our religion far and wide. The

Prince is just beginning to understand our religion. If I stay longer I am certain I can spread the faith of the Buddha beyond Tibet and, thus, help my country. The Prince . . . tells me that it is in his hands to do good for Tibet and that it is in mine to do good for him. . . . I am getting old and will not live much longer. Have no fear on this account, for I have taught everything I know to my nephew, Phagpa.

The Mongols most likely brought Sakya Pandita to their court because they wanted an influential monk whom they could use to establish their rule over Tibet. Sakya Pandita saw the relationship differently: he believed that he could convert Godan and establish a religious relationship between Tibet and the Mongols, which would protect Tibet and spread Buddhism. In the Tibetan worldview, Sakya Pandita was a worthy priest who had found a dutiful patron. Each had responsibilities and rights. The Mongols probably did not accept these definitions of their alliance with the Tibetans, not at first.

The Fourteenth Dalai Lama believes that Sakya Pandita and Godan established a bond that was primarily religious, though he understands that it existed on other levels. Still, he thinks that it is difficult for us to comprehend that ancient tie between a priest and a patron. "Modern international law," he said, "or Western concepts about the relations between ruler and ruled, may not be able to translate this unique relationship that was established between the Mongols and the Tibetans. You see, nowadays modern international law is based entirely on Western concepts. I do not know that the unique spiritual and political relationship between a Tibetan lama and a Mongol emperor—I don't know that this can be translated into Western concepts. There is no room in today's definitions because these definitions come from the West."

The Dalai Lama is correct when he says that it is impossible to define the relations between a Mongol emperor and a Tibetan lama in modern terms. The Mongols, Chinese, and Tibetans of the thirteenth century did not share our concepts of nation, state, race, tribe, and legitimate rule. Thus it is impossible to say that the conquest relations between the Mongols, Chinese, and Tibetans give any legitimacy to the Communist rulers of China, or their claim over Tibet. Yet China's claim that Tibet has been an inalienable part of China since the thirteenth century is based primarily on the false argument that Mongolia was part of China when it subjugated Tibet.

After Sakya Pandita's death, Phagpa remained with the Mongols. It was a time of great confusion among the Mongolian princes, since a succession battle had erupted between two grandsons of Genghis. It is unclear how many Tibetan principalities actually submitted to the Mongols during the ensuing chaos: Sakya Pandita's agreements with Godan may have been only on paper. In 1253, two Mongol princes invaded Tibet from different directions, and though they did not reach as far as Lhasa, they killed many monks and destroyed many temples and houses. Despite this, other Mongol princes offered patronage and protection to various Tibetan monasteries. Young Phagpa remained in Godan's camp, where his teachers continued to train him as a Tibetan monk. But he learned to speak Mongol and grew accustomed to Mongol ways. At the time, Kublai Khan was on his way to winning the succession battle, and he showed an interest in Buddhism. He asked Godan to surrender Phagpa to him, and Godan complied.

Five years later, the young Mongol prince Kublai Khan began to receive instruction in Buddhism from twenty-three-year-old Phagpa, who was now a guest in his court. Not long after, Kublai Khan defeated his brother and became chief of the Mongol world, Khan of Khans. As the Great Khan, he became the paramount lord not just in Mongolia and in the conquered Tangut and Jurchen lands but as far away as Persia and Russia: theoretically he ruled the entire Mongolian Empire, although his fractious relatives each held one of the four divisions of the empire as their own fief.

The same year he became the Great Khan, in 1260, Kublai appointed Phagpa as his imperial preceptor. Sakya Pandita's work now bore fruit, as Phagpa had patronage to spread Tibetan Buddhism throughout the Mongol Empire. Phagpa had an excellent explanation of why Buddhism was essential for anyone who possessed power and wealth. He told Kublai:

> I wish to present you the gift of my Doctrine.
> He who possesses the worldly riches,
> But is not familiar with the true Doctrine,

It is like attending a feast mixed with poison,
It brings only unhappiness and sorrow . . .
He who possesses both of these riches [Buddhism and wealth]
Brings benefit to himself and others.

Phagpa rationalized Kublai's power and wealth for the emperor, as well as for his subjects. According to Mongolians today, he was the first "to initiate the political theology of the relationship between state and religion in the Tibeto-Mongolian Buddhist world."

Mongols developed Phagpa's ideas in a book entitled *White History*. "The cornerstone of sacred religion is the Lama, the Lord of Doctrine," the work says, "the head of power is the Khan, the Sovereign of terrestrial power." The two powers, "throne and altar," cannot be denied and are interdependent.

Such ideas also percolated into Tibet, although they may have come from India to Tibet and were then transmitted by Phagpa to Mongolia. Clearly, these concepts bear no relation to contemporary principles about what a nation is, let alone relations between countries, nor does traditional Chinese philosophy appear to have influenced them.

As imperial preceptor, Phagpa did more for the emperor than teach him Buddhism and provide him with a philosophical framework for his rule. He developed a new script, to ensure accurate communication between the emperor and all the subject nations. It was impossible to transliterate Tibetan or Mongol accurately with Chinese ideograms, or with the Uighur script Mongols had been using. The empire needed a new alphabet, designed for this purpose. When faced with this challenge Kublai Khan turned to his preceptor, since Tibetans' linguistic genius was legendary. During the preceding centuries when they translated so many Buddhist texts, Tibetans had developed lexicons so that a given word or concept in Sanskrit would be translated exactly the same every time. It was centuries of work to translate the vast collections of texts from India, and that task honed Tibetans' linguistic skills over generations. The alphabet invented by Phagpa, based on Tibet's script, served as a universal script and contributed to the unification of the empire. When completed in 1268, Kublai Khan declared Phagpa's alphabet, not Chinese ideograms, to be the official script of his empire. The alphabet was used for 110 years. So far-reaching was its influence that scholars believe the modern Korean alphabet is an adaptation of Phagpa's script. In this way, and others, Tibet had an immense impact on the intellectual evolution of Asia. Despite widespread use, Phagpa's script died out after the Mongol Empire collapsed (except for the adapted form in Korea) because it had been so forcefully imposed by the Mongols that resistance to its usage developed. Despite the ultimate fate of his script, Phagpa's faithful service to the emperor reaped tremendous benefit for Tibet.

Like Phagpa, many other Tibetan teachers received patronage, and they instructed students from across the Mongol Empire. As a result, Tibetan Buddhism spread—and not just to China and Mongolia. As late as 1291 there were Tibetan temples, monks, and monasteries in Iran, patronized by the Mongol khan of the region. One present-day Mongol historian believes that Kublai Khan gave priority to Tibetan Buddhism because he feared that Mongol identity would be lost in the sea of Chinese or Iranian subjects. Kublai wanted to avert any chance of spiritual or cultural domination by the subject people, and he realized that Tibetan Buddhism would provide such protection. There were other ways in which Kublai Khan tried to keep the Mongols separate from the Chinese. For example, the walled Forbidden City in Beijing, begun by Kublai Khan, was built as a Mongol enclave. Entrance was essentially forbidden to Chinese, because the area served as a sanctuary for Mongol culture in the midst of its subject people. Moreover, the Mongols, for the most part, refused to learn Chinese and used translators to communicate with and rule their Chinese conquest.

No matter how we interpret it today, the relationship between Kublai Khan and the Tibetan monk Phagpa began as one between a student and his teacher. One day I summarized a passage from Marco Polo to the Dalai Lama. I was curious why Kublai trusted Phagpa so much.

"Marco Polo said that the magical arts of the Tibetan lamas could cause the khan's cup to rise up in front of his mouth," I said. "It's a famous passage in his book. Do you believe that this sort of magical display was one of the things that convinced Kublai Khan to convert to Buddhism?"

The Dalai Lama thought for a moment in silence before he began. "Yes, there is a story in the Tibetan texts where Phagpa was giving an initiation to Kublai Khan. He drew a mandala for the initiation, in front of him, and then that whole mandala appeared in the clouds of the sky above as well. It was Phagpa who did this."

Intrigued, I said, "This is a classic way of inspiring faith. This is one of the few correct uses of magical abilities acquired by a Bodhisattva from *siddhi* [spiritual power], isn't it?"

"This is possible," the Dalai Lama replied. "And this is a correct use of the *siddhi*. I think that at the end of the forty-six secondary precepts of a Bodhisattva, there is the mention of a Bodhisattva wielding these powers. The Bodhisattva realizes that he or she can help others discipline their minds with such displays, even though you learn that you shouldn't use these powers all the time. So this means if there is a real purpose, not just for showing off but for the benefit of others, then if there are no other negative circumstances, you should use these powers."

Checking to be sure that he has me hanging on every word, he peered over his glasses and continued with his most solemn expression. "The best thing is not to possess any of these qualities so you don't have to watch for any of these circumstances." He burst out laughing. "So I have nothing even if I wanted to show it!"

The Dalai Lama had me, as always, laughing with him. "Well, you know," I said, "Westerners all think that you are a telepath. You're not a big believer in psychic powers?"

After laughing with me for a moment, he grew more serious. "Of course, I am a *(Buddhist)* practitioner," the Dalai Lama said. "And so if you see something . . ." His voice faded away without finishing his sentence. "Like both my tutors when they gave instructions on altruism. They wept. That is a real sign *(that a master has developed psychic powers)*." Talking with him, I could easily forget that he believes in miracles and psychic powers—though he says he has none himself—and he believes that those powers are an outgrowth of one's spiritual development.

Looking carefully at me, the Dalai Lama continued. "And perhaps I can say there are some experiences about altruism because of my practice and understanding of *Shunyata*." It was the first time he had mentioned this Sanskrit word, which has no real English equivalent though, roughly translated, it means "emptiness."

"Sometimes I feel it is necessary to tell other people about this," the Dalai Lama said, "even though I am not fully developed. But some experience is there. I am telling other people and also I can feel some experience."

Amazed that the Dalai Lama could go from Mongols and self-deprecating laughter to speaking about one of the fundamental steps that lead to enlightenment in a matter of seconds, I asked, "You have had realization of Shunyata?"

"Yes, I think some experiences are just beginning," he said. "When I think about it, I can see that everything looks unreal or like a mirage." He was quiet for a moment before he continued. "There is good, bad, positive, negative, right and wrong: everything is there. These little experiences make a difference; they are very beneficial. I have no doubt about my peace of mind now. The peace of mind from Shunyata gives you equanimity."

Returning to the patron-priest relationship in the thirteenth century, I said, "Phagpa's job—whether he used *Siddhi* or some other tool—was to deal with the spirit, and the emperor's was to deal with the material world."

"Yes," the Dalai Lama replied. "The religious king has his own domain and the spiritual teacher has his own domain." It was interesting to see that the Dalai Lama had the same understanding of this relationship as is extolled in Mongol texts on the subject.

Kublai Khan agreed to prostrate to his spiritual teacher, in private, before he received Buddhist teachings. In public, Phagpa prostrated to the emperor. Phagpa was only nineteen or twenty years old when he told his student that he must prostrate before him in private if the student was to receive Buddhist teachings. Was Phagpa teaching, to the ruler of the Mongol Empire, the devotion felt by Milarepa for his teacher Marpa? Humility is a fundamental lesson of Buddhism, the antidote to pride; devotion to the master expressed by bowing down on hands and knees to your teacher is a basic practice.

Even the Dalai Lama bows to his spiritual teachers. "Though I am the Dalai Lama, to my teacher, Khunu Lama Tenzin Gyaltsen, I am just a very ordinary Buddhist practitioner, almost a beggar," the Dalai Lama said.

"So when my teacher receives me, I make prostrations to him. If someone interprets this to mean that the Dalai Lama is socially or politically lower than this person, that's just nonsense. The prostration to a teacher is to be taken purely from a religious viewpoint." There is impatience in the Dalai Lama's voice when he says the word "nonsense." He cannot believe that anyone could misinterpret such a gesture.

As part of a religious meeting, the emperor bowed to Phagpa. Phagpa then bowed to demonstrate deference to the emperor in worldly affairs. The Chinese have cited these prostrations as evidence that Tibet was in actuality a subject of China's. This is specious reasoning on two counts. First, the emperor was not the physical representation of either Chinese power or a Chinese state. Both the Tibetans and the Chinese were part of a Mongol state, and both were subject to a higher authority. Neither state had greater power than the other. Second, the gesture was part of an ancient relationship that cannot be interpreted using contemporary definitions of sovereignty or legality. The "bow" gesture was simply a sign of respect and recognition for the supremacy of the Mongol emperor. It did not acknowledge that Tibet was a subjugated nation.

In exchange for offering Kublai Khan what Tibetans call the precious teachings, the student Kublai agreed to seek Phagpa's consent before making decisions regarding Tibet. This is the Tibetan version of these events. To the early Mongols, the Buddhist teachers of Tibet, like Phagpa, may have represented a tool to obtain political influence in Tibet. It was a mutually beneficial relationship, unique in the Mongol world: a spiritual leader directed the governance of a subject country within the Mongol Empire. These bonds between Mongols and Tibetans had nothing to do with China. When Tibet became a Mongol subject, Song China was still an independent country.

Phagpa officiated as priest at the enthronement ceremony of Kublai Khan in 1260, two decades before the Mongols finished the conquest of Song China, and by then he had been Kublai's priest for seven years. While Kublai made plans to use Phagpa to establish Mongol supremacy over Central Tibet, he incorporated the old eastern provinces of imperial Tibet, Amdo and Kham, directly into his empire. In 1264, Kublai sent troops to subdue Amdo.

Finally, in 1265, the khan allowed his teacher to return to Tibet, and the Tibetan chieftains came to pay homage. Kublai ordered Phagpa to establish Mongol supremacy over Tibet, in ways that were acceptable to Tibet and that reflected its native culture. Phagpa ruled Tibet for the Mongols as an ally and a vassal. Tibet received a tremendous opportunity, considering that Mongols often imposed dominance in brutal ways. Mongols made this offer to the Tibetans because they respected Phagpa and Buddhism, but also because Tibet was not wealthy. Since the sparsely populated state could not generate the kind of tribute or taxes that China could, the Mongols preferred to subdue the Tibetans in the most cost-effective way.

Not all the independent princes of Tibet accepted their new status without a fight, and, in 1267, Kublai sent a small army into Tibet to crush any resistance. Within a year, the Mongols had established their domination of Tibet and set up an administration. They conducted a census and established a courier system for imperial messages from Sakya Monastery to Beijing, Kublai's new capital. The Mongols created thirteen administrative zones, or myriarchies, as well as militias, and the Tibetan families who worked for this system became hereditary nobles. There was the occasional revolt. As many as ten thousand Tibetans died during one such revolt in 1290. The Mongols marched in, suppressed the revolt, and then were, once again, able to leave. Despite such problems, much of the territory unified by Songzen Gampo, except for parts of Amdo and Kham, was once again under a single Sakya administration, mostly run by Tibetans. Tibet had largely escaped the fate of millions of Chinese, whom the Mongols were exterminating at the same time. When Phagpa died at Sakya Monastery, in 1280, thirty-six years after he had set out with Sakya Pandita on his long journey to meet the Mongols, the broad outline of Tibet's strange victory was visible.

The domination of Tibet took place, as the Fourteenth Dalai Lama says, *before* Kublai Khan took the name Yuan for his dynasty, in 1271, and before the Mongols completed the conquest of Song China, in 1279. The Mongols were not unifying what is now modern China; they were simply conquering or subjugating as many of their neighbors as they could. The Mongols' administration of Tibet was not linked to their administration of China, and in no way unified the two countries into a Chinese state.

The Mongol conquest of Song China began about 1258 but it took two decades to complete because the Chinese resisted so ferociously. Song China was a proud nation with a strong military. The Mongols sacked, looted, and pillaged their way from one Chinese city to the next. They converted large swaths of fertile fields to pasture, and exterminated millions of farmers in north China, in the lands just south of the Great Wall. Once the Mongols depopulated north China, their garrison troops brought in Chinese slaves to farm the land allotted to them by the emperor. Some educated Chinese served the Mongols as bureaucrats, in a desperate attempt to spare their ethnic compatriots, but the effort was inadequate. Despite this painful experience—or probably because of it—Chinese ethnic nationalism, which would not coalesce into its modern form until the nineteenth century, began to emerge under the Mongols.

Tibet, a nation in which nomads were a large fraction of the population, surrendered virtually without a fight, and the Tibetans received a trusted place within the empire, like the Uighurs before them. China, a nation of farmers who despised nomads and built the Great Wall to prove it, fought to the end; as a result, the Mongols never trusted the Chinese.

The lack of a united Tibet, coupled with the appeal of Tibetan Buddhism, spared Tibet during the Mongol conquest. At the same time the unique nature of Buddhism in Tibet wounded, perhaps fatally, the birth of Tibetan nationalism. One afternoon I tried to summarize what I understood of this chapter of history to the Dalai Lama.

"From what you have told me and what I have read," I began, "modern Chinese have distorted the history between the Mongols, the Chinese, and the Tibetans to help rationalize their 1950 invasion of Tibet. They want to say, 'Tibet has been part of China since Tibet became part of the Mongol Empire.' You say and, in fact, historians seem to agree with you that Tibet became a subject of the Mongols in the 1250s at a time when the Mongols had not yet conquered China. But even though the Chinese have distorted this key moment of history, it is still very important, but for a different reason. Tibetans began to look outside of Tibet for the first time, for political and military power to control events inside of Tibet. The unique state of Tibet that we find in 1950 has its roots in this moment with Phagpa and the Mongols."

"Yes, it looks like that . . . hmmm . . . I agree," the Dalai Lama said. "You forget one thing. Either Sakya Pandita or Phagpa sent one letter back to Tibet. He mentioned the Mongols' fearfulness. He advised the Tibetans that they should be very careful. He indicated that they should be fearful of the Mongols. So there was pressure."

"Yes, they were afraid of the Mongols," I said, "and I have read that letter you mention. The Tibetans did not turn to foreigners to end their lack of unity. They were forced to acquiesce to a stronger power. Still, beginning with a disunited Tibetan state submitting to the Mongols, out of fear, and Tibet being unified by a foreign power, this smells like Tibet to me. The Mongol subjugation of the Tibetans was the first intervention of a foreign power in Tibet—the first of many—which ultimately led to the tragedy of today." I felt terrible dissecting his country's history so abstractly. "There is a small seed of all of this in the thirteenth century, isn't there?"

He sensed what a solemn moment we had arrived at together, and took a long moment to respond. "Yes, you can say that. Today's tragedy did not develop overnight. It developed during decades, centuries, generations. I entirely agree that, right from the beginning, there was some lost opportunity."

It was late, and we were both tired. The Dalai Lama's secretary looked at the clock, yet the Dalai Lama could not quite let go of the thin roots of the fate of his country, hidden in the history of the Mongols eight hundred years earlier. He shook his head and sighed as he reached out his hand to sweep up his prayer beads. As we walked to the door, he spoke, in an infinitely sad tone I had not heard before.

"This is a tragic situation which was caused over many centuries," the Dalai Lama said finally. "So the worst things have happened and now to overcome that, it is very difficult. So our generation's task seems almost impossible. Very difficult."

7

A MASTER PLAN:
THE FIRST TO THE FOURTH
DALAI LAMAS, 1357–1617

It was monsoon in Dharamsala. Black rain clouds covered the old British colonial hill town for days at a time. When the clouds finally part briefly, you can make out the brilliant green rice fields on the stepped terraces below. Farther south the terraces flatten out into the Indian plains that stretch out to the distance.

In Dharamsala, it seemed more like Tibet than India. Many of the Tibetans in exile since 1959 have flocked here to live near the Dalai Lama. Tibetans are nearly the sole inhabitants of the upper part of the town, called McLeod Ganj, where Tibetan monasteries and offices of Tibet's exile government dominate the skyline. As I crossed a square, headed toward the Dalai Lama's residence, I made my way through a crowd of young monks clad in red robes. The monks gathered in small groups to practice their debate techniques. One monk defended his position while an encircling group of monks peppered the defender with rapid-fire questions about fine points of Buddhist logic. The monks shouted, clapped their hands, and pointed dramatically at one another as they debated. An occasional peal of laughter punctuated the loud debates. The monsoon cloud hovering over Dharamsala was so thick that the monks vanished when I was just twenty yards beyond them, though I could still hear their disembodied voices as they debated.

The Dalai Lama's residence materialized slowly from the ground-hugging cloud. Called Thekchen Choeling, his home in exile comprises about eighteen cement bungalows scattered among pine trees and gardens in a five-acre fenced compound. The Dalai Lama lives in one of the smallest bungalows, while staff offices, dorms for bodyguards, a temple where he gives teachings, and a library occupy the others. In the guardhouse at the front gate—set into an imposing wall—Tibetan body-guards, their jackets bulging with revolvers, patted me down, passed me through metal detectors, checked my ID, and signed me in. I trudged on uphill, as mist turned to rain, under a bower of dripping bamboo, toward what everyone calls the audience bungalow. I dropped my um-brella into the rack at the door, tramped the mud and rain off my feet. An old monk then ushered me into the audience room. A row of small gold-plated statues dressed in colorful brocade robes stands on an altar on one wall, while a large map of Tibet fills another wall. It was perfect timing. Just as I arrived, the Dalai Lama's tapping footsteps on the ce-ment floors and the clicking prayer beads in his hands announced his arrival. His secretaries, who were normally present for our meetings, were late.

"They are late. Let's start without them," the Dalai Lama said. As we sat down to begin our discussion about Tsongkhapa, founder of the Gelug school of Buddhism (the Dalai Lama's order), a steady monsoon rain began to fall.

In Tibet's far northeastern province of Amdo, there is a region called Tsongkha. The founder of the Gelug order was born there in 1357, and when he later moved to Central Tibet, he was called Tsongkhapa. He had just been ordained as a monk at the age of ten when the Mongols left Tibet. At age fifteen, he was a charismatic young monk from the provinces who studied with more than one hundred of the most respected teachers, from all of Tibet's schools of Buddhism. By the 1370s the lines between the schools of Buddhism were clear. As disucssed in Chapter 5, the Nyingma was the oldest school, whose founding is attributed to Padmasambhava, though Nyingmapa emerged as such only after the arrival of the other sects. The devotees of the Kagyu order followed a path established by Marpa and Milarepa. The followers of the Sakya were renowned as great scholars, and their chief lama, or hierarch, had been viceroy of Tibet under the Mongols. Finally, there was the reform Kadam order, founded by Atisha. Tsongkhapa studied with great teachers from all the orders, even as conflict between the schools intensified after the Mongols left Tibet. Tsongkhapa was upset by what he saw as the state of ethical decay among monks, particularly those who drank alcohol and were not celibate, but also by the battle for supremacy between them. He wanted to return to the pure roots of Buddhism, abstinence included.

The Dalai Lama emphasizes Tsongkhapa's links to Atisha, the Indian reformer of the eleventh century. "Lama Tsongkhapa followed Atisha's traditions. He was a reformer too," the Dalai Lama said. "Like Atisha, he helped bring back a strict obedience to the code of conduct for monks, to restore respect for the *Vinaya*." The Dalai Lama explained how the teachings of Atisha and Tsongkhapa fused into the New Kadam order, which eventually became the Gelug. To me it seems that the focus on academic excellence, and attention to strict monastic vows, distinguishes the Gelug from the older schools of Buddhism.

I asked the Dalai Lama what sort of personal connection he felt to Tsongkhapa.

"I have had some dreams" he replied, "and of course his work is very remarkable, wonderful. When I studied his commentaries on one Indian Buddhist text, I saw that whenever the teaching was obvious, he made little comment, but when the original text was difficult, then he wrote a long commentary. He tried hard to understand fully what *(the text)* was about. That was Lama Tsongkhapa's way."

"Were there large monasteries in Tibet before Tsongkhapa," I asked, "or did they emerge only after him?"

"In some monasteries," the Dalai Lama said, "the number of monks reached ten thousand even before Tsongkhapa. By 1950, the largest monastery was Drepung, and it was founded by a disciple of Tsongkhapa. I believe it had nearly eight thousand monks, and as I told you, by then I think half were rubbish and only about half were true scholars." He laughed thinly as he bitingly summarized how, in time, even the Gelugpa strayed from their founding principles.

Tsongkhapa founded Ganden, the first Gelugpa monastery, in 1409. On his death, in 1419, his disciples entombed his preserved body there.

The Dalai Lama remembers Ganden because of a visit he made there just before he fled Tibet in 1959. At the time of his visit, Ganden had two dozen substantial chapels with large statues of the Buddha. The biggest chapel seated 3,500 monks during rituals. One of the temples still housed Tsongkhapa's silver-and-gold-encrusted tomb. In the 1960s, during the Cultural Revolution, Red Guards destroyed the monasteries at Ganden, as well as Tsongkhapa's tomb, and forced a monk, Bomi Rinpoche, to carry the mummy on his back to a fire. The remains of Tsongkhapa were as sacred for Tibetans as the remains of Saint Paul would be for Christians. Bomi secretly saved the skull and some ashes from the fire after the Red Guard burned the mummy. Reconstruction, including a new tomb for Tsongkhapa's preserved relics, began in the 1980s and is still under way. When the Dalai Lama visited the tomb, he had a strange experience that shows how deeply connected he feels to the founder of the Gelug sect.

"In 1958, for my final degree examination, my debate was in a court-yard at Ganden," the Dalai Lama recalled. He raises one hand and points it firmly at me, striking one of the debate poses I had seen the monks using at the gate, and smiles as he continues. "One day I was in front of Lama Tsongkhapa's tomb in Ganden, during my free time. I was not there for any special sort of ritual or ceremony. I was alone and I made some pros-trations in front of his tomb. I felt so moved, I felt like crying. It was some sort of very special feeling." He looks at me, assuming I have understood that this "special feeling" indicates a direct link to Tsongkhapa in a previ-ous life.

According to two reliable sources, the Dalai Lama believes that he spent an earlier life as a disciple of Tsongkhapa, forming a karmic con-nection with the master. Buddhist tradition decrees that it is inappro-priate for a monk who has developed the spiritual attainments that allow him to be aware of his past lives to discuss those lives in public. Doing so would exhibit pride, incompatible with the teachings of the Buddha. When I asked about his past life, as a disciple of Tsongkhapa, the Dalai Lama looked at me severely. "That is private," he said. When I pressed him doggedly, he laughed and said, "Let them talk about this after I am dead!" The "human soul" Tenzin Gyatso has had many human incar-nations prior to his life as the Dalai Lama. While he is a manifestation of the grace of Chenrizi, the Bodhisattva of Compassion, in this life, he retains other strands of karmic connection from other lives; one of those bonds is with Tsongkhapa.

Turning back to the religious biography of Tsongkhapa, I asked the Dalai Lama about the Bodhisattva of Wisdom Manjushri, who is in many ways the twin to Chenrizi the Bodhisattva of Compassion. I had seen murals in Lhasa that depicted Manjushri, in a rainbow halo, appearing to Tsongkhapa. I wondered how such visions compared with visions in which Jewish, Christian, and Muslim prophets received divine guidance from apparitions that also appeared within halos of light.

"Tibetans believe that Manjushri appeared to Tsongkhapa during one of his teachings at Ganden," I said.

"This happened frequently, not only at Ganden," the Dalai Lama replied with utter conviction.

"Why?" I asked.

"Why?" he responded, looking curiously at me as he scratched his face and repeated my question. "When he was a young monk, Tsongkhapa had no direct visions of Manjushri," the Dalai Lama said finally. "Those visions began only after he met his teacher from Kham, Lama Umapa Pawo Dorje, who was from a poor family. When *(Lama Umapa)* was young, he was a shepherd. Once, while he was with the animals in the pasture, he fainted, and when he awoke, there in front of him was Manjushri."

"And after that he often had visions of Manjushri," I interjected. Though I had not read about Lama Umapa's experience, it was so similar to Saint Paul's fainting episode on the road to Damascus that I could guess the ending.

"Yes, after that Lama Umapa saw Manjushri regularly," the Dalai Lama said. "So Lama Tsongkhapa received teachings from this teacher. Then eventually during one of Tsongkhapa's meditation retreats *(when he was about thirty)*, a blue light appeared, a small ball." He wrinkled his face as he gestured with his fingers in front of his eyes to indicate how small the blue ball was. "In that blue light was Manjushri. After that, whenever he had questions, then the Manjushri image always appeared."

"And many people saw this?" I asked.

"No," the Dalai Lama said. "Only on a very few occasions did others see Manjushri."

"But still you are saying that Tsongkhapa was taking direct teachings from Manjushri," I observed.

"Yes," the Dalai Lama said. "And slowly he became quite a famous scholar and teacher. Hundreds of people came to receive teaching from him. So one time Manjushri told him, 'Now your teaching is good, but still you are without proper understanding yourself. And this might not be so effective. So you must stop teaching and go to southern Tibet and put more effort in practice and accumulate more virtue and then you will have more realization.'" A tiny smile flickered on the Dalai Lama's lips as he told this story.

"After some of his disciples heard this, they complained to him." The Dalai Lama mimicked their complaints convincingly. "So many people get immense benefits from your teachings, if we stop these teachings, how will we save these people?" The Dalai Lama laughed deeply, almost as though he has heard such arguments himself. Then he continued in the same high, complaining voice. "And also for the Buddha Dharma, if we stop these teachings, it is also harmful!"

He chuckled as he continued. "The next day, Lama Tsongkhapa repeated these complaints to Manjushri. Manjushri said, 'So. You will present your teachings whether it is good for Buddha Dharma or not? Listen to me. I know better, and if others complain to you, well, fine. You can practice tolerance as you listen to their complaints.'"

The Dalai Lama laughed loudly at the punch line to this spiritual joke. "So this is very good," he said, "and disciplined. Manjushri was a very stern teacher. Tsongkhapa went to southern Tibet to do the retreat as he was ordered. And Manjushri even told him how many disciples could go with him."

Since I have no faith that there is divine guidance of human affairs, I could not contain my disbelief as I said, "Manjushri was directing the daily life of Lama Tsongkhapa?"

He considered my words and the tone of my delivery, saying nothing for several seconds. "Yes, it was almost like that." Acknowledging the disbelief in my voice, he admonished me, "But judging these experiences, these are true and confirmed. Lama Tsongkhapa did extraordinary things," the Dalai Lama said. "Even in my generation, these things can happen. So I am convinced."

His utter conviction made me wonder, sadly, what it would feel like to have such faith. It also made me recall his explanation of such "miracles." They were visible to any human who transformed his or her mind through intense meditation practice. There are two levels of human understanding, he had said, and for him both are real.

For me, Tsongkhapa was the founder of a school of Buddhism. He was a historic person. The Dalai Lama shared that vision, but he saw more— Tsongkhapa was guided. Since I lack faith in that concept, I asked the Dalai Lama to compare Tsongkhapa to Milarepa, the yogi-poet. I hoped that his comparison would help explain the mysterious force that the Dalai Lama sincerely believes has guided Tibetan history. "What is similar about the lives and methods of Milarepa and Tsongkhapa, and what is essentially different?" I asked.

The Dalai Lama's face relaxed as he pondered my question for thirty seconds in silence. Apparently this issue was something he had never thought about; I was thus confirmed in my understanding that he and I saw the world in vastly different ways. He began slowly, "Of course, both are really great masters, genuine practitioners. Both had highly developed spiritual experiences and achieved enlightenment. It is generally believed that for Milarepa, this happened in this life and that for Tsongkhapa, just after death. In this life Tsongkhapa was first a monk and then also more scholarly, so he was the more deeply studied of the two."

If it had seemed strange to him at first, the Dalai Lama soon warmed to the idea of comparing Milarepa and Tsongkhapa. "Milarepa captured the essence of emptiness. He hit the real essence without much scholarly study. So because of that, the followers of Milarepa *(the Kagyu order)* emphasize direct practice and meditation. In Tsongkhapa's case, study is very important. He wrote major books. But his emphasis was on practice. His books offer an explanation of different Buddhist schools of thought according to Indian history. But he emphasized that *(these books)* were for the real practice of Buddhism, not just to read."

"There is a literal difference between the two men," I said, "and their lives convey two aspects of Tibet, don't they?"

"Yes," he said. "Milarepa sang his songs spontaneously, and others wrote them down. And they are short. Tsongkhapa wrote his own treatises, and they are long. But both men achieved enlightenment. That is certain."

The Dalai Lama had extracted the heart of Tibetan Buddhism. These two paths, meditation and study, are two approaches to the same goal. Tibetan monks and nuns from all orders, depending on their natural inclinations, pursue one or both of these paths today. Still I could not understand how the Bodhisattvas of Wisdom and Compassion guided the lives of the men who created these paths, literally. Yet the clarity with which the Dalai Lama saw the essence of Tibetan Buddhism increased my respect for him. It also increased my determination to probe the origins of his unshakable faith that there is a force that has guided key developments in Tibetan history.

Tsongkhapa's fame as a Buddhist teacher spread throughout Asia, even to the Ming emperors, during his life. When the Chinese evicted the Mongols, they installed a Chinese emperor who founded the Ming dynasty. The Ming worked to rebuild the Great Wall to keep the foreign nomads out. As their power grew, they reached out to nearby states, hoping to contain or subjugate them. When the Ming heard of Tsongkhapa and the power he had over Tibetans, they sent him an invitation.

"He was twice invited to the Ming court and he refused," I said to the Dalai Lama. "Other Tibetan lamas of this period visited the Ming court and received fancy Chinese titles. Some even made money by engaging in trade while in the Chinese capital. Why did Tsongkhapa refuse the Ming emperor's invitation to visit Beijing?"

The Dalai Lama said, "This, I think, shows that he doesn't bother about his fame or money . . ."

"Or politics," I blurted out.

He looked up at me sharply. "Politics," he said, grumbling as if it were a dirty word. "Politics, I don't know. Lama Tsongkhapa was not interested in name, prestige, and other things. I think some Tibetan lamas, like the Karmapa *(head of the Karma Kagyu sect)* or the Fifth Dalai Lama, when they visited China, it was not necessarily for political reasons. I think *their* motivation was simply trying to propagate Buddha Dharma. Though, frankly speaking, sometimes, some of *(the other Tibetans who visited China)* were expecting some wealth."

Some Tibetan monasteries and princes eagerly sought invitations from the Ming emperor because when they gave gifts, or paid tribute to the emperor (as the Chinese saw these gifts), they received gifts of much greater value in return.

"And that wealth which they received," the Dalai Lama continued, "was not necessarily used privately but to build monasteries and things like that. But actually, I think they were seeking some wealth. So they repeated nice empty words to the Chinese emperor, and those were returned with solid things, like gold. There was not necessarily a political motivation in these visits by the Tibetan lamas, but its impact was also political." The emperors of the Ming dynasty recorded these trade missions as "tribute missions," though they were trading missions. Even now, the Chinese government cites such missions" as evidence that Tibet was a vassal to the Ming dynasty.

"So Lama Tsongkhapa had no such interest," the Dalai Lama said as he concluded. "He declined the invitation. But then he sent one of his closest disciples."

Tsongkhapa's list of accomplishments is a long one. He is famous for his direct guidance from the Bodhisattva of Wisdom, Manjushri, for his commitment to monastic reformation, and for his thorough and incisive commentaries on Buddhist scripture. He is also famous for the monasteries he and his disciples founded, including Ganden, the first Gelug monastery, in 1409.

Despite what the Dalai Lama had taught me, I still saw Tibetan monasteries in a secular light. "Weren't monasteries bastions of culture, built to preserve Buddhist scripture and art from destruction in a violent world?" I asked.

"Yes, that's true," the Dalai Lama said, "but the protection of these material things are by-products. For me the most important purpose of a monastery is to protect the spiritual purity of a spiritual practice and the spiritual lineage that transmits it. That is what is preserved in a monastery."

The Dalai Lama's meaning is precise. Tibetan monasteries are places where Buddhist teachers meditate, study, and teach. The Buddhist scriptures about specific meditation practices serve only as an outline for the oral teaching of those practices. Teachers receive training from their master and, in turn, pass their learning on to their students. The Dalai Lama attaches great importance to the oral transmission from one generation to the next. He believes that the meditation practices used by monks today are the same as those used thousands of years ago, all the way back to the Buddha. Through the millennia, the careful word-of-mouth transmission from one generation to the next ensures the unbroken veracity of the Buddhist heritage. Tibetan monks will not embark on a meditation practice without receiving the oral instruction. As the Dalai Lama spoke, I understood that, for him, the buildings, texts, and art are only the by-products of the preservation and transmission of the oral spiritual tradition. He looked at me intently to see if I had comprehended his point and then said, "Lama Tsongkhapa was very strict about *Vinaya* because he wanted to protect the practices." The strict code of ethics that a monk must follow is also a means to protect the Buddhist practices.

I thought carefully about the Dalai Lama's words before I replied. "You say that monasteries were tools built to preserve and transmit Buddhist practices. Yet the monks collected great wealth to build the monasteries. And you have said that many monasteries were corrupted over the centuries. Did Lama Tsongkhapa worry that the wealth needed to build and maintain monasteries might corrupt the monasteries?"

"One time, Lama Tsongkhapa intentionally placed his begging bowl upside down, to receive nothing," the Dalai Lama explained. "He worried that the precious teaching we have received from the Buddha could be destroyed because of monks running after wealth and enjoyment. When Tsongkhapa placed his begging bowl upside down, he was saying that this wonderful and beautiful teaching we have inherited from our spiritual masters—all of it can be corrupted by evil influences and practices. He worried that, later on, false people could claim to be very good teachers, and this would pollute and corrupt the Buddhist teaching."

The Dalai Lama's face is filled with concern as he continues. "In fact, as I have told you before, Tsongkhapa said that though the Gelug order, in terms of material appearances, might one day look pompous and magnificent, what if it is then devoid of any content or spiritual practice?" The pain in his voice was raw. Tsongkhapa's six-hundred-year-old concern that the lineage which transmits Buddhism might be corrupted had a personal effect on the Dalai Lama.

Despite Tsongkhapa's reservations, his disciples followed their master's precedent and founded three more monasteries. All eventually grew into monastic cities, housing thousands of monks. They would become Tibet's four largest, wealthiest, and most powerful monasteries. After Tsongkhapa founded Ganden, in 1409, his disciples founded Drepung in 1416 and Sera in 1419: all are near Lhasa. A disciple of Tsongkhapa named Gendundrup founded Tashilunpo in 1445, in Shigatse, Tibet's second largest town. Though Gendundrup was only a very holy monk in his own lifetime, retroactively he would be recognized as the First Dalai Lama.

"When the First Dalai Lama started construction of the Tashilunpo Monastery, he was quite old," the Dalai Lama said. "Still, his daily routine was to give Buddhist teachings to his students, and then instruct them about the design and construction of monasteries. Finally, he gave instructions for people to collect money to help build the monastery. There was one old monk who spent his youth raising money for Tashilunpo, and later, when he was old, he went into meditation retreat. At one point, he said, 'If I had spent my youth in retreat, then I would have reached a much higher spiritual stage. But I sacrificed that in order to establish this monastery and serve Buddha Dharma and a greater number of sentient beings.' So you see this is why the First Dalai Lama told his disciples at Tashilunpo, 'Sometimes I teach you Dharma, sometimes I instruct you in constructing buildings, sometimes I instruct you to raise money. Now all these teachings are for your benefit, and if you are not intent, then all my effort becomes useless.' He told them that the main purpose of this was to propagate and preserve the Buddha Dharma and one's own spiritual tradition. And there was something positive and necessary and also welcome in all this work."

The Dalai Lama smiled like a pragmatic father. The purpose of monasteries is clear for him: money, too, can be an effective tool, if used properly. Despite potential pitfalls, monasteries are a means to preserve the transmission of spiritual techniques for human self-development. As families pass their genes from one generation to another, so, too, a monastery passes its teachings from one generation of a spiritual family to the next. As in families, a genetic flaw is deadly.

However, monasteries in Tibet became more than a means to preserve the teachings. They became the homes of lineages of reincarnate monks, like the lineage of the Dalai Lama. The Second Dalai Lama was the reincarnation of the monk Gendundrup, as well as a manifestation of Chenrizi. Gendundrup took the Bodhisattva vow. He attained a spiritual state near enlightenment and then refused to take the final step into enlightenment, until all other sentient beings (not just humans) achieved enlightenment.

The First Dalai Lama had already founded Tashilunpo, and his master Tsongkhapa had been dead for decades. "The First Dalai Lama was getting old," the current Dalai Lama said, "around eighty-two. One day he was explaining the Buddhist scriptures, as he did every day. Then with a deep sigh he said, 'Now I am near to dying.' One disciple responded, 'Now according to your past indications, you are going to go to the Pure Land of the Buddhas.'

"'No,' the First Dalai Lama said. 'I have no wish for that. My only wish is to take rebirth wherever there are more problems and suffering.'

"This is wonderful," the Dalai Lama told me, looking up with a smile of radiant happiness. "Many years ago I read this and was really impressed." He spoke softly, reverentially, as he continued. "I wept when I read this the first time. His way of thinking, *(it)* deeply influenced my mind. I prefer rebirth in this world continuously. Many lamas would prefer to take rebirth in Shambhala *(a near-heaven realm)*, but not me. My strong feelings about this were influenced by what I read long ago in the biography of the First Dalai Lama." Even I, an unbeliever, am moved.

The First Dalai Lama inherited many essential ideas from India through Tsongkhapa and Atisha, which he transmitted to the Fourteenth Dalai Lama unchanged. The current Dalai Lama's vision of Tibetan history and many of his philosophical, spiritual, and political ideas came to him through this lineage. His belief about the purpose of a monastery is identical to that of Tsongkhapa and the First Dalai Lama. He explains the proper use of wealth, just as the First Dalai Lama explained it. The First Dalai Lama's idea that a Buddhist monk should take the Bodhisattva vow and consciously seek a human rebirth, in the human world, to guide others toward enlightenment is, again, an Indian Buddhist ideal, which has been transmitted through the prism of Tibet, from the fourteenth century right up to the current Dalai Lama. Many aspects of Tibet, as it was until the Chinese invasion of 1950, begin with the life and death of Tsongkhapa and the First Dalai Lama.

While such spiritual ideals have clearly shaped Tibetan history, it was because the Gelugpa ultimately acquired immense political and military authority that the leaders of the order became the rulers of Tibet. The transformation of the Gelug, from a reformist spiritual order into a Buddhist school, which also wielded great military power, was a key event in Tibetan history. Ironically, it was the large number of devotees attracted by the spiritual commitment of the early Gelug masters that ultimately gave succeeding Dalai Lamas political and even military power.

The emergence of the Gelugpa as the rulers of Tibet took place against a backdrop of political turmoil, which began once Tibetans expelled the Mongols from the land.

The Mongols maintained a loose suzerainty over Tibet from about 1249 to 1368. Throughout this period, the power of the state remained with the Tibetan viceroy and with the monasteries and nobles, who followed orders from the Mongols. Except during the last ten years of the era, every viceroy was also a high-ranking Sakya priest. Two monks from the Sakya order, Sakya Pandita and his nephew Phagpa, established the priest-patron *(cho–yon)* relationship with the Mongol emperors; because of their religious authority, each was appointed viceroy. After the death of Phagpa, in 1280, the Mongols named successive Sakya leaders as imperial preceptors; they also became the viceroys of Tibet. The Sakya monks farmed out local control to the ruling princes in various provinces of Tibet. Some of the princes were also Buddhist monks. One such regional chief, Chang-chub Gyaltsen, revolted against Sakya hegemony from about 1352. During six years of war, Gyaltsen defeated the Sakya. At first, rather than challenging the Mongols and the Sakya at the same time, he presented himself to the Mongols as simply their new viceroy. In 1358, the Mongols, preoccupied with a growing uprising against their rule in China, accepted Gyaltsen as their viceroy, even though they knew his goal was Tibetan independence.

After he had killed the ruling Sakya lama and been recognized as the new viceroy, Gyaltsen replaced the Sakya administrators of Tibet with his loyalists, not men recommended by the Mongols. In this and other ways, he showed the Mongols that he was not their vassal. He posted Tibetan troops to the Chinese border, redistributed land more equally, and reduced taxes. Returning to the Tibetan judicial system established by Songzen Gampo and his heirs, he reinstituted trials for suspected lawbreakers. Under Mongol rules, *all* suspected violations brought an automatic death sentence. Despite these steps, which established de facto Tibetan independence, Gyaltsen never formally broke with the Mongols. Still, he had essentially freed Tibet of Mongol control a full ten years before China would do so. China and Tibet had succumbed to Mongol rule at different times, were ruled by the Mongols under different terms of subjugation, and were emancipated from Mongol rule at different times.

Gyaltsen died in 1364, six years after freeing Tibet, and his nephew, a monk, inherited rule over Tibet at the head of what was called the Phamo Drupa government. Four years later, in 1368, the Chinese defeated the Mongols in China, pushing them back north across the Great Wall, and established the Ming dynasty within the Great Wall. The dynasty never ruled the territory that the Mongols had governed, except for China itself.

At the same time, the Phamo Drupa cut its last ties with the Mongols, and Tibet regained full independence. The Phamo Drupa ruled over much of Tibet, with little challenge, until about 1434—although, during parts of that time, many Tibetan princes ruled autonomously rather than as part of any central government. Modern Chinese historians dispute the claim of Tibetan independence by asserting that Tibet was a part

Ancient Indian beliefs about the origins of the universe have influenced Tibetan ideas since the sixth century.

Murals in Tibetan monasteries depict a vast central mountain (left), with four sides where billions of world systems exist, from the highest heavens, through the human and animal realms, to the lowest hells. Other aspects of this worldview are depicted in a cosmological mural (top right), in Bhutan.

The first human inhabitants of the Tibetan Plateau settled there twenty or thirty thousand years ago. Ancient rock paintings (bottom right), often depicting people on horseback—as well as archaeological evidence—testify to this.

The Dalai Lama, who is particularly interested in archaeological discoveries in Tibet, has studied Buddhist theories about the origins of the universe and humankind. He says that the Buddha gave people freedom to follow whatever evidence they uncover even when that evidence contradicts ancient texts.

Tibetan origin myths say that the Bodhisattva Chenrizi (top) sent what the Dalai Lama calls "energy" or a "positive karmic connection" into a male monkey as the Bodhisattva guided the evolution of the first Tibetans. The rainbow is a metaphor for that energy.

The Dalai Lama says that Songzen Gampo, the Yarlung dynasty emperor who unified Tibet in the seventh century (bottom left), had a "connection" to the Bodhisattva Chenrizi and that when the emperor died he was transformed into a rainbow, which dissolved into a mysterious tiny wooden statue of Chenrizi (bottom right).

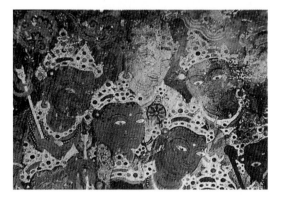

Tibetans believe the first two Buddhist statues brought to Tibet came with Songzen Gampo's Chinese and Nepalese wives. The Chinese Buddha, the *Jo* (top right), came with Princess Wencheng, the junior wife, from Chang'an, while the Nepalese princess brought a Buddha now said to be in Ramoche Temple, Lhasa (top left). Today both are nearly invisible beneath an accretion of gold, diamonds, turquoise, and coral offered by pilgrims over the centuries. In the seventh century the Jokhang, oldest Buddhist temple in Tibet, was built in a unique Tibeto-Nepalese-Indian style to house the Jo. Despite numerous invasions and lootings it still contains fragments of statues and murals (left & bottom) from the era of its foundation showing Indian and Nepalese (and even Greek) influence on the development of Tibetan art.

Though Tibet is famous for its Buddhist art, Tibetans mastered the arts of war as well. Tang dynasty chronicles tell how Yarlung dynasty warriors were famous for donning chain mail that left men and horses invincible to arrows. While the arms and mail (above) were made in nineteenth-century Tibet, there is no evidence that Tibet acquired any of its iron-making technology from China.

The Dalai Lama's favorite image of the Buddha (facing, top left), circa AD 200 (Lahore National Museum, Pakistan), was made in the kingdom of Ghandara. It shows Greek influence on the development of the first Buddhist images. The Dalai Lama says the emaciation in the statue is a graphic reminder that enlightenment is achieved only with intense effort. He does not have much appreciation for the aesthetic beauty of Buddha images; for him their purpose is to inspire devotion and effort. The Buddha mural from Drathang, Tibet, eleventh century (facing, top right) is one the oldest surviving in Tibet today and shows how some Greco-Indian iconography was transmitted from India to China, and then to Tibet. Tibet received all of the teachings of the Buddha, and the vast majority of its artistic inspiration, directly from India. Buddha, Mustang, circa 1800 (facing, bottom left), shows Indian and Nepalese influence. The early realism of the first Buddhist statues as well as stylistic elements of Indian, Chinese, Nepalese, and Inner Asian art were ultimately transmuted into a unique Tibetan style. Image of the Buddha, 1920 (facing, bottom right), Chensalingka, Lhasa.

The Yarlung dynasty collapsed after Lang Darma was murdered—shot between the eyes—by the monk Lhalung Palgyi Dorje (top): in front of the Jokhang; Tang/Tibet treaty pillar in foreground. Detail from mural, Norbulingka, Lhasa, circa 1956.

The elderly Sakya Pandita was summoned by the Mongol prince Godan to his camp to provide Buddhist teachings (bottom left). He brought his young nephew Phagpa (bottom right), who survived his uncle and went on to become imperial preceptor to Kublai Khan. Detail from *thangkha*, circa 1550.

Padmasambhava helped introduce Buddhism to Tibet in the eighth century (top left). Atisha helped to reform Buddhism in Tibet in the eleventh century (top right). Milarepa, Tibet's great yogi-poet of the eleventh and twelfth centuries (bottom left). Tsongkhapa founded the Gelug order of Buddhism and Ganden Monastery in the fifteenth century (bottom right).

Before his death Dusum Khyenpa, the First Karmapa, told his students where he would be reincarnated, and thus initiated the unique Tulku system where realized Buddhist masters return to guide the same order, or monastery, generation after generation. His teacher, Gampopa, disciple of Milarepa, is above him. This portrait with its strong jutting chin, said to be historically accurate, is a masterpiece of Tibetan art, painted circa 1750.

Tsongkhapa, founder of the Dalai Lama's Gelug order of Tibetan Buddhism, receiving instructions from the Bodhisattva Manjushri, Norbulingka mural, Lhasa. The Great Fifth Dalai Lama, also Gelugpa (left, circa 1750), started construction of the Potala, about 1645, shortly after the Qoshot Mongol Gushri Khan (bottom) helped the Great Fifth unify the Tibetan Plateau. Mural, Jokhang, Lhasa.

The Great Fifth Dalai Lama was invited to Beijing, the Manchu imperial capital, by Emperor Shunzhi, in 1653. Tibetan mural of the meeting, Norbulingka, Lhasa (top).

Vast Tibetan monasteries did more than house giant statues—and this is a small statue in Gyantse circa 1700—they were also libraries and schools (bottom left). A Nyingmapa mural illustrating one Tantric yoga pose. Sherpa, eastern Nepal, 1920s (bottom right).

Some Buddhist yogis, often of the Nyingma or Kagyu order, flouted the rules of *Vinaya* that traditional monks followed. Roaming yogis, like this *Nagpa* (top left) with his human thighbone horn and human skullcup, practiced esoteric Tantric forms of Buddhism that were said to lead to enlightenment in this very life. Austere monks shaved their heads, wore traditional monk's robes (top right), and followed strict rules of celibacy. Both types of Buddhists often engaged in long meditation retreats, but the traditional monks would first engage in years of academic study and preparation.

Tibetan farmers and nomads (left) supported monks of all types and visited monasteries and temples to earn merit.

In the 1890s, British officials in India at first tried to negotiate border agreements regarding the line between Tibet and Sikkim with Manchu officials (top). Ultimately Lord Curzon (bottom left) realized that despite Manchu claims to sovereignty over Tibet, the Manchu had no control over the nation, which had at least de facto independence. He ordered Sir Francis Younghusband (bottom right) and a small military expedition into Tibet in 1904.

After the British invasion of 1904 and the Manchu invasion of 1908, the Thirteenth Dalai Lama realized the importance of building a modern army and Tibetan troops were trained by a variety of foreign advisers (top), while weapons and uniforms were bought from Britain. Detail from a mural, Chensalingka, Lhasa, circa 1920. A saddle rug from the Tibetan cavalry (left), private collection. Tibetan coin (middle), private collection.

The invasions by the Manchu and British empires, along with his years in exile, convinced the Thirteenth Dalai Lama upon his return to Tibet in 1912 to initiate a campaign of reform. Lungshar Dorje Tsegyal (top, center) was sent to Europe not only to accompany four students whom the Dalai Lama hoped could return to Tibet with much needed technical knowledge, but as the Dalai Lama's representative. Upon Lungshar's return to Tibet, he was appointed commander in chief of the Tibetan army, where he tried to convince the monasteries with their large

population of monks (right) that taxes needed to be raised to finance a modern army. After the Thirteenth Dalai Lama's death, his reforms were gutted and ultimately Lungshar was arrested and blinded, which killed him.

Traditionally Tibetan prisoners might serve part of their term while living in shackles and a wooden collar or stock. This punishment was also common in Manchu China and even Bhutan. The Fourteenth Dalai Lama was so distressed by this method of punishment that he freed such prisoners in 1950.

Tibetan woman, with distinctive headdress, burns incense above Lhasa Valley, 1949

The Thirteenth Dalai Lama (seated), with Sir Charles Bell, circa 1907, with an attendant.

of the Ming dynasty. The dynasty did bestow honorary titles on the princes and monks in eastern Tibet, who were eager to trade with China and rarely accepted the supremacy of the Phamo Drupa. These alliances with eastern Tibetan principalities are the evidence China now produces for its assertion that the Ming ruled Tibet. In fact, after the Mongol troops left Tibet, no Ming troops replaced them.

After eighty years of Phamo Drupa rule in Central Tibet, a hostile group within the government began to usurp power from Gyaltsen's heirs. The Rinpung faction of princes supported the Kagyu order of Buddhism, and by about the year 1500, the Kagyupa were eager to check the growing strength of the Gelugpa. The monasteries founded by Tsongkhapa and his disciples grew rapidly, and the other schools saw the Gelugpa as a threat to their power. The princely factions in government allied themselves with different Buddhist orders, which led to sectarian and regional violence as one province raided another and the monks of one order razed the monasteries of another.

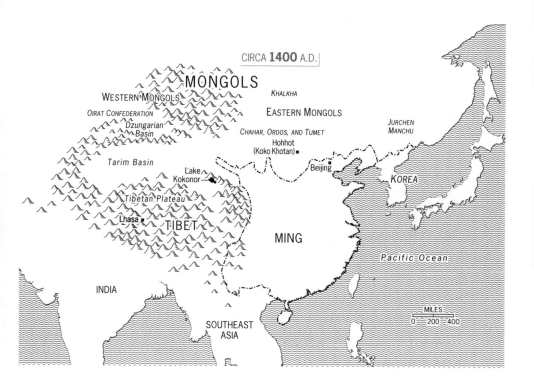

From 1450 onward, war was common, and the battles between orders were not about differences in philosophy but about wealth and control among rival factions. By 1565, the princes of Tsang Province, centered in Shigatse, had seized power and become the kings of Central Tibet. Since they supported the Kagyupa, the Gelugpa and their supporting princes in Lhasa were under constant attack. It was against this backdrop that the Dalai Lamas emerged as political as well as religious leaders.

The first four Dalai Lamas, from 1391 to 1616, devoted their lives to building the monasteries and the order established by Atisha and Tsongkhapa, despite the political chaos around them. When the current Dalai Lama discussed this period, it was clear that he saw a pattern within the chaos. Just as the Bodhisattva Chenrizi had earlier manifested through Songzen Gampo and other great Tibetans, now Chenrizi worked through the first Dalai Lamas to fulfill the promise Chenrizi had made, long ago, to the Buddha. Chenrizi had promised to guide and protect the Tibetan people, and his oath manifested itself now as a master plan.

"The master plan meant a new beginning," the Dalai Lama said. "It was a period where there was a possibility of a longer-term plan. It was a plan for more than one or two generations, and it benefited not only the Dalai Lama institution but the whole nation, and Buddha Dharma. This plan for the nation involved the First through the Fifth Dalai Lamas. They came one after another, successfully, for one purpose. They were all moving in one direction.

"Here is my summary," he began. "The First Dalai Lama established a sort of power base, not military or political but one of popular support, in the Tsang area around Tashilunpo. Of course, because of the construction of Tashilunpo, the First Dalai Lama became an even more important lama. So his reincarnation *(Gedun Gyatso, the Second Dalai Lama, born 1475)* then came to Tashilunpo Monastery and remained until he was sixteen or seventeen. Then there were some controversies or jealousy, and the young Second Dalai Lama was compelled to leave the monastery. He went to Lhasa and studied, and became abbot of Drepung. So his popularity developed in Lhasa and Central Tibet. Later, he went to southern Tibet and built his own monastery, Chokhor-gyal," in 1509.

"There for the first time," the Dalai Lama continued, "he formalized the system of recognizing another Gelugpa incarnate, including using the vision lake of Palden Lhamo." Monks went to a sacred lake named Lhamo Latso, where the goddess Palden Lhamo resides, to meditate in search of visions that would guide them to the new incarnation of Chenrizi. This method survived through the quest for the Fourteenth Dalai Lama. "Meantime, he also made some connection with two other areas of Tibet, Kongpo and Dhagpo. So during the Second Dalai Lama, he was now established in Central and southern Tibet." For the Dalai Lama, the master plan of Chenrizi was guiding the First and Second Dalai Lamas as they created a base of popular support and then extended the base to encompass more adherents, in larger regions of Tibet. They had prepared the way for the Third Dalai Lama to go to Mongolia and convert the Mongols to Buddhism.

The Third Dalai Lama, called Sonam *Gyatso* (with what now became the traditional last name "*Ocean*"), was born in 1543, near Lhasa, and recognized as a reincarnation of the Second Dalai Lama. He studied at Drepung Monastery, where, after exhibiting remarkable scholastic abilities, he became abbot, just as his predecessor had been. As head of one of the four largest Gelugpa monasteries, his influence grew so quickly that soon the monks at Sera recognized him as the abbot of their institution. The monks of Tashilunpo also welcomed his representative. His powers were far-reaching: when one of Tibet's kings (supported by the Kagyupa) died in 1564, it was the Third Dalai Lama, at the age of twenty-one, who presided during the funeral rites.

By the 1570s, the rising power of the Gelug lamas had reached a critical mass in Tibet, and the fame of the Third Dalai Lama spread to neighboring countries. For Mongolians, nomads who were just building their first permanent city, Tibetan culture was advanced and attractive, with much to covet: the intellectual and spiritual ferment in Tibet, the rigorous training of Tibetan monks, the massive library of translated Indian Buddhist text, and the construction spree of monasteries with fine statues and murals. Hearing that Sonam Gyatso was a living manifestation of the Bodhisattva Chenrizi, the Mongols were eager to meet him.

Between the fourteenth and sixteenth centuries, the Mongols survived two centuries of historic reverses and catastrophes that shaped and reshaped Asia and Europe. In 1368, the Chinese evicted the Mongols and founded their national dynasty, the Ming. The last Mongol emperor of China, Toghan Temur, along with sixty thousand troops, retreated north of the Great Wall to their former grazing lands in Inner Asia. When the Mongol army returned to a homeland it had not seen in decades, if at all, it wreaked havoc on the fragile nomadic economy of the Mongols who had remained behind while Genghis Khan conquered the world. Accustomed to living in the luxury that only conquest can bring, the former lords of China now fought over the grazing lands, which yielded only meat, cheese, and milk. When an avenging Ming army of 100,000 Chinese invaded Mongolia in 1388, the Mongols were defeated in their homeland and the Mongol princes assassinated the grandson of Toghan. The Chinese did not stay in Mongolia, but the humiliation suffered by the heirs of Genghis Khan allowed the Mongol princes to reclaim their autonomy. In the coming centuries, Mongol unity was rarely achieved and then only briefly. The dream of retaking the throne of China never died, even as tribal factionalism made it impossible. If the Mongols wanted more than what their herds of sheep and horses could provide (such as wheat, rice, or silk), they still raided Chinese cities to obtain it. From 1368 until the Manchu subjugated them in the seventeenth century, the tribes raided the Chinese and fought among themselves for ever-elusive supremacy. Each tribe looked to its own prince, and there was no sense of nationhood. Though the greatest Mongol princes had earlier studied Buddhism as they conquered the world, the average Mongol had not. Whatever imprint Buddhism had made among the Mongols vanished in the centuries of chaos after 1368. Mongolians had reverted to their faith in shamans and blood offerings.

The tribes were divided roughly into two camps, the eastern and western Mongols. Though they had lost Ghenghis Khan's empire, the two tribal confederations ruled an area much larger than modern Mongolia.

The eastern Mongolian tribes included, among others, the Khalkha, who lived in what is now the northern part of Mongolia, and the Chahar, Ordos, and Tumet, who resided primarily in territory that is now within the Autonomous Inner Mongolian Province of China. The eastern tribes included the direct descendants of Genghis Khan and so claimed the right to be the emperor of the Mongols, but they were unable to enforce their claim. The Oirat confederation of the western Mongol tribes, including the Qoshot, Torghuud, Khoyid, and others, based themselves in the Dzungarian Basin, one thousand miles to the west, in what is now the province of Xinjiang. The Oirat rejected eastern Mongol claims of supremacy. For a time the Oirat subjugated nearly all the eastern tribes. In 1449, under Oirat leadership, the briefly reunited Mongols killed more than 100,000 Chinese troops and captured the Ming emperor Ying-tsung. But the Oirat leaders could not follow through on their invasion of China, and ultimately they were again driven north of the Great Wall. The Mongols released the much-abused Ming emperor a year later. The invasion of Ming China was just one of many Oirat raids against their neighbors. The Mongols did not become part of a Ming-led pan-ethnic Chinese state.

Oirat hegemony over the eastern Mongols waned from 1455 but was not broken until Altan Khan, a prince of the Tumet tribe, recaptured the ancient imperial Mongol capital of Karakorum about 1550. Altan was the most prominent prince among the eastern Mongols during his reign, from 1543 to 1583, but despite his military supremacy, he was not emperor. That title passed down to Ligdan Khan, through another branch of Genghis Khan's descendants, though Ligdan was too weak to enforce the claim. Altan was famous during his youth for the piratical raids he led against Chinese towns just south of the Great Wall. In 1529, 1530, and again in 1542, he led raids and all who followed him brought home livestock and plunder. In 1550, he set fire to the suburbs of Beijing, but by then his plans extended beyond plunder. Although such raids had become the primary source of income for Mongols, Altan felt that the tribes should trade for what they could not raise, if the Chinese would reopen the border markets. They had been closed by the Ming to punish the Mongols for their raids and to drive them from the frontiers of China.

By 1571, Altan had defeated his eastern Mongol rivals; though he could not unite the far-flung Mongol nomads, he overthrew the Oirat confederation's hegemony, and most of the eastern Mongols followed his lead. As Altan aged, he began construction of a capital, Koko Khotan, the first permanent Mongol city of modern times. He also tried to end two centuries of Mongol attacks on China. He made peace with Ming China in 1571, and within two years had forced the Ming to reopen their border markets so the eastern Mongol tribesmen could unload their excess horses on the Chinese at a good profit. The Ming felt that appeasement of the Mongols through trade might work; in any event, they had nothing to lose, since they were unable to stop the Mongol raids with military force. In the opinion of later Mongols, Altan forced the Ming to treat him as an equal. Despite these facts, Chinese historians argue that the Mongol warlord was actually a loyal Chinese citizen.

During raids in China and into the fringe of Tibet, Altan heard rumors about Sonam Gyatso, head of the Gelugpa. A nephew of Altan's persuaded the prince that after defeating the Oirat and taking revenge on the Chinese, Altan had fulfilled his political destiny and now, as he grew older, it was time for him to think of higher things. The nephew said, "Now it appears that in the western land of snows [Tibet] there dwells, in corporeal form, the Mighty Seer and Pitiful One, the Bodhisattva Avalokiteshvara [Chenrizi]." Here Altan referred to learning that the Tulku Sonam Gyatso was believed to be a manifestation of Chenrizi.

In 1577, Altan Khan invited the Third Dalai Lama to visit Mongolia. That Sonam Gyatso traveled 1,500 miles to meet Altan says much about the Mongol prince's military power. When the two met, in June 1578, they exchanged the customary honorific titles. Altan translated the Tibetan word *Gyatso* "ocean," or "oceanic virtue," into Mongolian: *Dalai* means "ocean." *Lama* had long been a Tibetan honorific for any reincarnate Buddhist teacher—not for all monks, but for those recognized as a Tulku, or for one's own teacher or guru. The Mongolian title *Dalai Lama* was only later retroactively applied to Sonam Gyatso's two predecessors. No one called the First and Second Dalai Lamas by that title in their lifetimes. More confusing in our time is that many writers have mistranslated *Dalai Lama* as "Ocean of Wisdom." The full Mongolian title, "the wonderful

Vajradhara, good splendid meritorious ocean," given by Altan Khan, is primarily a translation of the Tibetan words *Sonam Gyatso* (*sonam* is "merit"). Only some of this information was clear to me when I first asked the Dalai Lama about his most famous title. He grew slightly agitated. He too had seen the mistranslations of the title.

"Now, I have something I have to say," he began sternly. "The very name of each Dalai Lama from the Second Dalai Lama onwards had the word Gyatso *(in it)*, which means 'ocean' in Tibetan. Even now I am Tenzin Gyatso, so the first name is changing but the second part (*the word "ocean"*) became like part of each Dalai Lama's name. All of the Dalai Lamas, since the Second, have this name. So I don't really agree that the Mongols actually conferred a title. It was just a translation."

I was caught off guard, unable to accept that so many modern writers had made the mistake of translating *Dalai Lama* as "Ocean of Wisdom" and that so few see his title as Tenzin Gyatso does. "Does the ocean word, *Dalai*, in the Mongolian title, imply something? Wisdom?"

"No, there is no implication," he nearly shouted at me. "It's just a name!

"Look, my sweeper was named Sangye, which is Tibetan for Buddha," he continued exasperated, "but he was quite lazy and silly. Sometimes I had to say something about his work, like, 'Oh, that Buddha!'"

He laughs and continues, "His name had nothing to do with the meaning."

In 1578, when Altan Khan and Sonam Gyatso met, the conferring of titles was a minor detail. Tibetans believe that the Third Dalai Lama converted Altan to Buddhism. The conversion of the most powerful of the Mongol princes encouraged other princes to convert as well. When Altan Khan sent presents back to monasteries in Tibet and financed the printing and translation of Buddhist texts, other princes did the same. Altan allowed the Third Dalai Lama to burn all the wooden carvings his family had kept as shamanic totems. In fact, he ordered all his subjects to burn their totems and to renounce shamanism, or to face execution. Other Mongol princes followed course. The Mongol princes banned blood sacrifices. Buddhist monks were accorded the same status Mongol laws gave the nobility, whereas active shamans were now subject to execution. Some shamanic practices survived the mass conversion of the

Mongols to Buddhism in the sixteenth century, but the nation as a whole took another path. The Mongols' loyalty to their princes, and the military structure of Mongol society, made mass conversion possible. When the princes converted, the people followed.

When Altan Khan and the Third Dalai Lama met, the monk gave a long Buddhist teaching to a large crowd of Mongols. They gathered at Koko Khotan, Altan's capital, which is now Hohhot, capital of the Chinese province of Inner Mongolia. The site of these teachings became blessed ground, and Altan financed the construction of Mongolia's first monastery, Thegchen Chonkhor, there. Mongolians describe the Third Dalai Lama as the teacher responsible, more than any other, for converting the Mongol tribes to Buddhism. Besides founding the monastery, Mongol devotees of the Third Dalai Lama commissioned the translation of Tibetan Buddhist texts into their language. They also paid to have Tibetan texts copied with letters of silver and gold for use in Mongolia. Within fifty years, nearly all Mongolians were Buddhists, while tens of thousands became monks. The majority of Mongols became devout followers of the Gelug order, intensely loyal to the Dalai Lama, their most revered guide.

Tibetan Buddhism, and the institution of the Dalai Lama, morphed into Central Asian Buddhism, and as the religion spread, the Dalai Lamas gained tremendous influence as a pan-Asian spiritual and political leader, almost akin to a Buddhist pontiff. During the next century, nomadic Mongols roaming from the borders of Russia to the borders of Korea, China, Tibet, and modern Kazakhstan converted to Buddhism. Mongols across Asia looked to the new Buddhist Mecca in Lhasa. While this was a religious transformation, it was one fraught with military and political consequences.

The Chinese watched these developments with interest, though few Chinese ever became devout Tibetan Buddhists. Chinese emperors had built the Great Wall to keep Mongols and other northern nomads out. Now the Ming dynasty devoted much of its energies to rebuilding and reinforcing the Great Wall, to the point of obsession. But a new strategy soon emerged. What if Mongol devotion to the Dalai Lama could be a tool to help the rulers of China keep the Mongols at bay? In the next few centuries, this idea became a constant theme in the political relationship between Mongolians, Tibetans, Chinese, and the Manchu.

Altan Khan and the Third Dalai Lama ascribed a singular worldview to their actions as they founded a spiritual empire: belief in reincarnation was an absolute given. The biography of the Third Dalai Lama indicates that his visit to Mongolia was predestined by past karmic connections. Mongolians believe that the Third Dalai Lama, on meeting Altan, said, "The khan and I have the signs that, because we have performed meritorious deeds in our former lives, we will meet and together propagate the religion [in this life]."

According to the current Dalai Lama, the Third Dalai Lama continued the efforts of the First and the Second. He sees essentially the same meaning in this history as Altan Khan and the Third Dalai Lama saw. The master plan was moving ahead.

"The Third Dalai Lama worked to spread the Dharma among the Mongols," he said, "and many became his students, which increased the power of the Dalai Lamas. This helped to open the way for the Fifth Dalai Lama to unify Tibet."

If we look beyond the personal spiritual relationship between the two men, it is clear that they had a mutually beneficial relationship that encouraged the spread of Buddhism. Both Altan Khan and the Third Dalai Lama were rising powers in their own countries. The Gelugpa were fighting the Kagyupa, and Altan wanted to unite the Mongol tribes and become their emperor. The Third Dalai Lama publicly proclaimed that he was a reincarnation of the priest Phagpa and that Altan was a reincarnation of Kublai Khan. This interpretation was extremely useful for Altan as he struggled to become emperor, especially since the true descendant of the Great Khan happened to be another prince. The Dalai Lama, whose Gelug order was being harassed by the Kagyupa and the princes in Tibet who supported them, could now claim the backing of the greatest military power in Mongolia. The two men could say that their cooperation in past lives explained their devotion to each other, as priest and patron, in this life—although others might have considered that explanation to be pious veneer for political maneuvering. This curious form of "reincarnate politics" continued into the next generation. After the Third Dalai Lama died, he was reborn in Mongolia as the great-grandson of Altan Khan. The discovery of the Fourth Dalai Lama in Mongolia, and his enthronement in Tibet, was to have far-reaching consequences.

Altan Khan died in 1582, just four years after meeting the Third Dalai Lama. Sonam Gyatso survived until 1588. During the rest of his life, his power and prestige grew continually because of his newfound role as a revered teacher of the Mongols. After initiating their conversion, he headed back to eastern Tibet. En route, he received a plea from local Chinese officials to use his authority among the Mongols to prevent them from mounting attacks on China, which had continued at a slower pace in spite of Altan's agreement with the Chinese in 1571. The Dalai Lama's rising influence was again confirmed when the Ming emperor invited him to visit the Chinese capital, but he declined because of a prior commitment, though he was only 250 miles from Beijing: the power of the Ming emperor did not reach very far at the time. In another sign of the Dalai Lama's power, devout princes, or khans, of Mongolia requested that the Dalai Lama grant them their titles. Already the Third Dalai Lama wielded a unique fusion of religious and political power, one that would come to define the institution of the Dalai Lamas and would have enormous impact, throughout Asia, in the coming decades.

In 1580 the Third Dalai Lama founded the monastery of Lithang, in Kham. The king of Lithang renounced his allegiance to the Kagyupa—who were still at war with the Gelugpa—and switched his devotion to the Gelugpa, at a time when the kings of Lithang did not accept interference from the princes of Lhasa or Shigatse and ruled their region as a de facto independent kingdom.

On the death of Altan Khan, two years later, the Third Dalai Lama accepted an invitation back to Mongolia. En route he founded another monastery, Kumbum, at the site where the Gelugpa's founder, Tsongkhapa, was born 230 years earlier. Kumbum grew to become one of the largest monasteries in Tibet. By 1585, the Dalai Lama was back in Mongolia, working with Altan Khan's son to continue the spread of Buddhism among the Mongols. More princes converted, and more tribes came with them. While in Mongolia, the Dalai Lama received a second invitation to visit the Ming emperor, and this time he accepted. However, in 1588, while returning to Tibet, he died, just ten years after he had received the name with which the Dalai Lamas would ultimately achieve global recognition. His accomplishments during his forty-five years of life were astounding, and many of them were the fruits of his relationship with Altan Khan. But for devout Tibetans and Mongols, their relationship did not end with death. In 1589, the Fourth Dalai Lama reincarnated as a young Mongol boy named Yonten Gyatso, who happened to be the great-grandson of Altan Khan. Several delegations of Tibetan monks investigated reports about a precocious child, and all were convinced that he was the reincarnation of Sonam Gyatso.

For the only time in the history of the Dalai Lamas, the manifestation of Chenrizi was born into a non-Tibetan body. The boy, a descendant of Genghis Khan, was recognized by the abbot of Ganden Monastery as a true incarnate and then educated by Tibetan monks who were sent to Mongolia. The Fourth Dalai Lama first traveled to Lhasa when he was twelve years old. He left Mongolia in 1601, with a contingent of Mongolian cavalrymen. In Lhasa, the Gelugpa formally installed him, in a magnificent ceremony. While the Gelugpa gained the interested support of the Mongols by recognizing the young man as the Fourth Dalai Lama, they also opened the door to foreign involvement in Tibetan affairs.

When I mentioned to the Dalai Lama how obvious it was, to many historians, that the Gelugpa had let political motivations influence the selection of the Fourth Dalai Lama, he dismissed that interpretation as speculation.

"The search party looking for the Fourth Dalai Lama found the young boy through many spiritual investigations, just as in my case," he said. "They searched through visions and spiritual indications and happened to find that he had been reborn in the family of one Mongol chieftain. I don't make any political link in this."

"But many historians have ascribed political motivation to the discovery of the Fourth Dalai Lama as a Mongol," I said. "He was related to Genghis Khan. That gave the Gelugpa military allies at a time when they needed military power to end the Kagyupa attacks on them. How could it be an accident?"

"If you are politically minded," he snapped at me, "then maybe the Buddha was a politician and had a political party. Maybe. But I don't know. Maybe it didn't happen through political calculation, but once it happened, then the politicians saw that there was something to gain. So then they politicize it for political gain. That is possible," the Dalai Lama conceded.

The young Mongol Yonten Gyatso had excellent tutors. One of his teachers was the First Panchen Lama, who was a great scholar of his time. The title *Panchen Lama*, in fact, means "Great Scholar." The Panchen Lamas are a reincarnate lineage of Gelugpa Buddhist teachers, *Tulku*, like the Dalai Lamas. However, the Panchen Lamas are manifestations of Amitabha, just as the Dalai Lamas are manifestations of the Bodhisattva of Compassion, Chenrizi. In time, the Panchen Lamas became a power that rivaled that of the Dalai Lamas, but there was a strong spiritual link between the two lineages of reincarnate teachers. In many cases, as with the First Panchen Lama and the Fourth Dalai Lama, an elder Panchen Lama was one of the senior teachers for a young Dalai Lama. It was also traditional for a Panchen Lama to help identify an incarnation of a Dalai Lama, and for a Dalai Lama to help identify an incarnation of the Panchen Lama.

Despite his religious role, the Fourth Dalai Lama was also an object of political contention. The eastern Mongolian cavalrymen who followed him to Lhasa stayed to defend him, as fighting between Tibet's Buddhist sects and their princely supporters continued unabated. Yet the presence of these foreign fighters was dangerous, particularly at a time when Tibet was fractured into many states and Tibetans were vying to unify the nation. In one incident, the Mongols attacked a Kagyu establishment to avenge a perceived slight. After a rumor spread that a poem written by a Kagyu monk was insulting to the Fourth Dalai Lama, the avenging Mongols sacked a stable and houses belonging to Kagyu supporters. In 1605, one of the princely defenders of the Kagyu led a large body of troops to Lhasa and expelled the Fourth Dalai Lama's eastern Mongol cavalrymen. Five years later, the fratricidal Tibetan nobles and monasteries were again at each other's throats. During a skirmish in Lhasa Valley, a party of anti-Gelugpa warriors attacked Drepung Monastery, where the twenty-one-year-old Fourth Dalai Lama was studying. He fled to safety, but such skirmishes were a constant occurrence. Regional and sectarian conflict left Tibet disunited and the Tibetans constantly at war with one another. The Mongols were such a strong military presence and their devotion to the young Dalai Lama was so intense that it seemed inevitable that the cavalrymen would return and intervene in the war between the Tibetan Buddhist orders and the noble families. However, in 1617, when he was only in his mid-twenties, the Fourth Dalai Lama died. Some historians say that he was poisoned, though the current Dalai Lama rejects this as speculation. There is no hard evidence either to prove or to disprove the claim, but the assertion itself indicates just how bitter the political atmosphere was in early-seventeenth-century Tibet.

The stage was now set for the birth of who Tibetans call the Great Fifth Dalai Lama. As I studied the lives and deaths of his predecessors, it was obvious to me that the Gelugpa's search for dominance over their religious rivals drove them to seek military and political patrons among the Mongols. But the Fourteenth Dalai Lama heartily disagreed.

"Their work was seen in a political way by others, but that was not their motivation," the Dalai Lama responded. "As I said, maybe their work was politicized, for political gain by others. But then my master plan, that is something different!"

It is the master plan of Chenrizi, and not politics, that he sees in the remarkable growth of the spiritual and temporal power of the Gelugpa from the First to the Fourth Dalai Lamas.

"So when I look at all these developments," the Dalai Lama observed, "it seems almost that there is a creator or some planning. Of course, here *creator* does not mean the creator of everything, a god. No, not like that. As we discussed, there is a link between Tibet, as almost a chosen people, and this positive karmic connection with Chenrizi, as we saw in the life of Songzen Gampo. It might be as though the first four Dalai Lamas laid the groundwork or prepared the way for the Fifth Dalai Lama."

The Dalai Lama had a sly smile on his face as he concluded. "Normally this is not explained in this way, but this is my belief."

"So this was the Bodhisattva Chenrizi guiding a master plan for Tibetans?" I asked skeptically.

"In theory, I'd say yes," he replied, "but if I say yes, then you might get the impression that there was some absolute creator, and that is a mix-up.

All these are spontaneous, effortless achievements. If you gather the impression that there is some independent creator, some god, and that this is different from the Buddha, that is not reality."

"Why? What is reality?" I asked, without pausing to consider whom I addressed or where our dialogue had gone.

"Reality?" he asked. He paused and looked at me carefully.

"You see," the Dalai Lama said, "there are the individual Bodhisattvas, Chenrizi or Manjushri. Manjushri is the embodiment of the Buddha's wisdom. Chenrizi is the embodiment of the Buddha's compassion. Not only one Buddha but all the Buddhas, but these are kind of inexpressible things, unless we study or see the complete picture of Buddha Dharma."

"So it is not one factor like politics, "I said, "but many, many interdependent factors that shape the course of these historical events?"

"Yes, that's right," the Dalai Lama said. "I think that the collective energy of the myriad sentient beings who inhabit this world system, their collective energy shapes this whole universe. And one of those factors is the Tibetan people's karma. That is also involved, you see."

"Their motivations and actions shape what happens," I said.

"Yes," he continued, "but not only the Tibetans at that time but the future Tibetans, including myself. Our karma now, and in the future, also made these things, in the past."

The future affects the past. My mind was reeling. Physicists speculate that seeing the past, present, and future separately is a delusion. Past, present, and future may be parts of one reality, which our limited senses are so far unable to glimpse. The Dalai Lama reached a similar conclusion through spiritual insight. His words opened many doors all at once, in every direction. Political motivations are never more than one thread in the infinitely complex web of human affairs. I was shaken, unprepared for the Dalai Lama's lesson to affect me so profoundly. What did I think I knew about any of this? The Dalai Lama watched me and waited in silence.

"The master plan," I asked, humbled, "that you see shaping the lives of the first five Dalai Lamas in the past is also reflecting the karma and actions of future Tibetans?"

"When we talk of karma or the future," the Dalai Lama responded, "thousands of different sorts of opportunities are there that *could* be, since all of these emerging possibilities are interdependent. You see, the events in Tibet are often related to America, or even lives on other supposed planets. Now, for example, I feel the coming Tibetan generations or future Tibetans. Some of them may come from a great distance. So their activities on that planet, or in that galaxy, in the future, that also makes a difference here and now, and in the past."

I listened in rapt silence as he concluded. "So judging from that, the future is something *very* powerful and vast. There are many possibilities. According to one possibility, a plan emerged, the master plan, which guided the lives of the first Dalai Lamas."

Leaving the Dalai Lama that day, I doubted everything I had ever believed, including my disbelief, and wondered at the infinite possibilities he hinted at.

8

THE FIFTH DALAI LAMA AND
THE RISE OF THE MANCHU,
1617–1720

The Fifth Dalai Lama, Ngawang Lozsang Gyatso, was born in 1617. The Fifth reunified Tibet after centuries of factionalism and transformed the Dalai Lama institution. Whereas his predecessors had led a Buddhist order, he led a nation. He sat on a throne beside the first Manchu emperor of China, received in Beijing on equal terms. Marauding Mongol bands from one end of Asia to the other fought, or stood down, on his orders. The Fifth reforged a mountaintop in Lhasa into the Potala, home of all future Dalai Lamas, which became an enduring symbol of the Fifth and a unique icon of the nation. It's easy to see why Tibetans call him the Great Fifth Dalai Lama.

The Fifth's father was a noncelibate Nyingma Buddhist yogi, not of the reform Gelug order. He could father a son, though he spent much time in meditation practice. The current Dalai Lama leaned forward in his chair as he spoke about the Fifth's father, who was a Nagpa, or yogi with dreadlocks. The infant had to be "looked after by one woman at his village of Chongye," the Dalai Lama said. "She brought him to Drepung Monastery when he was very young, only five years old. This young woman mentioned before she left that the Fifth Dalai Lama had very good behavior, never cried, and was very easy to care for. But she said he used to drink *chang (beer)* a lot!"

The Dalai Lama laughed at the thought of the infant Dalai Lama developing a taste for home-brewed barley beer. *Vinaya* forbids alcohol to the Gelug monks of Tsongkhapa's reform order but, for the average farmer and nomad of Tibet, *chang*, then and now, is akin to water.

The Dalai Lama laughed as he finished the story. "So he was cut off and not allowed to drink again!"

Gelug monks discovered the boy in the fashion prescribed by an established spiritual tradition. A year after the Fourth Dalai Lama's death, his chief attendant, Sonam Rapten, sent out search parties to look for the reincarnation. One of the search teams reported an unusual child in Chongye. In 1619, Sonam tested the child, carrying objects personally used by the Fourth. The young boy recognized "his" property at once, although it was mixed in with items belonging to other people. The Panchen Lama went to see the boy and concurred that he was the reincarnation of the Fourth Dalai Lama.

The rivalry between Buddhist orders, and the princes who supported them, remained so intense that the king of Tsang, based in Shigatse and allied with the Kagyu Buddhist orders, tried to forbid the search for the Fifth. The Gelugpa, supported by the Tumet tribesmen of the eastern Mongols, conducted the search for the Fifth Dalai Lama in secrecy because of the continuing violence with the Kagyupa. Though the Kagyu had expelled the armed Mongols from Lhasa earlier, some returned in 1619 and again camped outside Lhasa.

"In spite of this rejection from the king of Tsang," the Fourteenth Dalai Lama said, "Sonam Rapten searched for the reincarnation of the Fourth Dalai Lama. Then he had to make a lot of gifts to the king as he sought permission to reinstall the reincarnation of the Fourth Dalai Lama."

While Sonam Rapten offered gifts to the king of Tsang, additional pressure was applied. In 1620 the eastern Mongols, camped outside Lhasa, defeated the troops of the king of Tsang stationed there. The Mongols expelled the Kagyupa military forces from Lhasa, and a quiet period ensued. Two years later, with the military pressure relieved, at least in Lhasa, the Gelugpa felt safe enough to reveal that they had found the Fifth Dalai Lama and had brought him to Lhasa. Soon after, there was another skirmish between the Tibetan factions, and the Fifth retreated into hiding. In 1625, during another lull in the fighting, the eight-year-old Fifth Dalai Lama traveled to Drepung Monastery, in Lhasa, where the Panchen Lama initiated him as a monk.

During that time, warriors of the Buddhist orders frequently attacked and razed monasteries of their opponents; some Gelug monasteries were forcibly converted into Kagyu establishments. Fighting between the orders, between regions, and between regional lords was so intense that the provinces were virtually independent of central authority.

The power of the eastern Mongols was waning, and they were less and less able to protect the Fifth Dalai Lama, and the monasteries of his order, from attack. In fact, the authority of the Mongol tribes such as Altan Khan's Tumet, as well as the Chahar, Ordos, and Khalkha—all the eastern Mongols who had supported the Fourth Dalai Lama—had declined since Altan's death. That event, in 1583, led to renewed conflicts between the Mongol tribes. The western tribes of the Oriat confederation, living in the Dzungarian Basin, tribes like the Qoshot and others, slowly regained their influence. By 1620, some Qoshot had migrated eastward onto the Tibetan Plateau, where they established themselves around Lake Kokonor, today's Lake Qinghai, in Qinghai Province. There they fought for control of the grazing lands, against Tibetan nomads as well as eastern Mongols, such as the Khalkha and the Tumet, who had settled in the region. The eastern tribes that had remained in Mongolia were simultaneously under attack. By the 1620s, tribes from Manchuria had begun their war with the Chinese, though they would not take Beijing until 1644. But by 1620, the Khalkha, Tumet, Ordos, and Chahar tribes were under siege from the Manchu, and some had already surrendered to the Manchu—two decades before the Manchu conquered the Chinese. The eastern Mongols were in decline even as the western Mongols, particular the Qoshot, were in ascendancy. One of the Qoshot princes who had migrated from the Dzungarian Basin to the high Tibetan Plateau around Lake Kokonor was Gushri Khan.

"While the Fifth was being trained and looked after as a young reincarnation," the Dalai Lama told me, "in the meantime messages were sent to Gushri Khan informing him how difficult it was in Tibet for him and seeking some help." Gushri Khan, a young and rising prince of the Qoshot Mongols, responded to the Fifth Dalai Lama's plea for aid by promising to defend the Dalai Lama with his armies. With this step, the Gelugpa plunged

Tibet into the larger war between the eastern and western Mongols, ongoing since the Mongols' eviction from China in 1368.

Prince Gushri Khan's march east to Lake Kokonor, on the borders of Tibet, Mongolia, and Ming China, was one battle in the war of supremacy between the eastern and western Mongols. When Gushri arrived at Lake Kokonor, he fought the eastern Mongols, who were already there, for local control. In fact, a prince of the Khalkha, Tsogtu Taji, had fled from Manchu attacks in the 1630s; he was one of the leaders who faced Gushri at Lake Kokonor. Like all who opposed Gushri Khan in his youth—Mongol or Tibetan—he was killed.

The young Dalai Lama's regent, Sonam Rapten, hoped to use Gushri's armies, and their devotion to the Dalai Lama, to crush his opponents in Tibet. But when Gushri attacked Tsogtu Taji, the eastern Mongols around Lake Kokonor allied themselves with the king of Tsang and the Kagyupa. The eastern Mongols, who had supported the Gelugpa since the Third

Dalai Lama converted the Mongols, had suffered in battles with the Manchu, and it was the western Mongols, led by the Qoshot prince Gushri, who had the strength to support the Dalai Lama. Ironically, the old supporters of the Third Dalai Lama entered the war in Tibet on the side of those fighting against the Gelugpa.

This was tangled history, and I wondered when the Dalai Lama had first learned of it. Growing up in Tibet, he had not studied it formally. Later in China and in India, when he was in his twenties, he read about the events.

"When did you first hear of this as a child?" I asked.

"I don't remember. Of course, I think from very early I understood, as the common people did, that the Third Dalai Lama went to Mongolia, the Fourth Dalai Lama was Mongolian, and then the Fifth Dalai Lama, with the help of Mongolians, became ruler of Tibet and eventually built the Potala. My teachers made no special effort to teach me about history. In their curriculum there was only Buddhist philosophy."

"Do you regret not studying this history as a child?"

"No, no regrets," he said with a small laugh.

"So you learned just by listening to people talk, and often their comments were sparked by paintings?"

"Yes," the Dalai Lama said, nodding, "through people talking about paintings in the Potala. I remember that wherever there was a painting of the Fifth Dalai Lama, he was in the center and on the right there was his regent, the *Desi*, and on the left was Gushri Khan, and his face was large and kind."

Walking through the Potala one day in 1985, months after China opened Tibet to foreign tourists for the first time ever, I tried to identify some of the figures in the murals that cover the walls of every room. I found most temples illuminated with paintings of religious teachers, Buddhas, former Dalai Lamas, and Bodhisattvas. There are also murals that chronicle the major events of Tibetan history, such as the building of the Potala and of the Jokhang. It was an overwhelming task to interpret just a few of these murals, even with a history book in hand. There are thousands of square feet of religious and historical paintings. Some murals are twenty or thirty feet high; some panels stretch for fifty yards down hallways. Some of the intricate murals were painted in the time of the Fifth Dalai Lama as the Potala was constructed, from 1645 to 1695, though others were created from the seventeenth to the twentieth centuries. As I explored with a headlamp in the depths of the Potala that are closed to tourists, I even found images of Mao Tse-tung painted over ancient Buddhist murals during the Cultural Revolution. The centuries of murals provide a rare glimpse into Tibet's history, and the young Fourteenth Dalai Lama walked past these works every day. One of the most frequently painted themes in the Potala, and I saw dozens of them, was a triple portrait of the Fifth Dalai Lama with Gushri Khan and the Desi (the Fifth's regent), just as the Dalai Lama described. This icon appears in many rooms of the Potala.

In the ancient cathedral in downtown Lhasa, the Jokhang, founded by Songzen Gampo, I encountered a larger-than-life mural of the same three-some. As I studied it one day, an old monk pointed at the mural and began talking with great fervor to a crowd of farmers. The farmers held their black fedoras in their calloused hands, behind their backs, and bowed toward the mural. They glanced up only occasionally from beneath downcast eyes as the red-robed monk explained the history of Gushri Khan and the Fifth, as well as a myth about that particular painting.

Listening to the Dalai Lama discuss these paintings, I asked him about the myth the monk in the Jokhang had spoken of. "The people in Lhasa told me that one painting of Gushri Khan occasionally speaks, at least according to local folk belief. And one time, one of the paintings of Gushri Khan bowed to the Dalai Lama as he entered the Jokhang. You never heard these stories as a child?"

"No, I never heard that story," he replied, "but I still remember one painting of Gushri Khan in the Potala with his mustache and a special sort of hat, and heavy robes, and the Dalai Lama sitting beside him. His face struck my mind. So through such paintings in the Potala, there was some sort of knowledge about the Mongolians and their relations with the Dalai Lama and the Dalai Lama institution. I first heard about many people in Tibetan history from these paintings." Then he remembered the biographies, usually of famous lamas, that he read as a boy. "And then there are the *namtars*. I read some of those. But unfortunately I read only the *namtar* of the Fifth Dalai Lama in India, after I left Tibet."

I laughed. "You had a very restricted education in your youth."

The Dalai Lama laughed along with me. I was starting to become a good judge of his self-effacing sense of humor. Afterward, he said, "No regrets," and chuckled.

"But there was no political history education for you to become head of state," I said.

"No," the Dalai Lama agreed, "just through experience."

The Fifth Dalai Lama was educated in the same way, as he waited for Gushri Khan to come to Lhasa. According to the Fourteenth Dalai Lama, some years went by after the Desi sent the first message to Gushri Khan, asking for help. The current Dalai Lama learned the details of what happened next from the biography of the Fifth Dalai Lama.

"The Mongols were quite interested," he said, "and when the Fifth Dalai Lama was grown up, around fifteen or so, then there was an indication that the Mongol army would come. The attitude of the Fifth Dalai Lama became bolder, and in the meantime, the regent decided to have the Dalai Lama do a ritual in public. He gave the young boy some instructions for the ritual. The Fifth Dalai Lama then performed a Tantric ritual and specifically cursed the name of the Tsangpa king, against whom the ritual was targeted. Many people felt apprehensive, that he shouldn't have mentioned the king's name specifically. So in his autobiography the Fifth told them, 'I have already said it, so it is too late no matter what the consequences.' Before then, he was an honest, innocent young boy, but the regent instigated the Dalai Lama to do this against the king of Tsang."

It was a dangerous moment. After the public attack against the king, by name, the regent worried that the king might attack the Fifth before Gushri Khan could reach Lhasa. The Dalai Lama laughed cynically, then cited from memory the Fifth's reply to his frightened regent.

"'It was you who instigated me when I was not interested in politics! You made me do it, and now you are apprehensive?' Fortunately, the Mongol soldiers reached Lhasa, and the Fifth Dalai Lama became head of the Tibetan government."

It took three years for the western Mongol cavalrymen of the Qoshot tribe, led by Gushri Khan, to install the Fifth Dalai Lama as leader of a unified Tibet. In 1639, as the campaign was prepared, the Fifth's regent, Sonam Rapten, justified war by saying that the Gelugpa had been persecuted and Tibet had to be unified. He told the young Fifth that the Gelugpa had needed a strong backer and, now that they had one, good use should be made of him. Gushri was eager to attack the eastern Tibetan provinces, including Kham, where the Kagyupa and others opposed to the Gelugpa had their strongholds. When the war plans were discussed with the Fifth Dalai Lama, he wanted no association with the violence, whether it was a justified preemptive strike or not. When his militant regent asked him to send a letter to Gushri Khan, ordering him to crush their opponents, the idealistic young Fifth refused:

> I am supposed to be a lama. My duty is to study religion, go into meditation, and to preach to others. . . . Too many people have suffered in the past and even been killed because of this kind of political activity. I feel that if we are unnecessarily active, we might find ourselves in the same predicament.

Rapten, however, ignored the young monk and, in the name of the Dalai Lama, ordered Gushri to attack. The Fifth heard the whispering in the next room as the letter was being prepared for Gushri. He had told his regent to send a message of peace, but he wondered if "the tune of the flute had not been changed to the song of the arrow."

During the winter of 1640, Gushri crushed military resistance in Kham with an army of Qoshot cavalrymen reinforced with willing Tibetan fighters. Ironically, some of those Gushri fought against were eastern Mongols from the Khalkha and Chahar tribes who had allied themselves with the king of Tsang and the anti-Gelug forces in eastern Tibet. Altan Khan and the Third Dalai Lama would have been amazed at this turn of events. But the western Mongols, led by Gushri, were victorious over all who opposed him. The eastern Mongols fighting in Tibet were defeated, even as invading Manchu troops destroyed the eastern Mongols in Mongolia. The tide had turned against the eastern Mongols. Soon only the western Mongols and Tibet remained independent of the expanding Manchu Empire. The linkage between military events in Tibet and those in the wider Central Asian world now became more and more common.

In eastern Tibet, the western Mongols defeated the Tibetan princes and their armies who had opposed the Gelugpa and resisted any central government. Gushri often put the Tibetan princes to death after their armies were overwhelmed. In 1641, after Gushri crushed opposition in eastern Tibet, Sonam Rapten ordered him to attack the king of Tsang, in his fortress at Shigatse, south of Lhasa. Rapten was determined to unite Tibet and end the attacks against the Gelugpa. Again, the Fifth opposed his regent, who ignored the Dalai Lama's advice. While Gushri besieged Shigatse, Rapten worked with Gelug supporters to force the surrender of small outlying districts loyal to the king of Tsang. Most collapsed without a fight after the Mongol army marched to Shigatse. Once the Mongols besieged Shigatse, the town mounted a stronger resistance than Rapten had imagined. For a while the outcome was uncertain, and Rapten had doubts. He asked the Fifth Dalai Lama if he would mediate between the two armies. The Fifth was "so disturbed" that he told Rapten, "I have no alternative but to reproach you. Did I not tell you a number of times that it would be unwise to engage in a war with the Tsang ruler?" But by now even the Fifth felt that Tibet must pursue the war. "We now must go through with this war, which you have so carelessly begun. If Gushri Khan wins, well and good. If he loses, we shall have to leave Lhasa and find some other country to live in."

After this stinging rebuke, Rapten redoubled his efforts. In 1642, the Fifth's militant regent achieved his objectives. The Mongol army breached the fortress at Shigatse and slew the king of Tsang. The might of the Qoshot army defeated all Kagyu supporters and ended Tibetan factionalism. Gushri's military muscle, combined with the strategic direction of Rapten, had prevailed.

In the early summer of 1642, the Fifth Dalai Lama marched in state to Shigatse and was seated on a throne in the impressive audience hall of the deposed king of Tsang. Gushri Khan and the regent, Sonam Rapten, took seats on slightly lower thrones to his left and right. Tibetan painters turned this image from the enthronement into an icon: the Great Fifth with Gushri on one side and Sonam on the other. Artists copied it onto murals in temples across Tibet, particularly on the walls of the Potala when construction began a few years later. This icon of the coronation was the image the young Fourteenth Dalai Lama saw so frequently as a boy. It was the moment when the Fifth Dalai Lama became supreme religious and political leader of Tibet.

Once in power, the Dalai Lama issued numerous proclamations. Lhasa would be the capital of Tibet. He appointed governors to the districts, chose ministers for his government, and promulgated a set of laws. The young Dalai Lama also transformed his regent into a prime minister, or, as Tibetans called him, the Desi. Administrative authority remained with the Desi and military power with Gushri, who was entitled king of Tibet. The Fifth could then focus solely on religion. When sporadic regional and anti-Gelug rebellions broke out in the next few years, Gushri's army defeated them, and monasteries that offered support to the rebels sometimes burned; if they were not set alight by the rebels during the conflict, then they were torched by the victors. In the early years after 1642, Gushri and Sonam often jointly led armies against any who dared oppose the Gelug victory. The wars fought in the Fifth's name were universally successful, except for a foray into Bhutan, a stronghold of the Kagyu sect even today, where the Mongol-Tibetan army was defeated. The following year, Indian and Nepalese kings sent envoys with gifts to congratulate the Fifth on his ascension to the throne. When Gushri died, his sons inherited his position as king, though his heirs were in fact without influence, because, later in life, the Great Fifth eclipsed all who surrounded him. He assumed a mantle of awe, and even the Mongols looked to him as the supreme leader.

When I asked the Dalai Lama to summarize the achievements of his revered predecessor, he said, "I think one unique thing about the Fifth Dalai Lama was that he established his authority over all of Tibet. So before the Fifth Dalai Lama, there were Tibetan kings who were theoretically the central Tibetan government, but in reality their power was very limited and regional. Then the Fifth Dalai Lama unified all of Tibet quite effectively."

"He was in some ways almost a warrior king, wasn't he?" I asked.

The Dalai Lama responded with a quote from the Fifth's *namtar*, or biography. "I think he was in Namgyal Monastery," the Dalai Lama said. "He made one humorous, one very sarcastic remark. 'People in all directions are turning against you, then things are questionable.'"

"What do you think the Fifth meant by that?" I asked, confused.

"He had fought with the king of Tsang," he replied, "and then after that victory still there was a war with Bhutan. He had enemies in every direction. He was being very sarcastic when he said this. How could he be the Dalai Lama when he was fighting with so many people?"

"Well," I said, "isn't there a contradiction when war is waged in a monk's name, even if he did not command the armies, even if he initially rejected the use of violence?"

"This is natural," the Dalai Lama said. "He sort of set up a central power. So this will cause some problems naturally."

"Yes," I prodded, "but don't you see a contradiction between political and religious power?"

"True," the Dalai Lama responded. "True. Especially for a religious leader, especially for a monk."

The contradictions between the Great Fifth's role as ruler and monk were many. Gushri Khan remained the power that held the newly unified Tibet together. He put down each rebellion, but according to the Dalai Lama, "he considered himself a Tibetan, not a foreigner. He became a citizen of Tibet. First, he came as a foreigner in order to help the Dalai Lama. There was this constant threat to the Fifth Dalai Lama from the king of Tsang and the Kagyupa. So Gushri Khan's basic aim was simply to destroy the opposition facing the Fifth Dalai Lama or the Dalai Lama institution. He came to defend the Dalai Lama at first, and then it evolved. But later, after victory, he never returned to his home *(in the Dzungarian Basin)*. He remained in Lhasa during wintertime, and in summer he was with his animals herding in a pasture north of Lhasa. He had a palace in Lhasa for the wintertime. So he was no longer a foreigner."

I pointed out to the Dalai Lama that even if Gushri was seen as a Tibetan, when the Gelugpa used his armies in Tibet they were opening the door for other foreign powers. "No matter that this strategy worked in the short term. It is exactly what caused problems for Tibet later, wasn't it?" I asked.

"True. Yes," he said. Then he looked at me in silence.

Tibetans unable to end their factionalism had relied on a foreign military power to achieve national unity. This fateful step would have long-term consequences. Although it was not clear at the time, Tibet's dependence on the Mongols paved the way for the Manchu invasion of the country.

In 1644, two years after the Fifth's unification of Tibet, the Manchu people (formerly the Jurchen), a non-Chinese ethnic group originally living in Manchuria, stormed south through the Great Wall, conquered Beijing, and embarked on a seventeen-year war of conquest to defeat the Ming pretenders. Already the rulers of a large empire, they now added all of Ming China to their territory. They methodically conquered the other non-Chinese tribes around them, north of the Great Wall, before they turned on Beijing. The Manchus had seen how disunity among the Mongols—particularly between the Mongols left on the steppes and those living in luxury in Beijing—had cost the Mongols control of China earlier.

The princes and tribes of the eastern Mongols, including the Chahar and the Tumet, who lived just north of the Great Wall, surrendered to the Manchu by 1636, before the invaders reached China. Two years later, the Manchu conquered Korea. By the time the Manchu overtook China, they had unified the nomadic tribes just north of the Great Wall. Only the western Mongols, in the Dzungarian Basin, and Gushri Khan's bands of western Mongols in Tibet remained independent. The Khalkha tribes of the eastern Mongols were also still independent, but they were farther north (not adjacent to the Great Wall); the Manchu would deal with them in the next few decades. The Manchu now enforced the unity that had eluded the eastern Mongols since the Chinese expelled them in 1368. The Manchu knew that it would be disastrous to attack Beijing until they had subdued at least those Mongols along China's northern border, a feat the Ming had never

164 THE STORY OF TIBET

achieved. And so for the first time in nearly three hundred years, the people just north of the wall were unified under the rule of one strong tribe. Ultimately, all Mongols would kowtow before the Manchu throne and accept their status as Manchu subjects—except, of course, for those the Manchu exterminated.

Just as the Mongol conquerors of China had done, the Manchu gave their conquest dynasty a Chinese name, which they had adopted before they invaded China—much like the way Chinese corporations assume English trade names before they do business in the United States. The Manchus called their dynasty the Qing (pronounced *ching*), which means, literally, "clear or pure." They also adopted Chinese administrative tools to rule their new colony, just as the Mongols had done. Once again, many of the Chinese bureaucrats who had served the Ming rulers were spared; they learned to serve China's new foreign master instead. Because the Manchu were never more than 2 percent of the population of the empire, their emperors sought to prevent them from becoming Chinese. Intermarriage between the Manchu and the Chinese was forbidden. Manchu officials had to speak and read Manchu, and they had to earn their positions in government. Manchu officers were also assigned to oversee every Chinese bureaucrat, to ensure thorough domination.

After the conquest, the Manchu subdued the rest of the eastern Mongols, the Khalkha far to the north of the zone around the Great Wall, and consolidated their administration of China. As the Manchu emperor solidified his authority, one of his most serious concerns was that the western Mongols, including Gushri Khan and his Qoshot band in Tibet, as well as the half dozen tribes in the Dzungarian Basin, would be a threat to his rule. Not only did they have military power; they had faith in the Dalai Lama around which to rally.

For the Manchu, the Fifth Dalai Lama's influence over the Mongols was a key issue. After studying this idea carefully, one day I said, "The Dalai Lama slowly became a great power with sway over all the Mongols. The Dalai Lamas were almost creating an empire, but it was a religious one, not a military one."

The Dalai Lama nodded his head and said, "That is correct."

Despite the unity forged in great part by Mongol military power, there was still occasional resistance to the Fifth's rule over Tibet. The Mongol forces in Tibet, supported by Tibetans loyal to the Gelugpa, defeated each new rebellion, and the ferocity of these uprisings began to fade. One of modern Tibet's first historians, Tsepon Shakabpa, wrote that, in at least one instance, the army forced monks of several Kagyu monasteries to convert to the Gelug sect, in 1648.

The Dalai Lama's refusal to believe that the Fifth would have allowed forced conversions led to another one of the many dialogues in which we discussed the forces that underlie Tibetan history.

"Do you remember," I began, "when you told me that the Fifth did not destroy some of the monasteries of the Kagyupa and the Nyingmapa? You were very insistent. But when I read various historians about this, some insist that there were forced conversions. You said that some of these people converted but that violence was not used against them. There seems to be a contradiction," I concluded.

"If you use the word *forcibly*, OK," the Dalai Lama replied. "In a sense, I think those monks of the Kagyu Monastery would voluntarily take the new tradition, but sometimes there *was* force. I think some kind of instruction was given to them, like now you should follow Lama Tsongkhapa's tradition and you must give up Kagyu. Still, I don't believe this was for political reasons."

"But do you admit," I added, "that there was resentment from the adherents of the other schools of Buddhism in Tibet and that some force was used?"

"Well, my point is that these changes were not necessarily for a political reason," he said. "If only the Kagyupa had converted, then you could say that there was almost revenge behind it. But then, look—Sakya monasteries also changed. And the Nyingmapa were not changed. I remember one *namtar* by a Nyingma master from Western Tibet. It was handwritten at the time of the Fifth Dalai Lama. That monk met the Fifth Dalai Lama at the Potala and was told, 'It would be wonderful if both Gelug and Nyingma teachings were spread widely.' The Fifth Dalai Lama showed great wisdom when he followed a nonsectarian path, officially and formally. In order for him to become head of all of Tibet, to lead the Tibetan government, that was very necessary."

In the nineteenth century, a nonsectarian Buddhist movement developed in Tibet. Many great monks tried to unite all the schools of Buddhism, since they felt the divisions between the orders were spiritually insignificant. They called this movement Rimey. The Dalai Lama's words reminded me of the Rimey. "Are you saying that the Fifth Dalai Lama was almost a Rimey?" I asked. "That he wanted to see a fusion of the different orders long before that movement began?"

"That is right," the Dalai Lama responded with great excitement. "Usually we consider him as a great Rimey. Everyone does except the Kagyupa. He received Nyingma teaching and Sakya teaching. From an early age, he was interested in the Nyingma tradition. After he studied at Drepung Monastery, then of course he grew more interested in the Gelug teachings. But then later in life he grew interested the Sakya teachings. Still later, at the end of his life, he was more interested in Nyingma and especially its Tantric Dzogchen teachings. One of the unique things about him was that he was a great scholar of the Nyingma, Sakya, and Gelug traditions. He wrote one verse, I think in the autobiography, where he says that even though he composed texts about the Gelug tradition, he did not enlist into the Gelug order, just as when he composed a work about a Nyingma text, he did not enlist in the Nyingma. He was very nonsectarian. It's also true he did not study the Kagyu tradition much and that his relations with the Kagyu and the king of Tsang were not very good."

The Dalai Lama saw the grand pattern in Tibetan history and he clearly wanted to see Tibetans united over their past rather than divided. Even so, the issue of the division between Kagyupa (and Nyingmapa) and Gelugpa in the time of the Fifth Dalai Lama remains sensitive. When he said the Fifth's relations with the Kagyupa and the king of Tsang were "not very good," I rolled my eyes. He caught my gesture.

"Still," the Dalai Lama insisted, "I feel he might have had different motivations. They were not political. He really felt that the Gelug tradition, as far as scholastic study is concerned, is the best. So he deliberately propagated the Gelug tradition. But then some monasteries—yes, like Sakya monasteries—were forcefully converted. That is also possible. With these things, it very much depends on your view of the history, and not just history. For example, in my case. Sometimes in an interview, I say or do something without any political motivation. Some people who are politically minded, they study what I say word by word. Especially the Chinese. They think that the Dalai Lama says carefully worded things, but for me I just use the first English word that comes. So someone who is always thinking about politics, then they always think that everything has political significance, but actually that is not so."

I spent four years of my youth in the Himalayas, living alongside Nyingmapa villagers: Sherpa in Nepal's Everest region. They taught me a different version of this history. The Sherpa in Nepal believe that their ancestors fled Tibet in the 1640s and took refuge in Nepal, because they were Nyingmapa. To this day, all Sherpa are Nyingmapa. Sherpa myths say that their ancestors worried that if they stayed in Tibet, they might have to fight the Gelugpa, or face conversion. As Buddhists, they did not want to kill anyone, or so Sherpa myths record. So I persisted with the Dalai Lama, trying to understand the root of this conflict—between the Nyingmapa, the Kagyupa, and the Gelugpa—that has carried so much emotional weight over so many centuries.

"Let me play the devil's advocate for a moment," I persisted. "If I were a Nyingma or Kagyu leader, and I heard the head of the Gelugpa saying this, and I was very sectarian, I might say, 'He is defending the Fifth Dalai Lama because he doesn't want to admit that politics dominated the actions of the Fifth, and that in fact the Fifth wanted to unify Tibet. So he crushed all the other orders.' I have heard monks say this."

"It is possible," he said as soon as I stopped speaking, but he was not finished. I saw in the way he looked silently at the prayer beads in his hands that he wanted to say more. He counted his prayer beads for a few seconds, and I caught the whisper of a mantra on his lips.

"Two months ago," he began, "I received a letter from Beijing from one Kagyu monk. He is now ninety. He wrote me quite a long letter, and he explained that he came from Kham, and in that area they are traditionally Kagyupa. He said the Fifth Dalai Lama made many Kagyupa monasteries convert to Gelugpa. He wrote that for the last three hundred years, the people in that area have had very bad feelings toward the Dalai Lama. So therefore, in 1954, when I first gave the Kalachakra (a Tantric Buddhist practice) initiation in Lhasa, he deliberately avoided taking it. And then in

1954 to 1955, when I was in Beijing, though he visited the Panchen Lama, he deliberately avoided meeting me, because of the last three hundred years of pain. Now he had heard, and realized, that I genuinely follow Rimey, and he wanted to make some kind of confession before his death. So he wrote me the letter."

I struggled to absorb how quickly the Dalai Lama could leap over the most difficult barriers that separate people, always in search of the common human heart that unites us all. He has no ordinary thirst for power, and this attitude shapes the world he sees.

"He realized," I said, "that *you* were not working for political reasons. So it was sinful to hold on to these ancient fights?"

"Here," the Dalai Lama said, "we see the confusion of motivations. But in reality it is there. Negative feeling *is* there. For the last three hundred years, some people have held on to this."

Our conversation repeatedly returned to the accomplishments and personality of the Fifth Dalai Lama. We spoke about the many books written by the Fifth. The Dalai Lama proclaimed they were "excellent. His style of writing was unique and very beautiful and clear. His autobiography was not only lucid but very humorous. As a person, he was very funny and never lived a luxurious life. He was a very simple and careful person." The Dalai Lama chuckled as he told how the Fifth measured the soap for monks headed out to do laundry by the river. He even measured how much tea went with the laundry detail and deducted some if one monk could not go.

The Dalai Lama told several stories about a very short, very strong monk in the Fifth's inner circle. "This man," he said, "always made sarcastic remarks to the Fifth Dalai Lama, who used to tease him. One day the Dalai Lama asked him to hang a *thangkha* [a painted scroll], and he made sure that there was no stool or other things for him to stand on. When the short monk looked around, he couldn't find any stool. He got hold of one box in which Buddhist scriptures were kept and climbed on it and tried to hang the *thangkha*." The Dalai Lama paused in his telling of this story and then continued in a voice thick with false piety, "The Fifth Dalai Lama said, 'This is very improper. There are many sacred scriptures in this box.'

"The monk said, 'It doesn't matter because the scriptures are inside, and you have the covers of the box.'" The Dalai Lama laughed as he told this story, as if the Fifth Dalai Lama were telling us a joke about the uselessness of false piety.

He then told me another story, which also illustrates how the Fifth Dalai Lama was more interested in Buddhism as a means to transform the human mind than he was in empty ritual and false piety. The second story turns on the simple fact that the Gelugpa are sometimes called the Yellow Hats, because of the distinctive headwear they donned during some rituals.

Quoting lines from the Fifth's autobiography from memory, he said, "'It is an easy task to contribute to the flourishment of the teaching of Tsongkhapa if you do that by just putting a yellow hat on your head. But in actuality, I find many people remaining empty-handed, as the teachings that have been inherited from the past great masters are lost.'" As I listened to him recite these lines, I realized that the Fourteenth Dalai Lama is far more pragmatic, in a hardheaded way, than people imagine. I began to believe that this had probably been true for the Fifth as well.

In 1652, just a decade after the Fifth and Gushri Khan unified Tibet, the newly founded Manchu Empire sent its third letter of invitation to the Dalai Lama, urging him to proceed to its new court in Beijing. As he wrote in his autobiography, the Fifth seized on the chance to pursue his life's work of continuing to "convert China, Tibet and Mongolia" to Buddhism.

The Manchu emperor was simply "one of the many rulers in Tibet, Mongolia and [now] Manchuria, who were [the Dalai Lama's] Worshippers, Patrons and Protectors." There were dozens of ways in which his trip to Beijing reinforced key ideas, like this one. Curiously, the Chinese who served the Manchu court witnessed the same events and were convinced that they proved Tibet was a province ruled by the Chinese. The Manchu perceived the visit from yet a third vantage point. They were obsessed with using the

Dalai Lama to subdue the Mongols who still threatened their conquest of China. Clearly, the three nations each interpreted their alliances according to their own goals.

The Fourteenth Dalai Lama watched my face carefully as I summarized the unfolding of these events. "Just as with the Mongols, the Tibetans established relations with the Manchu conquerors before they took China. The Manchu emperor invited the Fifth to visit him before he conquered China. The first Tibetan delegates traveled to the Manchu capital of Mukden, before the Manchu occupied Beijing. Though the priest was ready to meet the new patron, there were many delays in the trip. In fact, the Manchu invited him three times. The Fifth was finally able to make the trip only after the Manchu had settled in their new capital, Beijing. So it is very clear that this invitation had nothing to do with China. It was from the Manchus."

"Now," the Dalai Lama laughed, "you have become a historian! Very good." As I laughed with the Dalai Lama, I also knew, as did he, that those working for the Chinese government today interpret this history differently. To them the Fifth was a faithful vassal of China and China's new rulers, who were Chinese of Manchu ethnic-minority origin.

Evidence that the Manchu invited the Dalai Lama to Beijing for help in controlling the Mongols is available. Shunzhi, the first emperor to rule Manchuria, and most of Ming China, was only fourteen, but he knew why so many in his court insisted that he invite the Fifth Dalai Lama to Beijing in 1652. In the time of Shunzhi's father, Emperor Hong Taji, the eastern Mongol tribes had only begun to submit as vassals to the Manchu. So Shunzhi wrote, "Considering the fact that *all the Tibetans and Mongols obeyed the words of the Lamas,* the Dalai Lama was sent for but before the envoy had reached him, the Emperor Hong Taji died." Thus the Manchu did not invite him as a vassal; they invited him because of his power, not his servility.

In the fall of 1652, the Fifth was at last en route to China, with an escort of three thousand mounted and armed men. Some of them were western Mongols, the most serious threat to the Manchu's conquest of China. Although the young emperor was concerned about allowing this menacing party through the Great Wall, he himself had issued the invitation. Emperor Shunzhi wrote, "We would like to go outside the border to meet him, but reflect that if he enters the country in a year of poor harvests with such a multitude, the country may suffer injury. On the other hand, if we do not go to meet him . . . he may go back to Tibet . . . and the Khalkhas [the eastern Mongols north of the Great Wall who were still independent] will not render their submission." Again the reason for inviting the Dalai Lama is made clear. The Manchu hoped that showing reverence to the Dalai Lama would help them control the last of the eastern Mongols who remained beyond their control.

The emperor turned to the Manchu and Chinese counselors at court for advice on this foreign policy problem. The Manchu officials said, "If the Emperor meets him in person, the Khalkhas will make their submission, from which great advantage will result. . . . What objection can there be to our reverencing the Lama, without entering the Lama sect?"

Chinese officials, however, told the young emperor that since he was "Lord Paramount of the whole world" he "ought not to go to meet" the Dalai Lama. Moreover, since three thousand men accompanied the Dalai Lama, they "ought not to be allowed to enter the country."

Shunzhi decided to ignore his Chinese advisers. Such was the threat from the Khalkha tribes. The emperor was more concerned with protecting his recent conquest, China, than with defending the abstract Chinese idea that he ruled the whole world. Clearly, the Chinese at the Manchu court had not yet shaped the emperor's view—for him it was a Manchu empire, not a Chinese one. Accepting the recommendations from his Manchu advisers, Shunzhi sent a letter informing the Fifth Dalai Lama that he would travel beyond the Great Wall to welcome the visitor. No ruler of China had ever accorded such an extravagant gesture of respect to a foreign ruler. Before the emperor could set off, the Chinese at court mounted a second attempt to scuttle the journey. They noted signs in the sky.

"Venus has dared to challenge" the brightness of the Sun, a Chinese secretary wrote. A brilliant Venus in the morning sky meant that the Dalai Lama's power was a threat to the emperor. Again, the advisers urged Shunzhi not to travel beyond China to meet the Dalai Lama. "Being outside the frontier is not as secure as being inside the Palace. Journeying abroad is not as peaceful as repose. The Dalai Lama is coming from a distant country." They pressed the emperor to send high envoys to greet the Dalai Lama, saying that such a gesture would be enough to "subdue the hearts of the Mongols."

These Manchu court documents are quixotically cited by the People's Republic of China as evidence that Tibet was under the administration of China's central government. In fact, they describe Tibet as "abroad" and "outside the frontier" and therefore clearly suggest the opposite of what the Chinese assert they prove. When I pointed out this fact to the Dalai Lama, he smiled and said, "The Great Wall was seen as what we call an international border then. Yes, history says that Mongolians and Tibetans lived beyond the wall, as independent peoples."

The superstitious Emperor Shunzhi bowed to the omens from the stars—but not because he believed Tibet or the western Mongols were part of his empire. Perhaps to apologize for breaking his promise to meet the Dalai Lama outside the Great Wall, the emperor overcompensated. He sent an equestrian party of three thousand, bearing rich gifts, to invite the Dalai Lama to Beijing. When this Manchu army approached the caravan of the Dalai Lama, thousands of silk banners and flags snapped in the stiff wind of the steppes. The Fifth was impressed by the "striking display of sword, umbrella, banner, flag and music" that accompanied the approaching Manchu imperial envoys. This colorful representation of Manchu power—which would have been all the more impressive marching out of the barren desert steppes just north of the Great Wall—"was a sign that I was the legal King [of Tibet], of whom there was not the like in Tibet." Of course, this was *not* the message the Chinese at the Manchu court had intended the Dalai Lama to receive.

I said to the Dalai Lama, "Your opinion is that he was an independent ruler making a visit."

"Yes, we believe that," he replied. "That is what the Tibetans believe."

"And the Manchu records," I pointed out, "they say the same thing."

"Yes," he said, raising his hands listlessly, with the air of someone who has examined this idea ad nauseam. "Yes, the records are clear."

"There are so many instances where the Manchu emperor treated the Dalai Lama as an equal during the visit," I said.

"Yes," he observed, "there was equal seating and equal status when they met."

In January 1653, Shunzhi and the Dalai Lama greeted each other and sat down to drink a cup of tea. The visitor dismounted from his horse inside the imperial palace. "The Emperor descended from his Throne and advanced for a distance of 10 fathoms," the Dalai Lama wrote in his diary. "He seized my hand with his hand . . . he enquired after my health." The emperor and the Dalai Lama sat down, though the Fifth noted that his seat was "a little lower than the Emperor's throne."

This point is another used by Beijing as evidence that the Fifth Dalai Lama was a Chinese vassal. The Fourteenth Dalai Lama says, "Yes, the Fifth Dalai Lama's autobiography mentions that the emperor's seat was higher. In ancient times, I think we treated China as a great country. They are equal, but China is a bigger country, so maybe the Manchu emperor's chair was a bit higher. The Tibetan viewpoint is like that."

The Manchu court records are silent about the first meeting in Beijing except to note that the Dalai Lama was permitted to sit in the imperial presence. The Fifth Dalai Lama, meanwhile, recorded every detail. "When tea arrived, although he asked me to drink before he did, I submitted that this was not proper, and he granted that we drink at the same time. Such and other showing of mutual respect, we did very much." The Dalai Lama was impressed with the fourteen-year-old emperor. "A person of royal lineage, though young in age, by the greatness of his lineage, will outshine old ministers," he wrote. And although the boy was young, "no matter where he was placed, among peoples of many tongues and countless numbers, he seemed the very pattern of a fearless lion roaming without bridle. He was extremely hospitable."

The Fifth Dalai Lama spent several months in Beijing, but like all highlanders he was fearful of lowland epidemics, particularly smallpox. Though he wanted to leave, the emperor asked him to settle a religious dispute that arose at court that winter. From this and other indications, it seems that both the Dalai Lama and the emperor realized the essentially religious character of the Dalai Lama's visit.

"The Fifth Dalai Lama's motivation," his present-day successor told me, "the reason he went to Beijing and met the emperor, was simply to propagate Buddha Dharma."

According to Shunzhi himself, "the Dalai Lama was sent for" because the "Mongols obeyed the words of the Lamas," in the hope that the Mongols would "render their submission." It was not just that the emperor recognized the religious power of the Dalai Lama but that he knew how much the Mongols respected the Dalai Lama as a spiritual influence. The American historian W. W. Rockhill summarized these facts well in 1910, when he wrote that the Fifth Dalai Lama was treated

> with all the ceremony which could have been accorded to any independent sovereign, and nothing can be found in Chinese works to indicate that he was looked upon in any other light. . . . The temporal power of the lama, backed by the arms of Gushri Khan and the devotion of all Mongolia, was not a thing for the Emperor of China to question.

The Potala is one of the Great Fifth's most enduring accomplishments, a physical structure that symbolizes his other achievements. Wherever you are in Lhasa, the Potala is the first and the last thing you see, an axis around which all of Tibet seems to revolve. Architecturally, it expresses a sense of upward flight and, at the same time, domination of the surrounding valley. The soaring walls, which seem to sprout organically from the cliffs, harken back to the Tibetans' most ancient forts, built on cliffs.

Its blinding whitewashed ramparts and dark burgundy walls appear suddenly on a summer afternoon as a high fortress at the horizon. The golden roofs that crown it sparkle in the sunshine high above green barley fields, even from thirty kilometers away. The fortress grows out of a craggy mountain spur and stands as a solitary sentinel in the center of the fertile Lhasa plain. It commands all approaches to the city. Often you see a tourist bus parked alongside the road, with fifty foreign visitors hauling out their cameras to capture that first glimpse of this icon of Tibet. Once you are in Lhasa, the soaring masses of cut-stone walls loom above the rooflines, making it visible from anywhere in the city.

The Potala affects everyone who sees it, and Hugh Richardson and David Snellgrove, two of the greatest contemporary scholars of Tibet, were not immune.

If only this survived of all Tibetan achievements, they would have staked an incontrovertible claim to the unique genius of their own national culture.

Today in Lhasa, you sometimes glimpse the Potala, in the distance, floating above the roofs of a dozen houses of prostitution. Young Chinese women in their bright polyester pants and tops gather in front of their shops to chat and spit out sunflower shells onto the cracked pavements. The scene makes you think that the day has already arrived when "only this survives"—when someone looking for Tibet must keep the eyes focused tightly on the Potala, started under the guidance of the Great Fifth Dalai Lama in 1645.

I am not the first Westerner to romanticize the Potala as the heart of Tibet. The first large number of Europeans who reached Lhasa were part of a British army that invaded the city in 1904. The illustrated magazines of the day inevitably ran double-page spreads showing the troops marching in formation just beneath the soaring ramparts of the Potala. It's the same today: most magazines and books about Tibet display the Potala on the cover.

Tibetans also see the Potala as a symbol, though what it symbolizes to them is different. Thousands of citizens walk around the structure every day: nuns and monks, old women and men, young boys and girls. For Tibetans, it's a sacred walk. They believe that they will earn a more beneficial rebirth by this meritorious action. Thousands throng the walkway every day. On festival days, their numbers swell to tens of thousands.

Many of the pilgrims don't actually walk around the Potala. Instead, they prostrate their way around it. I watched one old woman throw herself full length on the ground to bump her head on the earth, and I listened to her groan as she pushed herself back up. Then she moved her bowlegged, arthritic legs forward to the spot where her head had marked the earth, and started all over again. Pilgrims in Lhasa commonly "walk" around the Potala several miles a day in this fashion.

For such faithful Tibetans today, and for all Tibetans since the Fifth Dalai Lama started the Potala in the mid-seventeenth century, the building is holy because it houses manifestations of Chenrizi, who come to guide the Tibetan people, and because it houses the tombs of most Dalai Lamas. In Buddhist mythology the Bodhisattva Chenrizi lived on a mountaintop in South India, called Mount Potala. The Potala in Lhasa is home to the manifestation of Chenrizi in Tibet. Tibetans continue to prostrate at the base of the Potala, and prostrate their way around it, though the Dalai Lama has not lived there since 1959.

The Dalai Lama's quarters in India are not a replica of the Potala and are unimposing. You look out the large modern windows from inside his bungalows and see pine and bamboo surrounding the buildings. Beyond are the thickly forested hillsides of the Himalayas: during the monsoon months, more than three feet of rain falls here. His Indian home is composed of small cottages, with no more than a few dozen rooms combined. The number of rooms in the Potala is estimated at thousands, but no one has counted them. Despite the differences, I still found Tibetans walking around the Dalai Lama's Indian quarters, just as they do in Lhasa, seeking his blessing through ritual circumambulation of his residence, as if it were a temple.

Peering from the tiny wooden windows of the Potala is like looking through a window in the one skyscraper in a flat city. Everything is remote except the darting ravens and soaring falcons that whiz by so close you hear their wings whistling in the air. The Potala soars up 380 feet, so the only view from inside is a distant one of the treeless mountains surrounding the Lhasa Valley. They are khaki brown in winter, or white with snow, and brilliant green in summer. The valley floor far below, at 12,000 feet, is nothing like the lush semitropical landscape that surrounds the Dalai Lama in India. Lhasa is lucky to have ten inches of rain a year. Directly in front of the Potala today stands a 300-yard-wide flagstoned square modeled after Tiananmen Square in Beijing. In the 1990s, when China built the square, an immense 100-foot-high flagpole was erected right in front of the Potala, and the Chinese flag flies proudly from the top.

When our conversation first focused on the Potala, I asked the Dalai Lama about its importance, and he replied that it was just a building. After that conversation, I tried to understand how he saw the Potala. To elucidate his views, I asked him to compare it with the Jokhang, the first Buddhist temple, built by Songzen Gampo.

"For the Tibetans, which do you think is more important as a pilgrimage site?" I inquired.

"Which is more holy in the Tibetan mind, the Jokhang or the Potala?" He restated my question as he thought about it. "People usually go on pilgrimage to see the Jokhang," he said, "and then once they reach the Jokhang, they go to see the Potala. People from Kham and Amdo, when they go on pilgrimage, say they are going to the Jokhang. So for me the seat of Tibetan Buddhism is the Jokhang."

"Yes, but the Potala," I interjected, "is the seat of nationalism."

"The Potala," he continued, "is considered the palace of the Dalai Lama. Because of that, there *is* a special feeling. It was first started by Songzen Gampo as a royal fort or residence. So naturally, the Potala was already something important from that time. It was built on Marpori. *Marpori* means *red* hill or mountain. The Potala was constructed on top of the red mountain. Potala is the name of the building, and Potala is a sort of heaven, or habitat, for Chenrizi." The Dalai Lama refers to Mount Potala, a mythological mountaintop in South India, which was the home of Chenrizi. "So the Potala in Lhasa," he concluded, "is also considered a similar seat of Chenrizi, or residence of Chenrizi."

The building on Marpori had fallen onto hard times by the time Tsongkhapa arrived in Lhasa in the 1380s. As the Dalai Lama said, "There was just a small temple there where any lama could teach. So Lama Tsongkhapa also gave a teaching there. It's mentioned in his autobiography."

"And so," I summarized, "the First through the Fourth Dalai Lamas lived just out of Lhasa, in Drepung Monastery, but after Tibet was unified, the Fifth moved to the ruins on Marpori and began the construction of this vast palace in 1645, just three years after Gushri Khan unified Tibet."

"Yes, that's right," he replied.

"But listen for one moment," I began. "I met a Tibetan in Lhasa and we spoke about what it was like for him to see the Potala for the first time, in 1968. He grew up in a tiny village outside of Lhasa and never traveled in his youth. He was just a farmer. It was during the Cultural Revolution, and everything about his life was controlled by the Chinese when he was growing up; his school, where he was taught in Chinese; the history he was taught there; the work of his father; whether his family starved or not. Everything was controlled by the Chinese, and he said he had been taught to think of himself and his people as barbarians by his teachers from coastal China. Then he saw the Potala for the first time. He was in awe. And the thing he said to himself out loud when he first saw it was, 'We Tibetans built this place with our own hands!' For him, and many others, it is a deep symbol of Tibet. You lived inside, and it was a cold place for you, and I know from what you have said that in some ways you disliked living there, and much preferred the summer palace. So maybe it was not a place you have fond memories of."

He brought my monologue to a halt with a loud burst of laughter, and after a second I joined him. "Of course, for everyone on the outside, it *is* graceful," he said. "And even more than that, for many Tibetans there are psychological or perhaps religious factors, especially after I left. When I left, the radiance or magnificence did not exist there anymore. The light stopped."

"So why did that man try to pull down the Chinese flag in front of the Potala?" I asked.

"Of course, it is a symbol," the Dalai Lama replied grudgingly. "Actually, the Fifth Dalai Lama mentioned in his autobiography that his teacher Yongzin Konchok Choephel advised him that the seat of the Tibetan government should be built on Red Hill, on Marpori. Why? First, because this is the center of Lhasa Valley. Second, two big Gelugpa monasteries, Sera and Drepung, are very close. At that time, big monasteries were like big armies; they needed a power base. And then after it was built, it became the seat of the Tibetan government. In that way, it slowly became like a symbol of the Tibetan nation. Then I think that because it had been Songzen Gampo's place, it was more political or national. There were ancient historical echoes linking it to the past."

"Choosing to build in that place," I said, "the Potala and the institution of the Dalai Lama were linked to the past, and that gave them both great power in the minds of the Tibetan people."

"Yes," the Dalai Lama said. "So that place is considered a sacred place of Chenrizi. It is religious. The father of Tibet was born there. But I think the immediate political and power reasons, when it was chosen, were about location. It was strategically placed. Also there was a wall around it as well, for protection, constructed during the time of the regent."

When he mentioned the wall around the Potala, I recalled the central gatehouse in the wall, which is now locked, while the gateway itself has been transformed into a small shop.

"What do you feel," I asked, "when you hear that the main entrance through that wall, the main gate to the Potala today, is locked? In that gateway today, an old Chinese man is living there, and he runs his bicycle repair shop out of it. He lives there in that gate where every Dalai Lama, from the Fifth to the Fourteenth, came and went from the Potala. The Chinese don't do things like this by accident, do they?"

"No," he said, looking at me gravely. "I don't think so. This is symbolic, of course. The collapse of Tibetan power and government. That is it."

"So when a Tibetan goes to pull down the Chinese flag," I responded, "just fifty yards in front of that closed gate, doing it even though he knows he will be beaten and jailed . . ."

"That is very sad," he agreed.

"But also very strong," I noted.

"It is a symbol of the Tibetan spirit, culture, and determination," he said. "I was telling some people, Tibetan people I think, that of course their culture is very sophisticated. They have a long cultural heritage and a long Buddhist tradition. I think you can almost say the best of the Buddha's teachings were kept in Tibet, and also the nation is quite tough and unique. So because of these things, Tibet is seen as a proud nation. Tibetans are confident and determined."

"Yes, and some of that strength you can see in the Potala," I said.

He laughed again at my dogged hounding of this metaphor. "What the meaning is, I don't know. But, yes, the Potala was constructed very strong. So during the 1910 Chinese invasion, even though there was some bombardment, there was not much damage. Then in 1959, when I left, there was artillery fired against the Potala. The Chinese say it didn't happen, but it did. Many shells, but nothing happened. The building as a whole remained very strong. The wall was very strong. It caused some destruction inside, but the building as a whole was fine."

"Who built the Potala?" I asked. "Were the workers, serfs, wage laborers, or did some people come to work out of love for the Dalai Lama?"

"I think it was a mixture," he answered. "Some came from love, some came as corvée labor. The people were asked to come and contribute to the construction, but they were given food and shelter."

I knew it was a vast undertaking; estimates say there were more than seven thousand workers on the site, from 1645 until it was finished fifty years later.

"Who designed the Potala?" I asked. "Or was it based on some design from traditional architecture?"

"I don't think so," the Dalai Lama said. "I think the Fifth Dalai Lama's last Desi *(the prime minister and regent Sangye Gyatso)*, the one of his elder years, drew the design. The Fifth Dalai Lama had the desire to extend the building *(from the ruined fortress that was there since Songzen Gampo)*. The work started and then he passed away. Then it took fifteen years to complete the whole work, and that was done by the Desi."

Now that our discussion moved to the end of the Fifth's life, I asked a question that had been in the back of my mind for some time. "You said that Songzen Gampo and the Fifth are part of what you have called Chenrizi's master plan. And the Potala also?"

"Yes," he replied instantly, and with great conviction. "The Potala is part of the master plan. And from that aspect it is a symbol of Tibet."

"And the Fifth? Was he part of the master plan?" I asked.

"Yes," the Dalai Lama said. "As I explained earlier, the master plan is difficult to explain. There are many possibilities. One possibility, in my opinion, is that there was a master plan working from the First to the Fifth Dalai Lamas, but then during the time of the Sixth Dalai Lama, unfortunately, that plan collapsed."

Before the Fifth Dalai Lama died, he had a premonition that disaster lay ahead. He expressed fears to his last Desi about the potential for instability in Tibet after his death. Desi Sangye Gyatso was just twenty-seven years old when the Fifth appointed him in 1679, and there are unsubstantiated, though persistent, rumors that he was the son of the Fifth. Despite the Desi's youth, the current Dalai Lama said, the Fifth had great faith in him. In fact, Desi Sangye Gyatso is highly regarded today as a renowned scholar. According to the Dalai Lama, the Fifth so trusted the Desi that he instructed him to "keep the Fifth Dalai Lama's death secret for thirteen years. Then the Desi extended that period by two more years."

Though during the four hundred years before 1682 Tibetans had used the unique system of finding reincarnate Tulku as a means to identify the heads of monasteries, the death of the Fifth was the first instance in which they used that system to find the head of state. On a political level, the first attempt was a disaster.

"Was the Fifth worried before he died," I asked, "about potential political instability during the fifteen years it would take to find and train the new incarnation?"

"Yes, the Dalai Lama was worried about the period of regency, so he told the regent, 'Hide my death,'" the Fourteenth Dalai Lama said. "He was frightened before he died, it seems. Even a politician can sort of see the future. Then the Dalai Lama was also a highly developed person spiritually, and certainly he could see what would probably happen."

The Dalai Lama then volunteered what he called "my own feeling or speculation" about the most controversial of all Dalai Lamas, the Sixth. The Dalai Lama felt that the master plan called for the Sixth to renounce his celibacy and found a hereditary kingship in Tibet. "I read in the Fifth Dalai Lama's biography," the Dalai Lama said, "where the Fifth Dalai Lama praised very much the father-to-son tradition of the Sakya lineage for being more stable. He said that this was not like the Gelugpa system of reincarnation. He said our tradition *(of Dalai Lamas reincarnating)* is very unstable. When the Dalai Lama passed away, you had to wait and then begin to search. Then you must wait until the young boy becomes mature. It's risky; there is more opportunity for problems. And this is what happened when the Fifth Dalai Lama died."

In 1682, when the Fifth died at the age of sixty-eight, the Desi hid his death. As a result, he had to conduct the search for the Sixth in secrecy. The Desi discovered a three-year-old boy, Tsangyang Gyatso, in 1685. Three years later, the Desi verified the incarnation and took the boy to a remote monastery, where he was educated by tutors. In 1696, the year after the Potala was completed, the Desi announced that the Fifth Dalai Lama had died fourteen years earlier and that the reincarnation was already thirteen years old. Tsangyang Gyatso was enthroned in the Potala as the Sixth Dalai Lama of Tibet in 1697. Though the Desi, the Panchen Lama, and his tutors gave the boy a traditional monk's education, he exhibited distinct inclinations at an early age. He enjoyed archery more than studying Buddhist texts and often left the confines of the Potala for archery contests in the park with a group of friends. Despite many appeals to the young boy that he should not "lead a frivolous life," Tsangyang Gyatso pursued his own path. He delayed taking the full vows of a monk until a very late age; when he was pressed to take the monk's vows at age twenty, he simply refused. Worse, he returned the preliminary monk's vows he had taken as a boy.

In 1702, after the Sixth took this radical step—every Dalai Lama before him had been a celibate monk—the abbots from the three largest Gelugpa monasteries, as well as the grandson of Gushri Khan, who had become king of Tibet, pleaded with the Sixth to change his mind and take his vows as a monk. Instead, the Sixth Dalai Lama remained a member of the laity and began to roam the streets of Lhasa at night from one *chang* house to the next. He had numerous girlfriends and made no secret of it. The teenager who went drinking in the brothels composed romantic verses and songs that he supposedly sang in the streets during his carousing, songs that became quite popular in Lhasa. Though he did not write commentaries on Buddhist texts, as the first five Dalai Lamas had, his unique Tibetan love poems are memorable:

> When I'm meditating, my lama's face
> Fails to appear in my mind.

When I'm not meditating, my lover's face
Comes clearer and clearer into my mind.
If I thought of Holy Dharma,
As consistently as I think of her,
Then in just one lifetime, in just one body,
I'd become a Buddha!

Tibetans have long held that, in the common view, the Sixth was a lover of wine and women. Simultaneously they point out that at the "uncommon level"—for those with a purified mind—the Sixth was a master of Tantric sexual yoga practices, initiated at a young age into the ancient Nyingma traditions by the Desi. Many have wondered if the Sixth Dalai Lama was a Tantric master or a libertine, or both. It is possible to read his poems either way.

Is this girl not born of a mother?
Or was she born of a peach tree?
She fades quicker than
The peach tree's blossom.

A superficial reading of this poem reveals a boy's fear that the astounding beauty of his girl must perish. To others—say, a yogi—it speaks of the impermanence the Buddha said underlies all human joy and suffering. Someone with a purified mind might even say the Sixth's lovers reminded him of the Buddha's teachings.

The Fourteenth Dalai Lama has thought a great deal about the short life and strange death of the Sixth and has developed a nuanced explanation of the most provocative of all Dalai Lamas. He has found a middle way between the two extremes. He does not think that the Sixth disrobed just so he could practice the secret sexual teachings associated with some of the Nyingma Dzogchen meditation practices.

The Dalai Lama said that, in his opinion (and he cites the Fifth's biography to support it), the Sixth gave up his monk's robes and became a layman for a reason. "The Sixth Dalai Lama disrobed according to some plan," the Dalai Lama said. "If the Sixth had disrobed and still remained the Dalai Lama, and the popular support for the Dalai Lama remained, then he would have had a son who would have become king. That would have been better. The Dalai Lama's position would have been very strong, from father to son. Then there would have been no need for help or protection from the Manchu emperors. Then the disturbances of the seventeenth to the nineteenth centuries *(several foreign invasions of Tibet)* may not have happened. This is my feeling, or speculation."

This interpretation of the life and behavior of the Sixth Dalai Lama goes beyond the conventional versus uncommon views of reality that the Dalai Lama had explained several times. With the Sixth, it was not just a matter of how a yogi or a layman might see the same event in a different light. The Sixth Dalai Lama tried to transform the Dalai Lama institution at both the common and the uncommon levels, and the Dalai Lama believes that this step was planned by Chenrizi.

"You shouldn't think that the Sixth Dalai Lama disrobed because he wanted to practice Dzogchen," the Dalai Lama warned. "There's no connection. He received Dzogchen teaching right from the beginning, from Desi Sangye Gyatso and other teachers. He disrobed because of the obvious reason that he was fond of girls." He laughed at the simplicity of this logic and then continued. "I think that is the common reason. And I have told you the deeper reason, my opinion, though it might not be correct," alluding to the idea that the master plan of Chenrizi called for the Sixth to disrobe and found a lineage of married Tibetan kings.

But this was not to be. Instead, Mongol warriors and the Manchu emperor ensnared this self-professed lover in plots and counterplots while the Fifth's Desi fought unsuccessfully to manipulate the competing forces for the benefit of Tibet.

No matter what plan, if any, history was following during these turbulent years, the fate of Tibet was at stake. The Fifth seemed to have guaranteed unification and independence for generations, though he used foreign military power to do so. Just a few short years later, however, during the regency of Desi Sangye Gyatso and the life of the Sixth Dalai Lama, the Manchu emperor Kangxi's powers grew and Tibet—for only the second time in its history—lost its total independence.

9

THE SIXTH TO THE TWELFTH
DALAI LAMAS, 1705–1900

I could hear the Dalai Lama's laughter through a window in the waiting room of his bungalow. He had just finished an interview and was now being photographed out in the garden. Such sessions are so frequent that I could hear the photographer laughing as the Dalai Lama tried to help set up the tripod. Next to the window where I stood was a display case containing some of the Fourteenth's many awards. The citation for his Nobel Peace Prize (but not the gold medal) is in a leather case next to dozens of honorary degrees from universities around the world. The mementos reminded me that the Fourteenth Dalai Lama is a figure on the world stage, just as earlier Dalai Lamas were, in their day, major figures in Asia.

Gushri Khan had been content to be king of Tibet in name only, leaving real power to the Great Fifth and his regent, or Desi. A product of Inner Asia's nomadic culture, Gushri spent the last years of his life with his herds in pastures north of Lhasa. When he died, in 1642, his son seemed content to follow the same path. In 1697, however, Gushri's grandson Lhazang Khan seized the throne and became leader of the Qoshot band of western Mongols in Tibet, by killing his brother. That same year the Desi belatedly announced that the Fifth had been dead for fifteen years and that he had already found and educated the Sixth in secret. He immediately enthroned the Sixth in the Potala. The Desi planned to continue his rule as the Sixth's regent, just as he had ruled Tibet while he hid the Fifth's death. Lhazang was insulted that the Desi had dared to keep his family ignorant of these major events. Lhazang and the Desi were soon in deadly conflict, and both sought foreign allies.

Lhazang, the new king of Tibet, allied himself with the Manchu emperor of China, while the Desi found allies among the Qoshot of the western Mongols, who were still based around the Dzungarian Basin. Though Lhazang was a Qoshot, his long residence in Tibet had led to a break with his tribe. The western Mongols, known as Dzungars, were the most potent threat to Manchu supremacy; they were eager to use the Dalai Lama's sway over all Mongols to rally those who remained independent of the Manchu to make a last stand. These soldiers were quick to leap to Desi Sangye Gyatso's support when he and Lhazang Khan fell out. The Fifth Dalai Lama's Desi, and even the Fifth himself, had long-standing ties to the Dzungars, as well as support from Gushri Khan.

Galden, who had already made himself king of all the Dzungars except for the Qoshot in Tibet, was in the midst of a vicious war with the Manchu. He sought unity so he could then turn on the Manchu and challenge them for control of China. As the drama unfolded, the Dzungars marched far to the east of their normal grazing lands and attacked the last remaining independent eastern Mongols, the Khalkha. In 1688, this attack stampeded the Khalkha into the arms of the Manchu. The battle between Mongol banners was so intense that the Khalkha preferred to be subjects of the Manchu than to be united with the Dzungars. In 1696 the Manchu inflicted a heavy blow on Dzungar armies at Jao Modo—King Galden died a year after the battle— but still the Dzungars would not give up their dream of unifying the remaining Mongols so they could attack the Manchu and seize control of China for themselves. The Manchu pressed on, expanding their control steadily westward. However, it was only after the Manchu slaughtered nine of ten remaining Dzungars in 1759 during battles around Kashgar and Yarkand that the Dzungar threat to the Manchu was finally eliminated. During this century of warfare between the Manchu and the Dzungar, the institution of the Dalai Lama played a key role. It was against this wider backdrop, in 1705, as the war between the Dzungarian Mongols and the Manchu exploded, that Lhazang marched on Lhasa to depose the Desi: he accused the regent of usurping power and installing a fake Dalai Lama. The Sixth's behavior, especially his many lovers, made this accusation easy.

It is at this critical juncture in Tibet's history that I would pick up our discussion. With his photo session finished, he came out of the garden, smiled, and shook my hand and led me into the audience room, a simple living room with two sofas and four chairs. The Dalai Lama sat cross-legged in a brown upholstered chair across from me. While he knew the history, which I summarized to him from my reading, his thoughts veered away from the political explanations I saw in the history. To explain the Sixth Dalai Lama to me, the Fourteenth went back to terms he had introduced at the start of our talks. It was the same framework he used in describing why meditation masters saw the yogi Milarepa perform miracles though average people sometimes did not. Where I perceived political machinations in the story of the Sixth Dalai Lama, the Fourteenth observed a conflict between conventional and unconventional visions of the world.

"You see, the internal practice of the Fifth's Desi was Nyingma," the Dalai Lama began. "And the Sixth Dalai Lama was chosen by the Desi. Then the Desi gave the Sixth Dalai Lama the Nyingma Dzogchen teachings," which can involve sexual yoga. "And then later the Sixth Dalai Lama also disrobed"—that is, he cast off the robes of a novice and refused to take the monk's vows of celibacy. "Conventionally"—and the Dalai Lama emphasized the word, so that I understood it as he did—"the Sixth Dalai Lama's behavior was also not very good. Now Lhazang Khan was a follower of the Gelugpa. I think this was one reason for the trouble between Lhazang and the Desi. Lhazang disrespected the Sixth and his behavior and he blamed the Desi, who also had women and children."

"You have said that the Fifth wanted to, in a sense, unify the different orders of Buddhism in Tibet," I said. "But Lhazang saw the Sixth as a fake, a ladies' man who violated the vows of celibacy that all Gelugpa should embrace. He was angry that the Sixth was not pure. But also Lhazang Khan had a thirst for power and had sectarian feelings against the Nyingma . . ."

"And personal dislike of the Desi," the Dalai Lama interjected. Some argue this personal dislike stemmed from the fact that Lhazang's queen was in love with the Desi.

"You say that at this point the master plan for Tibet failed," I remarked. "When you say this, you mean the evolution of religious and political power that led to the Fifth Dalai Lama, who planned for the Sixth to father a hereditary kingship."

"That is what I mean. But it is pure speculation," the Dalai Lama responded.

"Speculation?" I asked. "Isn't this your historical analysis?"

"Yes," he said, "both historical, personal analysis and spiritual. A mixture."

"But Lhazang Khan understood none of this. He saw only the conventional level of reality," I said.

"Poor Lhazang Khan!" the Dalai Lama laughed. "His head is very small. This is what I am saying. And then some of the *(Tibetan)* Gelugpa monasteries, they supported Lhazang Khan, as well as his troops. In this way there was a sectarian conflict between the Nyingmapa and the Gelugpa." The Dalai Lama explained the underlying motivations between the Desi, Lhazang, and the Sixth Dalai Lama much more clearly than any historian had done. He showed me that Lhazang was a strict Gelug sectarian, horrified at what he saw as Nyingma corruption destroying the institution of the Dalai Lama.

"The history books speak of many covert plots back and forth between Lhazang and the Desi that led finally to open war," I said. "But it was based on more than just sectarian conflict, wasn't it? Lhazang Khan came and said to the Desi, I want to be a real king. At a *conventional* level, Lhazang used the sectarian division you talk about as an excuse to seek power, though he said to the Sixth, you are not a pure lama."

The Dalai Lama smiled as I summarized this chapter of history, and noted with a lifted eyebrow how I emphasized the word *conventional*, as I had heard him do. "Yes," he said, "continue."

"Lhazang Khan killed the Fifth's Desi, or regent, in 1705," I observed. "Then in June 1706, Lhazang deposed the Sixth Dalai Lama and sent troops to seize the twenty-three-year-old from the Potala. Lhazang and the Manchu emperor planned to send the Sixth into exile in China. Tibetans feared he would not return alive. Lhazang and the emperor said the Sixth was not an incarnation of Chenrizi. They were working at a *conventional* level and so had no faith in your idea that all the actions of the Sixth were, *unconventionally*, part of Chenrizi's master plan for Tibet. They saw a false Dalai Lama appointed by a

Desi who was killed because he tried to seize power. The Manchu and Lhazang were using the sins of the Sixth Dalai Lama as a pretext to take power in Tibet."

"The blame is not on the Manchu," the Dalai Lama insisted, "but on the Tibetans' internal fighting. The sectarian conflict in Tibet allowed this to happen."

Once again, I was amazed at the Dalai Lama's assessment. It wasn't Lhazang's and the Manchu's thirst for control over Tibet that caused the death of the Sixth; instead, it was conflict between the Tibetan orders of Buddhism that allowed the Manchu into Tibet. As I had now seen him do several times, the Dalai Lama placed the blame on Tibet, not on foreigners. How many other world leaders would assume historic blame in this way?

"So when Lhazang said that the Sixth was not a manifestation of Chenrizi," I asked, "and took him from the Potala, had the people of Tibet also lost their faith in the Sixth?"

"When he left the Potala, I have not read any mention that people of Lhasa came to protect him," the Dalai Lama explained. "Or that they tried to stop Lhazang from taking him away. It was only when the Sixth Dalai Lama passed by Drepung Monastery that the monks came out and tried to stop Lhazang. The Gelug monks were very supportive and were ready to die for him. The monks were devoted."

"Yes," I replied, "the history books say that a crowd of monks surrounded Lhazang's troops and the Dalai Lama, in June 1706, as they neared Drepung Monastery. The infuriated monks attacked the troops with sticks and stones, seized the Sixth Dalai Lama, and brought him to Drepung. But the next day Lhazang's troops surrounded Drepung and aimed their artillery at the monastery as they prepared to set it on fire. At that point, the Sixth Dalai Lama walked outside with just a few companions, toward Lhazang's troops in the middle of the battle. When everyone who went out with him had been killed—they fought to the last man—then he allowed himself to be taken by the troops."

"Yes, if he had stayed at Drepung," the Dalai Lama said, "if he had taken the protection of the monks, many would have been destroyed. So he thought that it was just his one life, it doesn't matter. So, you see, he accepted. He calculated the circumstances. The Mongol forces were much stronger than the Tibetan forces. There were seven thousand armed troops. It was not that he chose to go with the Mongols to China. He went because of religious motivation. If he refused, many Tibetans would have suffered. He felt he must deal with this."

"So the Sixth felt that he had to sacrifice himself to spare others?" I asked.

"Yes," the Dalai Lama said. "I think in that situation the Sixth Dalai Lama risked his own life in order to save the lives of the monks and Drepung Monastery."

Historians overlook the Sixth Dalai Lama's self-sacrifice and focus instead on his poems and his lovers: the Fourteenth Dalai Lama does not. The Sixth wasn't the only Dalai Lama who was faced with a decision about his own life and the fate of his nation. The Fourteenth Dalai Lama was likewise confronted with the same choice (or lack thereof) after the international community ignored the Chinese invasion of Tibet in 1950.

"You did this in 1954," I said. "You didn't want to go to China when Mao summoned you. You wanted to go to India, but no one would help you. There was no choice. You had to go to China to deal with the Chinese. You appealed to the UN, and it was rejected. You felt that if you did not go to China, your people would suffer."

"Yes, you are right," the Dalai Lama said. "There was no choice, so it is similar."

"When you knew you had to go to China to deal with Mao Tse-tung, just as the Sixth was forced to go to China to meet the Manchu emperor, what did you feel?"

"It was a really lonely sort of feeling." He paused for a beat, and his gaze turned inward. Then with a sigh he looked back at me and said one word. "Helplessness."

This was such a frank admission that it took my breath away. The room was silent for a long time. Finally, I found my voice again.

"And so what happened to the Sixth Dalai Lama on the road to China?" I asked.

The Fourteenth Dalai Lama answered, "There are two versions about the death of the Sixth Dalai Lama. Conventionally, it is said that he died or was killed on the road to China. At the unconventional level, he disappeared on the road to China and then he appeared in southeastern Tibet, then traveled in southern Tibet and then reached Lhasa and finally he reached Mongolia. Then he remained there for another thirty years or so. This is the nonconventional view."

As with Milarepa, Songzen Gampo, and all the great figures of Tibetan history, the Dalai Lama saw two levels in the life and death of the Sixth Dalai Lama. At the conventional level, the Sixth was perhaps a libertine, who died on the road to China. At the unconventional level, something the Dalai Lama was convinced existed for people who trained their minds, the Sixth used esoteric, erotic yoga to achieve higher states of consciousness, and then eluded his captors to lead a secret life in Mongolia long after his supposed death. For the Dalai Lama, both the conventional, or historic, view and the unconventional, or mythical, view were true: reality for him was composed of both these visions, interwoven with each other. As he had said to me earlier about conventional and unconventional perceptions of reality, "Both are true." Or, at the very least, both are possible, and it is impossible to pin reality down any further than that.

Historically, at the conventional level, Lhazang, grandson of the Qoshot Mongol Gushri Khan, became king of Tibet and then, with the aid of the Manchu emperor, killed the Desi and the Sixth Dalai Lama. He then agreed for Tibet to become a protectorate of the Manchu. In doing so, he turned his back on the Dzungar Mongols, his own tribes.

The Manchu sent their first imperial representative to Lhasa in 1709; this figure, called an Amban, was the first foreign representative ever to reside there. Once Lhazang suppressed the Tibetans, he installed a "legitimate" Sixth Dalai Lama. Tibetans never accepted the replacement as a true manifestation of Chenrizi, establishing a precedent that would make it difficult for an alien ruler to manipulate Tibet's incarnation system for political purposes.

Distraught at this turn of events, Tibetan monks sent secret envoys to the Dzungar Mongols, with whom the Fifth and the Desi had long been in touch, hoping to rid Tibet of Lhazang and his Manchu protectors. In 1717 the Dzungars responded to the request. As part of their long-running battle with the Manchu (though they cloaked their invasion as aid to the Tibetans), the Dzungars marched into Lhasa. At first the Tibetans welcomed the Dzungars, who promised to kill Lhazang for deposing the Sixth and to install the just-discovered Seventh Dalai Lama. The young boy, as the Sixth had predicted before his death, had recently been reborn in the eastern town of Lithang.

Unfortunately, when they invaded Lhasa, the Dzungars failed to capture the child. The Manchu emperor's troops fought to hold the boy, as he was the key to power in Tibet. Nevertheless, in 1717, the Dzungars finally seized Lhasa and killed Lhazang. Yet in so doing, they unleashed a chaotic reign of looting and murder that turned the Tibetans against the Dzungars. In 1720, after three years of Dzungar rule, a Manchu army approached Lhasa. By then, Tibetans were ready to welcome the Manchu, if only because they succeeded in bringing the Seventh Dalai Lama with them. Now the Tibetans resumed self-rule, free of their entanglements with the descendants of Gushri Khan. It was during this period that a loose Manchu protectorate was born.

The new relationship with the Manchu rulers of China was a key event in Tibetan history. "Wasn't the army that brought the Seventh Dalai Lama to Lhasa the first Manchu army to march into Tibet?" I asked. "Isn't this the moment when the rulers of China now began to use their armies in Tibet for the first time?"

"Yes, you are right," the Dalai Lama said.

"So Tibetans welcomed the first Manchu army, which had some Chinese troops, because, for the Tibetans, the Manchu came to protect and install the Seventh Dalai Lama?"

"Yes. I think the Manchu emperor had that sort of motivation," the Dalai Lama replied. "To protect the Dalai Lama institution. The Manchu even sent some officials, the Ambans, to protect the Dalai Lama. But Tibetan sources always refer to a patron-priest relationship between the Dalai Lama and the Manchu emperor. It began when the Fifth Dalai Lama visited Beijing, or some say even earlier. Originally, both sides were sincere about this unique relationship. Then later *(during the next 150 years of the Manchu protectorate)*, the spirit changed and the relationship became more political, more power-minded. So then there was trouble."

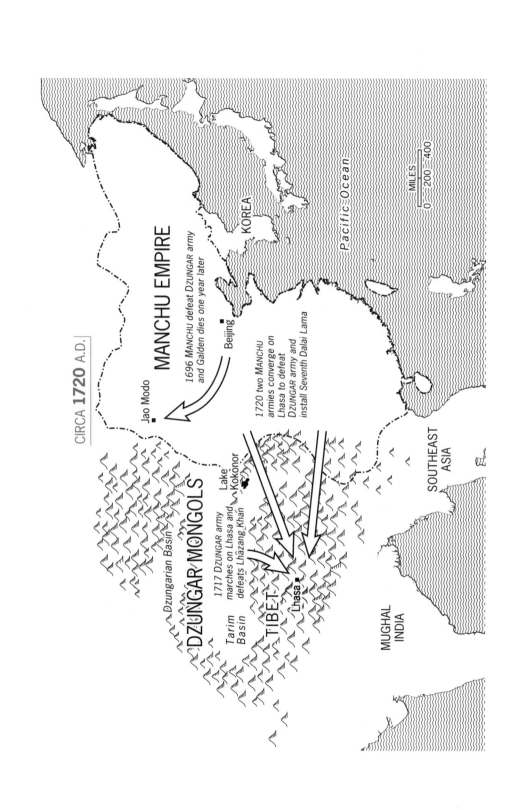

CIRCA **1720** A.D.

MANCHU EMPIRE

KOREA

Pacific Ocean

MILES
0   200   400

Jao Modo

Beijing

1696 MANCHU defeat DZUNGAR army
and Galden dies one year later

1720 two MANCHU
armies converge on
Lhasa to defeat
DZUNGAR army and
install Seventh Dalai Lama

Dzungarian Basin

DZUNGAR MONGOLS

Lake
Kokonor

1717 DZUNGAR army
marches on Lhasa and
defeats Lhazang Khan

Tarim
Basin

TIBET

Lhasa

SOUTHEAST
ASIA

MUGHAL
INDIA

In fact, the first Manchu army stayed only three years—long enough for the Manchu to install the Seventh Dalai Lama—and then withdrew, whereupon factional Tibetan fighting resumed. At this point in history, the Manchu were more concerned that the Dzungars controlled neither Tibet nor the Dalai Lama. The Manchu showed no interest in occupying Tibet. Even after their eviction from Tibet, the Dzungars remained a threat to the Manchu's grip on China, until the 1760s. Tibet was simply a buffer zone in the Manchu's long war with the Dzungar—to control the spoils of China—while Tibet held too little wealth, and remained too distant, to incorporate within the Manchu Empire.

That night, when I thought about the day's interviews, what came back to me was the terrible despair in the Dalai Lama's voice when he spoke about his trip to China—"Helplessness." No doubt the Sixth Dalai Lama must have shared that sense of helplessness when he was taken by his Mongol captors to China. For me, the monks of Drepung who tried to prevent the abduction of the Sixth Dalai Lama with sticks and stones became symbols of what Tibet would become over the next two hundred years—a weak nation under an ill-defined Manchu protectorate status—until the Thirteenth Dalai Lama tried to create a modern army, in the early twentieth century. The nation first unified by Songzen Gampo in the seventh century as a great military power, open to cultural influence from all sides, had become an insular and impotent land.

During my next interview with the Dalai Lama, I asked about Tibet's relationship with the Manchu. "After 1720 it changed and slowly the Manchu became a much more dominant power in Tibet—before 1720 they had no political power in Tibet?"

"Yes, true," the Dalai Lama replied. "I think it is very important to mention one thing, though. It was not the mere increase of Manchu powers that caused this. There were also Tibetan internal quarrels, and the very institution of the Dalai Lama was unstable after the Fifth Dalai Lama. Therefore, the Manchu emperor of China sent the Amban to Tibet to help during the time of the Seventh Dalai Lama. And then you see the same thing when the Nepalese invaded Tibet during the time of the Eighth Dalai Lama *(in 1792)*. The Tibetan army, I think, was disgraced, they were defeated, so the Manchu came to help, as patrons of the Dalai Lama. They came to help evict the Nepalese, but then when that was finished, that army left."

When the second Manchu army left Tibet after the Nepalese attack, one of the Manchu officials warned the Tibetans that they must do a better job of governing themselves and defending their borders, because next time the Manchu would not come to help them. There is clear historic evidence that the Manchu emperors never wanted to garrison and occupy Tibet. What they wanted to maintain was a loose status quo in Tibet to ensure that other forces did not use Tibet to cause trouble for Manchu rule in China.

Tibetans and Mongolians share the belief that Buddhism eroded their natural martial spirit. Speaking about this, the Dalai Lama said, "The Tibetans disarmed themselves!" Tibet as a religious power, with no concern for military power, emerged in the years after 1720.

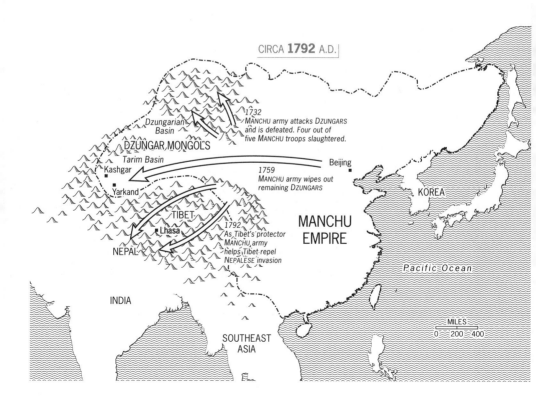

As for the Seventh through the Twelfth Dalai Lamas, none ruled Tibet as the Fifth had done. Most died before they reached the age of majority. Of the few who survived and tried to rule, the Dalai Lama said that they were "not very capable." From the Sixth Dalai Lama through the early years of the Thirteenth Dalai Lama, Tibet was ruled by a string of regents.

"Do you feel a strong connection to the Seventh through the Twelfth Dalai Lamas?" I asked.

"No, not much connection," he said. "I have never dreamed about them. Only the Fifth Dalai Lama and the Thirteenth Dalai Lama have I dreamed of." Though he did not say it, I understood that his dreams of connection to the two Dalai Lamas he mentioned were evidence of his past-life links to these men. It was the goals of the Fifth and Thirteenth Dalai Lamas that he was carrying out in this life.

"And what about Chenrizi's master plan?" I asked.

"During the time of the Sixth Dalai Lama, the master plan that started from the First Dalai Lama's time failed," he said. "I feel that during the Seventh Dalai Lama there was another period with a possible plan. But from that point on, I feel there was no sort of plan. So the Eighth Dalai Lama died young. The Ninth Dalai Lama died when he was only ten years old. He was remarkable. If that young boy had survived, I feel, he would have corrected things. He could have been like the Second Dalai Lama, a great master with a lot of visions. The Second Dalai Lama, as soon as he closed his eyes, had a lot of visions of Buddha and Bodhisattvas. The Ninth Dalai Lama was also like that, but he, too, very soon passed away. The Tenth and the Eleventh also passed away quickly, and then the Twelfth, same. So it was only during the time of the Thirteenth Dalai Lama that another master plan started, it seems."

Because the Dalai Lamas kept dying at a young age, the regents ruled Tibet for 160 years under nebulous Manchu protection. Several Western historians have suggested that many of these young Dalai Lamas were poisoned, perhaps by the regents who wanted to maintain their power, or perhaps in collusion with the Manchu emperors, who wanted to maintain a series of pliable regents rather than risk having a charismatic Dalai Lama in power in Tibet.

"One of the major historical debates for this period," I said, "is a division between Western and Tibetan historians about what happened to all of these boys."

"Whether they were poisoned or just died naturally," the Dalai Lama said, demonstrating how carefully he follows such debates.

"And you have insisted that it wasn't poisoning," I said.

"Yes," he said. "I don't accept that they were poisoned. It was just really carelessness. Of course, the possibility is there, but I feel that it was mainly negligence or foolishness that caused so many young Dalai Lamas to pass away. Look at the case of the Tenth, or the Eleventh. According to the biography of his life, he was sick for a few months and coughing. To me, it sounds like tuberculosis. Among the elderly people who cared for the Dalai Lamas, they had great devotion, but they really didn't know how to take care of them. They considered this young man as Chenrizi, and a cough for them was minuscule. So they were somewhat useless and foolish. Even today, when people get sick, some will say, 'Just do your prayers. You don't need medical treatment.' That is foolish." The Dalai Lama laughed at the idea of spirituality without practicality.

"What about the shining pill?" I asked. "Just before most of these boys died, their doctors gave them a pill that made their face shine, or so the records say."

"No, this wasn't poison," the Dalai Lama said. "Why would they do that? The shining that the documents speak of is from internal spiritual experiences. Westerners do not understand that this light around their heads, this shining they speak of, is the emanation of their own realization and not about pills or poison."

"Since political power remained with the regents during this period," I asked, "what was the effect on the Tibetan nation?"

"I think it had a very great effect," the Dalai Lama said. "I think the public was not educated, and those who were educated were mainly educated through religion, so usually they were not interested in politics or the national self-interest. The rest of the people, because of a lack of education, had a very limited vision. Under such circumstances the central authority is very important, but, at that time, the central authority was very weak in all fields. It was all very bad. There was a lot of corruption, and then also I think the regents had no experience about what was happening outside in the rest of the world. They had a false sense of their own power and the actual power of those around them. The main problem was ignorance, because Tibet was so isolated. Monastic institutions became an obstacle for development of the country, and also there was sectarianism."

"And if those are the negative effects of the regency, what was the positive side of this long period of regency?" I asked.

"I am not saying everything was negative," the Dalai Lama explained, "nor am I defending this situation, saying that all was positive. Both positions are extreme, I think. But yes, religion and Buddhism in the Tibetan case may have hindered further material development. And certainly the population was kept low because there were too many monks and nuns. Also the polyandry system *(two brothers sharing a wife)* restrained population growth. There is no doubt of this. Still, because of this, the economy was self-sufficient. Still, there were too many monks and rich monks. The monastic institutions had too much spiritual importance. In one way, it was a hindrance for the development of the nation, but at the same time, in spite of political ups and downs, the whole Tibetan race remained one because of Buddhism. Of that also there is no doubt."

During the long period of regency, the relationship between the Manchu emperors and the regents who ruled in the Dalai Lama's name was, from a modern perspective, ambiguous and confusing. Modern Chinese and Tibetans draw different conclusions from this history. Chinese government sources use the Manchu intervention as proof that Tibet was part of China, at least from this time, if not earlier. Tibetans living in exile—and in Tibet—deny that the Manchu had any real power over their country. The Tibetan Exile Government, based in India, pointedly says that the nation was never part of China. The Dalai Lama has a nuanced interpretation of this history.

"You have said," I began, "that between 1720 and about 1900, from the Seventh to the Twelfth Dalai Lamas, there was a special relationship between Tibet and the Manchu—though you know many Tibetans reject that idea totally."

"That is my viewpoint," he replied.

Pressing him on the issue, I asked, "Was Tibet officially a vassal of the Manchu?"

"My point is that it was a unique relationship," he responded. "We Tibetans call it a priest-patron relationship. *Cho-yon* we say in Tibetan."

"I think we talked about this before," I said, "when we discussed Phagpa's relations with Kublai Khan, didn't we?"

"Yes, and as I said then, there really is no room for this in today's definitions, because those definitions come from the West," the Dalai Lama said. "There were some cases where the Manchu influenced or controlled Tibetan affairs, but Tibetans saw this as an act of protection. So Tibetans accepted it. But that relationship, between priest and patron, we may not be able to translate it according to modern international law. Modern international laws between states come from Western concepts. So the unique relation between a Tibetan lama or leader and a Manchu emperor—I don't know that we can translate that concept into modern terms."

"Perhaps this would be clearer if we compared the relationship between the Dalai Lamas and the Manchu emperors to the relations between the pope and the kings and emperors of Europe," I said.

"Yes. I think we can compare the relationship between the Manchu emperors and the Dalai Lamas to relations between the European imperialists and the popes," he said.

When I approached Dr. Erberto Lobue, an Italian professor of Tibetan history and art, and explained the Dalai Lama's ideas, Lobue expanded knowledgeably on the subject.

It is easy to understand the political history of Tibet if you know the Italian one: until 1861 Italy was for centuries but a series of independent kingdoms and principalities constantly conspiring and fighting one against the other, regularly inviting foreign rulers—Spanish, French, German—with their armies into the country in order to get rid of their Italian rivals; in spite of that—or perhaps because of their very competitiveness—they created a wonderful civilization, at least in artistic and cultural terms. . . .

To a limited extent, one finds the application of similar political strategies in Tibet since at least the 13th century. In the early 18th century, in particular, Gelugpa religious leaders invited the Manchu emperor to rid them of the Dzungars, whom they had previously invited to eliminate the Qoshots, whom the 5th Dalai Lama had called in to get rid of the indigenous kings of Tsang and Beri, and to establish the supremacy of his own religious order all over Tibet.

The subsequent imposition of the Manchu protectorate over Tibet with the destruction of the walls of Lhasa, the appointment of two imperial representatives in the capital, the setting up of a garrison there and so forth meant the end of the . . . independence of Tibet, while the excessive conservatism of the Buddhist clergy hindered the birth of a lay political class which might have led to the creation of a lay state—such as Nepal or Bhutan—able to withstand the expansionist threat posed by China. Hopeless, just like Italy!

When I suggested to the Dalai Lama that the Manchu emperors manipulated Tibet for political reasons, without true piety toward the Dalai Lama—just as European kings had done with the popes—he disagreed. "My feeling about the Manchu is that some were religiously sincere, and some were very political minded. So I don't think you can categorize all Manchu and say that they all were politically minded and manipulated the situation. I don't believe that. Both sides at the start were not very conscious about the political side of the relationship. It was spiritual, and then there was corruption, but it wasn't planned. And then later, today, more political-minded people look back at this relationship and explain or interpret it with new ideas." The Dalai Lama was so convinced that the original relationship was purely a spiritual one (and thus not subject to political interpretation, either then or now) that he said some Tibetans, at the time, "appreciated some of the interference from the Manchu emperor in order to protect the Dalai Lama's future. It was part of priest-patron relations."

Manchu history substantiates the Dalai Lama's view. Once he became emperor, in 1744, the Manchu prince Yonghegong converted his palace into a Tibetan Buddhist temple in Beijing. The Lama Temple remains one of that city's best-known tourist destinations. To emphasize the Manchu's religious devotion to Tibetan Buddhism, the emperor Qianlong built a massive replica of the Potala at the Manchu summer palace, in Jehol—thousands of miles to the northeast of Lhasa—and it too survives as a tourist attraction, its walls still decorated with eighteenth-century Tibetan Buddhist frescoes. Like the Mongols before them, the Manchu identified with Tibetan Buddhism, in part, as a means of maintaining their cultural differences from their Chinese subjects. The Chinese subjects, on the other hand, remained Confucian and never hid their disdain for the Tibetans and their religion.

The Manchu emperors promoted cultural and ethnic differences between Manchu and Chinese, to prevent the absorption of the Manchu into the numerically larger Chinese population. Devotion to Tibetan Buddhism was part of that effort, though commitment to their shamanistic religion survived as well. The Manchu built a several-hundred-mile-long fence to demarcate the ancestral Manchurian lands from China and forbade Chinese farmers to cross it; they also banned all intermarriage (and even trade) with the subject Chinese peoples, as they strove to maintain their ethnic purity and, by extension, their rule over the Chinese. Nonetheless, as a means of legitimizing their rule, the Manchu encouraged Mongol princes, especially those from the line of Genghis Khan, to intermarry with the Manchu imperial family. Little additional evidence is needed to show that the Inner Asians saw the Chinese as a distinct, subject people, not as equals within a Chinese state. Nor do we have to look much further than these regulations to understand why the Chinese despised the Inner Asians as barbarians.

Though the Manchu defended their ethnic identity, they freely adopted those aspects of Chinese culture that helped them to rule their subjects. The Manchu took a Chinese name for their empire—the Qing ("Pure") dynasty—but they made sure it remained a Manchu state, ruled for Manchu benefit. China's bureaucratic machinery was absorbed almost completely intact, though a Manchu was placed at every level to guarantee Chinese loyalty. Chinese collaborators were essential to the Manchu subjugation of China. They were available because service to the Manchu offered Chinese a path to prosperity, though many Chinese disdained those who helped aliens dominate the Chinese people.

Once the Manchu completed the conquest of what is now Mongolia, between 1688 and 1691, the homeland of the eastern Mongols, they at first forbade their Chinese subjects to travel there or to reside there. The martial prowess of the Mongols was useful and thus had to be protected (i.e., segregated). One Manchu emperor referred to the tribes of Mongolia as the real Great Wall defending the northern borders from attack. If Chinese culture spread among the Mongols, the Manchu feared the Mongols would become soft and useless as warriors.

Over the centuries the Manchu rulers absorbed some Chinese cultural attitudes toward the world; they were, to a degree, sinicized. For example, the Manchu emperors eagerly accepted the Chinese conception of the status of those who ruled China. In 1775, Emperor Qianlong, writing to the king of Thailand, made the point clearly. "The celestial Court reigns over the whole world, and all the states therein are one family." While Chinese scholars attempt to convert the Manchu and Mongol conquests beyond Ming China into Chinese conquests—to justify Chinese occupation of Tibet and other lands—that is revisionism. In fact, the Manchu insisted that Chinese become Manchu, or at least display their subservience. All Chinese were forced, upon threat of death, to wear the traditional Manchu pigtail, or queue, to signify their status as subjects. The Chinese were additionally forced to abandon their style of clothing and wear Manchu robes. In the West, the pigtails and robes are often presented in popular culture as a Chinese stereotype. For patriotic Chinese, they were a sign of shame for centuries.

However we define them, Manchu claims over Tibet were part of the empire's hegemony in Asia, not of Chinese rule. From about 1750 to 1910, the Manchu claimed to be suzerain over Tibet, though the Tibetan regents continued to rule and the Manchu never based more than 1,500 troops in Tibet, an area larger than Texas and Alaska combined. This sort of security detail for the Manchu representative in Lhasa did not allow the Manchu to rule Tibet, or even to collect taxes there. Nevertheless, Qing imperial records claim Tibet—like the rest of the world—as a fief of the "celestial Court." Countries bordering the Manchu did not bluntly reject those vague Manchu claims. Europeans also spoke casually about the Manchu Empire as "China," though the region included all of what is today Mongolia. While European travelers recognized that the Chinese were subjects of the Manchu, this nuance was lost on casual readers of Chinese history, and the confusion is still common today.

The Dalai Lama was curious about the idea of Manchu supremacy in Asia, enacted through the ancient Chinese system of tributary relations, when I raised the topic.

"I am very eager," he said, "to compare Manchu relations with Tibet, to Manchu relations with the Korean, Vietnamese, or Thai kings. Since the Manchu emperors considered themselves supreme, I wonder about their attitude, or the way they dealt with others, and how that can be compared to the way they dealt with Tibet."

"If we use modern terms," I replied, "it would be curious to know if the Manchu considered themselves to be the 'suzerain' over these countries the way that the Chinese government today claims to have been 'suzerain' over Tibet from ancient times. Also the tribute missions . . ."

"Yes," the Dalai Lama agreed. "The Chinese government today always puts forward Tibetan trading missions during the Manchu period as tribute missions and talks about the titles the Manchu gave Tibetan priests. But if the Manchu dealt with other countries that are now independent the same way they dealt with Tibet, then it would be very difficult for the Chinese government to say that these ancient things were proof that Tibet's relations with the Manchu were those between subject and ruler."

"Yes, I think you are right," I said. "It should be investigated."

"Yes," the Dalai Lama replied eagerly. "I think some research work can be done on this. It would help us understand the reality of the relationship between Tibet and the Manchu." He looked at me in such a way as to make it clear that I should do my own investigation, and then, before he sent me on my way, he mentioned work on the subject done by Tibetan researchers.

What I discovered after digesting Manchu relations with Southeast Asia was fascinating. The rulers of Thailand, Laos, Burma, and Korea told the Manchu emperors that they accepted the Manchu as their suzerain (though sometimes they revolted), just as Tibet did for two hundred years. There was no tie to the Manchu Empire except as defined by Chinese cultural norms, adopted by the Manchu, which were based on the assumption of the emperor's absolute supremacy. All foreign affairs were part of the tributary relationship. I found that scholars—whether past masters such as John Fairbank, or those now active in the field, such as Princeton's Perry Link or Harvard's William Kirby—concur with the Dalai Lama when he says that this ancient diplomatic custom cannot be precisely translated into modern terms. Despite China's claims to the contrary, no support exists for the position that nations who sent tribute to the Manchu gave up their independence. There is general agreement that tributary relations, during the period of imperial conquest, cannot be used to define borders between modern states.

For example, Thai kings accepted the Manchu emperors as their "suzerain" in 1650, long before the Tibetans did. The representatives of the rulers of both Tibet and Thailand both kowtowed to the Manchu emperor in Beijing, but the so-called tribute missions these representatives led were actually trade missions—a profitable monopoly allowed foreign rulers, since the emperor permitted only those it recognized as government officials to present tribute.

Once enthroned, Thai kings sent a tribute mission to China to ask for a title and acceptance of their reign. According to Manchu documents from the period, Tibetans did the same with each Dalai Lama. The Manchus claimed the formal right to entitle Thai kings just as they claimed the formal right to recognize the true reincarnation of a Dalai Lama. In fact, Thais and Tibetans made decisions in these matters, and the Manchus rubber-stamped them. It was a useful system for the senders of tribute as well as for the Manchus. Thai kings used the grandeur of the title given them by the emperor to enhance their political standing in Thailand and elsewhere in Southeast Asia. Tibetan priests went to the Mongol, Ming, and Manchu emperors to receive titles, which they then used in Tibet to add to their power in Tibet and throughout Inner Asia. The Manchu thus gained status throughout Asia by pointing to the procession of tribute bearers as proof of the power they wielded.

The Manchu emperors faced one problem with Tibetan and Thai tribute missions: they became too frequent and too costly. As a result, the Manchu ultimately limited their number. They always gave more valuable gifts in return. Tribute from Tibet, Korea, or Thailand to the Manchu rulers of China and the Qing Empire provides no rationale for modern China to claim that these nations were part of China since the Manchu Empire. Nevertheless, this is exactly what the Chinese government argues in the case of Tibet. The view is promoted in Chinese schools, is widely accepted in China, and is cited by government leaders and publications as a reason why Tibet is part of China today. During the 1960s, China published maps based on the "Manchu claim" argument, in which Thailand, Vietnam, and other surrounding countries were shown to be part of China.

When I discussed my findings with the Dalai Lama, he was not surprised—they concurred with his understanding—but he pointed out one important thing. "You see," he said, "relations between Tibetan leaders and the Chinese emperors were more spiritual. With the Thai and the Vietnamese, their relations with the Manchu emperor never had the spiritual side. So while some things are similar, others are different. And still all of this is impossible to interpret in modern legal terms. Also there is the fact that Tibetans had the system of reincarnation. During all the Manchu years, the Manchu had no power to say this man is, or is not, a reincarnation in Tibet. They would just agree with whatever the Tibetans said about those decisions. The patron-priest relationship was a unique relationship, one that is hard to define today. It was based on Buddhism and faith, not politics. Even though that relation was more spiritual in nature, sometimes it was manipulated in the political field, and that is what caused trouble."

Another crucial difference among countries in the Manchu Empire is that some, like Mongolia, were directly occupied and administered. Others, like Thailand and Tibet, had a head of state, and there were few if any Manchu troops. The king of Thailand and the Dalai Lama both had a corvée labor system, so that they could command free labor from their subjects, a primary form of tax in both countries. While the Manchu emperor had a corvée system in China and Mongolia, he didn't have the luxury of demanding labor from the subjects of the Dalai Lama or those of the king of Thailand. The Manchu set up this complex economic web for one reason: to prevent threats to Manchu rule in China from springing up in bordering nations. The Dzungars had hoped to use the authority and prestige of the Dalai Lama to urge the Mongols under Manchu rule to revolt. The Manchu were determined to nip such efforts in the bud. Their ultimate goal was to maintain their grip on China because of its wealth. But the system the Manchu used in suppressing the Chinese backfired. Corruption eventually set in, and the Chinese learned to use the Manchu mechanisms of power for Chinese benefit—the opposite of what the Manchu intended.

Mongolia is the clearest example. At the start of the Manchu Empire's conquest of Mongolia, in 1688, the Chinese could not enter Mongolia, which was seen as one giant military training camp for the Mongols, the Manchu's best warriors. The system of corvée labor the Manchu had set up forced the Mongols to provide Manchu government employees with horses for the next day's journey or food or housing for the couriers. In an odd twist, the Chinese learned to exploit a system designed to perpetuate Manchu rule; the profit made by Chinese businessmen in Mongolia gave the Chinese great power over Mongol affairs.

By 1850, the Chinese had set up shops in every Mongol encampment. After bribing Manchu officials, they would use horses and couriers, obtained under the Manchu corvée system, to transport their own goods into Mongolia free of cost. No Mongol merchant could compete. In addition, Chinese merchants assumed the role of local moneylenders. Every Mongol family had to pay a tax to the Manchu emperor. But because Mongol wealth was on the hoof, in horses and sheep, they borrowed silver from the Chinese to pay their taxes. The interest was so high that soon most Mongols were perpetually in debt to the shopkeepers and moneylenders. If a Manchu bureaucrat created a problem, a Chinese moneylender simply bribed the official. Their corruption of the Manchu system of government slowly let the Chinese take over Mongolia from within, where it generated intense dislike for the Chinese.

A similar series of events unfolded in China, and with the tributary relationship with Thailand as well. Chinese merchants in Canton worked with Thai merchants in Bangkok (and expatriate Chinese in Thailand) to corrupt the tribute system so that Chinese and Thai merchants could make money from trade that the Manchu forbade. The merchants wanted more tribute missions—the only venue for foreign trade—and they bribed Manchu officials to allow it. Eventually the Manchu emperors had to shut down the tribute missions from Thailand because of the expense. What emerged was real foreign trade, though the Manchu maintained the fiction, to the end, that all the Southeast Asian countries were their vassals. The history of tributary relations, based on two-thousand-year-old Chinese ideals and enacted by the Manchu throughout Asia in the seventeenth century, would play out in a significant way in the twentieth century.

When I explained how the Chinese had penetrated every Mongol encampment and ultimately used the Manchu corvée system to colonize Mongolia in the nineteenth century, the Dalai Lama was shocked. In Tibet the situation from 1750 to 1900 was different in several major ways.

Since the Mongol nation was destroyed, to a large degree, by the Manchu's imposition of high taxes, payable in silver, which could be obtained only from Chinese moneylenders, I asked the Dalai Lama, "What taxes did Tibet . . ."

"Tibetans never paid any taxes to the Manchu!" he interjected with great surprise. He had no idea that Manchu domination of what is now the Republic of Mongolia (and Inner Mongolia in China) had ever been so thorough. He was taken aback when I compared Mongolian and Tibetan history during the Manchu period, because it was obvious that Tibet had remained more politically autonomous and economically free of Manchu and Chinese interference. As a young boy, the Dalai Lama had heard about his country's relations with the Manchu from the men who had governed Tibet during the Manchu period. He had not heard how extensively the Chinese had colonized Mongolia.

"At least we in Central Tibet," he said, "under Tibetan jurisdiction, never paid taxes to any Chinese government including the Manchu." Here he alluded to the fact that parts of what had been Eastern Tibet under the Fifth Dalai Lama and Songzen Gampo were incorporated into the Manchu provinces of China in the late nineteenth and early twentieth centuries, and so people there might have paid the Manchu taxes.

"And the corvée labor that Tibetans gave to the Tibetan government— that wasn't given to Manchu officials in Tibet?" I asked.

"No, that was only for the Tibetan government's use," the Dalai Lama replied. "If the Manchu representatives in Lhasa needed that, then the Tibetan government had to issue the orders for it to be given." It was obvious why the Dalai Lama was shocked. Manchu administration in Lhasa consisted of two representatives and a few hundred troops, not the countrywide net of thousands of officials and tens of thousands of troops that blanketed Mongolia.

"Were there hundreds of Chinese shops all over Tibet," I asked, "and did the Chinese merchants use the corvée labor to have their goods carried into Tibet to sell to Tibetans?"

"There were not hundreds of Chinese shops in Tibet!" the Dalai Lama exclaimed. "In Lhasa, there were perhaps a few shops. And in southern Tibet, perhaps a few Chinese were there, but they were there so long that they became like Tibetans. But there were never large numbers of Chinese living in Tibet." Chinese government figures from 1943 support the Dalai Lama's assertion that there were only approximately five hundred Chinese families in all of Central Tibet.

"Most important," the Dalai Lama continued, "it was impossible for the few Chinese merchants that were in Tibet to use the corvée labor system. Those few Chinese businessmen could not use the government system. It was for government use."

"Well, it was used very differently in Mongolia during the last decades of Manchu rule," I said. "There was a corruption of the Manchu, or Qing Empire's, corvée system for colonial purposes by a vast wave of Chinese, especially during the late nineteenth century. I think it's very important to understand that this never happened in Tibet."

"That is right. We certainly didn't have thousands of Chinese shops in Tibet," the Dalai Lama agreed. "And use of the corvée system could be authorized only by the Tibetan government, while from what you tell me in Mongolia's case the Chinese used it themselves. The big difference, in any case, was that the authority to use corvée labor in Mongolia was with the Manchu officials. In the Tibetan case, that was never so. Only the Tibetan government had that authority."

"Yes," I said. "In that sense, Tibet and Thailand are a closer comparison. Both had corvée systems used by the rulers of the two countries as a tax over their subjects, and the Manchus never had authority to demand use of that in either country. There is another similarity between Tibet and Southeast Asia. The Tibetan regent's government ruled Tibet, just as the Thai kings ruled Thailand. The tribute missions and other ritual ways they showed their respect for the Manchus were only a polite fiction, or at least the Thais and the Tibetans viewed these missions differently than they were viewed by the Manchus and the Chinese. They never felt it meant they were part of China, and they continued to rule their own countries."

"Yes, that is true," the Dalai Lama said. "I think the Thai example is similar to that of the Tibetans."

"So the Manchu, like the Chinese, or the Mongol rulers of China before them, said we are rulers of the world," I responded, "and insisted that everyone must kowtow to them and pay what they called tribute. The Thais and the Tibetans said fine, let's pay what they call tribute, if we can use that as a means to make money through trade with China, or if they felt they could exploit the titles the Manchu granted to gain local respect. The Thai historian I read about this points out these two things very clearly. This was also true in Tibet."

"Yes, that profit motive was true in the Tibetan case," the Dalai Lama said. "And also if someone claims that they have connection with the Chinese emperor, it added power to their image within their own locality. Even at the entrance of the temples and monasteries, they would put some of these gifts that they received from the Chinese emperors or the letters or titles they managed to get from the Manchu. This was true even in the Potala and at Drepung and Sera Monasteries in Lhasa."

He gave me an example. He referred to Tsongkhapa, founder of the Dalai Lama's own order, the Gelug. When the Dalai Lama visited Sera Monastery in the 1950s, before he fled Tibet, the monks were using a special black hat during a ceremony. A Ming emperor had given the hat along with a title to Tsongkhapa's cook. Monks from Sera, like all Gelugpa, are supposed to wear yellow hats during their rituals, as specified by Tsongkhapa, but the Dalai Lama found them using this hat from the Ming emperor in one ritual. The Dalai Lama teased the monks at Sera. "I jokingly told them that they regard the Chinese emperor as more important than Tsongkhapa and the Gelugpa lineage. This is clearly against *Vinaya* rule. *Vinaya* rule was created by the Buddha and we are followers of Buddha, and then we disregard Buddha's rule in order to show our greatness because of the backing from a Chinese emperor."

"And the purpose of the Manchu emperors through these things," I said, "was to control the so-called barbarians on the border, through gifts and titles. Titles and trinkets were cheap compared to what it would cost them to send troops to the border. Control was their motivation."

"Yes, that was the Manchu motivation," the Dalai Lama replied. "But worst of all in Tibet *(during this time)* was that there was stagnation and no one had any real control over the government."

"Is there some story," I asked, "that you heard as a young boy that can describe this period of stagnation in Tibet, when the regents ruled for so long? It is such a long period during which no Dalai Lama ever ruled, and thus I will not linger here, so I wonder how you would summarize it."

"I heard one phrase repeated continually when I was a boy," he said. "I think it was true earlier, too, during the period you talk about. They always said how we must follow the traditional way of doing things: it was repeated continually. It clearly shows some kind of stagnation. There was no sense of creating progress. If there was some new creative habit, then they would look at it as negative. They wanted to keep what was there and preserve the past. That was the greatest mistake. In that way, Tibet became weaker, and no one bothered to know what was happening in the world around them."

10

THE THIRTEENTH DALAI LAMA, 1876–1933

The Dalai Lama and I had been discussing Tibetan history off and on, as he had time, for fourteen months when we turned to his direct predecessor, the Thirteenth Dalai Lama. From what he'd said earlier, I knew he felt a strong "connection" to the Thirteenth. Although he was unable to describe precisely what this word means, he had repeatedly indicated that he believed he was a reincarnation of the Thirteenth Dalai Lama, as well as a manifestation of Chenrizi, and that he did not experience both of these connections with all the Dalai Lamas. It was a constant small thread in our conversation. To understand the history of modern Tibet, and his place in it, we need to know the personal story of the Thirteenth Dalai Lama, as his successor comprehends it, and the story that's familiar to historians.

Thupten Gyatso, the Thirteenth Dalai Lama, was born on May 27, 1876, in the southeastern village of Thakpo Langdun "one day by car, southeast from Lhasa," as the Dalai Lama said.

"How did you first hear about the Thirteenth?" I asked.

"I heard things from various people, many who worked for the Thirteenth Dalai Lama," he said. "I think I first heard about him from the sweepers in the Potala and the Norbulingka, and also from the monks at Namgyal Monastery in the Potala, and from officials who worked closely with me. I didn't read his biography."

"I studied a number of histories about the Thirteenth Dalai Lama," I said. "When the monks sought indications of where the Twelfth had been reborn, they went first to the vision lake, Lhamo Latso, as tradition dictated. One of the monks in the party saw a vision in the waters of the lake. While following those indications, the searchers found the Thirteenth quickly, but since he was only ten months old then, they had to wait a year before they put him to the test. When they placed the prayer beads and other personal objects of the Twelfth Dalai Lama in front of the boy, mixed in with the belongings of other people, he chose those of the Twelfth. The historical record says that the regent and others were quickly convinced that this infant was the true reincarnation, so the regent publicly confirmed Thupten Gyatso when he was about eighteen months old. That's what is recorded, but what do you remember about his early life?"

The Fourteenth shrugged his shoulders. "His education was very normal." Sir Charles Bell, an officer in Britain's Indian colonial government who spent many months with the Thirteenth Dalai Lama between 1908 and 1912, also wrote about the Thirteenth's education. The description amazed me, because Bell could just as well have been discussing the education of the Fourteenth Dalai Lama:

> He had not, during his youth, been taught the history or geography of other countries, but only of Tibet; but later in life, after visiting China and India, he learned these subjects by personal observations, travels and enquiries. He was especially interested in the Great Powers and learned all he could about the kings and different nations of the world.

The current Dalai Lama remembered a few details about his predecessor's education. "His tutor was the great scholar Phurchok Jampa Gyatso Rinpoche, and from a young age he was rather tough," he said. Then his eyes lit up as he recalled a memory. "There is one rather strange story. One day, as the Dalai Lama was studying, something happened, and his tutor scolded him, and His Holiness lost his temper. He was trying to prove that he was the smartest, as most young boys will do. The tutor got upset and said that if you don't study properly, then there is no use of my presence here. I have come here to teach you from a small meditation hermitage, and it is better for me to return back to the hermitage if you are not going to study. So the tutor left. His Holiness didn't say anything to stop him because he was also a tough person. And then His Holiness wondered if he would come back. He wondered about that often. So later, whenever the Thirteenth Dalai Lama mentioned the name of his tutor, he was always very emotional."

"It sounds like he was very hardheaded even when he was young," I observed. "You would have never done this," I laughed.

"Yes, that is right, he was," the Dalai Lama said. "I don't have that kind of courage."

"The Thirteenth Dalai Lama was very willful," I said.

"Very tough," the Dalai Lama replied, shaking his head in amazement. "My junior tutor Trijang Rinpoche told me that during the Thirteenth Dalai Lama's time, that type of character, being so serious and tough, that was useful. In my time, he said, my nature is softer, and that is needed at this time."

The Thirteenth Dalai Lama, perhaps because of his tough nature, was the first Dalai Lama in 120 years to survive past the age of twenty. His was not the brief powerless reign of a boy trapped in the Potala, while others ruled in his name. He was born at a time when Manchu power was waning. Like the Great Fifth, he ultimately ruled Tibet, though he had to play off the major foreign powers of his day—British, Russian, and Chinese—to achieve it. He was cosmopolitan for his era. Widely traveled (if under duress), he thrived during a peripatetic exile in Mongolia, China, and India. His was a tumultuous life in an era torn by strife. Tibet was invaded twice: by the British in 1904 and by forces of the Manchu Empire in 1910. After the second invasion, he created a Tibetan army—rather than relying on untrained villagers who came to Tibet's defense if there was an attack—and drove the last Manchu and Chinese troops out of the country. In the midst of war, the Thirteenth sent envoys to both imperial Russia and imperial Britain, and met personally with the emperor and dowager empress of the Manchu Empire and the British viceroy in India. He rode horseback across the wilds of Inner Asia and traveled in automobiles, trains, and steamships in China and India. He camped in Mongol yurts and stayed in British colonial mansions in Calcutta and Darjeeling. By the end of his life, he had regained full Tibetan independence and reunified the state. He restored control over lands in Eastern

Tibet, which the Manchu had incorporated into Chinese provinces, drove the Chinese out of nearly all of ethnic Tibet, and declared the nation's absolute independence.

The Thirteenth Dalai Lama did not start his reign under auspicious international conditions. By the time the young man was enthroned and assumed power from his regent, in 1895, predatory Japanese and European colonial powers ringed the Manchu Empire and Tibet. As early as the 1870s, during negotiations with the imperialist Japanese regarding hegemony over Korea and the Ryukyu Islands, the Manchu discovered that the ancient tributary relationship imposed on Korea and all border countries—which they believed made Korea part of the Manchu Empire—bore no legal weight in the modern world. Japan demanded Korea's independence, under its protection, and eventually forced the Manchu rulers to accept. The ensuing Japanese colonization of Korea was used as a stepping-stone to the eventual colonization of large parts of China.

Korea was but a foreshadowing of events to come. In 1880, despite the Manchu claim to "special rights" over Vietnam—again based on the ancient tributary relationships—the French added Hanoi and Haiphong to their expanding colonial empire in Southeast Asia. Not only were the Manchu's tributary relationships outmoded and not recognized by the neighboring states to whom the Qing Empire had tried to apply them; they were dismissed outright because the Manchu lacked the military might to enforce the claims. During a naval battle in 1884 between the Manchu and the French navies over Vietnam, for example, the French sank an enemy fleet and killed 521 Manchu and Chinese sailors, while only five French soldiers were lost. At the same time, Russians were pressing down on the Manchu Empire's northern borders, even showing an interest in Mongolia—which, unlike Southeast Asia and Tibet, paid direct taxes in silver to the Manchu.

Still trapped under Manchu domination, the Chinese developed a sense of aggrieved nationalism as they watched European and Japanese colonialists march through Asia. This growing sense of Chinese nationalism now demanded the Manchu Empire incorporate the old tribute states as parts of a Chinese state. By the late nineteenth century, newspapers and literacy were widespread and the Chinese people watched foreign affairs closely, though as subjects of the Manchu they had no say in them. The foreign incursions left the Chinese feeling doubly victimized—first by the Manchu, who had occupied China since 1644, and then by the Japanese, French, British, and Russian powers, who were stripping China of what its people saw as their ancient right to rule all bordering nations. For the budding ethnic Chinese revolutionaries, the Manchu were an alien people. As revolutionary fervor developed, it was based, at first, on the dream of a Chinese state from which all other races would be expelled. To ethnic Chinese like Sun Yat-sen, who eventually overthrew the Manchu to establish, initially, an ethnic Chinese Republic in 1911, the Manchu were allowing other foreigners to rob the Chinese. "Powerful foes encroached upon the territory of China," proclaimed Sun Yat-sen, "and the dynasty parted with our sacred soil to enrich neighboring nations." To Sun Yat-sen, it was not Manchu territory; the land belonged to the Chinese, and the Manchu had no right to give it away.

As European and Japanese colonialism intensified, ethnic nationalism exploded. China as a modern nation, distinct from the various empires that had ruled the land, had never existed, and today there is a consensus among scholars that Chinese nationalism is a creation of the twentieth century. It bubbled up among a prostrate people stifled under Manchu rule, unable to defend their country either from European imperialism or from Manchu invaders. The first questions about China, as it emerged, were simple. What were its borders? Should they be the borders of the Ming Empire? Were they to be determined by looking at where Chinese-speaking people actually lived? Or would Chinese conflate the borders of their territory with those determined by ancient Manchu conquests?

By the early 1900s, Chinese saw the Manchu tributary states as rightfully Chinese, even though the Chinese states that had existed before the Manchu conquest—the Tang, the Song, and the Ming—had never ruled them. Under a very real foreign threat, a virulent nationalism emerged. In time, Chinese nationalists would depose the Manchu and seize on the "solution" of colonizing the borderlands of Mongolia and Tibet, which the Manchu had until then prevented the Chinese from settling. Beijing was convinced that the Mongolians and Tibetans—whom they saw as illiterate barbarians, vulnerable to foreign manipulation—could not achieve real independence. As one Chinese observer saw it:

This is like the young sparrow boasting that it can fly, or the young rabbit bragging that it can run. They will surely not escape the mouths of the hungry vultures or ravenous tigers . . .

The vultures circling the Manchu Empire and Tibet drew closer. As British power in India increased, it reached into the southern foothills of the Himalayas toward Tibet. Sikkim was a Himalayan kingdom Tibet claimed as a vassal or tributary state. Its people adhered to the Nyingma and Kagyu orders of Tibetan Buddhism, and many were of Tibetan ethnicity. In 1890, the British, eager to finalize their slow annexation of Sikkim, negotiated a treaty with representatives of Manchu China, who claimed to control Tibet, and defined the Tibet-Sikkimese border. Tibet was not invited to the talks. The British then planted border markers, between Tibet and Sikkim, which Tibetans immediately tore out. During a series of armed skirmishes, Lhasa insisted that the Manchu and the British alone could not negotiate the border treaty. Slowly the British realized that the Manchu claim of dominion over Tibet was as fictitious as Manchu claims over Korea, Burma, Vietnam, and Thailand. Tibet would not recognize treaties negotiated by the Manchu, and thus if India wanted to control events in Tibet, or along India's border with Tibet, it would have to deal directly with Lhasa.

The viceroy in India, George Nathaniel Curzon, tried to establish direct contact with Tibet's true ruler, the Thirteenth Dalai Lama, but his letters, much to Curzon's annoyance, were returned unopened. Worse, some were returned, apparently unopened but filled with dried dung. Through intermediaries, Tibet informed the British that it had an agreement with the Manchu that Lhasa would not enter into communication with any foreign power without the permission of the Manchu. Yet as the British soon discovered, Tibet was using the fiction of Manchu power to deflect any discussion with the British, because the Dalai Lama had no interest in establishing relations with London. This ruse was only the beginning of the Thirteenth Dalai Lama's juggling of competing colonial empires.

The young Fourteenth Dalai Lama discovered the amazing history of his predecessor, bit by bit, through stories he heard growing up. It came to life as he opened boxes of strange gifts presented by foreign envoys, which the Thirteenth had put away in the personal rooms of the Dalai Lama. Though later in life the Fourteenth was entranced by a collection of ancient paintings he found in the Potala, which taught him about the spirituality of Milarepa, in his childhood he found pleasure in more mundane treasures hidden in the Potala.

"How did you find these things left by the Thirteenth?" I asked.

"When I was very young, I was fond of hunting for treasure," he said. "So I would open old boxes and see what was in them. That was just my habit. Then later, if the need arose to tell someone what these boxes contained, I could tell them. What kind of box was in which room and what kind of things were in the box. I knew them quite well."

"And no one else would have touched these boxes since the death of the Thirteenth?" I asked.

"No," he said gravely, shaking his head. "No one had the right to open them." Here he pointed at his chest and smiled mischievously. "No one except this person."

"What did you find in these boxes?" I inquired.

"A variety of things," he said. "In the Potala there were some monk's robes from the previous Dalai Lama which now were useless. They were, of course, very clean. He wore very clean clothes. But they were very old and worn out because of repeated washing."

"So you never wore any of his clothes?" I asked.

"No, never," he said. "Some were worn out, but also because of the years he spent in Mongolia, the Dalai Lama used to wear the Mongolian style of clothes, and I found those, but I always wore monk's robes, so I could not wear his. And the shoes. There were two boxes full of Western shoes. I was very interested in wearing a pair. This caused trouble because, on the one hand, they were too big for me, and on the other, I was restricted to wearing only Tibetan shoes when I was young. They were too Western or stylish for monks to wear when I was a boy. I think there were twenty or thirty pairs of shoes. He had never worn them. He just had them in boxes."

"And you liked these shoes of his?" I said, laughing.

"Yes. In fact, you can see the scar." He laughed and leaned over. He pulled down a sock to show me a pink scar on a delicate ankle that had seen little sunlight.

"You got that from just wearing them?" I asked.

"No," he laughed. "One shoe had iron nails in the sole. So it was fun to wear those shoes and tromp loudly around, listening to the great sound. They were too big, so I had to put paper in the toes to be able to wear them. Actually, I fell down and the nail on one shoe went into my ankle. The sweepers were very angry with me when I took out the shoes and insisted on wearing them. I think I only took them out twice, before I received power in 1950. Although I wanted to wear them when I was young, I was afraid! Then later, after I received power, I was also physically bigger, so I could use these shoes. So I did, during lessons, and once on a holiday I wore them to run in."

"And what else did you find of the Thirteenth Dalai Lama's when you were young?" was my next question.

"There were some watches that belonged to the Thirteenth Dalai Lama," he said. "Some were from the eighteeenth century and one probably from the seventeenth century. One watch was given to him by the Russian czar, and it was diamond studded. I also found a lot of silk brocades. There was a wide variety of articles, which were produced in China, Russia, India, and in the West. These were all there when I lived in the Potala. There was even more variety in the Norbulingka at the Chensalingka."

"The Chensalingka was a residence and temple built by the Thirteenth Dalai Lama in the walled compound of the summer palace, or the Norbulingka?" I asked.

He nodded and continued. "At the Chensalingka there was a collection of his guns, and some were very beautiful. The Thirteenth Dalai Lama was very fond of these guns. And I liked them, too."

"Did you shoot them?" I asked.

"No," he answered sternly, "never. I was not allowed. Even when I was allowed to look at them, there were a lot of restrictions."

"You say the guns were beautiful. Why?" I asked.

"They were very smart," he said, "and some were very old and some new. There was even some Russian-made machine guns, quite a big one, and then the tackle for horses to play polo."

"Did the Thirteenth Dalai Lama play polo?" I asked.

"Never," he said. "But then the bodyguards would play polo and perhaps he would watch. So there were many boxes. Some were shipped together with him from China and India. Some of these were just left in the storerooms, as they were, never opened after they arrived in Lhasa. But I, his successor, opened them and used the little pencils, sharpeners, and paper. It was almost like a small market, full of very useful things. There was even a diamond cutter!"

"So you didn't have to buy things. You had everything already."

"Yes," he laughed. "There were also many gadgets for pruning the flowers. Some were really good quality. I think those were all English."

"He was very happy to spend time in the garden, wasn't he?" I asked. "In one book I read, it said he sent cuttings from Tibetan roses as a gift to the Russian czar."

"Yes, he liked flowers," the Dalai Lama said. "In fact, when I lived in the Norbulingka, there was an old monk whose responsibility was to look after flowers. He had done the same work for the Thirteenth Dalai Lama. The monk was very short-tempered, and even in a few cases he lost his temper with me. The Thirteenth Dalai Lama knew this person had a very short temper, so one day he walked in those areas where that monk looked after the flowers and then he asked, 'What are the names of these flowers?' The monk was very quiet and didn't answer. Then a second time he asked, and still no answer. And then a third time he asked. The monk replied, 'It is what you already know!'" The current Dalai Lama laughed when he told this story. "The Thirteenth Dalai Lama had nothing left to say except 'You are really angry and upset today,' and then he left."

"Were there other times when the Thirteenth was tougher than this?" I asked.

"Oh yes. Some of the sweepers, they were scolded by him," the Dalai Lama explained. "Or even beaten by the Thirteenth Dalai Lama. But then some of them were very superstitious, and they had strange experiences. After a beating from the Dalai Lama, they said they were healed of their chronic illnesses. Some were alive when I came, and some of them raised me. They told me stories about him being so tough. One old monk in the Norbulingka told me that the Thirteenth Dalai Lama lost his temper with him one day and picked up his cane *(as if to beat the monk)*. The monk jumped into a deep pond there in the Norbulingka. Because of his robes, he started floating, not sinking. Still, the monk tried to put his head in the water to drown himself. Then the Dalai Lama stretched out his cane, which the monk had been so fearful of being beaten with, and pulled him out."

"It seems like you learned much about the Thirteenth Dalai Lama from the sweepers and the treasures in the boxes you found in the Potala and the Norbulingka," I remarked.

"Yes, but I was not so interested in learning," he laughed. "I was just looking for treasures! Of course, one thing I found also was the telescopes. They were very helpful to develop my interest in astronomy from a young age. I think they were just a gift to him that was packed away; he never used them. But they were a treasure for me when I found them. I remember setting one up on the roof of the Potala, looking through the telescope at the moon. That is when I first saw the mountains on the moon, and the shadows from the mountains on the crater walls." This was an important discovery for the Dalai Lama. When he saw these shadows, he knew, contrary to the teachings of the Buddhist scripture, that the moon did not generate its own light. That discovery encouraged the development of a faith in science that has stayed with him throughout his life. But that was not the only use the Dalai Lama found for the telescope.

"Also," the Dalai Lama said, "I used the telescope to watch prisoners in the prison yard at the foot of the Potala." Seeing the conditions in which the prisoners lived was one of the discoveries that led the young Dalai Lama to begin questioning Tibet's government.

Speaking of the telescopes and other gifts from his predecessor that changed his life, he said, "The Thirteenth Dalai Lama was very careful to preserve all these gifts, even though his own lifestyle, his eating habits, all of those were very simple."

"I noticed that you found a number of Russian things that belonged to the Thirteenth Dalai Lama," I pointed out. "A watch studded with diamonds, from the czar, and some Russian guns. The first time that the Thirteenth Dalai Lama fled Tibet was just before the British reached Lhasa in 1904. The British said they invaded Tibet in 1904 because they feared the Russians were plotting to use Tibet as a base to attack India."

"Obviously," the Dalai Lama said, "the Thirteenth Dalai Lama had a keen desire to establish relations with Russia, and also I think he was a little skeptical toward England at first. Then there was Dorjiev. To the English he was a spy, but in reality he was a good scholar and a sincere Buddhist monk who had great devotion to the Thirteenth Dalai Lama."

Agvan Dorjiev (1854–1938) was one of the most intriguing figures in twentieth-century Tibetan history. Dorjiev was a Buddhist monk born among the Buryat tribe of Mongols in what is now the Russian Republic of Buryatia, located in the south-central region of Siberia along the eastern shore of Lake Baikal. Buryatia was invaded and then colonized by European Russians starting in 1666, but the Russians did not eradicate the native Buryats who remained Buddhists, though they became subjects of the czar. For Dorjiev, just as for Buddhists in Mongolia, Lhasa remained the holy land and the Dalai Lama, because of the Third Dalai Lama's work with the Mongols, remained Buddhism's greatest teacher and hierarch. Dorjiev began his studies of Buddhism when he was fourteen, but soon traveled to Mongolia for further studies and eventually to Lhasa, arriving there in 1890, at the age of thirty-six. He became such an excellent Buddhist scholar that Tibetans appointed him as one of the assistant tutors to the young Thirteenth Dalai Lama, despite his being a foreigner. Through close contact with the young Dalai Lama, he ultimately became one of his most trusted political advisers. Dorjiev was pleased with the Russian Empire's treatment of the Buryats, compared to the Manchu treatment of the Mongols in their homeland, and was a crucial advocate encouraging the Thirteenth Dalai Lama to look to Russia as a potential patron against Chinese and British influence.

In 1897, just two years after he assumed power from his regent, the Thirteenth Dalai Lama was confident enough of his authority that he no longer bothered to consult the Manchu emperor's representatives about his appointment of officials in Tibet. The illusion of Manchu control over Tibet had disappeared. As he assumed real power, the young Dalai Lama watched the British incursions along the nation's southern border with increasing concern. British spies caught secretly mapping the region further agitated Lhasa. Dorjiev, the Dalai Lama's foreign policy adviser, told the young ruler that he would need a new patron if the powerless Manchu were going to participate in the dismemberment of Tibet—as Tibetans felt they did with Sikkim—rather than protecting Tibet, as the patron-priest relationship required. Dorjiev recorded his views in his own hand:

> The necessity of seeking the patronage of a foreign country was secretly debated at the highest level in Tibet from the moment when Chinese officials bribed by Englishmen deprived Tibet of the land [of Sikkim]. I was present at one such meeting and expressed the opinion that Russian should be given preference.

Speaking of this period, the current Dalai Lama said, "Tibetans, at that time, we usually described people like the Englishmen who were very strong, as *tendra,* or enemies of the Dharma. I think some of the Chinese monks and the Manchu officials had this attitude at that time as well. There was a common perception that the English and Westerners were the enemy of Tibet and the Manchu were the patrons of Tibet." Since Tibet was a religious state, the concept of *tendra* included revulsion and fear of foreigners, which explains why the Thirteenth Dalai Lama refused even to open the first letters from the British. The conservative monasteries, which the Dalai Lama relied on for his power, were encouraged to continue their support of the Manchu, because of their common Buddhist beliefs. Meanwhile, fear of Christian missionaries, who Tibetans believed were supported by British India, was one of the factors that helped create the perception of the British as *tendra.*

"So naturally," the Dalai Lama said, "there was no trust of the British. Since we had no contact with them, there was not even the courage to meet the enemy of Dharma." In this case, especially with Dorjiev urging the Thirteenth Dalai Lama to turn to the Russians, there was only one recourse.

Once the decision was made to seek a new patron, Dorjiev was worldly enough simply to go to Russia and ask to speak with the czar directly. Lhasa had no idea that a diplomatic envoy of the Dalai Lama, seeking an audience with the czar, would send Britain into a panic. Dorjiev did nothing to keep his trip to Russia secret, nor did the Russians, as accounts of the trip appeared in British papers. Viceroy Curzon saw a clandestine Russian plot to threaten India from a new base, in Tibet. Dorjiev was obviously a Russian spy—his homeland, Buryatia, was part of Russia and Dorjiev was a Russian citizen—so Curzon decided it was "necessary to preserve the status quo in Tibet," which meant that London had to ensure that no Russian troops, or weapons, were allowed into Tibet. Reports from journalists in Beijing, in 1902, followed on the heels of accounts of Dorjiev's trip to Russia. According to the press, a Russian diplomat was discussing with the Manchu the prospect of an independent Tibet, under Russian protection. Korean and Vietnamese independence from China had been a euphemism for colonial occupation for decades, and this, along with wild rumors about the "Russian spy" Dorjiev, ignited Curzon's worst fears.

Ultimately, the Russians had no interest in an alliance with Tibet, rejecting all of Dorjiev's appeals. Nor did Moscow ever discuss Tibetan independence with the Manchu: the press report was a complete fabrication. Tibet was too remote and too inaccessible, with no markets for Russian goods and no known commodities worthy of extraction. The conservatives in London, however, refused to accept these explanations, offered by the Russian Foreign Office, at face value. By November 1902, Curzon was determined to send an army into Tibet—he was convinced he would find either Russian troops or Russian arms in Lhasa, the result of a secret treaty between the two nations. Events proved Curzon wrong on all counts.

Both Manchu China and Russia protested the British invasion of Tibet in 1904, though neither country assisted Tibet in any way. Once the British marched into southern Tibet under the guise of a trade mission, Lhasa refused to negotiate until the British returned to the border. London insisted that they would march straight to Lhasa. The tiny Tibetan militia—not an organized body but merely peasants who rose up to defend the nation, armed only with matchlocks and swords—massed to block the road to Lhasa.

In the decisive encounter, 1,500 ill-equipped Tibetans faced off against 3,000 British soldiers, some of whom were armed with an early version of a machine gun. Called a Maxim, it discharged seven hundred rounds in ninety seconds. The British killed six or seven hundred Tibetans at the massacre of Guru; not a single British, Nepali, or Indian conscript died.

When the surviving Tibetans retreated after the machine guns opened up, they did not run, but instead—perhaps unaware of what was happening— they walked away, very slowly, even as the British continued firing. The British officers and troops alike were horrified at their gruesome work. One British soldier confided in a letter to his mother, "I hope I shall never have to shoot down men walking away again." A second wrote his mother, "I got so sick of the slaughter that I ceased fire, though the General's order was to make as big a bag as possible."

The British army faced no further resistance. On July 30, 1904, the Thirteenth Dalai Lama appointed a regent to govern the affairs of Tibet in his name and fled into exile, after a three-month horseback ride to Mongolia, joined only by a few followers, including Dorjiev. On August 2, the British marched into Lhasa—a city no Englishman had visited since 1811—where they discovered no proof of Russian involvement in Tibetan affairs.

"Why did he run away to Mongolia?" I asked the Dalai Lama. "This was one of the most fateful decisions of his life. Why did he leave?"

"I personally feel that was a mistake," the Dalai Lama responded. "Of course, you cannot blame him, because at that time, no one knew who the British were, and no one knew what the British army would do. But then later the British military seemed disciplined. Whenever they faced some obstacles or resistance as a military, yes, they killed people. But otherwise there was no burning of monasteries, no robbing or pillaging of people. When they reached Lhasa, they camped in their own camp and negotiated with the Tibetan government. They were disciplined and, later, Tibetans compared their actions with those of the Manchu and Chinese during their invasion *(of 1910). (The Manchu and Chinese)* would burn monasteries and rob the villages. And when they arrived in Lhasa, they occupied people's houses. So judging from the *(comparatively)* good behavior of the British army, if the Thirteenth Dalai Lama had stayed in Lhasa and talked with them, maybe there would have been a more positive result."

"So looking backward and from your viewpoint, it was a mistake," I said.

"Yes," he replied. "When he left, the thinking was to go to China, through Mongolia. But all these things were hurriedly decided, just as my escape in 1959 was also hurriedly decided. When the Dalai Lama reached Reting Monastery, the Reting lama offered all the proper facilities to the

Dalai Lama, including tents, food, and more horses. So they rode on, and in this way reached Mongolia."

The Thirteenth Dalai Lama was twenty-eight years old when he rode into an exile that would last eight years. After three months of hard travel—across northern Tibet, a wild, treeless, windy plateau, much of it above 16,000 feet, and then the Gobi Desert—over a distance of 1,500 miles, he arrived at last at today's Ulaanbaatar. Because of Mongolian devotion to the Dalai Lamas, Mongols received him very well.

"His relationship with monks and monasteries was excellent," the Dalai Lama said. "At this time in Mongolia, there was a tradition of the monks approaching a scholar and requesting a debating session with you. So he accepted such requests, and they would debate with him. Because of this, he spent a lot of time fiercely studying the scriptures. Since he had to debate, he had to study. He debated and won many times, often against many highly placed scholars. Later on, he spent time explaining Buddhist texts, not in the form of a public teaching but very seriously explaining the philosophical text to a few monks. In fact, in Mongolia he acted like a teacher, not like the Dalai Lama. In Lhasa, the Dalai Lama gave public teaching, but otherwise he did not act like an ordinary teacher. So while the Thirteenth Dalai Lama was in Mongolia, he carried out Dharma both informally and formally. In fact, I learned about this on one of my trips to Mongolia when one of the senior Mongolian monks told me how his teacher had received teachings from the Thirteenth Dalai Lama in this way."

"His stay in Mongolia had a large influence on him?" I inquired.

"Yes," he smiled. "The sweepers told me that the Thirteenth Dalai Lama also learned Mongolian and spoke it quite fluently, and the influence of wearing Mongolian dress was very strong on him. For the rest of his life he wore the Mongolian dress. So anyway, in spite of the political situation and some misunderstanding with one Mongol priest, he developed a very special relation with the monasteries and the public. The Mongolians were very devoted to Buddhist teachers anyway, and so they were very devoted to the Dalai Lama."

"And what was happening politically between Britain, Tibet, and the Manchu while he was in Mongolia?" I asked.

"The political side I don't know. You will have to do research."

The British invasion aroused Chinese and Manchu fears of an English-occupied Tibet. The Qing Empire was already confronted with imperialist foes on its borders in Southeast Asia, and a British colonization of Tibet would have put English forces on its western borders, poised just a few hundred miles from heavily populated Chinese provinces of the Qing Empire. The fear that Tibet would be used by foreigners was one of the issues that ultimately provoked the 1910 Manchu invasion and the 1950 Chinese invasion of Tibet. The British incursion forced a harsh redefinition of Tibet's ancient priest-patron relationship and helped to ignite Chinese ethnic nationalism.

The Manchu, or Qing, Empire became Tibet's overlord in 1720 when it installed the Seventh Dalai Lama, but this relationship was not rigorously defined and the Manchu made no move to absorb Tibet as a province. Tibetans paid no taxes to the Manchu, as Mongolia, which is independent today, did. Tibet also maintained its legal and administrative systems, with its own officials, while Chinese and Manchu authorities directly ruled Mongolia. As early as 1792, the Manchu emperor Qianlong knew that the Dalai Lama and his ministers were "able to do whatever they wished in the administration of Tibetan affairs, ignoring . . . the incompetent [Manchu] officials" who were theoretically supposed to govern Tibet. This nebulous relationship grew even more unclear throughout the nineteenth century because of threats the Manchu faced elsewhere. The Taiping Rebellion (1850–63)—inspired in part by a Chinese desire to overthrow their Manchu rulers—left an estimated twenty to forty million dead and nearly toppled the Manchu regime. Tibet fought two wars in the nineteenth century, defending itself against Nepal and Ladakh, Indian province, and in neither case were Manchu armies dispatched. By the time the Thirteenth Dalai Lama took power, in 1895, the Manchu's ability to intervene in Tibetan affairs had vanished. Manchu attention was focused elsewhere—until the British invasion of Tibet. The Chinese revolutionaries, who had not yet thrown off their Manchu masters, viewed the British assault very simply: Tibet was part of China, and the imperial British were invading it.

In the summer of 1904, Tibetan officials left in charge by the Thirteenth Dalai Lama capitulated to British terms in their eagerness to secure the withdrawal of troops encamped in Lhasa. In the resulting Convention Between Great Britain and Thibet, Tibet accepted London's annexation of Sikkim; gave British-controlled India the right to open trade marts in southern Tibet and to station British troops there to protect them; and agreed not to conduct relations with foreign states, including Manchu China. At the same time, London ordered Lhasa to pay war reparations to the British. Although Tibet became its protectorate, Britain did not assume any responsibilities to defend the Asian country. As the first document between Tibet and another state as defined by the European legal tradition, it recognized Tibet's right to negotiate and sign treaties, as any other state might. If Britain had lived up to the agreement, Tibet would have become a protectorate like Sikkim, but that did not happen.

Meanwhile, the Dalai Lama, in Mongolia, sent Dorjiev back to Russia to plead once again for the backing of Czar Nicholas II. The Thirteenth now wrote that he wanted "protection from the dangers which threaten my life, if I return to Lhasa as is my intention and duty." It was not forthcoming. Like the British, the Russians sought to ensure that no one else used Tibet to threaten them. It was not to the advantage of either nation for Tibet to be either an independent state or the vassal of an enemy. The political solution was for London and Moscow both to recognize a purposely vague Manchu claim over Tibet, in spite of the fact that Tibet had been ruling itself for some time. The timing was opportune; the Dalai Lama was essentially powerless, living in exile under a Manchu order deposing him. In Lhasa, the Manchu tried to open a school and laid plans to assimilate the elite of the Tibetan government into a Manchu administration. Worse was yet to come.

As the Dalai Lama waited in Mongolia for Russian intervention, the collapsing Manchu state moved to defend itself from foreign aggression. The 1904 invasion incensed the Manchus and their Chinese subjects. The original relationship between Tibet and the Manchus, no matter how ill defined, never veered toward Tibetan assimilation. In direct response to the British invasion and the resulting treaty, the Manchu's second-to-last head of state—the empress dowager Cixi—and the officials around her created direct Manchu rule in eastern Tibet, where they installed Chinese colonies. Manchu officials drove Tibetan administrators out of Batang and then attempted to limit the power of the monasteries. They forbade the monks to recruit new monks, and—even worse for Tibetans, who considered foreigners to be enemies of the Dharma—gave a land grant to French Catholic priests.

Tibetans revolted in March 1905. They massacred Manchu officials and two French priests, who, unable to convert Tibetans, had sided with the Manchu in their attempts to colonize the area with compliant Chinese farmers. In response, two thousand Manchu troops marched into the region and executed Tibetan officials, including the abbots of a monastery, and burned a monastery. Beijing praised the Manchu magistrate who directed the campaign, Chao Erh-feng, for helping the "advance of civilization."

The following year, in eastern Tibet, monks who had surrendered after a Manchu siege were executed, Chinese temples were built to replace Tibetan ones, and Lhasa was ordered to pay taxes to the Manchu government (for the first time) and to adopt Chinese surnames. Chinese colonization was promoted in many ways, including a proclamation, issued by the Manchu magistrate Chao, to potential ethnic Chinese colonialists, explicating the attitude toward Tibetans.

> The native Rulers have been abolished forever. . . . Who will now prevent you from going there? . . . Emigrants who bring their families will find that they can live much more economically than in China. The unmarried man . . . will find the women more numerous than the men . . . the females are industrious . . . the males lazy. A native girl taken as wife will prove of great assistance . . . for these women perform all the carrying of water, cooking of food. . . . Nor is any dowry necessary, for all that is needed are garments in which to clothe her.

Similar colonizing efforts in Mongolia, Inner Mongolia, and Manchuria occurred during the same time. While the Manchu emperors had always protected the Mongols and Tibetans as distinct races, and forbidden the Chinese to learn Mongolian or even to marry Mongolians (though the Manchu married Chinese in the later period), the cultural norms were changing. In the opinion of the Manchu, cultural assimilation was the only way to unify a state strong enough to defend its integrity. The Manchu Empire was laying the groundwork for incorporating Tibet, Mongolia, and Manchuria into Chinese provinces. The Manchu had administered each of these areas in unique ways, but the motivation was to prevent the Chinese, with their greater numbers, from racially absorbing the Manchu, Mongols, and Tibetans into the Manchu Empire. But the thinking had shifted. Chinese empires, such as the Tang and the Ming, had used ethnic assimilation of border tribes as a means to defend and expand the Chinese state. The Manchu understood the reasoning and, for centuries, had wanted none of it. Now on their deathbed, the Manchu were willing to reconsider.

Having helped to set these events into motion by their invasion of Tibet, British politicians decided that it would be too expensive to turn Tibet into a true British protectorate, as it had done to tiny Sikkim. Tibet was vast and would be expensive to defend. As a result, some clauses in the 1904 convention were repudiated by the Foreign Office in London, which felt that officers in the field had exceeded their mandate. To achieve its ends, Britain concluded two new treaties, one with Russia and one with the Qing Empire, called the Government of China in the English version. The 1906 treaty with the Manchu read, in part:

> The Government of Great Britain engages not to annex Tibetan territory or to interfere in the administration of Tibet. The Government of China also undertakes not to permit any other foreign state to interfere with the territory or internal administration of Tibet.

With the Convention Between Great Britain and China Respecting Tibet, Britain implied that the Manchu Empire was not a foreign state in relation to Tibet but did not say that Tibet was part of the empire. Britain had mentioned none of this in its 1904 treaty with Tibet, nor did London or the Manchus inform Lhasa of the 1906 agreement, between two foreign powers, about its fate. With the Manchus on board, and the start of a deal to protect Britain's interests in India in hand, London turned to Russia in 1907 and signed the second treaty, in which the two states agreed to recognize "the principle of the *suzerainty* of China over Thibet." Perhaps for the first time, the ancient relations between the Manchu and the Tibetans were defined by a European word and concept. By now, English documents commonly conflated the Qing Empire with China, though Manchu documents never made this mistake. Through its treaties with the Manchus and Russia, Britain granted rights to the Manchu Empire over Tibet that the Qing had never had. It was a huge victory for the empire, because the Western powers had dismissed Qing claims of sovereignty, stemming from its ancient tributary relationship with all its neighbors, in every other case. With this document in hand, the Manchu had become Tibet's "suzerain"—which, according to European legal precedent, meant that Tibet was, at least nominally, not fully independent. Neither the Thirteenth Dalai Lama nor the Tibetans were party to these developments. Under European legal precedent, the status of a state cannot be changed unless it is a party to the agreement. Thus it was impossible for the treaties between China, Russia, and Britain to alter Tibet's status.

In the first decade of the twentieth century, British documents began to equate China with all the territory held by the Manchu Empire. At the same time, the Chinese in the Qing Empire, as they started to think what a Chinese nation would be once the Manchu were overthrown, grew increasingly concerned that the ring of ancient tributary nations around the Middle Kingdom were being colonized or absorbed into European or Japanese spheres of influence. The Chinese conflated the Manchu Empire with what they felt their sense of China was, even though they had never ruled more than half the territory the Manchus had conquered. The Chinese obsession with the idea that foreign provocateurs—aided by Manchu imperialists—were tearing China apart encouraged a virulent sense of aggrieved nationalism, which persists today

China is deeply suspicious of any foreign involvement in its affairs, no doubt because of its belief that European and other powers had lied about its history to justify their nineteenth- and twentieth-century colonialist exploits. Chinese today remain angry that foreign imperialists stripped China of what, in their eyes, belonged to China. Ironically, the Great

Game imperial Britain and Russia played over Tibet ended with the recognition, by each country, of the Qing Empire's nominal rights over Tibet.

I came back to the Dalai Lama armed with my research. As I briefly narrated, with a sense of indignation and outrage, the game Russia and Britain had played, the Dalai Lama responded with bursts of loud laughter. He *had* already known the rough outline of the story before he sent me out to discover it for myself.

"Yes, there was a great deal of duplicity!" he laughed, probably shaking his head at how little attention Westerners paid to any history except their own.

"In order to check Russian influence," the Dalai Lama continued, "I think the British wanted some kind of Manchu influence. I think the British deliberately remained vague in the treaties because that served their interest. They simply tried to keep out the Russian influence or control from Tibet. They were just using the name of Manchu suzerainty over Tibet as something useful for them. At the same time, if the Manchu were to come to Tibet, they would not be interested in the British being there, or interested in British concerns in India. So it was better to keep a vague status quo. No real Manchu control, no Russian influence, no British India control."

The British were as surprised as Lhasa was when the Manchus responded to Britain's invasion of Tibet by invading the country themselves. The Thirteenth Dalai Lama watched these events unfold from exile. By 1908 he'd left Mongolia, stopped at Bodhisaltva Manjushri's sacred Mt. Wutaishan and then traveled to Beijing as a last resort. The Russians would not help. He had been "deposed" by the Manchus. But because of the Manchu actions in eastern Tibet and stories of increased Manchu presence in Lhasa, going home wasn't an option. The Thirteenth Dalai Lama went to Beijing in a desperate attempt to establish some accord with the Manchus so he could return safely to Tibet. William Woodville Rockhill, the American consul to the Manchu Empire and the first American the Dalai Lama ever met, pointed out that the monk had received many pressing invitations from the Manchu emperor to visit Beijing but that he refused them, insisting he would go to Beijing in his own time.

In September 1908, the Thirteenth finally arrived in the capital, putting the same priest-patron interpretation on the relationship that the Fourteenth Dalai Lama uses today. "I went," the Thirteenth wrote, "because the Great Fifth Dalai Lama and the Manchu Emperor had made an agreement to help each other in the way that a priest and layman help each other." The Manchus were eager to install the Dalai Lama as a figurehead, in Lhasa, to give legitimacy to their rule. Western journalists in Beijing reported that the Manchus had stripped the Thirteenth of temporal authority, and no one thought he could recover it.

In Beijing, his greeting from the Manchu differed dramatically from that given to the Fifth Dalai Lama in 1653. The empress dowager Cixi demanded that the Dalai Lama kowtow before her puppet emperor Guangxu, whereas the Fifth had been received as an equal. When the Thirteenth refused, imperial officials spent two days hurriedly negotiating a compromise. In the end, the Dalai Lama agreed to bend to one knee, or genuflect (just as Britain's Lord McCartney did in 1792). Just days after this meeting, as the Dalai Lama continued to negotiate details about his return to Lhasa (during which he was given assurances about the continuation of his rule in Tibet), the emperor died, under suspicious circumstances, and the next day Cixi—having been the real power since 1875—also died. As the Dalai Lama performed rituals for the dead, in his role as priest to the Manchu emperors, the two-year-old "Last Emperor," Pu Yi, ascended to the throne. In fact, his uncle seized power and became the new regent. Even in this terminal chaos, the Manchus had shown that, from their viewpoint, the Dalai Lama was subordinate, and so was Tibet; their new title for him made their point succinctly: "loyal and submissive vice regent."

The Fourteenth Dalai Lama has a different interpretation, especially on the genuflection to the emperor. "The Tibetans by then viewed the emperor as an incarnation of the Bodhisattva Manjushri," he said. "So why not bend his knee to the emperor? His motivation was not out of submission to the ruler but because of religion. We Tibetans have always identified this as a priest-patron relationship, so the Dalai Lama came as a priest."

As I pressed the Fourteenth about the political relationship between the Lhasa and the Manchu emperor, he grew frustrated that I had yet to grasp how apolitical the Tibetans of that day were. "There is one very clear example. One day the high officials in the entourage of the Thirteenth Dalai Lama joined a luncheon party given by the dowager empress. They took pieces of dumplings from the meal home in their pockets and cherished them as something blessed. They considered that since these were from the table of the emperor, they were very sacred and they distributed them, like *prasad (sacrament blessed by the gods given to devotees at Hindu temples)*. So actually there was some devotion and faith."

Ironically, while Tibetans around the Thirteenth in Beijing held such conservative beliefs, the Dalai Lama himself was losing his traditional piety. In *Portrait of a Dalai Lama,* Charles Bell, who would meet the Thirteenth a few years later in India and become the first Westerner to spend much time with a Dalai Lama, wrote that the monk doubted whether the emperor "was really . . . an incarnation . . . of the Lord of Wisdom [the Bodhisattva Manjushri]." The Thirteenth's experiences were changing his way of thinking about Russia, Tibet, and the Manchu state, as well as his traditional religious beliefs.

Even as the Manchu dynasty shambled toward its extinction, it exerted pressure on the Dalai Lama and Tibet. The same Manchu magistrate who led the invasion of eastern Tibet in 1905, Chao Erh-feng, was sent, four years later, with an army of two thousand troops, toward Lhasa and ordered to continue the assimilation of Tibet, even as the Dalai Lama was allowed to return. Chao's troops were so barbaric en route to Lhasa that Tibetans soon dubbed him the Butcher.

"How did the troops handle themselves?" I asked.

"Oh, they were very bad. Very bad," the Dalai Lama replied. "Without discipline. They moved like any ancient army. Whatever they saw they took. They killed and raped, just like that. As soon as they arrived in Lhasa, they shot toward some officials, and I think one lay official was injured. So that night the Dalai Lama, who had also just arrived from China, hurriedly left Lhasa for India."

The monasteries and nobles of Tibet had not thought to fund the development of a modern army.

"At such occasions they would gather the local people," the Dalai Lama continued. "At that time, there was not some organized sort of Tibetan army. Traditionally, when some crisis happened, every able-bodied man would help. For example, some monks from Sera Monastery, or at least a certain number of monks, would be recruited as soldiers. So there was no permanent army."

"The Thirteenth Dalai Lama had just been to see the emperor in Beijing, and then immediately these barbarians came and started murdering people. He must have been quite upset," I said.

"Naturally," he replied.

"Because of his anger or frustration with the Manchu," I said, "perhaps he realized that the British weren't that bad."

"That is true," the Dalai Lama said. "Just after he returned to Lhasa, one month later, the Manchu and Chinese army reached Lhasa and the Dalai Lama hurriedly left for India."

Before he began his second exile, the Thirteenth Dalai Lama issued an appeal to Britain and the rest of the world. "We are very anxious and beg the Powers to intervene and cause the withdrawal of the Chinese troops." In an ominous shadow of events to come, not a single country intervened as Chinese troops, under Manchu command, occupied Lhasa and took steps to establish administrative control over Tibet, something no Chinese or Manchu government had ever accomplished.

As the Thirteenth Dalai Lama fled Lhasa, the Manchus, unlike the British, pursued him with troops. Once again, the Manchus legally "deposed" the Dalai Lama, as they had in 1904, though Tibetans paid no attention to the ruling. With the help of loyal retainers who stayed behind at a river and laid down restraining fire, and with a disinformation campaign provided by Tibetan commoners (the Thirteenth later laughed as he described how villagers sent the Manchus in all directions except the one he had taken), the Dalai Lama reached India safely.

By March 1910, the Thirteenth was living in exile in Darjeeling, India, anxiously awaiting news from home. London sent one of the few Tibetan-speaking Englishmen, Sir Charles Bell, the officer responsible for overseeing Sikkim, to deal with the Dalai Lama. On their first meeting, Bell wrote that Thupten Gyatso at first sight . . . did not look like a king. A squat figure, somewhat pockmarked (from smallpox), the features showed the plebeian origin of the farmer's son. But in Tibet things do not happen as elsewhere. Besides he was completely out of his setting. His kingdom gone, he was without the trappings of royalty. No palaces, no priesthood, not even the proper clothes; so sudden and rapid was his flight. Yet he was the god-king of Tibet, the Incarnation of Chen-re-zi himself. . . . Poor Dalai Lama! First a flight from the British expedition in 1904 resulting in five years' exile in Mongolia and China. And now a flight from the Chinese to the British, with apparently no hope of ever returning to his own country.

After their first meeting, Bell forwarded Thupten Gyatso's repeated requests for assistance to the viceroy in Calcutta. Bell and the Dalai Lama then settled into a pattern of frequent conversations as they awaited a reply. Bell told the Dalai Lama that British policy was to "give China practically complete control over Tibet, while insisting that we would not allow her to interfere in Nepal, Sikkim, and Bhutan," all of which were by then (de facto or otherwise) protectorates of Britain. The Dalai Lama responded that the Manchus, once in control of Tibet, would use the nation to threaten India or the British Himalayan protectorates. "It was not long," Bell wrote, "before his prediction was proved to be correct. As soon as they had consolidated their hold on Tibet, the Chinese Government made diplomatic claims over both Nepal and Bhutan as feudatory to China." Like Tibet, both Nepal and Bhutan had sent tribute to Manchu rulers in Beijing in the past, though the Manchus never administered the two states. By the same reasoning with which modern China claims Tibet, they were part of China. Ultimately neither the Qing, in its final years, nor China invaded either state.

Three months after the Dalai Lama's arrival in Darjeeling and his appeal for aid, and despite Manchu pugnacity in Tibet, Bell had the sad duty of telling him that the British "would not intervene between Tibet and China. When I delivered the message to him as we sat together in the quietude of his room, he was so surprised and distressed that for a minute or two he lost the power of speech. . . . His eyes . . . had the look of a man who is being hunted to his doom. Quickly, however, he cast it off, and discussed the matter calmly and clearly."

Bell met the Dalai Lama about fifty times during the latter's two and a quarter years of Indian exile. The Dalai Lama kept him abreast of his official requests to Nepal and to the king of England for aid but was astute enough not to tell Bell about his covert attempts to approach Czar Nicholas for aid through Dorjiev. Russia responded to Dorjiev's covert request by sending a diplomatic note to Britain. It was Bell's sad and uncomfortable duty to inform the Dalai Lama not only of Russia's latest rejection but of England's awareness of the request. According to Bell, "For a few moments he could say nothing. This was the only occasion on which I ever saw the Dalai Lama blush, but now he blushed deeply." The Dalai Lama explained to Bell that he approached the Russians only because the British had refused him and that he had done so covertly to spare Bell any embarrassment with his superiors. Bell was impressed with his political acumen. "Certainly one could not term the representative of Buddha slow-minded," he wrote.

The Dalai Lama taught Bell many of the insights that his successor has shared for this book. The Thirteenth said that "Tibet down through the centuries has almost always governed herself, though the Chinese histories will not tell you this" and that the Chinese "have always professed to regard the Tibetans as savages." He knew of Tibet's sack of the Tang capital and the equal ninth-century treaties between Tibet and the Tang. He complained how the Manchus distorted this history to say that the Tang had defeated Lhasa.

The Dalai Lama used secret couriers to guide forces in Tibet who continued to keep the Manchus on the defensive; during long discussions, the Thirteenth informed Bell of those efforts. The envoy noted how the Dalai Lama always spoke "in a low, quiet voice, varied at times with a cheerful laugh," even when describing betrayals that would have made grown men weep. Because Britain refused to sell them weapons, the Tibetans fought with their old matchlocks against a Manchu army supplied with armaments from Europe. The Dalai Lama continued his polite conversations with Bell, who he knew was only a messenger; more important, this Tibetan-speaking Englishman was one of his only advocates he knew in a dark time.

It was in India, under Bell's guidance, that the Dalai Lama learned about Western techniques of government. He was interested in the details of how London's administration governed the vast reaches of the Indian subcontinent, through a marvelous system of rails, schools, post offices, bureaucrats, and the many cantonments for British troops. I asked the Fourteenth how his predecessor's years in India affected him, Tenzin Gyatso.

"When I was young," he replied, "living in the Potala, and I first heard of it, I always thought that he must have had a great time. You see, for me, when I was young, going to India meant having a good time, and going on pilgrimage to Buddhist holy places. One of my attendants was also a member of the Kashag *(the Tibetan cabinet)*, and he used to tell me about his own experiences there when he was sent by the Tibetan government. He would tell me how big Calcutta was, and how big Howrah Bridge was. He talked about how when he traveled over the Howrah Bridge on a train, he would count the electric poles. He said that within the completion of one mantra, he would see another pole. And then of course what was of most interest to me was his story about visiting the Calcutta zoo and the many animals there. I had the impression that India was huge. I thought, how wonderful, and I was hoping to go myself."

In fact, the Thirteenth also visited the zoo in Calcutta and exhibited all the glee that the Fourteenth imagined in his childhood dreams. In particular, while staying at Hastings House, the great rambling mansion that served as the viceroy of India's state guesthouse, the Thirteenth Dalai Lama spoke for the first time on a telephone. Bell recounts that the Dalai Lama liked the device so much that he took every excuse to call him and ended every conversation with "a gurgle of laughter."

Despite such hospitality, British policy toward Tibet and the Thirteenth Dalai Lama in exile remained noncommittal for several years, until 1911. "My impression," the Fourteenth Dalai Lama said, "was that, in the beginning, the British government seemed to pay not much attention to him and they stayed neutral. So he was something like a guest. Just an ordinary person who came from Tibet and stayed in India, though he carried on some political activities in Tibet. In the beginning, it remained very low key, but then the situation greatly changed within Tibet and China. Then I think the British paid more attention to him."

It was the Chinese overthrow of the Manchu empire in 1911 that caused a shift in British attitudes. Since the invasion of Central Tibet the year before, London had encountered a number of problems with the Manchu government in Tibet. The Manchu raised questions about the exact border with India, claimed sovereignty over Nepal and Bhutan, and stirred up the tribes along the border against the British. When the Manchu Empire collapsed and a nation dominated by the Chinese rather than the Manchu emerged, London began to reconsider its policy of neutrality. Following guidance from the Thirteenth Dalai Lama in exile, sent via a stream of secret couriers, Tibetans took advantage of fighting between the Manchu and the Chinese in their country and attacked the occupiers. In a quick succession of events, Chinese soldiers in Tibet attacked their Manchu officers, and the Tibetans defeated the Chinese and the Manchus as the empire collapsed. Without resupply and guidance from China, which chaos precluded, the Manchus and the Chinese in Tibet were no threat. In June 1912, the Thirteenth Dalai Lama proclaimed Tibet's complete independence, and Tibetan forces—a volunteer army without much training, from every village and monastery—drove the Manchu forces in eastern Tibet back as far as the Mekong River. That autumn the remaining Chinese and Manchu, who had all surrendered, were marched out of the country to India. Finally, in January 1913, the Dalai Lama returned to Lhasa after eight years of exile.

The Mongols also reacted to the collapse of the Manchu Empire by declaring independence in 1912. With the fall of the Manchu state, neither the Tibetans nor the Mongols had any desire to join the Chinese Republic, which slowly emerged in the areas of the defunct empire where ethnic Chinese were the majority population. Since Mongols and Tibetans had never seen themselves as Chinese, the idea seemed absurd.

"I feel that once the Manchu emperor was overthrown and China became a republic," the Dalai Lama said, "the very nature of the old relationship between Tibet and the Manchus was no longer valid. So there was no reason to allow Manchu and Chinese forces in Tibet. All were expelled. As soon as the Manchu emperor was overthrown, Tibetans felt they were free of the old relationship. Since there was no more spiritual relationship, they expelled all these forces from Tibet. So long as the

Manchu emperor was there, there was still some control from the Manchus. We accepted this, because that was part of the patron-priest relationship. Once there was an attempt to change the very nature of the relationship, from a spiritual to a political one, then Tibetans were not willing to accept it."

"But the Chinese," I said "claimed that Tibet was part of the Chinese Republic, didn't they? They claimed that all the lands which had belonged to the Manchu Empire were now part of the new ethnic Chinese state."

"Yes, true," he said.

"In fact, after the Thirteenth Dalai Lama returned to Lhasa," I continued, "the government of the republic sent him a letter saying that his titles had been restored. They also asked him to join the Chinese Republic, an odd gesture, since China's claim is based on Tibet's already being part of China. The Thirteenth Dalai Lama replied, saying that he had not asked for any Chinese titles and that Tibet was now an independent nation."

"Yes, he did," the Dalai Lama replied. "The Dalai Lama declined to accept the Chinese title. He said, 'I don't want any titles from the Chinese, and you take care of your country. Don't worry about us.'"

"Today, Mongolia is an independent nation," I said, "but its legal basis for independence from China is no different from Tibet's. It separated from the Manchu Empire at the same time as Tibet did, for the same reasons. If China has some legal claim over Tibet, then it has that same legal claim over Mongolia. If history proves that Tibet is part of China, then that same history proves that Korea, North Vietnam, Thailand, Bhutan, and Nepal are also part of China. The argument is similar or identical in all cases but was applied only in the case of Tibet."

"True, very true," the Dalai Lama said with cheerful equanimity. "And then culturally, racially, linguistically, Tibet is completely different from the Chinese. Whereas China's links with the Vietnamese, or the Koreans, are much more solid. They have many connections. All of their classical texts are in Chinese. But that was never the case in Tibet. Tibet, right from the beginning, was never like this. None of our ancient records are in Chinese."

"The root of this," I said, "is when the Chinese leaders of the revolution of 1911, like Sun Yat-sen, decided the only way they could claim all the land that the Manchus had conquered as Chinese was if they could show that history proved all the people of the Manchu Empire were really, somehow, Chinese. But that change came late in the revolution. At first, Sun Yat-sen considered the Chinese revolt against the Manchus a revolt of one race against another."

"You must study that!" the Dalai Lama exclaimed. "But yes, Sun Yat-sen considered the Manchus as foreigners. That is true."

After Sun Yat-sen, the founder of modern China, overthrew the Manchus and established the Chinese Republic, he went in procession with his cabinet to the tomb of Emperor Yongle, the first emperor of the Ming dynasty (1368–1644). As the first Chinese leader of a Chinese state since the 1644 Manchu conquest, when the Ming were overthrown, Sun Yat-sen went to speak to his ancestors. After offering a sacrifice to them in the Confucian way, he addressed them as though they were still living:

> The policy of the Manchus has been one of . . . unyielding tyranny. . . . Actuated by a desire for the perpetual subjugation of the Chinese . . . the Manchus have governed the country to the lasting injury and detriment of the people. . . . The Chinese race of today . . . has at last restored the government to the Chinese people. . . . Your people have come here to-day to inform your Majesty of the final victory.

When I reported this to the Dalai Lama, I asked him if he had read how Mao Tse-tung also considered the Manchus as foreigners when he was a young boy, in 1911.

"I have not heard," he said.

"In Edgar Snow's book *Red Star over China,* Mao describes what he felt when he cut off the Manchu pigtail that all Chinese were forced to wear, on pain of death. He cut it off to show his freedom from Manchu oppression."

"He cut if off?" the Dalai Lama asked.

"Yes. Chinese all over China showed that they were no longer under Manchu domination by cutting off their pigtails, or queue, during the 1911 revolution. They had been forced to wear this Manchu hairstyle since 1644."

Like all Chinese, Mao knew that the 1911 revolution was an uprising against the Manchu. In Snow's book, Mao described, after a pitched battle, seeing "the Han flag raised. . . . It was a white banner with the character Han in it." *Han* is the modern word for Chinese. The revolution flew the flag with just one word on it: *Chinese!* That flag struck terror into all Manchus, since the Chinese had massacred them by the thousands during the revolution, just as they had during the Taiping Rebellion, in the nineteenth century.

For much of this period, from 1911 to the foundation of the People's Republic of China, in 1949, Manchus who lived in China did so by hiding their ethnic identity and by teaching their children the native language at home, in secret. In 1911, the extermination, or ethnic cleansing, of Manchus was so common that thousands fled back to Manchuria, their homeland, and talked about re-creating it as an ethnic state, separate from China. The fact that the Manchus were not Chinese, and thus Tibet's dealings with the Manchu Empire set no precedent for Tibetan relations with Beijing, is a distinction that the Dalai Lama is acutely aware of but one that Chinese scholars refuse to make. To Chinese historians, the Manchus, like the Tibetans and the Mongols, are Chinese of ethnic minority descent. Today, however, with the newly translated Manchu archives available covering the period from 1644 to 1911, scholars studying Chinese history are no longer willing to consider "Manchu" or "Qing" as synonymous with "China."

Scholars today are beginning to understand what Mongols and Tibetans knew in 1911. When the Manchus were overthrown, Mongols, Tibetans, and Chinese naturally sought independence—a horrifying development for the Chinese. In 1912, just a year after the Tibetan and Mongol revolutions and declarations of independence, Sun Yat-sen declared that the Republic of China was now a multiethnic state composed of Manchus, Mongols, Tibetans, Han, and Uighur (the majority ethnic group of Xinjiang Province). His declarations at the Ming tombs, extolling the Chinese and condemning the Manchu, were cast aside. Promoting a diverse population was the only way that Beijing could claim to have inherited the right to rule China despite the fact that ethnic groups who did not acknowledge this claim inhabited 60 percent of its territory. The People's Republic ultimately enforced most of the territorial claims, first made by Sun Yat-sen, through invasion (except of Outer Mongolia) and developed a vision of history, still taught in schools, to rationalize them.

For Chinese ethnic nationalists, Tibetan independence in 1912 was a farce, stage-managed by British imperialists, just as Mongolian independence was managed by the Russians (the only difference being that Moscow succeeded whereas London failed). For the Mongols and the Tibetans, independence was essential because of the many brutal attempts the Chinese had made to assimilate them culturally and ethnically, particularly during the final decades of the Manchu Empire. A union with China was seen as a move toward cultural and ethnic extermination.

Unfortunately, the 1911 revolution was not an end to conflict in China. It was just the beginning of decades of chaos and civil war, followed by the Japanese invasion and World War II, and then a return to civil war, during which there was no central state. As the Chinese were unable even to unify and govern their own people, for half a century, they certainly lacked the ability to subjugate Mongolia or Tibet. Thus the Thirteenth Dalai Lama's declaration of independence, in 1912, denied on paper by the ever-changing Chinese governments, stood as a reality until the Chinese invasion of Tibet in 1950.

From his return to Lhasa in 1913 until his death in 1933, the Dalai Lama worked for the independence of Tibet with little respite. In his remaining years, he focused on reforming the government, defending the nation, and dealing with elements in Tibetan society that resisted these efforts.

"I think overall he saw that the way Tibet was governed was backward," the Fourteenth Dalai Lama said, "so there was a need for modernization. That was the main thing. So he worked for modernization in Tibet. He started the postal system, and he did many things like that. And one aspect of modernization that he worked for was with the military in Tibet."

The people of Lhasa had a firsthand taste of what it meant to lack an army to defend them when the Chinese troops in the city revolted against the Manchu. For months, Tibetans fought the Chinese, and the fighting split the capital into two zones, one Chinese, one Tibetan. Soldiers sandbagged houses and dug trenches and tunnels; the ancient holy city resounded to the constant barrage of gunfire and explosions. At one point, the Chinese attacked Sera Monastery. The conflict, however, was not always on ethnic grounds. There were, for example, Chinese monks who fought for the Tibetans, and monks from eastern Tibet who fought for the Chinese, though such defectors were not crucial to the outcome.

"These Tibetan monks," the Dalai Lama said, "actually came from near the border with China, so mentally they were close with the Chinese. Because of this, when they would use their muzzle gun, they would pretend to turn it against the Chinese. But when the actual shooting began, they turned it against the Tibetans."

"And what did the Thirteenth Dalai Lama do to them when he returned?" I asked.

"He put restrictions," he said, "but others will know the details."

In fact, there were numerous pro-Chinese Tibetan officials. Tibetan forces arrested and executed many of them, including two members of the Tibetan cabinet, or Kashag, before the Dalai Lama returned to Lhasa. The Tibetans also disbanded at least one monastery after the Dalai Lama's return, and other monasteries restricted the admission of monks from eastern Tibet.

Curious about the idea of fighting monks, I asked, "So some monks fought in the war against the Chinese?"

"Monks from Drepung didn't have to fight," the Dalai Lama said, "since most of the fighting in Lhasa was done by Sera monks."

"When monks must fight, aren't they violating the *Vinaya*?" I asked.

"They have to offer their vows back to their monastery, and then start fighting," the Dalai Lama explained. "They do not fight with their monk's robes on. You cannot fight while you are a monk."

"After the fighting," I asked, "they then take back their vows as a monk?"

"Yes, it's OK, if it's properly done," he said. "They must disrobe before, and that must be done by going to a teacher and offering the monk's vow back. Of course, murder is still a sin. But at least you are not transgressing the fundamental precept of the monk, because you are offering the vows back. So he or she would become like a layperson, though of course killing is still sinful. But there are degrees; it depends upon your motivation. If one is killing to defend oneself, or others, or if one is killing for profit, those are different."

"After all his years of exile," I said, "after the war in Tibet to expel the Chinese, at last the Dalai Lama returns to Lhasa and declares independence. What is his main focus then?"

"Right after he took power, he began many changes," the Dalai Lama replied. "By the time he returned from India, he had matured and, most important, he had traveled in China and also India. He had experienced the effect of having a weak Tibetan government. So all of these experiences had an impact. It is very clear that he really started the modernization of Tibet. The death sentence was abolished as a punishment, and also the practice of cutting off the hands of a criminal. He opened a mint to make coins and money. He also talked about starting more representation in government, for the people of Tibet. He started a police force and the bodyguards for the Dalai Lama, and hydroelectricity in Lhasa. He opened a school in Tibet, in the Western style. He sent four boys to England to be trained at school there. And a fifth man, Lungshar, went with them, and he also learned a lot in England."

Lungshar Dorje Tsegyal was from an old aristocratic family, which had served the Fifth Dalai Lama. He was more than just a chaperone when he accompanied the four students to Britain in 1912. The Dalai Lama made him an ambassador-at-large. Lungshar studied Western democratic history and institutions, particularly the replacement, by elected governments, of hereditary monarchy throughout Europe. London was adamant that Tibet should not have any direct dealings with foreign countries, but both the Dalai Lama and Lungshar knew that it was in Tibet's best interests to cultivate as many foreign alliances as possible, just in case relations with Britain and China went badly. Lungshar traveled in six European countries, besides England, despite British objections. By the time he returned to Tibet, in 1914, he was convinced that modernization and reform were critical if the country was to survive. Lungshar was a crucial supporter of the Dalai Lama's modernization program.

"There were many aspects to the modernization campaign. The Thirteenth Dalai Lama started exams for high monk officials in the monasteries, didn't he?" I asked.

"Yes, he made monk officials start to take exams," the Dalai Lama said, "and monks who failed he expelled. He was very tough on the officials in government and in the monasteries. So I feel that is good—toward those high people you must be extra tough, though he was very gentle with the common people. And he even had a car in Lhasa, I think, with a driver. But he never learned to read and write English himself."

"And as you said earlier, one aspect of these reforms was the Tibetan army," I remarked.

"Yes," the Dalai Lama replied, "he also organized the military forces. I think at first he adopted the Russian model and some exercises were run by the Mongolian trainers according to the Russian style. Then one Japanese man came to teach the Tibetan army. He imported foreign military experience from different places. And then later, as he grew older and relations with the British grew, the Tibetan army followed the British model. Not only did they follow British training methods, but the British taught them the English national anthem for the Tibetan army band." The Dalai Lama laughed at the thought. "Silly."

"Yes, I have spoken with witnesses," I answered, "who saw the Tibetan army, in 1950, and they had a brass band that still played "God Save the Queen," though the Tibetans then did not know what it meant. Anyway, in this fashion the British sometimes gave the appearance of helping the Dalai Lama in this effort. They helped him to create his army."

"They supplied weapons to Tibet, sometimes," the Dalai Lama noted.

"But at the same time," I said, "they were selling weapons to the Chinese, and were always telling the Tibetan government to recognize Chinese suzerainty, even when Tibet was completely independent. In fact, they convinced the Tibetans to sign a treaty that recognized Chinese suzerainty over Tibet—the Simla Treaty of 1914—except the Chinese refused to sign it, so it never went fully into effect. Despite that, the British still used that treaty to negotiate a new border between India and Tibet, which ceded territory to colonial India that had been Tibet's. The British seemed to be using the Tibetans, even as they sometimes helped them."

"Yes," he said, "as I told you, there was a great deal of duplicity. At the same time during all of this, the Thirteenth Dalai Lama tried to copy some of the things he had seen in other countries. They built military headquarters, where the army and the bodyguards had their grounds, and he usually received foreign representatives there."

"You do not seem to think much of the rituals in the military," I observed.

"It's silly," the Dalai Lama said. "Actually, I really, as you know, I like informality, and the military formality is too much. It is rubbish. The Chinese are very into it, and it is silly."

"This process of modernization. Did everyone support what the Thirteenth Dalai Lama was doing?" I asked.

"A few were against him," the Dalai Lama responded. "A few were very much against him. There was a person serving in the Norbulingka who behaved very badly and was dismissed. Also, there was opposition when the Thirteenth Dalai Lama carried out some reforms with the high lamas. Some who were not able to keep the purity of the *Vinaya* were expelled. One of the expelled lamas, much later, was very much against the Dalai Lama."

"These high lamas and monk officials who were expelled," I asked, "were unable to remain celibate, or broke the *Vinaya* in ways like that?"

"Yes," the Dalai Lama said, "and later my junior tutor knew one of these men, and he told me that later one of the expelled monks always complained about the Dalai Lama. He said the Dalai Lama was not a human being but the devil."

"So there was real opposition to the modernization he began?" I inquired.

"Yes, correct," the Dalai Lama replied, nodding.

From the start, the Dalai Lama faced immense opposition to his plan to build a modern army. The army had some early success. It pushed the Chinese in eastern Tibet back. To maintain the fighting force that won that victory, and to improve the military, however, required investment.

The only way the Thirteenth Dalai Lama could modernize the army was to increase taxes on the estates of the largest monasteries and nobles. He aroused strong opposition when he suggested that he might remove the tax-free estates of some of the monks and noble lords. Scholars debate the exact number of people who were serfs, but one estimate says that a single monastery in Lhasa—Drepung—controlled 185 estates with 20,000 serfs (and peasants), 300 pastures, and 16,000 nomads herding animals. The tax income from these holdings, actually paid in barley and butter, was the primary means of support for the 10,000 monks at Drepung. These estates fed the monks when they performed religious services. Most Tibetans felt that these rituals were essential for the survival of the nation. Rather than the state paying for these services directly, it had given the monastery the right to tax a certain percentage of produce. Any new tax on these estates would be taken from the monks and, by extension, the religious services they carried out. The tax burden was already so heavy that the peasants and serfs could not bear another increase. Thus the attempt to create a modern army incurred the wrath of vast numbers of monks, the most conservative element in society, by attacking their revenue base. Monks may have been up to 30 percent of the population at the time.

Lungshar became a lightning rod for the Dalai Lama's conflicts with those who resisted the creation of a modern army. The Thirteenth appointed Lungshar to a position in government in which he could help generate income for the army, and soon Lungshar began to force some of Tibet's largest landholders, both monastic and aristocratic, to pay increased taxes. He was successful in his work at first—in 1929, the Dalai Lama appointed him commander in chief, and Lungshar increased the size of the army and pay for the troops—but his arrogance and disdain for the conservative monastic faction ultimately caused his fall from power. One of the most frightening things, for the monks, was that Lungshar dressed Tibetan soldiers and officers in British-style uniforms. That appearance alone gave ammunition to monks who said the British were enemies of the Dharma and that reformers would destroy Tibet.

The Thirteenth Dalai Lama's conflict with conservative segments of society increased dramatically when he tried to tax the estates of the Ninth

Panchen Lama, in Shigatse. The Panchen Lamas are one of the most spiritually respected lineages in Tibet: for Gelugpa, the Panchen Lama is second only to the Dalai Lama. Since the seventeenth century, Panchen Lamas
have been involved in the search for a new Dalai Lama, while Dalai Lamas
help to recognize a new Panchen Lama incarnate. Despite this spiritual
link—both are Bodhisattvas who have forgone nirvana to guide others
to enlightenment—the two lineages historically have been at political odds,
if only because Panchen Lamas had no official political position, whereas
Dalai Lamas were rulers of Tibet.

When the Dalai Lama asked that the Panchen Lama provide 25 percent
of the tax base required for building the army, trouble erupted at once. The
Panchen Lamas cultivated their independence from Lhasa and jealously
guarded their status and tax base. Both the British and the Manchu officials,
at different times, tried to manipulate the political animosity between the
Panchen Lamas and the Dalai Lamas for their own political ends. During
the two years the Thirteenth Dalai Lama was in India, the Manchus invited
the Panchen Lama to Lhasa, and while he refused to allow the Manchu to
set him up as the Dalai Lama's replacement, he moved into the Dalai Lama's
summer palace, the Norbulingka, and attended some ceremonies with
Manchu officials.

"The relation between the Panchen Lama and the Thirteenth Dalai
Lama," the Dalai Lama told me, "on an official level was difficult and negative, but in private there was a deep, special spiritual connection. There
were many examples of private communication between them that make
this clear, so if we say that their relationship is totally negative, that is a
big mistake."

"Nevertheless, there were problems about the funding for the army,"
I noted.

"Yes," the Dalai Lama agreed. "It began in 1908, when the Dalai Lama
was in India. There was at least a belief, a saying—and I actually saw some
pictures that prove it—that the Dalai Lama's throne was pushed aside and
the Panchen Lama's throne was in its place in the Norbulingka. Perhaps.
Because of these events, many Tibetan officials and many in the public
had hurt feelings."

"And how did that affect the funding for the army?" I asked.

"As a consequence," the Dalai Lama responded, "during the 1920s, Commander in Chief Lungshar and one high monk official in charge with him, Lobsang Tenkyong. These two were responsible for increasing the tax for the army. To do that, they put a rather heavy tax on Tashilunpo Monastery *(headed by the Panchen Lama)*, to fund the expansion of the army. The Panchen Lama appealed this to the Dalai Lama a few times, and the Dalai Lama refused his request to lower the tax. Because of that, the Panchen Lama escaped and went to China."

The event gave them leverage within Tibetan affairs and provided an opportunity to demonstrate to foreigners that the Tibetans were only a collective of feuding principalities who needed China to reign over them. So even though an army was being created—modernization of training and equipment was ongoing, and ten thousand troops had been hired—ultimately the search for funding caused a major dispute between the Dalai Lama, the Panchen Lama, and the conservative monks who saw no need for an army. After the Panchen Lama fled, the resulting uproar and public debate forced the Thirteenth Dalai Lama to back down on any new taxes.

"It's clear," I said, "that the Dalai Lama was forced to gut the heart of his reform program. He demoted all the promodernization officers in government. He shut down the English school, which had been set up in Tibet to offer some alternative to monastic education. Eventually, despite the success of the army fighting the Chinese in eastern Tibet, monks argued that the soldiers were a threat to Buddhism, to the Dalai Lama, and to the authority of the monasteries in Tibet. Tibet lost its best chance to create a modern state and to survive in the modern world."

The Dalai Lama listened to me and then said, in a quiet voice, "There are elements of truth to these statements. His Holiness *(the Thirteenth Dalai Lama)* mentioned very clearly that among officials and even among the public, there was a tendency to follow the traditional path, the way things were done in the past. And whenever people did something other than the traditional way, then there was opposition. *Ngarlam,* we say, in Tibetan *(following the traditional way)*. My opinion is that all this came from ignorance and carelessness and foolishness, and that it was not necessarily a smart political campaign led by conservative forces in government, with them making some plan, which caused this."

"It wasn't just the officials who saw no need for the army?" I asked.

"I think," the Dalai Lama replied, "when some old monks or some lama saw some of the modernization, they saw it as British, and they sincerely felt the British were the enemy of the Dharma. They saw modernization as atheism. And perhaps we can make one criticism of the Thirteenth Dalai Lama. After all, he was in power and saw the necessity of change. Then some resistance came, and he should have resisted this and carried forward with his plan, because in the end the truth would prevail. He should have taken his reasons to the public and they would have understood. But he did not, and that is his mistake. So yes, there is some criticism."

I was surprised at how readily he challenged the attitudes of the religious conservatives. "There was a great deal of conservative ignorance that he had to deal with," I said.

He looked at me in frustration. Apparently, the term "conservative ignorance" was a gross understatement.

"I'll give you another example," he said. "This problem did not end in 1920. As late as 1950, when the Chinese were already entering eastern Tibet, there was an official in Lhasa, Phuntsong Tashi, whose duty it was to listen to the Chinese radio from Beijing, and from time to time he would make a report to the Regents Office. This is just before I came to power. One day he carefully mentioned the danger of the Chinese invasion. Then Nye-droen (the Lord Chamberlain) comforted him by saying, 'You do not need to worry about that at all, because we are a place of high lamas and gods and deities, and we don't have to worry about the Chinese army.'" I was shocked at the vehemence in the Dalai Lama's voice. "This is stupid," he concluded. "This is just blind faith and ignorance."

In Lhasa one sunny autumn afternoon, I drove past tawdry Chinese houses of prostitution. Chinese girls from Sichuan Province who cannot find jobs back in Chengdu languished indolently in empty shop fronts. I drove on past the television station with its blue plate glass mirror walls, which is as modern as what you'd find in Europe or Japan. From the speeding taxi I watched fractured reflections of the Potala, as they jerked back and forth on its mirrored glass surface. At the Norbulingka, the summer palace since at least the Seventh Dalai Lama, my Chinese cabdriver stopped in front of a long white wall that encircled the vast compound at the edge of Lhasa. When the Chinese women at the front of the Norbulingka asked for a ticket, I pretended not to understand her and just walked on through the massive, brightly painted gate into the parkland within.

I strolled casually toward the Chensalingka, a whitewashed stone building, commissioned by the Thirteenth Dalai Lama in the last decades of his life, in the far western side of the walled parkland. Palace is too grand a word for the Chensalingka, which is no larger than many modern homes in Europe or North America. I looked at my watch—I was early—and then detoured down a path lined with tall poplars. Their leaves had just changed color; they were golden in the afternoon light, rattling on the gust of an end-of-summer breeze. Beside one of the whitewashed stone houses that dot the parkland, I found the Thirteenth Dalai Lama's baby Austin in ruins, with weeds growing up through the automobile's rusty motor.

Exactly at three in the afternoon I met a Chinese gentleman (who must remain anonymous, so he will not be imprisoned), and I paid him the agreed-upon price of five hundred dollars in cash. He led me to a small door in the back of the private quarters of the Thirteenth and unlocked it. As we walked up a flight of stairs, I could hear a group of tourists being escorted into the ground floor below us to see the state palanquins that had been used by the Fourteenth Dalai Lama. The ground floor of the Chensalingka is now a museum, but the upstairs, which had been part of the Thirteenth Dalai Lama's living quarters, remains closed to the public. I had heard that the rooms housed a few murals that might interest the Fourteenth Dalai Lama, so I bribed my way into the building with my cameras on my back, prepared to photograph them.

The five rooms were empty. Yellow silk curtains over all the windows cast a golden tint across the polished wood floors, which had once been covered in layers of ancient carpets. They were looted and taken to China long ago. The bare altars likewise had been stripped of statues. More important, all of the Thirteenth's records and ancient documents that had been stored there are also gone, unlikely ever to be seen again. The Chinese gentleman to whom I paid my five hundred dollars took me into the main room and pointed at his watch. I had two hours. He then left, and I could soon smell the crisp scent of tobacco as he sat on the stoop outside and smoked. I got out my cameras, set up the tripod, wired up my flashes, and began to photograph the murals on the walls.

I recognized this room as the place where the Thirteenth Dalai Lama had a black-and-white portrait of himself taken during the last years of his life, because the murals on the wall had appeared in the background of the photograph. The fine religious murals on most of the walls were not what I was in search of. Then, in one small room, I found a large map—an actual mural of the Norbulingka during the time of the Thirteenth Dalai Lama. There was the white outer wall, intact around the entire compound on the western outskirts of Lhasa. There was the Potala in the distance, and, beyond that, Lhasa. It was a three-foot by six-foot painted map. For me, it was a treasure because of the historic details that it preserved about Lhasa in the early twentieth century.

In one corner of the mural map, I found a drawing of the Tibetan army troops. This was probably the only painting in Tibet of the army at its quarters in the Norbulingka. The soldiers were captured in a lot of different activities: raising themselves on a chin-up bar, playing soccer, marching in ranks, doing target practice with their British Enfield .202 rifles. The soldiers' legs were wrapped in old-fashioned green leggings, used by British soldiers in World War I and in colonial India. They wore green uniforms, and the officers had British solar toppees on their heads, a bizarre sign of office that would have made sense to a British colonial officer of Queen Victoria. Finally, there was the Thirteenth Dalai Lama himself, standing in the courtyard of the Chensalingka, the very building I was in. Dressed in the Mongolian robes he favored, he was greeting the first in a long line of people who had come to receive his blessings. Nearby, several of his beloved Tibetan mastiffs lunged at their chains.

In the last years of his life, he seemed to have spent more and more time in his walled compound at the Norbulingka. He had his dogs, his flowers, and frequent audiences with people from all over Tibet who came to consult with him about the government or to seek his spiritual blessing. Despite these pressures, he took the time for a three-year, three-month, three-day meditation retreat: he locked himself up in the Norbulingka and remained in absolute isolation. Judging from photographs, he seemed to age quickly in the last years of his life. The few hundred troops who lived with him inside his compound—in barracks within the vast parklands— were not affected by the gutting of his reforms that might have saved Tibet. In his final years, he did his best to control the factions that seemed intent upon destroying the nation. But the factionalism grew intense and the British duplicity seemed endless. The complexities of the period sprang to life for me as I photographed the painted map in the Thirteenth Dalai Lama's rooms in Lhasa.

Later, when I traveled to India and showed the Fourteenth Dalai Lama photographs of the painted map, he knew exactly where it was and talked about each of the buildings in the mural.

"What is this building here?" I asked him as I pointed to the photograph.

"During the construction of this one," the Dalai Lama said, "the Kelsang Phodrang, the Dalai Lama put a restriction on the smoking of tobacco. The Thirteenth Dalai Lama would visit the construction site of that building, and one day he came up behind the wall and he heard one worker say loudly, 'That tobacco is very useful when you are hungry. And when you are thirsty it fills your mouth. But now the Thirteenth Dalai Lama has put this restriction, and what is the benefit of that?'" The Fourteenth Dalai Lama laughed and said, "The Thirteenth Dalai Lama heard this and quietly left."

"Did he lift the restrictions?" I asked.

"No," the Dalai Lama replied. "What I am saying is that when poor people were making such complaints, he wouldn't interfere with them. In the same period when they were constructing the wide wall around the Norbulingka, some Lhasa people *(a father and son)* made a donation of stones for the white wall. I knew both the father and the son, later. The father was a monk in the Namgyal Monastery *(located in the Potala)*, and when I met him, he was eighty or eighty-four, but still very physically fit.

When that wall was built, that old father went with a few stones on his mule to the Norbulingka. There, at the construction site, the mule started going off in another direction after he unloaded the stones. He suddenly saw one person in Mongolian dress carrying a cane. He yelled, 'Would you just stop that mule?' and the man used his cane to stop the mule. Later, he realized that the man in Mongolian dress was the Thirteenth Dalai Lama. So you see, his relations with lay people were very easy. With officials and higher monks he was stricter, but with ordinary monks and people he had very close feeling and contact, and I think that is something good."

"What else makes you think the Tibetan people had such a close relationship with him?" I asked.

"When the Potala was whitewashed," the Dalai Lama said, as he pointed to the photograph of the mural I had shot in Lhasa, "then people from Shol *(the town at its base)* came to work. It was quite dangerous work. One day a lady was holding on, up high, and she slipped. She was just above a place with a ten-story drop, and the copper utensil she was using to throw the whitewash slipped from her hand. It made a loud noise when it hit. And she also slipped, but fortunately she was able to sit down there safely. And one of my bodyguards, who was very old, told me that at the moment when that lady slipped, she shouted 'Thupten Gyatso!'— the name of the Thirteenth Dalai Lama. So that means that at the moment when she felt hopeless, her first reaction was to yell out his name. So this shows great devotion. The people believed in their heart."

That afternoon in Lhasa as I photographed the painted map, time went by quickly, and suddenly late afternoon light was streaking through the windows. The Chinese gentleman returned, insistent that we leave. Instead of turning toward the gate when we reached the ground floor, however, he took me to a tiny, nondescript one-room house next door. It was difficult to understand why he led me here, because he was so nervous and agitated as we approached a giant black howling mastiff, close by the building, pawing at the ground and clacking his teeth. The dog wore a Tibetan collar—thick red wool—around its neck, and its cinnamon markings stood out against its jet-black coat. The Chinese man clearly wanted to show me one more room, for a price, but we had to slip by the animal to do so. As I watched my guide gingerly edge by the howling dog—kept just out of reach by its chain—I remembered what the Fourteenth Dalai Lama had told me, during one of my earlier meetings with him, about mastiffs and his predecessor.

"Ever since the Dalai Lama returned from India," he said, "his life was very active. He wrote a lot and responded a lot to requests in his own handwriting, even for government business. Then he also spent time out in the garden, and he also looked after his large dogs. He would feed them at least once a week with his own hands. When the Dalai Lama would feed these dogs—some were offered by the people, and often they were very fierce mastiffs and there would be new ones, wild and untrained—but no matter how fierce or new they were, when the Dalai Lama fed them, they would become obedient, friendly, and humble."

This mastiff was not going to become obedient and friendly. I worried that it was going to break its leash. My guide had the same fear, so without further attempts to tell me what was inside, he flicked his cigarette away, pulled out a key, and led me into a barely illuminated room. Again, yellow silk covered the windows and amazing murals covered the walls, from floor to ceiling. Once I realized I was in the room the Dalai Lama had died in, I paid the man the extra money.

There was only one main room, and as I set up to photograph the murals, my guide sat down on an empty wooden box in the tiny antechamber and watched. A fine mural of gods and titans fighting over the tree of immortality was in one corner of the room, and its delicate lines and brilliant gold leaf sparkled each time I triggered the flash. In another mural rings of snowcapped peaks encircled and hid the kingdom of Shambhala, from which armies of warriors marched forth headed into a great battle with strange machines, in the global war that the Kalachakra Tantra predicts will erupt in the coming centuries. The murals were too strange to absorb in the little time I had; what was more, I felt like an intruder, knowing that the Thirteenth Dalai Lama had died here. When I finished shooting pictures, I looked out the windows at the trees. The sweet chirping of house sparrows sitting in the eaves of the building echoed in the empty room. I felt the years that had passed since his death and wondered again about the master plan his successor believed in.

"I know that you say the master plan for the Thirteenth Dalai Lama failed in the end," I said when we met in India to discuss the murals, "but tell me what you think the master plan for his life was?"

"I feel," he began, "that in the spiritual field, there was improvement in Tibet during his life, because of the exams he started and the way he removed monks who were not pure. And on the temporal side, according to the last testament that he left, before he died, he wanted to modernize. You see I disagree, but he mentioned that with China and India, and our small neighbors, we should have military forces to challenge, and he built some military factories. So these are the ways he improved temporal power. He thought about self-defense, including the military power of the Tibetan nation. And then he thought of the border that had not been finalized between Tibet and China. There was a temporary agreement, and he wanted to finalize that. Then obviously he had a keen desire to establish relations with Russia, and also I think he was a little skeptical toward England because of its invasion."

"But it never worked," I said. "The Russians refused him, the British in the end were not selling him the weapons he needed to keep the army strong enough, and even Tibetans would not allow him to build the army he felt Tibet needed to survive. Still you say that there was a master plan trying to work again during the Thirteenth and the Fourteenth Dalai Lamas."

"Not the Fourteenth," he said at once, "just for the Thirteenth. Yes, at the time of the Thirteenth there was a master plan. Then just a few years before his death, after that plan had not worked, he planned his death, he planned to send me, the great Fourteenth Dalai Lama." He laughed merrily at this idea, puffing up his face and thrusting out his whole body. "Or the stupid Fourteenth Dalai Lama. The Fourteenth Dalai Lama himself has nothing to do with the master plan. I am just following up the Thirteenth Dalai Lama."

There was nothing to see out the windows, just a stand of trees that were probably not there when he died, in 1933, and there was nothing in the room but the murals, but still I stood there, watching.

Again I asked the current Dalai Lama, "So what was the master plan behind the Thirteenth Dalai Lama's life and work? How would you describe the master plan motivating his life?"

"The Fifth Dalai Lama's master plan was disturbed," he said, "and then I think something like a vacuum or uncertainty followed for many years. The Thirteenth Dalai Lama's life span, according to the early period of the master plan, should have been one hundred years. That was one prediction."

"Who made that prediction?" I inquired.

"One famous Tibetan lama, Pema Garwang, a great lama, in his vision one day met one old lady, and she was presumed to be the mother of the Dalai Lama. That lady said, 'Originally this rosary had one hundred beads. Then after being used, the beads are worn out, and now there are only around fifty-eight or fifty-nine beads left.' The Thirteenth Dalai Lama's life was supposed to be one hundred, but then obviously all his efforts at sending students to England, the modernization and factories, and some other activities, it changed." For the current Dalai Lama, the life of his predecessor was shortened by the effort he invested in defending Tibet.

My guide opened the door and the dog, which had stopped barking after we went inside, began to bark again. My guide left me as soon as we stepped out of the room where the Thirteenth had died. I took one pathway through the parkland of the Norbulingka and he took another, so that I walked toward the gate in the evening dusk, alone.

Finally, I asked the Dalai Lama, "Who was the Thirteenth Dalai Lama?"

"On one level, the Thirteenth Dalai Lama was one lonely human being," he said with an utter weariness. "He was born and he died, he got sick, and also one time he fell from the horse when he was riding and after that he was more cautious." His voice alternated from weariness to cheerful laughter. "So that is the human or conventional level."

"But when you speak of the Thirteenth Dalai Lama falling off his horse, you are using this to show that he was also very human," I said.

"Yes," he replied.

"But also," I said, "there is the spirit of Chenrizi present."

"So again these two levels," he concluded, and he nodded at me as he did so, since by now we had spoken of this so often.

After the Dalai Lama died, on December 17, 1933, at the age of fifty-eight, his old commander in chief Lungshar made a last wild stab at reviving the drive for modernization. The historian Tsepon Shakabpa calls Lungshar's effort the work of "political bandits" who wanted to bring about a change in Tibet's government and civil service. The current Dalai Lama has a different view.

"Actually the Thirteenth Dalai Lama fully trusted Lungshar," he said. "Lungshar was the lay official who took the four students to England and then he returned with them. All of those boys did very good work when they returned. One set up electricity in parts of Lhasa and another set up a telegraph. And then Lungshar, after he returned, started the reorganization of the army, helping to create a modern army. Unfortunately, that plan faded because of the problems with taxes we spoke of. So after the death of the Dalai Lama, Lungshar had a reform plan for the regency between the Thirteenth and the Fourteenth Dalai Lamas. Instead of appointing just one regent, a monk, his idea was to have two or four men, and half would be laymen and half would be monks."

"He tried to dilute the power of the monks during the regency," I observed.

"He wanted a combination of monks and laypersons," the Dalai Lama said. "After the Thirteenth Dalai Lama, as tradition called for, a reincarnate monk, a lama, Reting Rinpoche, was appointed as regent. But then Lungshar organized a secret meeting *(of all those who wanted to continue the Dalai Lama's modernization campaign)*. A monk who was at that secret meeting later told me that their main aim was that the Tibetan government should be led by officials and not by lamas. Lungshar said that the lamas have no experience in administration and so forth."

"There is some truth in this statement," I said.

"Yes, that is very true. But the other side *(religious conservatives who opposed modernization)* and the regency accused him of trying to make a republic. It was not just the monks but also lay officials. They accused him of being a traitor to the government. He was put into prison and then blinded. Lungshar had his eyes taken out after the death of the Thirteenth Dalai Lama."

Only five months after the Dalai Lama's death, everyone drawn to Lungshar's reform movement—in fact, the very idea of reform—was smeared with the tar brush of treason. Lungshar's sudden arrest, rapid trial, and horrific punishment terrified and silenced anyone with reformist ideas. It had been so long since anyone had been punished by the government with blinding that the specialists paid to blind Lungshar had only heard of the method as described by their fathers. They botched the job, and Lungshar did not survive long after he was blinded. With this horrific act, the conservative faction in Tibetan power circles made it clear that during the coming regency, there would be no more talk of modernization, of creating a modern army, or of building modern schools.

11

THE EARLY LIFE OF THE
FOURTEENTH DALAI LAMA,
1935–1950

It was a wet monsoon morning in Dharamsala, eighteen months after we began our interviews, as I waited for the Dalai Lama in the greenhouse just in front of his tiny cottage. The audience bungalow, his personal cottage, offices, a temple, and all the buildings in his fenced compound on the forested hilltop above Dharamsala had disappeared under cloud cover. Standing out of the rain under a clear fiberglass roof, I inspected his colorful collection of potted plants until he appeared.

The Dalai Lama stepped out of his cottage, glanced at the dark sky, and took the opened burgundy umbrella, the same color as his robes, offered to him by a guard. It was Saturday, and though he normally does not see visitors on the weekend, he had agreed to continue our daily interviews, since we were near the end of our journey—living, learning, and engaging Tibetan history—and yet we had so much to discuss.

First, however, we enjoyed his flowers. "This cutting I brought from Massachusetts," he said, pointing at a large healthy begonia. "And these begonias and peonies are my favorites." Two dozen pots sat in precise rows on wooden risers under the transparent roof. Because they would have died in the constant monsoon rains, the gardener had arranged the roof. The Dalai Lama's garden, sheltered from the teeming crowds and noise of India, was quiet except for the sound of rain on the greenhouse roof. Every plant was carefully plucked of any dead leaves, and the flowers were immaculate. As he and I bent to smell his flowers and inspect their bright colors, I would not have known I was in India except for a quiet Indian solider with a black automatic weapon at attention nearby in the rain.

I followed the Dalai Lama along a paved walkway through a stand of trees toward the audience bungalow, to resume our conversation. We were at the most pivotal point in Tibetan history, one that the Dalai Lama is most qualified to talk about: his own life.

He was born Lhamo Dhondup on July 6, 1935, eighteen months after the death of his predecessor, in the village of Taktser, in northeastern Tibet. His birth province Tibetans call Amdo (today it is part of the Chinese province of Qinghai, not even within the truncated fragment of Tibet called the TAR on Chinese maps).

His parents were Tibetan subsistence farmers dependent on milk and butter from a herd of hybrid yak cows, wool from their eighty sheep, eggs from their flock of hens, and barley, buckwheat, and potatoes from their fields. His mother, Dekyi Tsering, delivered him on a straw mat in the cow shed behind the house, not far from manure piles and suckling calves; within days, she was back in the fields with newborn Lhamo strapped to her back. She ultimately bore sixteen children, though only seven would survive beyond infancy. His father, Choekyong Tsering, a horse trader, had suffered a bout of ill health and the loss of many of his animals. With the birth of Lhamo, his health improved at once. Neighbors later claimed to have seen a rainbow at the time of the boy's birth.

"Was there any significance to your birth in Amdo, in the same way that you spoke of the significance of the First through the Fifth Dalai Lamas' birth locations?" I asked.

"Of course, there is no sound basis," he replied, "but my own feeling or assumption is that the Panchen Lama and myself were born on the border with China, both born in Amdo. Today the Amdo people have a special feeling toward Tibet because both the Dalai Lama and the Panchen Lama come from their area. In the previous few centuries, they had been cut off from Central Tibet, but because we both come from Amdo, there is a closer feeling. In that way it had some effect."

The northeastern rim of the Tibetan Plateau slopes down into the lowlands of western China in Amdo. At higher altitudes, farming is impossible on the plateau, so only widely scattered herders can survive there. Though yaks thrive at up to 18,000 feet, they sicken below 8,000 feet. The village of Taktser, at about 9,000 feet, is astride two worlds, since both farming and yak herding are possible there. The entire region sits along a natural border that has become a political and ethnic boundary line. Until the eighth century, Amdo was inhabited solely by Tibetans, but as they clashed with Mongols and Chinese along the plateau's eastern edge, the area was slowly settled by other ethnic groups. The feeling of political connection between Amdo Tibetans and Central Tibetans weakened, and the dialect of Amdo grew more and more distinct.

In the past four hundred years, local Tibetan chieftains ruled Amdo, sometimes as subjects of Lhasa, sometimes as subjects of the Mongols, the Manchus, or, in the twentieth century, China's Nationalist government, with its capital in Nanjing. In the 1930s, the Muslim warlord Ma Pu-fang seized the northeast corner of Amdo in the name of Chiang Kai-shek's weak central government and incorporated it into the Chinese province of Qinghai. He ruled the area from the town now called Xining (pro-nounced *shi-ning*), capital of Qinghai Province. Tibetans in Amdo ordi-narily spoke Tibetan, so it was a surprise to hear the Dalai Lama say that in Taktser (nominally under Ma Pu-fang's control in 1935), although only two of the seventeen households were Chinese, his family did not speak Tibetan as its first language.

"At that time in my village," he said, "we spoke a broken Chinese. As a child, I spoke Chinese first, but it was a broken Xining language which was *(a dialect of the)* Chinese language."

"So your first language," I responded, "was a broken Chinese regional dialect, which we might call Xining Chinese. It was not Tibetan. You learned Tibetan when you came to Lhasa."

"Yes," he answered, "that is correct, but then, you see, my brother Lobsang Samten entered Kumbum Monastery before me and the Amdo dialect was spoken there. They spoke Amdo Tibetan in the monastery. In other villages, they spoke Amdo Tibetan. But in my village, I don't know why, my parents spoke broken Xining Chinese."

"Taktser was really a border area with China," I said, "so there had been a slow penetration of Chinese into the area."

"Yes," he replied, "it is a real border."

"I have heard the popular belief among Tibetans," I said, "that the Thirteenth Dalai Lama, having fought his whole life to free Tibet from Chinese influence, decided to stick his thumb in the Chinese eye with this rebirth. He was saying, 'Here, in the far northeast, this is also Tibet.'"

"I have not heard that," the Dalai Lama said, "but events now clearly show there was some benefit *(of the rebirth in Amdo)*, because the people of Amdo developed closer feelings for Central Tibet after several centuries of feeling cut off."

In 1934 the young and politically inexperienced Reting Rinpoche, from Reting Monastery, sixty miles north of Lhasa, was selected as regent. While Tibetans other than reincarnate Buddhist monks, or Rinpoche (Precious One), could become regent, Reting Rinpoche was chosen, in part, because it was assumed that such a high lama, with his spiritual insight, was well qualified to lead the search for the reincarnation of the previous Dalai Lama. Nevertheless, it was the political skills of the new regent, not his spiritual ones, that the Chinese government immediately tested. Would he resist absorption by China as skillfully as the late Dalai Lama had?

Reting Rinpoche allowed the Chinese to carry out what they called a condolence mission to Lhasa in 1934. According to the Nationalist government, the Chinese people wanted to express their sincere condolences to Tibet on the death of the Thirteenth Dalai Lama. The mission brought with it the equivalent of $3.5 million, and handed out vast sums to the powerful factions in Lhasa, particularly to Reting Rinpoche and other monks. Chinese envoys then pressed Tibet to sign documents acknowledging that it was part of China, as all Chinese governments had insisted after the collapse of the Manchu, in 1911.

Lhasa was intent on protecting the nation's independence. Tibet had relations with bordering countries, such as Nepal and Bhutan, while Mongolia and Tibet had recognized each other as independent states shortly after the collapse of the Manchu empire. But Tibet did not have diplomatic ties with the major powers except Britain, which studiously maintained an ambiguous and self-interested stance. Russia concurred with the British viewpoint that China had suzerainty over Tibet but also conceded that Tibet fell under the British sphere of influence. Meanwhile, China was convinced that Tibetan nationalism, along with the desire for independence, was the result of duplicitious machinations in London. Since the condolence mission gave nearly every monk in Lhasa two Chinese silver dollars, it is hardly surprising that a faction in the capital was friendly toward the Chinese envoys. Other Tibetans felt that the country must adhere to the legacy of the Thirteenth Dalai Lama, who had adamantly insisted on independence, used force to push the Chinese out, and refused to allow an introduction of Chinese influence.

Reting Rinpoche, and his supporters in the large monasteries, dismissed concerns about the Chinese. He also restricted arms purchases from India and began to disband the Tibetan army. When the condolence mission returned to China, the Chinese team convinced Reting Regent to allow a Chinese radio operator to remain in Lhasa, along with a few staff members. This small presence slowly grew, as opponents had feared, so that by the 1940s, China maintained a permanent mission in Lhasa. The Tibetan government said the radio was simply a means to discuss issues of mutual concern, especially conflict over the border in Kham. The two nations had never agreed on Tibet's eastern border with China, and clashes occurred frequently. China's view of the radio station, however, was stated frankly: "In order to cement the relations between the Central Government and Tibet and facilitate direction of affairs in that border territory, [the Chinese government] has decided to station a Resident in Lhasa."

By 1935 Reting Rinpoche began to unravel the life's work of the late monk, not only by opening relations with China, on the Nationalists' terms, but by refusing to buy weapons and properly train the army. The small army the Dalai Lama had recruited withered away. Despite such disasters on the political front, the Reting Rinpoche was only starting his work as regent.

A year after his selection, Reting Rinpoche undertook the most important part of his job: the search for the Fourteenth Dalai Lama. He went to Lake Lhamo Latso, the vision lake, and gazed into its depths during meditation. Five hundred years earlier, the guardian spirit of the lake,

Lhamo Dhondup, the Fourteenth Dalai Lama, age four (top left), photographed at Kumbum Monastery, Amdo, Tibet, circa 1939; and at age ten (top right) in Lhasa, circa 1945. Note the traditional white wool shoes and the monk's robes in the second photograph, taken after he took the initial vows of a monk.

Reting Rinpoche (left), regent of Tibet, about 1936, in the garden of his mansion, in Lhasa, with his dogs.

Reting Rinpoche (seated), regent of Tibet, circa 1936, in monk's robes with a brocade-covered water bottle. The man with Reting Rinpoche was a member of the *Dhob Dhob*, a class of strong monks who acted as both bodyguards and monastic police. They padded their robes to appear larger. He is holding a *khata* in his left hand.

Lhamo Dhondup at age four, with officials of Ma Pu-fang, Kumbum Monastery, Tibet.

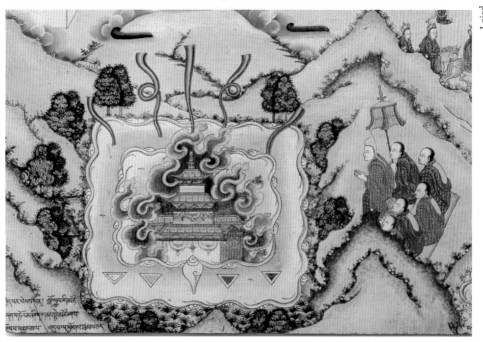

The regents of Tibet sought visions in Lhamo Latso lake to guide their search for each new Dalai Lama. Norbulingka mural, circa 1954, Lhasa.

At his home in Taktser (facing top), as his parents and monks from Sera Monastery watched, the young Lhamo Dhondup unerringly chose the objects that had belonged to his predecessor.

In Lhasa, the Dalai Lama's mother and father (facing bottom) were ennobled and given estates, and during this process his father became involved in Lhasan politics. Much about the young Dalai Lama's own life—including what shoes he wore (top)—was determined by tradition. His second regent, Taktra Rinpoche (on his left), became embroiled in a mini-war with Reting Rinpoche, the first regent. Gyalo Thondup, the Dalai Lama's elder brother (left), soon found a way to escape Lhasa and studied in China.

Pitt Rivers Museum, University of Oxford

The Fourteenth Dalai Lama (facing top left, photo 1949; facing top right, mural 1954) was politically powerless during the 1940s. He remained silent during meetings arranged by his regent. When he traveled in Lhasa, his palanquin (below) was part of a vast procession that included musicians and banner carriers. The mansion of the Phala clan outside of Lhasa (left) was typical of the homes of Tibetan aristocrats.

Laird

General Derge Sey's Tibetan flag (facing, top left), Markham, Tibet, 1949. It was probably given to the Chinese when Derge Sey surrendered in 1950.

Gold, diamonds, turquoise on a throne built for the Fourteenth Dalai Lama during the 1950s (facing, top right). Lhasa, Norbulingka.

Officials lunch with Lowell Thomas at the Tibetan Foreign Office, 1949 (facing, bottom). Official documents are filed in a traditional manner on the pillars, Lhasa, Tibet.

General Derge Sey, and part of the Tibetan army, in Markham, Eastern Tibet, 1949 (top), less than a year before they surrendered to the Chinese.

Nobles and officials from the Dalai Lama's court were at a picnic (bottom left), too busy to reply to a radio message about the invasion in the fall of 1950. Mural, Norbulingka, Lhasa, circa 1956.

(Left to right) The Panchen Lama, Mao Tse-tung, and the Fourteenth Dalai Lama, hand-painted photograph, 1954 (top).

The Dalai Lama and Chou En-lai, 1954 (facing, top).

(Left to right) The Panchen Lama, the Dalai Lama, and Nehru, in India, 1956 (facing, bottom).

The Norbulingka Institute, Sidhpur, India, 2

The Dalai Lama (top) on horseback, during his exhausting flight from Lhasa to India in 1959.

The Dalai Lama (left) and his entourage arrive in India. To his right is head valet Thupten Phala. The Dalai Lama's escape was one of the biggest media stories of 1959.

An image of Mao Tse-tung (facing, top left) and a slogan painted over Buddhist murals in Lhasa during the Cultural Revolution, 1992.

Young Tibetan women (facing, top right) sing songs in praise of Chairman Mao, Western Tibet, 1992.

Thousands of monasteries and temples across Tibet were destroyed during the Cultural Revolution (facing, bottom). Lhasa, 1992.

Drepung, on the edge of Lhasa, was once the largest monastery in the world. Devastated during the Cultural Revolution, today it is being rebuilt. The faithful gathered amidst the ruins of Drepung in 1997 to display and worship a large tapestry of the Buddha.

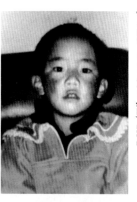

(Clockwise from top)

The Dalai Lama with Pope John Paul II.

Choekyi Gyaltsen, the Tenth Panchen Lama, shortly before his sudden death in 1989.

Gedhun Choekyi Nyima, the Eleventh Panchen Lama, widely known as the youngest political prisoner in the world, has been held in an undisclosed location since he was recognized by the Dalai Lama, while China has put forward another child as the "true" reincarnation of the Tenth Panchen Lama.

When it was still legal to own, display, and sell photographs of His Holiness the Dalai Lama, Tibetans sold large numbers of them, such as these in Lhasa, 1993. Note the images of the Dalai Lama with Bill Clinton and with John Major, as well as devotional images of the Dalai Lama and the Panchen Lama. Today the sale and display of such images in Tibet is banned.

Tibetan nomads (top left) still herd their yaks across the vast Barka Plain beneath Mount Gurla Mandhata, Western Tibet (top right). The Seventeenth Karmapa, head of the Karma Kagyu order of Buddhism, born in Tibet in 1985, recognized by the Dalai Lama and the Chinese government, fled to India in 1999 (bottom left). Ordinary Tibetan children still show tremendous devotion as they prostrate before the Jokhang temple in Lhasa, 1992 (bottom right).

Palden Lhamo, had promised the First Dalai Lama, in one of his visions, that she would protect the reincarnation lineage of the Dalai Lamas. Traditionally the goddess granted the regent a vision as he meditated and gazed into the lake, to guide him in the search for the new Dalai Lama. Reting Rinpoche was silent about what he saw in the lake, despite much prodding, until 1936. That year he summoned the National Assembly and announced that his vision showed that the Dalai Lama would reincarnate in the eastern province of Amdo. He had seen the Tibetan letter *Ah* in the lake and a few other details, which pointed toward a specific house in a specific village in Amdo. In the end, three search teams left Lhasa, all heading east, and one of them followed the omens given by Reting Rinpoche.

Following the regent's vision the search team that later found little Lhamo made its way first to the remote town of Jyekundo. There they met the Panchen Lama, who had fled to China in the 1920s after refusing to pay Lhasa the taxes that the Thirteenth had demanded of him to support the army, and was now unsuccessfully attempting to negotiate his return to Tibet. During long discussions between the Chinese and Tibetan governments (Lhasa refused to allow Chinese soldiers to accompany him), the Panchen Lama had been stuck in Jyekundo, where he quietly investigated reports of unusual children born in the area after the death of the Thirteenth Dalai Lama. As the Fourteenth mentioned, the spiritual link between the two lineages of reincarnate lamas never wavered, despite the political trouble. The Panchen Lama heard about a fearless boy in Taktser, and the name was added to the search team's list. The Panchen Lama died the following year, without ever returning to Tibet.

In May 1937, the search team reached the largest monastery in Amdo—Kumbum, founded on the birth site of Tsongkhapa—which they recognized from the regent's vision. Taktser was not far from Kumbum, but first the team went to pay respects to the local political power, Ma Pu-fang, delaying their arrival in Taktser until September.

To evaluate the boy in a natural setting, the head of the search team and also a Tulku called Ketsang Rinpoche traded clothes and position with his servant. The party posed as travelers and asked Lhamo's parents for food and lodging for the night. Ketsang sat quietly in the kitchen with the other servants while Lhamo's parents were busy entertaining the "high lama" in the main room of the house.

The Dalai Lama remembers nothing about the moment that was about to change his life, because he was only two years old. Ever since, however, he has heard reports about it from everyone who was present. He entered the kitchen and found Ketsang Rinpoche, a reincarnate lama from Sera Monastery, with an old rosary in his hands, sitting casually by the fire. The rosary had belonged to the Thirteenth Dalai Lama. The boy went fearlessly over to him and said, "I want that." Ketsang Rinpoche said, "If you know who I am, I will definitely give you this rosary." The child then called out, "Sera Lama, Sera Lama," identifying where Ketsang Rinpoche was from.

"When the search party reached us," the Dalai Lama said, "they said I spoke Lhasa dialect. I don't remember, but my mother told me that I spoke with the search party members in a language she didn't understand. So that means I used the language of my previous life." He chuckled and shook his head; he maintains a certain incredulousness about these stories even now.

Ketsang Rinpoche was impressed at being identified as a lama from Sera and at the way the boy kept holding the rosary. When the party set off the next morning, Lhamo reportedly cried, begging to go with the group. Convinced that Lhamo was probably the Fourteenth Dalai Lama, the search team returned to Taktser a few days later and notified his parents that they wished to test the boy officially. The parents thought the search party was merely looking for a reincarnate; it did not occur to them they were looking for the next Dalai Lama. Because, oddly enough, two of Lhamo's brothers had already been recognized as reincarnates, the family by now was not surprised.

Multiple items that had belonged to the late Dalai Lama—and similar-looking items that did not belong to him—were put before the boy on a long table. In every case, Lhamo selected the Dalai Lama's objects and discarded the fakes without hesitation: "It's mine." Of the dozen other boys tested, none selected more than one of the real objects, and one shy child refused even to come near the search party.

The team was eager to take Lhamo back to Lhasa, but Ma Pu-fang demanded a ransom for the boy—about 32,000 British pounds, in Chinese silver, or roughly $2.5 million today. The demand delayed Lhamo's departure for nearly two years, even though the search party assured the warlord that they were not certain about the boy and simply wanted to test him, among others, in Lhasa. The team looked for the money locally, and sent couriers back and forth to Lhasa seeking instructions. In the fall of 1937, Lhamo Dhondup's parents brought him to Kumbum Monastery, where he remained for the next twenty months. Eventually the search team was able to borrow the ransom money from a party of Chinese Muslims headed via Lhasa to Mecca. The pilgrims paid Ma Pu-fang in Xining, and the Tibetans repaid them in Lhasa, in what turned out to be a profitable transaction for the pilgrims.

The Fourteenth Dalai Lama stayed in Kumbum Monastery until July 1939. His two brothers who had been recognized as reincarnate lamas were already at Kumbum, studying to become monks.

"Do you have memories of Kumbum?" I asked.

"On one occasion," the Dalai Lama said, "I remember my elder brother was wearing monk's robes and studying in the monastery as he got his daily lesson. And I was free then, too young for study, and I just played outside. I remember asking him to come out and play, but he couldn't. And then I remember the teacher of my brothers. An old monk. I use to crawl up on his lap and sit inside of his monk's robes, where it was warm. It made me very happy that the monks were all disciplined and working hard to learn. Yet I felt completely free and went wherever I wanted to go. And then one day from inside the monk's robe I witnessed one student with a long red face. His face was so sad because he had not studied well and his teacher was about to beat him with a paddle. I was afraid. I remember the fear on the face of the student and the color of the paddle, even now. I remember that occasion. But the teacher was very nice to me, and he would give me peaches as I sat inside his robes."

The Dalai Lama's eldest brother, Thubten Jigme Norbu, was already sixteen when his infant brother came to Kumbum in 1937. Lobsang Samten, the other brother recognized as a reincarnate, was only four years old and still upset to be separated from his parents. Norbu and Samten knew what it was like to be raised by strange monks, with no women about. In his book, written with Heinrich Harrer, Norbu described how he and Samten spent their first night with their two-year-old brother, after their parents left:

> Lhamo Dhondup "dissolved in tears, he begged us to take him home. I was almost seventeen years old now, but I was still helpless in the face of such misery. Lobsang Samten was the first to join little Lhamo . . . in his sobs, but it was not long before I too dissolved into tears. A last attempt to distract my little brother by getting him to look at the dancing snowflakes outside the window . . . failed, and then we were all three in tears."

Finally, after months of waiting, just before dawn on the morning of July 21, 1939, Lhamo Dhondup was free to travel to Lhasa.

"I was put on a high throne," the Dalai Lama recalled, "and there was an attendant in front of me. His eye was very round and big. I remember that it was very early in the morning, and later that same attendant became my teacher in Lhasa. I remember sitting there on the throne and he was standing there before me. And some monk officials were there as well."

After early morning ceremonies to see them off, Lhamo Dhondup's caravan, which had by now swollen to 50 people and 350 horses and mules, set off overland, across roadless northeastern Tibet, to Lhasa. The Dalai Lama remembers little about this ten-week journey. He recalls the vast plains, the tiny settlements they passed, and the immense distances between them. Most of all, he recalls riding in a special palanquin designed to be carried by two mules. In it rode Lhamo Dhondup, who had just turned four, and his six-year-old brother, Lobsang Samten. The Dalai Lama's mother and father, and the second oldest boy in the family, eleven-year-old Gyalo Thondup, rode horses and mules. His eldest brother, Norbu, was left to continue his studies at Kumbum while his elder sister stayed on the family farm with her husband.

"Do you remember the journey to Lhasa?" I asked.

"Oh yes," he said, "a long journey."

"You were so small," I said, "only four years old. What was your impression of the wild country you crossed?"

"I just played with my father and my brothers and the people who looked after the palanquin. When Lobsang and I fought, we would sit on opposite sides of the palanquin and he *(the mule driver)* was happy because it was balanced. When we two boys were happy and friendly, then we were together in the middle, and it was much harder to balance the palanquin. Then I remember the trouble we caused for those men. Also, until we reached Nagchu *(ten days' march northeast of Lhasa)*, there were no bodyguards. Then the bodyguards came from Drapchi *(the bodyguards' base in Lhasa)*. They had brought a bunch of peas, in the shell. I remember the soldier giving me the peas while we were in the palanquin."

Lhamo Dhondup's caravan, led by scouts and muleteers, crossed swollen rivers, glaciated passes, and immense plains where herds of wild yak, wild horses, and antelopes roamed freely. While they were en route, and unbeknown to the members of the caravan, the regent, Reting Rinpoche, announced that the boy from Taktser was the Fourteenth Dalai Lama. He made the declaration, though, only after the party was out of the corner of Amdo controlled by Ma Pu-fang.

The caravan finally reached the outskirts of Lhasa, where the regent had erected a giant square of tents on a grassy plain. In the center was a yellow tent, which had belonged to the late Dalai Lama. Someone carried Lhamo Dhondup through the throng of thousands who had come out to welcome him and seated him on a throne in the tent. An official read a pronouncement declaring Lhamo Dhondup the Fourteenth Dalai Lama, and his peasant parents were ennobled. On October 8, 1939—the Dalai Lama was just four years old—he took the last lap on his trip to Lhasa.

"Did many people come to see you?" I asked.

"I don't remember," he replied with a laugh.

"You were seated on a high throne and many people came," I remarked.

"Yes, that's right," he said. "But I don't remember any of it. I remember one thing, though. After the ceremony, Reting Rinpoche wanted me to stay with him somewhere. I didn't want to stay there. I wanted to join my mother. So Reting Rinpoche called a huge bodyguard named Simkhang Tsugor Jhampa. He had big bulging eyes, and not only did they stick out, but they were very red. I was very afraid." The regent demonstrated his power, and the Dalai Lama's isolation, to Lhamo the moment the boy arrived in Lhasa.

As the Dalai Lama's entourage of thousands of people reached Lhasa, it stopped at the Jokhang, founded by Songzen Gampo thirteen hundred years earlier, to allow the young Dalai Lama to pay homage at the oldest Buddhist temple in Tibet. The procession then snaked its way beyond the Potala to the parklands of the Norbulingka. The Reting Rinpoche decided—and the Dalai Lama remains grateful even now—that the Norbulingka would be easier for the young boy to adjust to than the drafty Potala.

The Dalai Lama traveled in an enormous yellow-silk-covered palanquin. It was so large and cumbersome, almost the size of a small room, that two dozen men were needed to carry it. They were army officers, dressed in green robes, wearing bright red hats with a long tasseled fringe. Lhasa's nobility, in their finest silk robes, joined the parade of officers, horses, musicians, and banner bearers. The procession passed through the outer white wall around the gardens of the Norbulingka, only twenty feet high, and then approached the inner yellow wall, where only the Dalai Lama and his closest aides were allowed to enter. One section of the innermost yellow wall is twenty-five feet high, surrounding a small stone cottage, built during the reign of the Seventh Dalai Lama.

The boy dismounted from the palanquin and was led into the innermost courtyard garden, then up a short flight of granite steps into the three rooms of the Uyab Podrang. Here the Dalai Lama spent his first year in Lhasa, his house perpetually shaded by a dark ancient juniper tree that grew overhead. Murals illustrating aspects of the life of the Great Fifth Dalai Lama and Songzen Gampo, as well as secret yoga positions, covered the interior walls of the Uyab Podrang. A massive painted map of Lhasa in the eighteenth century filled an entire wall. It was in these rooms that his first tutors explained the basics of Tibetan history, in passing, as they taught him Buddhist philosophy.

During the next four years, the farmer's son from Amdo slowly entered into a new life. In his first year as Dalai Lama, he saw his mother, father, and brothers frequently in the Norbulingka, though he rarely traveled outside the walled compound. The government eventually granted the family a large estate in Lhasa. As his studies were gradually increased, the Dalai Lama saw less and less of his family. Just as the regent slowly separated the young Dalai Lama from his parents, the Reting Rinpoche slowly pushed aside every threat to his own absolute power. The boy was unaware of such political battles. He lived in a world apart, going out only in his palanquin, to face crowds of people who lowered themselves to the ground as he passed. To the prostrating Tibetans, the young Dalai Lama was so sacred that they were afraid to look in his eyes.

Today the Dalai Lama shows no curiosity about the devotion Tibetans in exile still demonstrate. He has been the object of such intense devotion since he was four years old that he has grown used to it. When I watched him in large crowds of devout Tibetans, I wondered how such adoration had affected him as a young man.

"How old were you," I asked, "when you first realized that you were a Tulku, a Rinpoche, a reincarnate lama?"

"Maybe five or six years old," he replied. "My mother told me that I insisted once that I would like to go the Chensalingka *(a building in the Norbulingka compound built by the Thirteenth Dalai Lama)*. She told me that we entered one room and I pointed to one box and said to open it. My teeth would be there. The officials opened it and they found the *(false)* teeth of the Thirteenth Dalai Lama in there. I don't remember, but my mother told me."

"In Lhasa," I asked, "do you remember anyone saying to you, 'Oh, you have returned'? Did they strongly believe that you were the same man returned?"

"There was one experience like that with Tsarong Dasang Damdul, whom people at that time did not consider to be very religious minded, since he was close with Western people and his lifestyle including his food and dress were more Western. Once he came to offer me a *khata*, a ritual white scarf, and we casually spoke about his own experiences with the Thirteenth Dalai Lama. Then he said, 'And now today the Thirteenth Dalai Lama has taken such a beautiful age,' and he cried and cried."

"What did it mean to you when you first realized that people thought you were a reincarnation of the Thirteenth Dalai Lama, or said that you were a true Dalai Lama?" I asked.

"I just took it for granted. I gave it no special attention," he responded. "There was a great scholar, Gen-nyima. Later, I received some teaching from him. For a few years after the Thirteenth Dalai Lama's death, there was no news about his reincarnation. So that scholar, Gen-nyima, became a little nervous and was worried. When I reached Lhasa, he deliberately came and witnessed the entire ceremony for my arrival. He returned to Drepung Monastery with great joy and satisfaction. It was a strange thing at that time—many officials like that great scholar Gen-nyima noticed how such a young boy behaved during all these functions. Even elder people were sometimes scared during those, but that young boy did not show any sign of fear or unfamiliarity. Gen-nyima told me later that after he saw that, he knew this was the reincarnation of the Dalai Lama. He said, 'Now I, as an old man, can die peacefully.' So these are the kinds of confirmation I received. When I was five or six, as a child, I developed this feeling that maybe I had the right to claim that I am the Dalai Lama."

Two months after the boy's arrival in Lhasa, his regent shaved his head, and he formally began his studies, though he had not yet taken the vows of a monk. He was officially enthroned in the Potala on February 22, 1940, and given a new name: Jampel Ngawang Lobsang Yeshe Tenzin Gyatso. The first two names were those of his regent, as was traditional. Because of a political firestorm that later erupted around Reting Rinpoche, he would lose those forenames. Today, he is known primarily by the last two names, Tenzin Gyatso. His family members and many Tibetans call him simply Kundun: the presence, or presence of the Buddha. Until recently, only English-speaking Tibetans referred to him as the Dalai Lama, though this ancient Mongol title, used so frequently in the world media, is now gaining favor even in Tibet.

Like the names given to him when he was four and a half, every detail of his daily life and education was now in the hands of monks, controlled by the orders of the regent, Reting Rinpoche; it included what he ate, what he studied, and whom he met. Meetings with his family were less frequent, and he spoke only to them, his tutors, servants, and the regent. During audiences with everyone else, he remained silent. Traditionally the regent had absolute power over the Dalai Lama until he reached eighteen, the legal age of maturity. But this course of events, for Reting Regent, was dramatically interrupted.

It was several years before the young Tenzin Gyatso realized that his first regent was notoriously corrupt. Apparently fonder of parties, horses, and women than of rituals or meditation, Reting Rinpoche abused his power, and that of the officials around him, not only by the sale of offices in government and the use of office for commercial advantage but by the destruction of any person or clan among the nobles who challenged him. The standards the Thirteenth Dalai Lama had imposed on the army, the monks, and government officials all eroded under the Reting regency. The army particularly suffered under him. He disbanded some units, and weapons purchases were restricted. At the same time, Reting Rinpoche accepted presents from the Chinese government, who wanted to weaken Tibet. Though the regent was praised for finding the Fourteenth Dalai Lama, which required the spiritual insight of a Tulku, he was condemned for his ignorance of administration, his vindictiveness, his disassembling of the army, and the violent political machinations that weakened the state in the years just before the Chinese invasion of 1950.

In February 1941, when the Dalai Lama was only six and a half years old, Reting Rinpoche abruptly resigned his position as regent. Though the regent was officially the Dalai Lama's senior tutor, young Tenzin Gyatso spent more time with his junior tutors, in particular the elderly monk Taktra Rinpoche, so Reting Rinpoche's departure was not a crushing blow. He probably resigned for fear that his not-so-secret lack of celibacy would have besmirched the ceremony in which the Dalai Lama would take his first vows as a monk, in 1942. It was considered vital for the fate of Tibet that a pure monk conduct the Dalai Lama's ordination, and the regent always presided over the ceremony. Taktra Rinpoche's strict observance of the rules of *Vinaya* was not in question, and the regent felt that monk could be counted on to return the seat to him at a later date, after the all- important ordination of the Dalai Lama was completed.

By 1942, the seven-year-old Dalai Lama had been enthroned and taken his vows as a monk. His life settled into a pattern of school in the morning, play, and then with more lessons in the afternoon. In winter he stayed in the Potala; in summer, in the Norbulingka. Male servants and monks surrounded him at all times. It is from this period that he has his first detailed memories, and it is his games and his odd collection of playmates that he recalls most fondly. As noted earlier, he refers to the lower-ranking monks and servants in the Potala and the Norbulingka as sweepers. They swept up the many chapels, tended butter lamps, carried water for the other monks, and cared for the Dalai Lama's daily needs. Nearly all were grown men, but as he was isolated from family and children, they became his true friends.

"My playmates were the sweepers and some monks who looked after the different chapels," he said. "Actually the first English I learned was from the sweepers who had been in the Tibetan military. They spoke a few words of broken English from their training, like, 'Present arms!' but in the Tibetan pronunciation they said, 'Prasan arm!' Tibetan officers were trained by British officers in the 1920s and their instruction had been pre-served. 'Attention!' became 'Tenion!' 'Stand at ease!' became 'Tand a eas!' and for 'fire!' they would say, 'Aim Tak!'" The Dalai Lama laughed as he mimicked the horrible pronunciation.

"Why did you learn these words from them?" I asked.

"I learned military exercises from these sweepers for our games. We were playing and we had wooden guns. I became kind of an expert in military salutations. Even today, when Indian police do a salutation (in an honor guard) and make a mistake, I can easily pinpoint it. We had the same teacher: the British."

"What sort of games did you play with the sweepers?" I inquired.

"There would be at least ten sweepers and we all had wooden guns," the Dalai Lama said.

"On the roof of the Potala?" I asked, trying to imagine this.

"No! In the Norbulingka!" he said with amazement at how dense I could be. "The old sweepers who were soldiers, they would all join me and we would march through the gardens."

"Were you the commander?" I asked.

"No," he said. "One of the ex-army people acted as the commander, and I would take his orders."

"Would you lie down in the grass and play war?" I asked.

"Oh yes!" he responded gleefully.

"What other games did you play with them?" I asked.

"Opera," he replied.

"You played army, and you played opera?"

"I only saw Tibetan opera for the first time in Lhasa," the Dalai Lama explained. "And it seemed quite jocular and fun. That's what I thought when I was young. I enjoyed the jokes *(slapstick between songs)* and only later did I acquire a taste for the whole opera. Later, you think about the meaning of the whole proceeding, the way they sing some opera songs, and so on."

"You saw the opera in the Norbulingka?" I asked.

"Yes," the Dalai Lama said, "but it was the opera dance that we played games with later. Actually, we copied each drama. First, we would play soldiers, and then we would play opera, and then, at the end of the day, we played soldiers again. So, yes, my games were first army, and then dancing. But I was not allowed to sing."

Thinking of the wildly acrobatic movements that Tibetan opera dancers perform, often leaping in the air and doing triple rotations before they hit the ground, I asked, "But what about the jumping dances? Did you try to do those?"

"There was one sweeper who did those very well, but we were just acting out the stories from the opera, just playing."

"You must have become very close to these men who were your first friends," I observed.

"Yes," the Dalai Lama said, "especially one attendant, the master of the kitchen, who I called Ponpo *(the boss)*. He had no stories to tell, but he was the one who fed me from the time I was four years old, until 1965 or 1966. He came with me to India in 1959. He was like a foster mother to me, though of course he was a monk." The Dalai Lama's affection for Ponpo—one of three personal attendants—is legendary. The master of the kitchen rode out to meet the infant Dalai Lama a few days before the boy first arrived in Lhasa. From that day, until his death, Ponpo and the Dalai Lama were inseparable. Ponpo had a large brown mole on his face, and when the Dalai Lama was four, after he was separated from his mother, he sometimes sucked at it for comfort. For many years, as the Dalai Lama grew up, he could not bear to let Ponpo out of his sight, even if it was only a glimpse of Ponpo's red robes scuttling about in the kitchen next to his schoolroom. The Dalai Lama felt great attachment to this ordinary monk, and has pondered the reason for the depth of his attachment for years.

"He was uneducated, but very honest," the Dalai Lama said. "But when he passed away, when his body gave up, I looked and it was very bright here," he said, pointing to his chest. "His inner soul was very light. I was moved and I wept. Even when my mother passed away, I did not cry."

"You were very close to him," I said.

"Yes, and when he died, I felt, 'Oh, human beings are the same species as monkeys.' It's the same with dogs. Deep inside, the most important person is the one who feeds them. So I think this is similar, with the one who fed me. He was uneducated and not very eloquent, and he had no stories to tell, but somehow I was very close to him, because he fed me every day."

The Dalai Lama's early years in Lhasa consisted at first of education and play, though a gradual awareness of his special role began to take shape.

"When you realized that you were a Tulku," I asked, "as a young boy one day, you must have realized that your whole life would be shaped by that. Perhaps you said to yourself, I can't be a farmer, I can't be a nomad, I must be a Tulku, I have no choice. It is determined now. Do you remember that feeling or when this happened?"

"Sometimes," he began wistfully and paused for a long moment before he continued. "Destination fixed. Eventually, you realize there is a purpose and a usefulness to serve. I realized that during one winter on a retreat. My senior teacher *(after Reting Rinpoche resigned)* was Taktra Rinpoche. He always looked toward me in a very stern way; he looked at everybody that way. During the winter retreat in the Potala, for a few weeks I was not allowed to go outside *(to play)*. I was always inside and in the morning there was one study session—and in the evening, one session. Each session was one and a half hours, and I must remain completely silent, except for the recitation of what I was learning. Then, especially in the afternoon when the sun went down, as the shadow of the mountains grew longer, I felt sometimes a little bit frustrated. My tutor Taktra Rinpoche recited *(the prayer or study text)* at the same time as I, but he would fall asleep peacefully, and still I would have to continue reciting alone."

The Dalai Lama paused, but by now I knew better than to ask anything during such moments. After a long silence, he resumed.

"Then there was a little bit of feeling closed in," the Dalai Lama said. "There was some frustration, like being in prison. At that moment, as the sun set, I would hear the shepherds returning from the pastures singing. I felt 'Oh, they are really happy and I am in a dark room with a tutor.' It was a lonely sort of feeling. So when I was very young, sometimes I had that sort of feeling or experience," he sighed.

"Did you feel angry," I asked, "or any resentment that you did not have a normal life?"

"No," he said confidently. "As I said, only on a few occasions on retreat when I was very young. Otherwise, I was happy and enjoyed life. The main reason was because of all my playmates. Despite their different age, they were very playful and very happy. They were full of fun and joy. They were always joking. Because of them I never felt isolated."

"And one of your playgrounds, in winter, when you were young, was the Potala. You told me about exploring and finding the things that belonged to the Thirteenth Dalai Lama, his telescope and so on. But when you were young, were there any special feelings about the Potala?"

"Yes, I enjoyed opening boxes," the Dalai Lama said, "and I found also manuscripts, ancient manuscripts, and then of course the tombs and the stupas *(of the previous Dalai Lamas)*, which are embedded with precious jewels. Then we have the treasure house, which is called the treasure house of the god Vaishravana, god of wealth, and there seemed to be quite a good amount of gold there."

"Did you see the gold?" I asked.

"No, I never went there," he said. "The ministers went there. Every year they would check if the gold was still there!"

"As you explored the many rooms of the Potala as a small boy, was it sometimes frightening?" I asked.

"Yes," the Dalai Lama said. "I didn't dare visit the dark places because of the demons. I was quite apprehensive about meeting one demon, called Arko Lhamo. Deep down in the Potala was a room where they kept the cement, and the sweepers called that place Arko Lhamo."

"And they frightened you with this?" I asked.

"Yes," he said. "When I was young, they said that Arko Lhamo was there. You see, it was dark there twenty-four hours a day. I sensed great fear. There are many records where the people saw some apparition; they saw different things in the Potala. There were many stories. Of course, when we accept that there are different types of spirits, we also accept these things."

"So the sweepers frightened you as a child with ghost stories," I said.

"Yes," he said.

"What about your positive experiences there?" I asked. "Besides learning some history from the murals there, and the wonderful time you had with the paintings of Milarepa, what else do you remember?" I asked.

"When I had a holiday," the Dalai Lama said, "and no lessons in the wintertime in the Potala, then usually I went and looked at the Fifth Dalai Lama's life story painted on the walls, and then also I went to see the paintings at the Thirteenth Dalai Lama's tomb. There are paintings at the tomb. The ones at the Thirteenth Dalai Lama's are not as fine as the ones on the Fifth Dalai Lama's."

Turning from his solitary explorations, back to his only friends, I asked about the sweepers again.

"Besides being your playmates, what did they teach you?" I inquired.

"I think they *(were the ones who first)* taught me about the negative side of the existing system of government in Tibet," the Dalai Lama said. "Slowly I learned about this from the innocent people like the sweepers, and I began to feel that it was important that there be some corrections. The regent and high officials were corrupt and dishonest. For example, one noble family, the Pala family, had a serf who came from their estate to accuse the Pala family of something. And then some punishment or judgment was given about the case brought by the serf, by the regent's office."

"What was the accusation?" I asked.

"That I don't know," he said. "One old person came several days to the office (*in the Potala*) and with the help of the sweepers, I joined them and listened *(secretly)* to what they were saying. The regent's officials really had a close link with the Pala family. So when they were receiving this old man's complaints—and he was very tough—they started arguing with him. The officials started bullying him, and they just would not allow him to talk. I felt that it was important for me to know about the dishonesty of these procedures and what was happening. It was quite rare that officials might give me a report that was critical. Especially during this period, before I had any power or responsibility over government, the sweepers, these ordinary monks, were my informers, and I think they were very helpful in educating me."

"They helped you spy on your own government," I pointed out.

"That is right," he said, "and I think it was very helpful. The sweepers helped me learn about the reality of the government. They were all quite poor. The noble people would not be there as a sweeper."

"For you it is obvious," I said, "but for us, we don't know these things. You lived in a very different world from people today. The servants of the kings of England and Russia were sometimes from a very high social class."

"The sweepers in charge of the temples in the Norbulingka and the Potala were all common people," the Dalai Lama said. "Then the monk officials in government, most of those were also from the common people. Only a few were aristocrats."

"You spoke earlier," I asked, "about using your telescope on the roof of the Potala to watch the prisoners in the village of Shol below. Did you begin to develop worries about Tibet from watching them as well?"

"No," he said. "It was from the sweepers where I got most of my concern. They showed me the way of life of ordinary people and all the different taxes they had to pay and the discrimination and injustice. I learned most of this from them. Of course, there was a prison in the Potala. In one part there was a place—almost like house arrest—for monks or for political prisoners. And the ordinary prisoners, I watched them in the yard below, from the roof of the Potala, with my telescope. Many of them were sort of my friends. I watched their lives every day *(though never met them)*. Many were common criminals, but still I could see their pain as a boy. Some were wearing the wooden thing . . ."

"That large wooden collar I have seen in pictures, as punishment?" I interjected. The collar was more like a stock, but one that the prisoner walked around with on his body for years.

"Yes," he replied. "And so when I first came to power, I released all the prisoners."

"So you saw these things as a boy," I said, "and slowly you began to develop a passion for reform."

"Yes," he said, "but also because of a growing knowledge about technology and modern machines. As I grew up, I was very eager for modernization."

"And one of the ways you learned about modernization and about the West, besides the few magazines you saw, and your eagerness to fix various machines, was through your meetings with your tutor Heinrich Harrer," I said, mentioning the author of *Seven Years in Tibet*.

"Tutor is too strong a word," the Dalai Lama said. "In the beginning, he came to the Norbulingka as a technician to work on the generators for the movie projector. Then we would sit together and talk, and he spoke Tibetan quite fluently. I was very eager to learn about the West and the countries and lifestyle, and then eventually I learned English. But before Heinrich, there was an electrician I also studied English with, and after Heinrich I studied with Jigme Taring. Even after 1951, Jigme occasionally came to the Norbulingka as a gardener. His main job was gardening, but in the meantime I spent time studying English, mainly grammar, with him."

"Through these friendships and your study, you grew interested in science and technology and grew ever more eager to see modernization in Tibet?" I asked.

"I once traveled on a narrow road," the Dalai Lama said. "I thought if we could widen it, then we could easily get a car on it. I grew very enthusiastic about this before taking temporal power *(in 1950)*. I really wanted to make a road from India to Tibet into Lhasa. When I was growing up, we had a few cars in Lhasa. So I thought, why not make a road? I enjoyed these few cars in Lhasa, but these cars were carried by people into Lhasa on their backs. It was foolish. Using a car is very pleasant and useful. But it would be far better to make a road from India to Tibet. Even the petrol supplies had to be carried to Lhasa on animals' and people's backs. This is later, in 1948, but by then when one diplomatic delegation returned to Lhasa in 1948, they brought a big refrigerator and big boxes."

"Some suffered a great deal to bring such things over the high passes, didn't they?" I asked.

"Yes," he said. "And these things were enjoyed by only a few people, and a lot of people suffered for them."

The Dalai Lama's informal education—from playing army to spying on his government—was hardly the main focus of his life, however. He spent his first years in Lhasa memorizing the five great Indian Buddhist classics, which had been translated into Tibetan centuries earlier. Once he memorized the texts, he studied them using logic and debate with his tutors. Finally, he read dozens of commentaries written about each of the texts. He had to master these subjects, and develop a fine public debating style, to pass the examination for his *Geshe* degree (a doctorate in Buddhist studies). A respected monk has concisely outlined the contents of the five texts. They range from "the study of the stages of mind needed for the realization of voidness, liberation, and enlightenment," to the rules of discipline for monastic vows and the "physical and mental constituents of limitless beings, rebirth states, karma, disturbing emotions and attitudes, paths to liberation, and so on." The Dalai Lama said that a focus on fine penmanship was one of the few areas in which his education was different from that of any other young Gelug monk. He had a calligraphy tutor who worked with him daily, as penmanship was traditionally a skill the Dalai Lama was expected to show particular mastery of.

It was through his calligraphy lessons, oddly enough, that he began to understand how his developing fears about the future of Tibet, and the need for more effective government, were similar to fears and prophecies written by the Thirteenth Dalai Lama. In 1932, a year before the Dalai Lama died, he predicted, in what is called his *Last Testament*, that he would soon die. His death was but the most mundane of the prophecies in this curious text, all of which came true.

"When did you study it?" I asked.

"I used that text to exercise my calligraphy skills," the Dalai Lama said. "It seems that my tutor intentionally chose that model for me to use."

Reading the fine English translation of the *Last Testament*, by Glenn Mullin, one can learn more about who the Fourteenth Dalai Lama is, and what his beliefs about Tibet and its history are, than from almost any other written source.

I am now almost fifty-eight years old, and soon it will be impossible for me to serve you any longer. Everyone should realize this fact, and begin to look to what you will do in the future when I am gone. Between me and the next incarnation there will be a period in which you will have to fend for yourself.

Our two most powerful neighbors are India and China, both of whom have very powerful armies. . . . Because of this it is important that we too maintain an efficient army of young and well-trained soldiers. . . . If we do not make preparations to defend ourselves . . . we will have very little chance of survival.

In particular we must guard ourselves against the barbaric red communists, who carry terror and destruction with them where ever they go. They are the worst of the worst. Already they have consumed much of Mongolia. . . . They have robbed and destroyed the monasteries, forcing the monks to join their armies, or else killing them . . . not even the name of the Buddha Dharma is allowed to remain in their wake. . . . It will not be long before we find the red onslaught at our own front door. It is only a matter of time . . . and when it happens we must be ready to defend ourselves. Otherwise our spiritual and cultural traditions will be completely eradicated. Even the names of the Dalai and Panchen Lamas will be erased. . . . The Monasteries will be looted and destroyed, and the monks and nuns killed or chased away. The great works of the noble Dharma kings of old will be undone, and all of our cultural and spiritual institutions persecuted, destroyed and forgotten. . . . We will become like slaves to our conquerors . . . and the days and nights will pass slowly and with great suffering and terror.

Therefore, now, when the strength of peace and happiness is with us, while the power to do something about the situation is still in our hands, we should make every effort to safeguard ourselves against this impending disaster. Use peaceful means where they are appropriate, but where they are not appropriate do not hesitate to resort to more forceful means. Work diligently now, while there is still time. Then there will be no regrets.

The future of the country lies in your hands. . . . I urge you all to rise up together and work for the common good. . . . One person alone cannot ward off the threat that faces us. . . . Avoid petty rivalry and petty self-interest. . . . We must strive together . . . for the general welfare of all . . . to assist the line of the Dalai Lamas in the task of caring for Tibet.

As for those who do not act correctly at this critical time, they will experience the fate they justly deserve. . . . Now they sit and lazily watch the time pass; but before long they will come to regret their apathy. . . .

I feel that the happiness and prosperity of Tibet will continue for the remainder of my life. After that, there will be considerable suffering, and each of you will individually experience the consequences of your ways in the manner I have described above.

Numerous external rituals have been and are being performed for my long life. But actually the most important thing people can do for me is to perform the inner ritual of holding this advice of mine in their hearts. . . . Think carefully about what I have said, for the future is in your hands.

Unfortunately, from 1933 until 1950, while Tibet had "the strength of peace and happiness," the nation made no effort to modernize the government or the army. The Fourteenth Dalai Lama grew up watching his predecessor's warning being ignored right before his eyes.

"Did you understand the meaning of the *Last Testament* even when you were young?" I asked.

"Yes, very much so," the Dalai Lama said, "and some portions I memorized by heart, since I read the testament of the Thirteenth Dalai Lama almost daily. My tutor helped me in the beginning to learn to read it word by word. And there it very clearly mentions the reds and the destruction of Mongolia."

Russian Communists invaded Mongolia before the Thirteenth died, and reports from the survivors had a great impact on him.

"So from a young age you were raised with the idea that there was some threat to Tibet, but particularly from Communism," I said.

"Yes," he said. "Also some old monks from Namgyal Monastery *(in the Potala)* had been in Mongolia. One was in Mongolia working for the Thirteenth Dalai Lama's business concern, so you see he, and others, witnessed what had happened in Mongolia. One of these monks told stories of how much destruction there was in Mongolia from the Communists."

After their 1911 revolt against the Manchu Empire, the Mongols had suffered an even worse fate than the Tibetans had. While the Chinese, embroiled in civil war, were unable to occupy either Tibet or Mongolia, several Russian armies invaded the state in the 1920s. By 1942, Stalin exterminated Buddhism in Mongolia. Everything the Dalai Lama predicted the Chinese Communists would do to Tibet, the Russians had done to Mongolia earlier. Because there were so many Mongol monks in Tibet, and because of the long connection between the two nations, Tibetans were well aware of the nightmare that was unfolding there.

"Besides the talk about Mongolia, what is the main intent and meaning of this political testament?" I asked.

"It is half prediction," the Dalai Lama said. "I think based on his past experiences and on what he witnessed, he made some predictions. He revealed the possibilities of the future based on the past, and that is exactly what happened."

"What he predicted is exactly what happened," I responded.

"Yes," the Dalai Lama said. "He warned that the Reds would come to Tibet, and he said that if we failed to defend ourselves through every means, then the same situation that happened in Mongolia would happen in our country. He warned that all the aristocrats would suffer, and all the ordinary people would also suffer, and that all the monasteries would be destroyed. He gave a warning like that."

"When you saw these problems in your youth, when you saw that nothing was being done, what did you think of the regent's government, your government?" I asked. "Did you sometimes question the regent? Did you criticize your regent?"

"Oh yes," he said.

"He didn't listen to you?" I asked.

"You see, there was no direct criticism," the Dalai Lama said. "Normally it was just backbiting, gossiping behind his back."

"You couldn't say anything to your regent directly, because he had great power?" I asked.

"Great power, sort of . . ." he paused, unsure of how to explain this to me.

"Did you feel a reluctance to criticize your regent?" I asked, surprised at how honestly he explored even delicate issues with me.

"There was a *kind* of reluctance," he said hesitantly, and it seemed that he truly was not clear about this, even now. He looked at his rosary of prayer beads in silence for a few seconds and then continued. "And also I was very young at first and actually at that point I was not involved in meeting people and talking to them. During any meetings with the Kashag *(the cabinet),* it was all very formal and ceremonial. I couldn't say anything. Theoretically, the Dalai Lama could intervene, but I was too young, and then *(perhaps I had a)* lack of interest. I don't know. Anyway," he concluded with regret, "I was not directly involved, and did not take an active role."

The historian K. Dhondup wrote that it is a "dismal fact of modern Tibetan history" that Reting Rinpoche and Taktra Rinpoche fulfilled the Thirteenth Dalai Lama's warning, "to the letter by their extremely callous handling of the Tibetan administration, treating it merely as a source of personal enrichment and an avenue to reward friends and supporters and punish enemies and critics. It was one of the darkest periods of Tibetan history."

This was the era in which the current Dalai Lama came of age, the decade before the Chinese invasion of 1950. While the administration of

Taktra Rinpoche at first bowed to the wishes of his predecessor, by appointing members personally recommended by Reting Rinpoche, Taktra soon took the opposite approach. He evicted from office anyone who supported the former regent. Although Reting Rinpoche had initially expected Taktra Rinpoche, after a few years as regent, to return the office to him, on demand, it was obvious, by 1946, that Taktra Rinpoche did not intend to do so. In addition, he took a more anti-Chinese stance than Reting Rinpoche had, and this policy may have created opposition to Taktra Rinpoche in some circles. Reting Rinpoche soon became involved in a plot to murder the older regent. The power struggle came to a head when Taktra Rinpoche saw incontrovertible evidence that Reting Rinpoche had approached the Chinese Kuomintang government of Chiang Kai-shek, agreeing to sign a treaty surrendering Tibetan sovereignty if China would provide Reting Rinpoche with military assistance against his enemies in Tibet, after Taktra Rinpoche was murdered. But Taktra moved first, and bloody fighting raged for several weeks in April 1947. Thousands of monk supporters of Reting Rinpoche revolted against the regent, and gun battles erupted around Lhasa. The Taktra regency finally defeated the rebels and Reting Rinpoche was captured, interrogated, and, before any sentence could be passed, murdered in the dungeons of the Potala.

The young Dalai Lama watched the battles from the roof of the Potala with his telescope, as shelling and gunfire echoed around Lhasa Valley. Yet even at the age of eleven, he was not completely surprised by this mini-war fought by monks, because of the education he had received from his sweepers, who had already shown him the reality of the government of Tibet.

"Actually, Reting Rinpoche and Taktra Rinpoche in the beginning had good relations," the Dalai Lama said. "Taktra Rinpoche was the disciple of Reting *(there had been a spiritual connection at first)*. But then, eventually, it was about power. Reting Rinpoche wanted to retake power from Taktra Rinpoche, and Taktra Rinpoche refused. Then eventually Reting Rinpoche attempted to kill Taktra Rinpoche."

"How do you know?" I asked.

"I saw one handwritten letter by Reting Rinpoche," the Dalai Lama explained. "It said, 'Make sure that the power does not remain in the hands of this old monk. What I mean is that this old monk should not be alive.'"

"That is what set off the fighting," I said, "but in the midst of all this, Buddhist monks were fighting and killing one another."

"Yes, a great mistake," the Dalai Lama agreed. "I was approached to see if I could intervene, but my position was hopeless."

"Did you become more cynical after this event?" I asked. "Before that time, did you think that all monks had only religious motivation?"

"No, it didn't change my opinions," he said. "Such fighting *(between monks)* was common in Kham *(in eastern Tibet, south of Amdo)*. Often during Tibet's history, monks in monasteries were fighting."

"And what did you think about the death of Reting Rinpoche? It wasn't an execution by the government when he was killed?" I asked.

"That was murder. . . . It was not legal execution," the Dalai Lama said. "There are two versions of what happened. Some say that they stuffed a *khata (a ritual scarf)* down his throat, and some say that he was castrated and that killed him."

"And this took place in the Potala," I said.

"Yes, in the Potala," the Dalai Lama replied.

"You were in the building when your first regent was murdered?" I asked. "Did you know this happened?"

"Yes, but I found out only afterward."

The young Dalai Lama faced more than the tragedy of such civil strife in 1947. His father, Choekyong Tsering, died the same year. Gyalo Thondup, one of the Dalai Lama's two elder brothers, claims that Tsering was poisoned by enemies he made during tense conflicts between the factions in Lhasa. The Dalai Lama called the poisoning charge unsubstantiated speculation, and, indeed, there is no proof to support it. We do know that the Dalai Lama's father supported Reting Rinpoche and that he died only a few months before the former regent was murdered.

Their father's death is but one of many issues dividing the Dalai Lama and Gyalo Thondup. Their education and lives dramatically diverged on their arrival in Lhasa. The Dalai Lama was only four when he arrived in

Lhasa, where he was educated to be a monk. He admits that his tutors did not give him any specific training to become a head of state, nor an accurate education about modern affairs. The monks had a stronger faith in Buddhism, the community of monks, and the importance of monasteries than they had in Tibet as a nation and the significance of nationalism. Indeed, the modern concept of a nation-state was alien to them. The Dalai Lama's education reflected that reality. It also reflected the traditional spiritual belief that greed, anger, ignorance, lust, and pride caused suffering in the world and that only a purified mind and heart—not politics—could ease human suffering.

Gyalo Thondup was eleven when he arrived in Lhasa, and members of the Chinese mission soon befriended him. A few Chinese officials had lived in Lhasa ever since Reting Rinpoche allowed them to establish a permanent radio station. After casually taking a few Chinese lessons from the mission, the Dalai Lama's brother was soon interested in Sino-Tibetan history. He learned that China was a modern state and Tibet a backward land in which it was impossible to receive up-to-date schooling. China's leader, Chiang Kai-shek, offered to pay for and supervise Gyalo Thondup's education in China.

In 1946 he persuaded his family, and the Tibetan government, to allow him to study in China. He argued that it was important that someone in the isolated court of Lhasa learn to speak Chinese. Despite the reservations of government officials, who believed that Chiang Kai-shek was seeking a lever with which to manipulate the Dalai Lama, Gyalo Thondup was permitted to go. From the 1950s until today, Gyalo Thondup, who speaks fluent Chinese, Tibetan, and English, has occasionally been sought out by Taiwanese, Chinese, British, and American officials in an attempt to contact the Dalai Lama. Beginning in 1946, Chiang Kai-shek groomed him for this role. In fact, young Gyalo Thondup ate his meals at the Chiang family table, from April 1947 until the summer of 1949, and tutors selected by Chiang educated the boy.

According to Gyalo Thondup, "Chiang Kai-shek wanted to train some of the Dalai Lama's family members to become more educated, so they could run Tibet. General Chiang Kai-shek and the Madame were very open about this and very kind to me. The Generalissimo told me, 'If you really want to get independence, I will support you. I will support the independence of Tibet.' "

In Gyalo Thondup's view, the monks did not give the Dalai Lama an education suitable to the future leader of a country. When I asked the younger brother about Gyalo Thondup's criticism, he waved the question away.

"He spent a long time in China," the Dalai Lama said, as if this fact explained everything. "He only spent one or two years in Lhasa and then he went to China."

"And in China," I said, "he received a historical and political education from a Chinese viewpoint. He says that you did not receive the historical and political education you needed as a head of state."

"I don't think so," the Dalai Lama said. "I don't regret the education I got. I think that is a different subject. Anyway, history is always something you can ask from historians."

The informal education in geography and international affairs the young Dalai Lama received came through contact with the few foreigners he met during his daily activities, and from magazines, maps, the daily news, and conversation.

"How old were you when you saw your first map of Tibet?" I asked.

"I don't know exactly, but I was already in Lhasa," the Dalai Lama said. "I had some maps which belonged to the Thirteenth Dalai Lama, with all the names in English, translated into Tibetan, from when I was young. I didn't study them but just looked at them. My main opportunity to learn about geography and maps was when I was attracted to pictorial books about the First World War, and then the Second World War. Also from *Life* magazine; some of those who spoke English arranged for me to receive it. So the geography of Europe was very clear to me, but Tibet and China were not very clear; *(American geography)* was not clear. But the war pictures in books and magazines, this really sparked my interest in maps and technology. Much came from the pictorial books."

"Was it the fighting and the battles you were interested in?" I asked.

"The pictures showing the machines was what I liked at first. Airplanes. The old tanks in World War I were so very clumsy, then came airplanes, and then the better machines in World War II."

"You were very impressed by these machines of war. Was it their technical prowess? Or was it just that you were a child and thought the machines were cool?" I asked.

"I think I was really impressed with war," the Dalai Lama said, "though of course the killing made me uncomfortable. But my main feeling, at first, looking at the map, was that Germany and Italy are not very big. They were only two nations. Then France, England, and America were all on one side. So I got the feeling that Germany and Italy were being bullied by those big nations. So at first, before I knew better, my sympathy was with Germany."

"So you really did not have any political education during World War II," I said. "But then you were only ten when the war ended."

"I had no knowledge about the Nazis," the Dalai Lama said, "or their atrocities or the Holocaust. I had no idea. I was just a child, looking at maps, and because of the sheer size of the countries on one side, and the smaller size of Germany, I had sympathy toward them. Then of course gradually I heard about the Holocaust and the war, and I learned what the Germans had done."

The Dalai Lama's tutors were monks who knew nothing about the outside world, so they could not educate the future ruler on that subject. What is surprising is just how much the Dalai Lama learned about the world despite his tutors.

"In the spring of 1947, President Harry Truman announced what was called the Truman Doctrine," I said. "At that time, the United States had an atomic monopoly. The Soviets made their first atomic bomb only in 1950. So it seemed easy for Truman to announce that the United States was ready to help free people anywhere who wanted self-determination. He said that it must be the policy of the United States to assist them anywhere."

"Is that so?" the Dalai Lama asked, with a tight smile. "But that is a very vague promise," he concluded with a laugh.

"I just wonder," I said, "how you first heard of this sort of broader political idea."

"I think I remember, vaguely, hearing a poor-quality radio channel once. There was a Tibetan paper published in Kalimpong and that was the only source of news in Tibetan. Through that monthly newspaper, *Sargyur Melong* (Tibetan Mirror), I saw some pictures, and I was very eager to read it."

"When did you first hear about America?" I asked.

"I had one letter from FDR in 1943," the Dalai Lama said, nonchalantly referring to a letter that President Franklin Roosevelt sent to him, along with some gifts, in the hands of a covert mission to Tibet undertaken by the Army's Office of Strategic Services (OSS) in 1943. The Dalai Lama was only eight years old at the time.

I had read about the letter, but the Dalai Lama always surprised me by how casually he mentioned such things. His offhandedness about the famous and the powerful of the world, bred through frequent contact with them, was a solemn reminder that the smiling monk seated before me had dealt, in some capacity, with every President from Franklin Roosevelt to George W. Bush. Few other people on earth can make such a claim.

When Roosevelt sent the letter, two years after Pearl Harbor, the United States had only one potential ally on the East Asian mainland: China. Imperial Japan had conquered the rest of the region. Facing this bleak reality, Roosevelt assumed that without air bases in China from which to attack Japan, the Allies could not defeat Tokyo. The only way to acquire such bases was to prop up Chiang Kai-shek's government, which had fled coastal China to the southwestern part of the country. Since southwest China was cut off from the sea, the United States flew cargo from British-occupied India, over the eastern Himalayas and Eastern Tibet. Supplying China was of such overwhelming strategic interest to the United States that the government was willing to pay any price. The cost of the air bridge over the Himalayas turned out to be an estimated fifteen hundred Americans who lost their lives flying the Hump. As an alternative, Washington considered building a road from the ports of India, through Tibet, to western China. In the 1940s, only a war could have justified this enterprise or brought the United States into contact with Tibet.

When China approached the Tibetan government on behalf of the United States about building such a road, permission was denied. In fact, the leader of one Chinese road team who ventured too far into Tibetan territory was killed. Tibetans feared any road from China to India through their country built during the war, because China might use it after the war to invade Tibet. Lhasa's refusal came as a surprise to Washington and embarrassed China. The fiction of China's control over Tibet had been exposed to the United States, which until then had not paid much attention to China's claim over Tibet.

Prior to World War II, America's only contact with Tibet had been the purchase of white yak tails, from which Santa Claus beards were made. Now, desperate to reach an accord with Chiang Kai-shek, Roosevelt agreed to help China assert control over all "its territory" after the hostilities had ended, if China would allow the United States to use its bases to attack Japan. To China, "its territory" included Tibet and Mongolia. Always opposed to European colonialism in Asia, Roosevelt assumed he was pledging to help China evict the colonial powers from the continent.

This broad agreement between China and America clashed with Tibet's refusal to allow any road on its territory. When Tibet rejected the road, Washington had to wrestle with the thorny reality of Tibet. China itself had to admit that it did not control Tibet, thereby acknowledging the smaller nation's de facto independence. If China did not control Tibet, was it then independent? Eventually Roosevelt and the OSS, still hoping to build the road to China, sent two intelligence agents, Ilia Tolstoy (émigré grandson of the Russian novelist) and Brooke Dolan, to Tibet to investigate the situation. America had its first glimpse of the depth of the conflict between China and Tibet when it asked for permission to travel to Tibet. Lhasa rebuffed the normal OSS request for visas, sent via the Chinese Foreign Ministry. Canny OSS bureaucrats then sent a visa request through Britain's colonial offices in Calcutta. For many years Britain had recognized Tibet's de facto independence. At the same time, it accepted Chinese suzerainty, not sovereignty, over Tibet, insisting on Tibet's full autonomy in matters of defense, foreign affairs, currency, and so on. Once the United States approached Tibet through British offices, the Tibetan government gave OSS agents permission to trek to Lhasa from India. The agents were under instructions to continue on to China so they could survey the terrain for a potential road. The Tibetans made it clear, however, that the Americans would have to return to India.

The eight-year-old Dalai Lama had an audience with the two agents, Tolstoy and Dolan, when they arrived in Lhasa.

"Useless!" the Dalai Lama laughed derisively as he recalled such formal meetings.

Tradition dictated that he say nothing to his visitors and that they say nothing to him. Instead, he accepted gifts from the foreign envoys, and they accepted a ritual *khata* from him in silence. The private audience was at an end.

While in Lhasa, the agents expressed sympathy for the Tibetans, and Tibet's foreign minister, Surkhang Dzasa, explained Sino-Tibetan history to the Americans. Tibet had never been part of China. Look around you, he said to the Americans. Do you see any Chinese here? Does anyone speak Chinese? As Surkhang explained, "Tibet owed her independence entirely to Great Britain . . . and the Tibetan Government wished to see . . . America backing up Great Britain in her effort to maintain Tibet's independence." Surkhang meant that Tibet felt Britain had helped to prevent Chinese incursions, an effort they hoped America would support. The minister's stance was entirely different from China's interpretation of the events, which was that Britain was actively lending a hand in fostering Tibetan independence.

Tolstoy and Dolan convinced the Tibetan government that the United States had great sympathy for the freedom of small, oppressed countries everywhere (in spite of the fact that Roosevelt had sent his letter and presents to the Dalai Lama in his role as a religious leader, not as head of an independent state, so as not to challenge Nationalist Chinese claims). Excited at the prospects of what it perceived would be increased foreign support, Tibet reversed its decision to force the agents back to India and allowed them to continue on to China. Ultimately, the OSS decided that it was unfeasible to build a road through Tibet, but relations between Washington and Lhasa had been established, though the two governments differed in their understanding of what was happening. Tibet was convinced that, at the end of the war, it would have a new ally to help it defend itself from the Chinese invasion. To more and more Tibetans, such an invasion was inevitable as soon as the Chinese freed themselves of the Japanese.

On the other hand, Tibet never realized that Roosevelt had accepted Chinese definitions of its borders without investigation. The American policy toward Tibet, which began at the onset of the war, remains fundamentally unchanged today, even though many Americans, in and out of government, have argued that the policy is not based on historical fact.

On the previous day, I had asked the Dalai Lama about the gifts from Roosevelt. The next morning, as we sat down again, he had a surprise for me.

"This is from Tolstoy and Dolan," he said as he put a box in my hands.

Inside was a gold Patek Philippe watch, which showed the phases of the moon and the days of the week. "Well, Roosevelt certainly had nice taste," I said. "How old were you when you received this from President Roosevelt?" I asked.

"I was seven or eight," he said.

"Has it been repaired?"

"Several times," he said with an embarrassed smile. By the time his brother left for China, in 1946, accompanying a Tibetan delegation who went to offer congratulations to India's colonial government and to China on their victory in the war, the timepiece already needed repairs. Even a Patek couldn't hold up to the wear and tear from young Tenzin Gyatso.

"Then after that, on one occasion in Lhasa," the Dalai Lama said, "I had it in my pocket and I also had a strong magnet. I was working on the movie projector. So the watch was sent out for repair again," he noted sheepishly. It was even out for repairs in Switzerland in 1959, when he fled Lhasa the last time. Regular maintenance is the reason he has the watch today.

He joked about the checkered history of Roosevelt's gift. "It seems that this watch has made the prayer that it will never be in the hands of the Chinese!" the Dalai Lama laughed.

"You have a memento of your first contact with the United States, which has remained with you all these years," I remarked. "But back in

1942, when you first met Americans, and then right at the end of the war, what were your first impressions of America?"

"Tibetans, you see, we generally considered America as a champion of Freedom, Liberty and Justice." I could hear the capital letters as he spoke. "A great nation. That kind of feeling or attitude was there from the beginning. So the Tibetans, I think unrealistically, expected too much from America. We thought that if there was ever any communist invasion or any attempt to invade Tibet, we thought America would help."

"Even though you didn't hear about the Truman Doctrine directly, the meaning of his proclamation in 1947 came through to you?"

"Yes, that is right," the Dalai Lama replied.

"Even to one boy who was locked up in the Potala studying very hard," I laughed.

"Not very hard," he laughed. "But yes, even to me in complete isolation it came, yes."

"It is a very powerful ideal," I said.

"Yes," he responded. "And then after the war, as we began to worry about how the Chinese Communists were defeating Chiang Kai-shek, Lowell Thomas came *(to Tibet)* in 1949. The Tibetan government considered Lowell Thomas to be a very important person in the American government. But actually he was just a broadcast journalist. So all during this time, the Tibetan government put a lot of hope on America."

"Tibetans put faith in America's ideals just after the war, didn't they?" I said.

"Yes," he said. "We obviously had the clear expectation or impression that since America supported Chiang Kai-shek *(as he fought Mao in the Chinese civil war)* America would help prevent a Communist invasion of Tibet. At that time, we thought that Communism was a real enemy of Dharma. And since America fought against Communism and opposed Russia, it was very clear, to us, that they would help." These assumptions proved to be false.

The end of World War II marked the beginning of the Chinese civil war. Americans believed that with funding and training by the United States, the Nationalist armies, led by the "Christian" Chiang Kai-shek, could defeat the Communists, led by the "godless Communist" Mao Tse-tung.

Yet in October 1949, the People's Liberation Army (PLA) defeated the Nationalist army, despite the billions of dollars Washington had given the Nationalists, including $750 million President Truman was convinced Chiang Kai-shek had personally skimmed. U.S. reporters in Beijing, the new Communist capital, watched the victory parades in awe. Almost half of all the PLA's weapons and vehicles had been made in America. Mao drove up to the podium in a U.S. jeep and officially proclaimed the foundation of the People's Republic of China. Corrupt Nationalist generals had sold, or turned over, much of the U.S. aid to the Communists.

During the first half of the twentieth century, except for brief moments, Britain and the United States essentially refused to recognize Tibet as an independent state. Both nations, for reasons based on self-interest, insisted that China was Tibet's nominal suzerain, even though Lhasa had expelled the Manchus, declared independence, and defended its de facto sovereignty ever since. After the Communist victory, Mao claimed that he had inherited "China's rights" over Tibet from the Nationalist government (which claimed to have inherited them from the Manchus). Chinese schools, now run by the Communist Party, taught history that proved foreign imperialists had used a feudal clique in Tibet in their attempts to split the Chinese motherland. By 1949, China was broadcasting radio programs into Tibet that demanded the "Peaceful liberation of Tibet." And who was Tibet to be peacefully liberated from? Imperialist American and British spies.

"How did you become aware of the Communist victory in China?" I asked the Dalai Lama.

"I received *Life* magazine," the Dalai Lama said, "and actually one article mentioned that the Dalai Lama was a regular reader and that my picture was also in it. In fact, it was a picture of the Panchen Lama. Anyway, the officials who spoke English translated the articles, and I saw the pictures of the Kuomintang defeated and the Communist movements, and then I became aware. Of course, every Tibetan was very much concerned."

His regent, Taktra Rinpoche, feverishly tried to revive the Tibetan army in the last few years before the PLA invaded Tibet. Britain also agreed to sell the Tibetans small amounts of ammunition and weapons. It was too little, too late.

Before the invasion of 1950, the Dalai Lama heard from many Tibetans who approached his regent to describe their worries about Chinese Communist intentions. Signs of the impending invasion grew.

"In 1949, when the Chinese started regular Tibetan broadcasts in Tibetan and English," he said, "there was one official who listened to Chinese broadcasts. Penpa Tashi approached the main chief secretary of the regent. He told him what the broadcasts said. He told him about the danger of the Communists coming. Then the chief secretary told him that 'Tibet is the land of great lamas and they cannot bring any harm.'"

For a moment it seemed to me the Dalai Lama exuded a quiet anger. "Such ignorance," he said finally.

"But immense faith, too. Both ignorance and faith, a faith that is hard for me to understand," I said.

"Yes," the Dalai Lama said. "Blind faith, not the proper faith."

This blind faith among religious conservatives saw the events that prevented China from invading Tibet before 1950—the defeat of the Manchu in 1911, internal chaos in China, and the subsequent attack by the Japanese in World War II—as divine intervention. Here was proof that Tibet had no need to build the army the Thirteenth Dalai Lama had pleaded for. Tibet was a special land, ruled by a living manifestation of Chenrizi, and as long as the tens of thousands of monks performed their annual cycle of rituals in the monasteries, the holy hermits sat in their remote caves at the bases of the glaciers, and Tibet remained devoted to Buddha Dharma, the patron protectors would secure this holy land.

Despite such attitudes, there were Tibetans within the ruling circles who managed to prod the government to assert independence. In 1947, a diplomatic delegation traveled to Europe using Tibetan passports. The Tibetans tried to send a delegation to the United Nations in 1949 to apply for membership, but Britain and the United States blocked the envoys. Both countries said that any attempt to join the UN, or for Tibet to arm itself openly, would only hasten a Communist invasion. Repeatedly, Washington and London killed Tibet's halfhearted attempts at self-defense, which were difficult to muster because of internal conservative resistance. The two nations insisted on legally recognizing Tibet as part of China for foreign policy reasons of their own, though they continued to deal with Tibet, behind the scenes, as an independent country. This duplicity increased Lhasa's belief that, because the Himalayan state was in fact independent, an invasion by China would prompt other countries to come to its aid. Britain's insistence that China respect Tibet's autonomy, and London's long-held nuanced view, only strengthened the Tibetans' false sense that other nations would respond to a call for help.

That assumption was deeply flawed. As Britain prepared to leave India and allow self-rule there, Tibet was no longer of any strategic value. Its value to Britain had been as a buffer to protect north India. Chiang Kai-shek—now in exile on the island of Taiwan—still insisted that Tibet was part of China. Because Republicans were sniping at Truman, claiming that he had "lost China," the president found it difficult to support Tibetan independence publicly. The State Department worried that Chiang might characterize any overt support for Tibet as an example of Washington's efforts to cut off more of China's territory. The White House also knew that with Chiang's veto in the UN, China could prevent Tibet from joining the organization if it applied. Because such a vote would have been embarrassing to the United States, it was much better to prevent the Tibetans from forcing a public debate of their nation's status.

I asked the Dalai Lama if he realized that Truman's fear of Chiang Kai-shek's influence in the United States and at the UN was one of the factors that prevented Washington from openly supporting Tibet in 1949, even after Chiang fled the mainland for Taiwan. The Dalai Lama said that if Chiang had "come forward to support Tibetan independence" as the Communists took over, then "in the eyes of millions of Chinese," Chiang and his political party would have been "a national disgrace." Though Chiang had never ruled Tibet, and though he might have wanted to support Tibet's independence after 1949, as a way to keep Tibet free of the Communists, his nationalistic rhetoric forbade it. The Chinese had been educated to believe that their neighbor was part of their nation, and no one could deny that claim without being seen as unpatriotic.

It was in such complicated circumstances that the United States sent its second, and final, secret mission to Tibet, led this time by the CIA officer Douglas S. Mackiernan. The State Department believed that any overt move to arm the Tibetans, in 1949, would precipitate or hasten the inevitable Communist invasion. Thus the Mackiernan mission was intended to be covert.

Tragically, Mackiernan was killed by Tibetan border guards who, in those tense days prior to China's invasion, had instructions to shoot any foreigners. The grievous outcome was caused by the CIA and the State Department, which had failed to alert the Tibetan Foreign Office to Mackiernan's arrival until it was too late to send word out to the jittery border guards. Worse, the Chinese knew Mackiernan's status as an intelligence officer prior to his arrival in Tibet. Ultimately, the Mackiernan mission had exactly the effect on the Chinese that the United States said it wanted to avoid. Fearful that the mission indicated Washington's willingness to provide covert military assistance, the Chinese sped up their plans to attack.

The Dalai Lama was not fully convinced that the Mackiernan mission hastened the invasion. "Maybe," he commented, though, he said, the United States had secretly begun to airdrop equipment to the Tibetan army just weeks before the October 1950 assault. The Dalai Lama knew how the Chinese perceived any American involvement with Tibet at that time.

"Before the Chinese Liberation Army entered Tibet," he explained, "their propaganda said that Tibet was full of imperialist influences, or the imperialist influences were very much alive in Tibet. That was the Chinese impression."

"And since Mackiernan was a blown CIA spy before he arrived in Tibet," I argued, "the CIA, by failing to keep this mission covert, reinforced this impression. In this way the CIA betrayed Tibet."

"I don't know," he said. "I always tell my American friends, when we were in Tibet we considered America as the champion of freedom, liberty, and democracy. Then in the 1970s, when the Bangladesh crisis happened, the American Seventh Fleet appeared and supported Pakistan. We all knew about Pakistan's brutality and the independence movement in

Bangladesh—East Pakistan at that time. It was a people's movement, but then America leaned toward Pakistan and its dictators, toward a military regime. That is the case."

"This is what I am talking about," I said.

"*(Henry)* Kissinger openly stated that in international relations, there is no room for morality and this is very sad, shameful, and disgraceful. America, the champion of freedom and democracy, does these sorts of things, and I think in this way many countries in Asia lost their faith, and that is a pity. The American people, I think, love freedom and liberty, but because of the administration . . ."

"Yes, I agree with you," I said, "and I think this all started after World War II. We abandoned our ideals, and American foreign policy has been adrift ever since. America's failure to support Tibet was just part of a wider pattern during the cold war."

The Dalai Lama then brought up his June 2000 meeting with President Bill Clinton.

"You see, in my latest meeting with President Clinton," the Dalai Lama said, "I also mentioned it. During the cold war, yes, sometimes, you may have to take a certain policy, which is not very truthful, but now times have changed and now the time is ripe. The greatest nation, the nation that champions liberty and freedom, must base its policies on its founding principles and inject this into American foreign policy. I told him this. I think now there is a greater chance, but we need political will."

"Yes," I said, "but when we examine the history of America's relationship with Tibet, we do not find any commitment to the founding principles of the United States."

"True, that is true," the Dalai Lama said. "The U.S. support for Tibet in the 1950s was not out of moral principle or sympathy but because of the worldwide anti-Communist policies that were there. So because of that, they helped. But once their grand anti-Communist policy toward China changed *(in the 1970s)*, then the whole thing changed. But nowadays the kind of support we receive from the outside world is sincere help and support. Because of the public concern and sympathy, now even the administration, in spite of inconvenience, is compelled to show attention. So that is positive."

For the fifteen-year-old Dalai Lama, the months prior to the invasion in October 1950 were tense ones. He was just a boy without any of the sweeping global awareness he exhibits so casually today. His regent still had absolute power, since the Dalai Lama was three years away from reaching the age of majority. From early 1950, rumors of China's preparations to invade Tibet circulated continuously in Lhasa. "I felt much anxiety," the Dalai Lama said. "All during the previous winter, and the beginning of that year, I remember very clearly not feeling well. The situation grew more and more tense and serious."

On October 7, 1950, the highest ministers of the government were all at a picnic, where beer flowed freely, when the first radio message came in from Eastern Tibet that the PLA had invaded. No one knew that this involved forty thousand troops. The desperate officer on the radio from the front did not have that information. He probably did not know that highly mobile Chinese troops, armed with modern weapons the Tibetans did not have, were surrounding the Tibetan troops. Still he demanded that the ministers be summoned from their picnic, so that they could issue orders about whether the army should retreat or fight. A low-ranking secretary in Lhasa told the officer that the ministers could not be disturbed. The field officer screamed over the radio, "Shit on their picnic!" and then hung up. That was the last radio message from the front. The Chinese moved so fast that further communication was impossible.

By October 19, five thousand Tibetan troops had been "liquidated" and the small army, underfunded ever since the Thirteenth Dalai Lama, surrendered. Captured troops handed over their guns; the Chinese gave them a lecture about Socialism and a small amount of money, and then told them they could return to their homes. The PLA could have marched on to the capital but instead, 200 kilometers from Lhasa, they stopped and demanded that the Tibetan government submit to "peaceful liberation." The position was consistent with the Chinese belief that Tibet was a renegade province, in rebellion because of support from Western imperialists. Many of the Communist cadres on the ground sincerely believed they were helping to peacefully liberate a Chinese province from "the reactionary ruling clique" that held the Chinese citizens of Tibetan nationality in thrall. This vision of Tibet has been maintained in China ever since. As recently as 2000, China's state-controlled media accused the Dalai Lama and his government in Tibet of rape, murder, and child cannibalism, saying they had presided over a system that was "the most gloomy, cruel, and uncultured in the history of mankind."

"What did you feel when you heard of the invasion?" I asked the Dalai Lama.

"Much anxiety," he said. "I remember clearly how my mind was unsettled and there was so much anxiety as this happened. Then eventually, as the situation became more tense and serious, even though I was only fifteen, the responsibility came heavier and heavier. Everyone looked to me for an answer. So then eventually I realized there was some purpose for me."

"From an early age you felt this sort of purpose for your life," I said. "Even though sometimes you didn't like it, you felt it."

"Yes. Then my senior tutor Ling Rinpoche and also Trijang Rinpoche gave me some encouragement at that time and that was helpful," the Dalai Lama said.

"Did they talk to you about the conflict that you are describing, the personal feelings of being trapped, but the need to serve others? How did they encourage you to deal with this?" I asked.

"They said, 'At this critical time in the history of Tibet, everyone will look toward His Holiness, and you must take this responsibility.' They gave me great personal encouragement. When I was a young boy, they always told me what great potential *(I had)*. Then there was the feeling of caring and compassion and that was a sort of strong seed or imprint *(in me)*."

"Did you speak with your regent about politics in the weeks just before the invasion of Eastern Tibet?" I asked.

"He knew that things were imminent," the Dalai Lama said. "I think *(I had)* a few conversations with the regent. Of course, the regent was my tutor and came to give me teachings or lessons, *(normally)* without talking of these *(political)* things. But then the regent eventually mentioned these issues to me."

"Did he seem afraid as he shared these things with you?" I asked.

"The regent told me that I must take responsibility," the Dalai Lama replied. "He said that since things were difficult and getting worse, the time had now come that the Dalai Lama should take full authority."

"If this old man who raised you like a father, who you trusted, if this man is suddenly afraid and handing power to you . . . Did he show any fear?" I asked.

"He seemed to have some anxiety," the Dalai Lama said with the chilly understatement that he uses when discussing critical events.

"What did you feel, as a fifteen-year-old," I asked, "when you saw that this older man was deferring to you in this situation?"

"Of course, on one level I was grateful for the respect," the Dalai Lama said. "But as a political leader, I had received many complaints about the regent and the public had little faith in him."

"How was power handed over to you?" I asked

"Somehow in the autumn *(of 1950)*, the state oracle and others said that the Dalai Lama should take full responsibility hurriedly," the Dalai Lama said. "Then that winter, I came into power *(November 17)* after they invaded Eastern Tibet. My immediate concern was that some officials told me that I should not remain in Lhasa and that I should go south to the Indian border. Some said no. At that point, I remember very clearly the indecisiveness. What should I do? There was so much seriousness, and so much risk, and so much discussion about what decision should be made, so I went back and forth. There were many people telling me what to do and in fact I asked many people, even the sweepers, about their views and there were so many different opinions."

As this debate raged into November, the government also tried to bring an appeal before the General Assembly of the United Nations. Only the tiny country of El Salvador agreed to sponsor Tibet's plea.

In their appeal to the UN, urging the international community to hear their case, the Tibetans drew heavily on years of history. The Kashag, or cabinet, sent a long telegram to the UN, saying that the Communists had misconstrued the meaning of friendship and interdependence, which had existed "between China and Tibet as between neighbors. To them

China was suzerain, and Tibet a vassal state," even though "Tibet had declared its complete independence" after the Chinese revolution of 1911 had dethroned the Manchu emperor and thus "snapped the last of the sentimental and religious bonds that Tibet had with China."

"The armed invasion of Tibet . . . is a clear case of aggression," the telegram read. "As long as the people of Tibet are compelled by force to become a part of China against their will and consent, the present invasion of Tibet will be the grossest instance of the violation of the weak by the strong. We therefore appeal through you to the nations of the world to intercede on our behalf and restrain Chinese aggression."

The State Department began to study its policy toward Tibet. The department's legal adviser noted that "as a matter of fact this Office believes that China does not have and has not had 'sovereignty' over Tibet." At the UN, no one was willing to stand up beside El Salvador. The other nations had overriding self-interests, which made it impossible for them to support San Salvador's attempt to bring the invasion before the General Assembly. A dissident official in the State Department wrote a long, classified assessment of why Tibet was being abandoned. London was concerned that if it irritated Beijing, the Chinese might interfere with Britain's claim over Hong Kong. Paris worried that if it challenged China's colonial "rights" in Tibet, others might look carefully at France's "rights" in Vietnam or Algeria. Less-developed nations wanted to show solidarity with China, as part of the emerging anticolonial front.

Meanwhile, the United States and China were at war with each other in Korea. Chinese soldiers invaded Tibet the same week they invaded Korea. Washington could not consider opening another front with China while PLA troops were driving U.S. forces down the Korean Peninsula, in the longest retreat in American military history.

The United States and Europe let newly liberated India take the lead with Tibet in the UN. India's first prime minister, Jawaharlal Nehru, believed that with Western colonialism defeated in Asia, he could take the moral high ground with Mao Tse-tung. He dreamed of China and India leading the world into a moral, revolutionary order, growing out of the disgraced ruins of colonialism. The Indian delegation to the UN said that China had given assurances that the Sino-Tibet situation would be resolved through peaceful negotiations. There was no need to bring the issue before the General Assembly, since the Chinese army had stopped short of Lhasa and had asked the Tibetans to discuss a peaceful settlement. The UN unanimously dropped the Tibetan plea from its agenda. The Soviet Union and the United States, for one of the few times during the cold war, voted together.

While this played out in New York, the Dalai Lama concluded the debate in Lhasa about whether he should remain there or flee to the Indian border, to the last town in Tibet, Yatung. "After much discussion, finally we decided to go to Yatung," he explained.

"As you fled south toward India," I asked, "leaving one set of ministers in place in Lhasa but taking an entire exile government with you, what did you know about how the invading Chinese forces were behaving in Eastern Tibet?"

He had heard that when the Manchu and the Chinese invaded Tibet during the time of the Thirteenth Dalai Lama, they burned monasteries and attacked civilians. "But this was not the case in 1950," he said. "The Chinese were very disciplined. They were like the British soldiers *(in 1904)*. Even better than the British, because they distributed some money *(to villagers and local leaders)*. So they carefully planned."

Mao and the Chinese Communist Party (CCP) controlled the actions of its troops right down to the last soldier. Troops were told not to take anything from the people, and instead to pay for all local materials and labor. The CCP, intent on winning the hearts and minds of the Tibetans, at first treated Eastern Tibet very well. Roads were built—headed back to China—and the peasants were paid to work on them. The Chinese gave local chiefs positions within the new administration and paid them for their work.

One of the officials captured in October 1950 by the PLA, along with several thousand troops who surrendered, was a governor in Eastern Tibet, Ngawang Jigme Ngapo. The CCP put him and others through a period of "reeducation." Party propaganda issued later said that they soon felt "like blind men" whose eyes had now, after their education, been opened. "Having received their traveling allowances and travel permits, they respectfully bowed to the pictures of Chairman Mao . . . before returning to their homes with their horses. They hoped that the radiance of Chairman Mao would soon be shed over Lhasa and all Tibet."

The captured Tibetans, who headed back west to Lhasa in the fall of 1950, spoke of their good treatment by the Chinese. At the same time, there were broadcasts promising the Tibetan elite that they, like the officials in Eastern Tibet, could retain their position, and their power, if they would only accept "peaceful liberation." The alternative was obvious. If they somehow fought the Chinese without an army, they would not retain their powers in a new Tibet.

Faced with the complete lack of international support, those around the Dalai Lama, now living in exile at Yatung, felt that they had no choice but to enter into negotiations with the CCP. The party demanded that the Tibetans send a delegation to Beijing to discuss "peaceful liberation" or face the military alternative. Chinese troops who were within 200 kilometers of Lhasa could have easily enforced the demand. The Chinese sent the message repeatedly: send a team to Beijing to negotiate. It was preferable for China, politically, if the Tibetans accepted the invasion; Lhasa's acquiescence would give the Chinese political cover, at least within China, for their actions.

"None of the great powers offered you real military aid before the invasion," I said. "Then after the invasion, the UN even refused to hear your appeal." Choosing my words deliberately, I concluded, "You were betrayed."

"Yes," he said coldly, looking away from me.

"But you have never expressed any anger at this betrayal," I said.

"What is the benefit of that?" he snapped. "If there is too much rain, should you lose your temper at the sky? That's foolish!"

"But now we are talking about history," I said.

"We were angry at them," the Dalai Lama replied softly. "I remember that. Regretfully, we would say, 'Now we have destroyed ourselves' or 'Now we have been completely betrayed by these people.'"

Without effective international support and after the defeat of the country's tiny army, the Dalai Lama and his government were forced to send negotiators to China. One of the negotiators was Ngawang Jigme Ngapo, the former governor who had surrendered in October and had been through a CCP reeducation program. The negotiators arrived in Beijing in April 1951, and after some brief discussion, the Chinese gave the Tibetans a finished document and told them to sign it. It is called the Agreement of the Central People's Government and the Local Government of Tibet on Measures for the Peaceful Liberation of Tibet, and since it had seventeen points it is commonly referred to as the Seventeen-Point Agreement. It stated first that Tibet "returned to the big family of the Motherland, the People's Republic of China," officially acknowledging Tibet as a part of China. Second, the political and religious institutions of Tibet would remain unchanged, and any social and economic reforms would be undertaken only by the Tibetans themselves at their own pace. It also stated that Tibet would retain self-government in all areas except defense and foreign affairs, which would be handled by Beijing.

The Chinese dismissed all pretense of negotiation as they pressured the Tibetans to sign this treaty. "Do you want a peaceful liberation or a liberation by force?" the Chinese delegates erupted loudly. When the Tibetans demanded that they be allowed to communicate with their government regarding the key point—that Tibetans were part of the People's Republic of China—the host diplomats said that it was not necessary to disccuss this with anyone since "other nations also regarded Tibet as part of China."

Lhasa had never given the envoys permission to sign anything in the name of the government, but nevertheless on May 23, 1951, the delegates were forced to sign the Seventeen-Point Agreement. The Dalai Lama says that the government's seal was forged and affixed to the document. With this document, Tibetans—for the first time in their history—publicly accepted China's vision of the two nations' history.

> The Tibetan nationality is one of the nationalities with a long history within the boundaries of China and, like many other nationalities, it has performed its glorious duty in the course of the creation and development of our great Motherland. But over the last one hundred years or more, imperialist forces penetrated into China, and in consequence also penetrated into the Tibetan region and carried out all kinds of deceptions and provocations.

"You had already fled Lhasa and were in Yatung, just near the Indian border, when you heard that the Seventeen-Point Agreement had been signed. Can you describe exactly where you were sitting when you heard?" I asked.

"There are three rooms above the main hall of Yatung Monastery, upstairs," the Dalai Lama said. "I used to stay in the smaller of these, by myself. I heard the news on the radio first, alone. But then there was a meeting with the Kashag immediately."

"Were people upset?" I asked.

"Yes, and I was worried," he replied.

"What was your first reaction?" I inquired.

"I felt shocked; great shock. We expected some draft agreement first, and then without that, things were just decided, so we were shocked. Of course we had trust in Ngapo and personally at that time I didn't know much, but we believed that these people *(the negotiators sent to Beijing)* would do something good, but then under what kind of circumstances *(they would have to work)*, we just didn't know."

"When you first heard that your negotiating team had signed the Seventeen-Point Agreement under duress," I asked, "did you think it was a decisive moment?"

"No, I don't think it was," the Dalai Lama replied. "On the first day of the invasion, we already knew what would happen."

"Still, the agreement was important," I said.

"I heard that, legally, until the Seventeen-Point Agreement, Tibet was not part of China," the Dalai Lama said.

"Yes, exactly," I concurred, "and it was signed under the threat that China would invade if the delegates did not sign the document. It was signed under duress."

"That is right," the Dalai Lama said. "Witnesses at the meeting have said that. And then the government seals used to sign it, even those were forged."

In the weeks after the agreement was signed in Beijing, Washington sent several messages to the Dalai Lama at Yatung. The United States urged the Dalai Lama to renounce the agreement, flee to India, and then to seek exile somewhere in Asia. Senior American diplomats at the State Department, such as Dean Rusk, wanted to turn Asian public opinion against China and hoped that even if the United States could not help Tibet retain its independence, the White House could use the Tibetan tragedy as a tool in America's cold war anti-Communist campaign. The Dalai Lama and his advisers decided that without a firm commitment of support from the United States— which the Tibetans felt they were not given—the Dalai Lama had to work with the Chinese. Perhaps China would live up to the Seventeen-Point Agreement and Tibet could have real autonomy within China. Messages flew back and forth from Beijing and Washington to Tibet.

"During all these tense negotiations, fear did not overwhelm you?" I asked.

"One of my experiences," the Dalai Lama said, "is that when the crisis is very far away, there is more anxiety, and when the crisis is very close, then less anxiety."

"The closer the Chinese got, the less anxiety you felt," I replied.

The Dalai Lama laughed. "Seems like that," he said. "And also maybe I got used to it."

In July 1951 a Chinese delegation and General Chiang Chin-wu arrived at Yatung. They flew from China to India and then traveled overland up to the Himalayan border with Tibet, and then across the border to Yatung. The tracks from China to Lhasa were still so bad that it was easier to travel from China to Tibet in a roundabout way via India.

"Tell me about when you met your first Chinese general," I said.

"Now that," the Dalai Lama smiled as he recalled that initial glimpse, "someone told me that the Communists are coming and I peeped from the upper window of the monastery, looking down at them when they crossed the courtyard. I was surprised, and I thought, 'Oh, they are just human beings.'"

"Was it frightening to meet him the first time?" I asked. "Besides the shock of recognizing your shared humanity, after all the horror stories you had heard, was it still frightening?"

"I felt very uncomfortable," he said. "We were very suspicious, but we had to smile and talk."

By the time the Chinese general arrived in Yatung, the Dalai Lama and his ministers had decided not to repudiate the Seventeen-Point

Agreement but to accept it at least for the time being. They hoped to renegotiate some of the terms later, but in the meantime, they would try to work with the Chinese in Tibet under the terms of the agreement. Some of the reasons for this decision were simple and yet are rarely discussed. The Dalai Lama was not sure that New Delhi would allow him to enter India or that he could trust the United States to offer any real support.

"Is it true that in 1950 you did not leave Yatung and go into exile in India—though you were not sure you could truly work with the Chinese—simply because India refused to grant you a visa?"

"I never applied for a visa," the Dalai Lama said carefully, "because the indications were very clear while I stayed in Yatung. We calculated that they *(Indian authorities)* were not ready to receive us."

"So you calculated, when you thought about your options, that you might not be able to go to India," I said, shaking my head at the endless levels of betrayal that had surrounded him.

"Not that way," the Dalai Lama said. "We calculated that the Indian government *(would not be)* happy, and then we actually decided. One group felt I should return *(to Lhasa)* and one group felt that I shouldn't, that I should go into exile."

"Did you return to Lhasa because of anything the State Oracle said?"

The Dalai Lama said, "No," that his decision to return to Lhasa was based on "some investigation. I still feel that all the major decisions at that time in Yatung, in 1951, were correct. And then in 1954 when I decided to go to China, and then in 1956 when I went to India and then returned to Tibet—I feel all these decisions were correct."

"While you were in Yatung in 1951," I said, "before you made the final decision to try to work with the Chinese in Tibet, and before you returned to Lhasa with the Chinese general, you still hoped that there would be help from America or Britain, and it did not come."

The Dalai Lama acknowledged, "We received one letter from the American consul in Calcutta."

Washington's offers were too vague and the decision that he must return to Lhasa and try to work with the Chinese was not an easy one.

"At that time also, in Yatung," the Dalai Lama continued, "we were indecisive, and were anxious to know what to do. It was a very black moment."

"Very dark, very scary, very painful," I said.

"Not painful," he said with a half smile.

"You were never depressed?" I asked.

"A lot of anxiety, doubt, and uncertainty," he said.

"In the worst of those moments, what did you feel?" I inquired.

"It was a really lonely sort of feeling. Helplessness," he said, shrugging his shoulders. "For all Tibetans." His spirits, unpredictably, lifted as soon as he said this. I could see why in his eye. He had thought of a funny story that summarized the period.

"There was this old monk from Namgyal Monastery," he began, and I knew from all the time we had spent together what was coming. Now it seemed the most natural thing in the world to me that he should tell a joke.

"There was a rumor in the streets," the Dalai Lama continued, "that the Americans will come and a flight will come to take the Dalai Lama to India. There had been all these rumors before and after Yatung. And so eventually, after many months, we returned from Yatung, to Lhasa, and no one came. And then several months passed and this old monk said, 'For a long time we have heard that the Americans are coming. But even if they were sliding on their backsides along the ground, they should have reached here by now!'" We exploded in laughter together.

As our laughter subsided, I said, "You are laughing now but at the time you were not laughing. You were very frightened."

"Yes, you're right, but you see that sadness was not there twenty-four hours a day. Occasionally there was a laugh like today. We are Tibetans, not Americans. If there is something wrong, Americans spend so much time worrying, and we cannot do it that way."

My mood had lifted with his joke and, somehow, everything he had ever told me was just there, before me. Tibetan resilience, self-sacrifice, and laughter—things the Dalai Lama so fully embodies—illuminate the vision of Tibetan history that the Dalai Lama had, in the past eighteen months, shared with me.

"But this has happened several times in Tibetan history," I said, "where there has been a dark moment, and the actions of the Dalai Lama have created history in those moments."

"Yes, and there is a Tibetan saying," the Dalai Lama replied. "What is burned by fire should be healed by using fire."

"What do you mean by this?" I asked.

"So trouble comes from the East, from the Chinese. The only way to deal with that is to go there, to have talks, with dialogue."

With that I knew why he returned to Lhasa even though many in his family had urged him to flee into exile. His childhood was over at sixteen. His true life had begun.

12

LIFE UNDER CHINESE
OCCUPATION, 1951–1959

The Dalai Lama sat down in his upholstered chair and kicked off his red plastic flip-flops. They still had traces of mud on them from his walk through the rain to the audience hall. Outside, monsoon clouds enshrouded the steep mountainsides of Dharamsala, and all the pathways were muddy and running with rivulets of water. Inside the audience room, I heard the falling rain echo off the white cement walls. I laughed to myself as I set up the tape recorder. The Dalai Lama was wearing the same plastic flip-flops that every farmer in India was wearing.

The Dalai Lama settled back in his chair, folded his legs and bare feet beneath him in one of his favorite postures, hoisted his prayer beads in one hand, and leaned forward for the microphone. I noticed, as I leaned closer to clip the mike to his robe, that the tank-top T-shirt he wore underneath had been dyed yellow. His robes were red, and so were his flip-flops, but his T-shirt was a pale yellow, washed so often it was frayed at the edges. He leads a frugal life despite the trappings of power that surround and protect him.

After nearly fifty hours of interviews, we had come to the most critical period of his personal involvement with Tibetan history. In 1951, when he returned to Lhasa, just after the first Chinese officials began to arrive there, he faced impossible political challenges. Yet as he had reminded me, his life was not only about serious matters of state.

In the summer of 1951, he was only sixteen years old and he still loved cars. He personally tinkered with the engine of an old car left by the

Thirteenth Dalai Lama. His childhood fascination with watches, telescopes, movie projectors, and everything mechanical continued to grow.

"There were three cars, at first, when I was young," the Dalai Lama began. "I think in 1948 when Shakabpa returned *(a diplomat returning from a foreign mission)*, he brought one jeep. The three cars belonged to the Thirteenth Dalai Lama, but for about fifteen years, no one looked after them. Around 1951 or 1952, soon after I came back from Yatung, I asked someone to repair the cars. Then I used them, and I also drove one myself, without permission from the driver. Because the jeep needed a key, I couldn't use it. The key was in the driver's hand. But the other three cars didn't need a key, so I could use them. I secretly went and got the car. Then one of these old cars crashed in the garden and the headlight glass broke. The next day, of course, I had to show it to the driver. But I was at a loss at how to do it."

"You mean you had to figure out how to hide the damage?" I asked.

"I thought for some time," he laughed. "Then I prepared a round glass using the diamond cutter that was left from the Thirteenth Dalai Lama. It was one of the things that I found in all the treasures I told you about— it was almost like a market. So I cut a piece of round glass. Then I thought it should be clouded to look like the other one. I boiled sugar until it became thick, and I put the sugar on the glass. I used a small cotton ball and put the sugar on the glass and then it looked similar *(to the unbroken one)* and then I put it in. I don't know if the driver ever found out." Again the Dalai Lama laughed.

"Did you spend longer driving or fixing the glass?" I asked.

"I fixed the glass in one day, but I drove the car for more than a month," he went on. "I took it out frequently. You see, I drove *(myself)* within the Yellow Wall *(compound of the Norbulingka)* and then, occasionally, I drove to Chensalingka *(half a mile away but still within the larger outer White Wall)*. But when I exited from the *(compound within the)* Yellow Wall, it was not convenient for me to drive, as there were many officials and people. So I would ask one of my attendants, an old monk, who was very clever. I trained him how to drive. One day we were driving out from the Yellow Wall and we bumped against a door. And he got frightened. I shouted 'Put on the brake!' Instead he put his foot on the accelerator!"

Again and again, the young Dalai Lama's life within a walled compound that he recalls so fondly was cut short by the demands of state. The first Chinese troops arrived in Lhasa in October 1951, a year after they had invaded Eastern Tibet.

Shrill horns, flapping red banners, and giant posters of Chairman Mao accompanied the troops as they marched in front of the Potala. The troops immediately enforced a number of demands on the Tibetan government, though the Seventeen-Point Agreement stipulated that China would not intervene in its neighbor's affairs. Lhasa's first obligation was to provide grain to feed the troops. Initially, the People's Liberation Army paid for grain as the Tibetan government issued it from storehouses, but within a year, as more troops arrived, the price doubled and government storehouses emptied. Tibet's agrarian economy could not support such a drain on its resources. Ultimately, the PLA stopped paying for the grain altogether, and began to requisition, without compensation, housing and land to maintain the army.

The situation grew to a national crisis. There were reports of famine among the troops and civilians. Since the PLA had not completed the first road from China to Lhasa, which it had begun building in 1950, food could not yet be imported from China. "The Chinese army came to Lhasa and the government stores were emptied by the army," the Dalai Lama said. The crisis could have spiraled out of control if the Indian government had not acceded to a Chinese request and allowed rice to be imported through India.

The grain shortage was indicative of the multitude of problems, both large and small, that erupted as ancient Tibet, which had so fiercely defended its isolation, was forced against its will into the modern world. Sporadic uprisings against the Chinese occurred despite the Dalai Lama's requests to the contrary. In Lhasa, amid daily acrimonious disputes, it required great effort to maintain the pretense of amicable relations between the prime ministers appointed by the Dalai Lama and the occupying army. Though China had promised, in the Seventeen-Point Agreement, not to interfere with the Tibetan administration, radicals among the PLA and Chinese Communist Party cadres longed to reform, or liquidate, what they saw as the "feudal ruling clique" in Tibet. Members of the Tibetan government, though under duress to cooperate outwardly with the Chinese, were ready to rebel. Relations between the Dalai Lama's officials and those of the PLA and the CCP deteriorated.

The young Dalai Lama was in the impossible position of seeking to encourage his government to cooperate with the invaders, even as he tried to defend the autonomy Tibet had been promised. According to the Dalai Lama, Chinese officials prevented him from pursuing social change, which he had longed to attempt ever since the sweepers in the Potala and the Norbulingka had brought the injustices in his country to his attention.

"And as you became aware of the many people suffering and the serf system in Tibet," I asked, "did you begin to feel that maybe you wanted to liberate the serfs?"

"I was not aware of terms like *serfs*," the Dalai Lama said. "But anyway, there was inequality, and I felt we must do something for poor people. In 1952 we started this reform committee."

"After the arrival of the PLA," I noted.

"The idea was there before the Communists came, but I had no power then," the Dalai Lama said with a hint of defensiveness. "Only once Communism reached eastern Tibet did I get power, and then I went to Dromo *(Yatung)*, and stayed there in early 1951. *(Only after)* I returned did this start. But the idea came earlier."

"You had earlier ideas to reform government and liberate the serfs?" I asked.

"That is right, *(but)* serfs I don't know. This word is too much," the Dalai Lama said abruptly.

"You have used the word *serf*," I interjected, recalling the time when he secretly watched a serf of the Pala family who had come to lodge a complaint about his treatment with officials of his regent.

"Yes, I use these words today," the Dalai Lama continued, "but at that time we had no particular words. These words became popular only later."

"What words did you use then?" I asked.

"*Nyamthag*, the weak and the poor; *Chabang*, poor subjects," he said.

"As a boy, you didn't think of them as serfs?" I asked.

"I did not know such terms," the Dalai Lama replied. "But when we started the reform committee, the first act was relieving the horse taxes. And then *(hereditary)* debts. Then there were more reform plans. For example, the estates which were owned by the wealthy families, we wanted those to be given back to the government. There was a step-by-step plan. But then the Chinese were reluctant to allow these reforms to go forward. They wanted their own way. That is true."

Peasants and serfs across central Tibet who lived near a road were required, on government order, to supply horses free of charge to passing aristocrats and officials. Such a tax was extremely onerous, as were hereditary debts, another practice the Dalai Lama wanted to eliminate. Many landless serfs had become so because of an inherited debt owed to a landlord. Sometimes hereditary debts kept peasants bonded to an aristocratic family for generations. The Dalai Lama's goal was to return lands of wealthy landowners back to the government, which would, in essence, free the bonded serfs attached to it.

The use of terms like *serf* and *feudal society* to describe socioeconomic relations in preinvasion Tibet is a contentious issue. One contemporary Chinese government source argues that in Tibet, before the 1950 invasion, "The serfs and slaves, accounting for more than 95 percent of the population, owned no land or other means of production." Another Chinese source says that 60 percent of all Tibetans were landowning peasants who paid taxes. China's argument that it liberated the Tibetans from slavery as a primary justification for its invasion has led to grossly distorted and politically motivated numbers. Tibet's foreign supporters, eager to challenge any rationale for the invasion, argue that there was no exploitation in Tibet before Beijing's invasion. The Dalai Lama has repeatedly condemned the corruption and exploitation that existed in Tibet, but the inequities and inequalities cannot logically be used to justify a foreign occupation.

Scholars actively debate whether it is accurate to use words like *feudal* and *serf* in the Tibetan context. The peasants paid various taxes, both in kind and in corvée labor, to the government, to monasteries, and to local nobles, but did that make all the peasants serfs? And, if so, how many were serfs?

In the opinion of one scholar, Tom Grunfeld, author of *The Making of Modern Tibet,* reliable documentation about the number of Tibetans who were serfs before 1950 does not exist. The government did not keep comprehensive records for past centuries, and many of the extant materials may have been destroyed. Moreover, any documentation that survives, much of it created after 1959, is in the hands of the Chinese and may reflect Beijing's need to justify its invasion more than it does the history of Tibet.

When forced to make an informed guess on this subject, Grunfeld gives some credence to Chinese claims, made in 1959, that 60 percent of the population were serfs, not 95 percent, as the Chinese widely claim today. But when we look at the number, we find that half of the 60 percent were landowning peasants who paid taxes in labor and in kind to the government, a monastery, or nobles. That leaves only 30 percent who might be classified as landless serfs, indentured to aristocratic families, a monastery, or the government. But the 30 percent who were monks were not bonded to anyone. Nomads, who made up 20 percent of the population, were often free of all government control. Unfortunately, discussion of this subject is handicapped by the lack of solid data. Furthermore, in some provinces, such as Kham and Amdo, many peasants had no lord at all. These easterners resented any attempt by the aristocrats of Central Tibet to impose their domination in the east. The complex reality of the socio-economic structure prior to the invasion—which differed in various regions throughout Tibet—is not a subject about which anyone can accurately make gross generalizations.

Curiously, China told Lhasa that the purpose of its takeover was to "liberate" the Tibetans from imperialist forces. There was no mention of liberating serfs. On the contrary, China promised it *would preserve* the existing social order: the Seventeen-Point Agreement makes that clear. It was only after the Dalai Lama fled his country, in 1959, that China began to collectivize the land and execute landlords, as it "liberated the serfs" in Central Tibet. It is an inconvenient fact of history that Beijing worked with Tibetan nobles, during the first nine years after the takeover, to preserve aristocratic rights over the serfs and that China prevented the Dalai Lama from initiating reforms during this time. China's first motivation was to occupy Tibet, not to change it.

During the 1940s, travelers who passed through both China and Tibet reported that Tibetan peasants were far richer than their Chinese counterparts were. Tibetans had a level of immunity from famine, while poverty and starvation were common in China.

"Everyone had something to eat and wear, the necessities were there," the Dalai Lama said. Yes, there was exploitation, but he condemned the practice as morally unacceptable. Still, he added, "I think the serf or feudal society *(in Tibet)* when compared to Chinese, Indian, and Russian cases —*(then)* perhaps the Tibetan situation was better. I think as a whole *(Tibet was a)* more compassionate society."

The Dalai Lama paused and then continued, "There were different categories *(of peasants)*. In some areas, they were happier because *(there were)* fewer taxes. However, in other areas they had a more difficult time. It depended on their location. If they were situated near the road, there were more taxes. Especially *(the demand)* for horses and porters. Then also there was an understanding that if you belonged to some monastery, it also meant they had some responsibility to look after you as well. In some cases, it was better, in some cases worse."

"And how can we compare the relations between those we might call serfs, and their masters, in Tibet versus in China?" I asked.

"I think it was much worse in China," he said, "and my reason is quite simple. After the revolution the struggle between classes was very active in China, because of the oppression *(the lower classes had suffered)*. In China, the serfs showed great hatred toward the landlords. *(Three million landlords were executed in 1953.)* And in Tibet there were also some cases like this, yes. But the majority of the serfs tried to protect the landlords."

For the average Tibetan, 1951 was a year of tremendous confusion. The isolated world they had known was gone. Six months after the Chinese invasion, Lhasa issued the following document in the name of the Dalai Lama:

> The Tibetan local government, the monks and the people have given their unanimous assent. Under Chairman Mao Tse-tung's and the central government's guidance, they are actively assisting units of the PLA to enter Tibet and strengthen national defense, expel

imperialist forces and safeguard the unification of the sovereign territory of the motherland.

I once asked the Dalai Lama about a fine set of murals in the Norbulingka, painted after the arrival of Chinese troops. He said, in passing, that yes, the history inscribed beneath the murals was reliable, except that the inscriptions might use a word "like motherland, because the Chinese were already there" when the murals were painted. Documents written between 1950 and 1959, when the young Dalai Lama tried to collaborate, under duress, with the People's Republic of China, are troubling for him today. Speaking about the inscriptions, he added, "Already the Chinese were there. I don't know. Maybe because of different circumstances there may be some different words *(such as "motherland")*. I don't know." It is not just inscriptions and state documents that trouble him, however. Many events in these difficult years still cause the Dalai Lama anguish.

Hoping to prevent bloodshed, the young Dalai Lama was compelled to participate in the forced resignation, or firing, of his two prime ministers, which he acknowledged was "very painful." The young Dalai Lama grieved for them but he saw no way forward except to work with the Chinese. Patriots who were unwilling or unable to cooperate with the Chinese were let go.

Between 1951 and 1954, as the teenage Dalai Lama tried to cooperate, other Tibetans continued sporadic armed resistance. Chinese news reports spoke of what they called bandit attacks. Widely separated, ill-armed parties of freedom fighters, desperate for training and weapons, continued their assaults on the well-armed Chinese. Two of the Dalai Lama's elder brothers—Gyalo Thondup and Takster Rinpoche—went into exile in India and the United States after 1950. They developed covert relations with the Central Intelligence Agency. As popular rage over the invasion slowly grew in Tibet, the CIA formulated plans to airlift Tibetan freedom fighters out of Asia (they walked from Tibet through India to Bangladesh and then were flown out), train them in the United States, and then airdrop them with a radio, some money, and a few weapons into Tibet.

Washington primarily hoped to use the Tibetans to collect intelligence, while the freedom fighters thought the United States supported their campaign to liberate Tibet. The Dalai Lama did not know of these developments with the CIA until years later. Awareness of such secret information would have put him in danger—and, in any event, he would have opposed the plans if he had known about them.

Only through dialogue with the Chinese, the Dalai Lama was convinced, could he protect his people. Any attempt to resist China by force of arms would have led to bloodshed, without hope of victory, because of Beijing's overwhelming military superiority. All of his decisions in the 1950s were made in light of that fact. He was under duress. The Dalai Lama normally keeps his feelings about the invasion and occupation of Tibet beneath the surface, but during one conversation they came into view.

In early 1954, Mao Tse-tung invited the nineteen-year-old Dalai Lama to visit China. Mao was eager to show foreigners that things were going well in Tibet.

"If you had refused to go to China . . ." I began.

"I think that is foolish!" He was angry, and his face was flushed. I understood my error immediately: was I so stupid as to think that Mao had issued an "invitation" that could be refused? "Already the Seventeen-Point Agreement was signed," he said. "Now, they are in Tibet . . . no response from the UN! No response from the Indian government! British government! American government!" His voice was quivering. "What to do?" he asked softly. His eyes locked on mine. "I had no choice," the Dalai Lama said finally. "Yes, I had to deal with the invaders."

If Tibetans fought back with their outmoded weapons, the Dalai Lama knew, the Chinese would exterminate them, but he had no idea what hardships the Chinese were enduring as the price for Mao's victory. In 1950, Mao began a rampage in China and Tibet that would ultimately result in the death of twenty million to forty million people. One political campaign after the next swept through China, each reaping another deadly harvest.

The Dalai Lama's teachers had not taught him history, or statecraft. Instead, they focused entirely on Buddhist studies, from an early age. As the Dalai Lama said once, his teachers planted seeds of compassion in his heart. How did that unique training affect his response to the invasion and his forced trip to China in 1954?

"Had you developed emotional detachment through spiritual practices, like *shunyata* [emptiness], back then?" I asked. "Now you have great development of *shunyata* and you are able to become very detached. You remember the Potala and just see a building. You might look at the suffering of your nation and you might not hurt as much as you would without detachment. There is nonattachment."

"Detachment does not mean that I am like a rock," the Dalai Lama said with some irritation.

"But back then you were really not like a rock," I replied. "You were young. You hadn't had the years of mind training you have had since. So sometimes you were going to feel very afraid."

"Even today also," he said gravely, as he peered over his glasses at me.

"But at that time you were so young and under such pressure, you must have felt very afraid sometimes. Or sometimes maybe you cried," I said.

"I never cried for national interests," the Dalai Lama responded firmly. "Sometimes if there was something about a Dharma practice, or I heard stories about some ill people or animals when they were being eaten by the vultures, sometimes then I cried. But for national interests, I never cried."

"Why," I asked, "if you can cry in empathy for suffering animals, why wouldn't you cry for your own suffering nation?"

"I don't know," he said, shaking his head. "But that is just a fact. I think those things are different from a national crisis. Now later, after I came to India in 1959, when Tibetans came and told me their stories about *(being)* tortured or having their children killed, especially in the 1980s, when people came from Tibet and told stories about torture, they cried and I also cried and I was very sad. Often tears would come. Nowadays again," he concluded regretfully, "there are too many stories, so now my mind is hardened a bit."

Yet there is another facet of who the nineteen-year-old Dalai Lama was as he set off for China in 1954.

"One time one senior official sent a message asking to see me," the Dalai Lama explained. "So I said yes. Then he expressed his concern about the Chinese motivations and activities. Then he wept as he showed his concern. He said, 'His Holiness is very humble, and has a bit of a child nature.' He said, 'Chinese are brazen and will not hesitate to exploit this.'

And then he wept like a child. I was very touched at that time. He said, 'You are weak and the Chinese might exploit you,' and that was his concern."

"And did he have reason for this fear?" I asked.

"I think some reasons. When someone asks me forcefully, then I find it very hard to say no. Anyway," the Dalai Lama concluded with a sigh, "this happens. My temper is not developed, and in that way I am very weak."

Historians debate exactly how many people Mao killed during his reign over China; some say it was twenty-five million, others say it exceeded forty million. Phillip Short, in *Mao: A Life,* notes the essential fact underlying the debate. "His rule brought about the deaths of more of his own people than any other leader in history."

Mao was sixty-one years old in 1954, when he met the young Dalai Lama, and he was the absolute master of China by then. Maoist cadre implemented every one of his orders without question, as though he knew the will of heaven. During the Four No's campaign, Mao told millions of people to eradicate rats, sparrows, flies, and mosquitoes and promised the highest crop yields in the world. Instead, caterpillars—free of predation from the now-dead birds—infested the crops. The ensuing famine killed uncounted millions. Another folly, the Great Leap Forward, exacerbated the hunger. Mao said he would bring China up to a Western standard of living in one great leap, by building backyard steel furnaces in every household. The number of trees cut down to fuel the furnaces created massive deforestation, which caused widespread floods, while the steel produced was useless.

The Dalai Lama had his first meeting with Mao in Beijing on September 12, 1954.

"What were your first impressions of Mao?" I asked.

"I thought he was great and powerful and revolutionary," the Dalai Lama answered. "And I still feel that the early part of his life *(was)* really dedicated to the people. With Chairman Mao, there was some basis of respect for him, until he became like another emperor *(later in his life).*

He was a great leader, naturally, because he worked so hard and was very determined. One thing that impressed me was Mao's conversation. Although I didn't speak Chinese, there was a perfect interpreter. Mao spoke very slowly and each word carried weight. All of his words were very selected and economical, and no word lacked meaning or value. So that was really impressive. Also he was not overly polite and he seemed very straightforward, unlike Chou En-lai, who was very shrewd. At once with Chou you could see, 'Oh, that person is very clever, too clever.'"

"And did you speak about Tibet much?" I inquired.

"He mentioned," the Dalai Lama said, "that in the past, Tibet was once a great nation . . . I don't remember the exact translation, but the meaning was that Tibet was once a great nation. He said that we had even expelled the *(Tang)* Chinese emperor. But today Tibet is a very weak and backward nation, so we have come to help you. So after twenty years you might come to a stage when it is your responsibility to help us. Chairman Mao said like that. So this meaning is very much as though we were separate . . . nations. And he also inquired of the Tibetan national flag. I was a bit hesitant because I was not sure what to say . . . Chairman Mao asked me if there was a Tibetan national flag or not. With some hesitation, I said yes. Then he said it is very important to keep, to show your identity."

I was surprised at this. "Mao said that, even though it is illegal to display the flag in Tibet today?"

"Yes," the Dalai Lama replied. "Chairman Mao felt that in the international movement of the proletariat, there are no national boundaries. And particularly if we Tibetans voluntarily joined with China, then it could be very powerful. Then Tibetans could go to Shanghai and Beijing with no problems."

"The problem is that the Chinese can also go to Tibet with no problem," I joked.

"That is right!" the Dalai Lama laughed. "So in my view, from a global perspective, Chairman Mao's words had a lot of meaning. But then with the Communist rule, unfortunately, everything is hypocrisy and everything is artificial."

"There is no rule of law," I observed.

"That is right," he readily agreed.

"So at the most dangerous moment in modern Tibetan history," I said, "after the preceding regents have failed to resolve the situation with China, after China invades, you are just a sixteen-year-old boy, and you are asked to take over responsibilities. You are to be the hero of the nation—the whole nation believes in you. Now there is no choice the Dalai Lama must take power. But we cannot, of course, compare your political abilities to those of Mao. Correct?"

"Yes. He was experienced," the Dalai Lama acknowledged, "in age, in everything."

"And so there is no question but that he could have manipulated you politically," I continued.

"Yes, he could have," the Dalai Lama said.

"Well, do you think he did?" I asked.

"Now here," the Dalai Lama said, "my impression is that in the early 1950s, all the revolutionary-minded Chinese leaders, I think, were sincere *(about their)* goals and ideology. There was one political commissar who met us in Chamdo when we were traveling to China. He cried and said, 'We brothers, you see because of the imperialist manipulation of the Westerners, due to their activities, now we two brothers have had to fight.' He actually cried. I don't think this was an act. I don't feel that."

"Of course they believed that," I said, "and you were very moved by their ideological sincerity."

"I was full of suspicion *(when I first went to China)*," the Dalai Lama said. "But when I returned from China, I was more confident. Because when I was in China proper, I had the opportunity to meet many Chinese party members and leaders in the province level and the central government, including Chairman Mao *(and others)*. These people really interested me."

Mao and the Dalai Lama met perhaps fifteen times that winter and the following spring, before the Dalai Lama returned to Lhasa in June 1955. When he was not in meetings with Mao, party functionaries escorted him on tours of Potemkin villages and factories, designed to impress the young Tibetan with the tremendous strides being made under the glorious leadership of Chairman Mao. He traveled cocooned within the same sort of privileged world the Communist Party prepared for Mao himself to see. Even without that special preparation, China's growing industrial base and achievements would have amazed the young Dalai Lama: compared to Tibet, China was a modern, scientific wonderland. And the Dalai Lama, who grew up in a land where science was almost forbidden by law, had idealized science. Still, he traveled in China on special trains, with Communist Party officials in his entourage, one of whom was even assigned to teach him about the history of the Chinese revolution.

"You grew to have an appreciation of Communism," I noted.

"You see," the Dalai Lama explained, "Chairman Mao at his last meeting *(with me)* told me that religion is poison, so this I felt *(showed)* that he really trusted me, otherwise *(there was)* no reason to mention that. Then afterward, when I was returning to Tibet, I stopped in Chengdu for two to three weeks *(and Chou En-lai came to visit)*. Chou En-lai told me that I was well versed in politics. He praised me, saying that I would become very well versed politically. Then during conversation, he also praised religion very much. Remembering what Chairman Mao said to me on religion, and I thought now Chou En-lai was trying to repair that. That was my feeling. The reason for Chairman Mao's comment on religion was straightforward. Of course my mind is more scientific and I love science and technology. I believe in the scientific explanation. My mind was scientific and open. Actually, Mao himself told me this. He said, 'I have watched your thinking and activities all these months. Your mind is a very revolutionary mind.' Then he told me that religion is poison. I think he told me this sincerely."

"But wasn't he manipulating you as a master politician?" I asked.

"I don't know," the Dalai Lama responded.

"Wasn't he manipulating a young boy who had no knowledge of the world? For the eight years when you were in Tibet working with them, they could say, 'Look, the Dalai Lama says that Tibet is a part of China.'"

"That is not what I said!" the Dalai Lama insisted. "The Seventeen-Point Agreement was signed under duress, and I had to accept it!"

"And from there Mao tried to gradually win you and the Tibetans over," I remarked. "He wanted to win you first. That's what all the touring was about. All the education about Communism. You were the great prize."

"It is difficult to say," the Dalai Lama replied. "We can say 70 percent or 80 percent, maybe that is true. But 100 percent no one can say. Even myself, I cannot say."

"But they were trying to win you," I insisted, amazed at how he refused to acknowledge what seemed obvious to me.

"Hmmmm," he said, as he scratched his face and thought about his reply. Clearly he had a more nuanced interpretation of these events than I did. "I think there was a close understanding. Yes, from their side, naturally, they saw a young boy, more open-minded, who could be a good Communist. From my side, I was very much impressed by Marxist ideology. The idea of taking care of the less-privileged people, of working-class people, this is wonderful. They didn't care about national borders or nationalism at that time. It was wonderful, but then eventually it was just the opposite."

"Buddhism is an ideal with a path that leads to fulfillment," I said. "Marxism is an ideal with no path to fulfillment."

"At that time, yes, there was *(a path to fulfillment),*" the Dalai Lama insisted. "Communism believed in achieving a classless society, through Socialism step by step. Through cooperatives, then communes, then a classless society. At that time, there was a clear sort of vision and path. Some of Marxist ideology is wonderful. To oppose all exploitation forcefully, and then *(to use)* distribution rather than profit making. What is lacking in Marxism is compassion. It lacks a holistic sort of view, and that is the mistake. But, you see, capitalism also has no goal. It's only about making profit. Profit! Profit! Profit! No profit cares about consequences!"

"No profit cares about knowledge!"

"Now Marxism," he continued. "I think the greatest sin in this system or ideology is that they totally neglect basic human values, human compassion, human care. And they deliberately promote hate. That is their greatest mistake."

Seizing on the word *hate*, I went back to where we had begun—the Dalai Lama's meetings with Mao.

"Mao promoted hate in a very brutal way," I said. "In the year before you arrived, he promoted a campaign of class warfare, encouraging peasants to butcher the landlords of China. More than one million people were executed. This man you sat with is one of the greatest murderers in human history. And when you saw him, he seemed like a nice man."

"Yes," the Dalai Lama acknowledged and then paused. It is one of his most impressive traits. He thinks about what you say. He began to move the prayer beads in his hands more quickly. Seconds passed in silence.

"It is strange, isn't it?" I asked. My words seemed to wake him from a reverie.

"Yes, it is strange," the Dalai Lama said, looking up at me. "But what I think is even stranger is that, at that time, it was difficult to say it was strange. It was a time when, yes, there was a possibility to change China. To change the world. *(To bring)* some kind of equality and prosperity with less exploitation. *(For such a goal perhaps)* you can justify some of these negative activities."

"How many people can we kill to justify this?" I inquired. "This is the problem."

"That is true. Too extreme the methods," the Dalai Lama said.

"Those in the Chinese government," I went on, "even today, though they condemn Mao, they keep his face on Chinese money, and they will not admit that he murdered at least twenty-five million people. It's even more than Hitler."

"That is right," the Dalai Lama agreed. "Hitler was explicit about his evil intention to exterminate a specific group of people, while the Communists were hypocritical about their goals. *(They said)*, 'I liberate you. I am helping you.' But in reality, these are just words." He seemed pained that Communism's ideals had been lost.

"Imagine this," I said, brutally. "Imagine twenty-five million dead people and then remember that you sat with this man and you say that he looked like a nice man . . ."

"Of course, if at that time I had known how many people he killed," the Dalai Lama said, "then my impression would be different."

"Yes," I replied. "It was because you did not know what was happening in the world, and in China."

"Yes," he said, "about Chairman Mao it was ignorance, it is true. I didn't know what really happened. My teachers did not spend the time to teach me about history. So in their curriculum, there was only Buddhist philosophy."

"And you have said several times that you do not regret that," I said.

"No, no, no regrets," he said, laughing again.

"But when you went to Mao in 1954, you had no historical education and Mao was a master of history. So wasn't it easy for him to manipulate you?"

"But we never discussed history. He never brought it up. It wasn't the issue," the Dalai Lama said with a merry laugh, and once again I laughed with him. Mao did not need historic excuses for what he did.

"Actually," the Dalai Lama said, "during my visit in China proper, I did have some sort of lesson *(about history)*. Whenever I had some leisure time one of the assistants, with one Chinese acting as a liaison officer *(Lu Ke Ping)*, he explained the history of the Chinese revolution. I think that is the only history lesson I ever had!"

"Your first history lesson was given by a Communist!" I said.

"And it was not about China's history," he said, "or about Tibetan and Chinese history, but just about the revolution!"

"Yes. I am sure that, for them, it was the only history worth learning!" I said, expecting a laugh, and I was rewarded with one.

As I watched his long face crinkle with mirth again, I thought about all that he had taught me, and in particular all that he had said about his education. Clearly, his spiritual training is the wellspring of his immense strengths: the source of the human wisdom he has carried to the world at large.

The Dalai Lama returned to Lhasa from China in June 1955, hopeful that he could apply the ideals he had seen there to the situation in Tibet. He hoped that the Chinese were truly seeking to develop a unified world order beyond ethnic identity and that, just possibly, the loss of Tibetan independence might be part of a global Communist revolution.

The impossible conditions he had left in 1954, however, had only gotten worse. While Lhasa at first remained quiet, the situation in the eastern provinces, like Amdo and Kham, deteriorated rapidly. When

China incorporated these historically Tibetan regions into the modern Chinese provinces of Qinghai, Yunnan, Gansu, and Sichuan as locally autonomous areas, they were no longer part of Tibet. The promises of local autonomy made to the Dalai Lama, in the Seventeen-Point Agreement, did not apply to Kham and Amdo, though more than half of all Tibetans lived there. Since Kham and Amdo were not part of what is today the Tibetan Autonomous Region but instead had been incorporated into Chinese provinces, Communist "reforms" began in those areas much earlier. In fact, Kham and Amdo were the first to be reached by the roads from China; therefore, it was easier for China to impose its will and initiate "socialist reforms." Eastern Tibetans who had happily accepted Chinese wages to build the roads soon realized that Beijing had manipulated them as part of a larger plan.

The Chinese Communist Party in 1955 and 1956 started down what it imagined to be a scientific path toward Communism in Amdo and Kham, through cooperatives to communes, and then a classless society, ". . . collectivization, measures to settle the nomads, active discouragement of religious practice and the arrests and even murders of uncooperative tribal chieftains and lamas. Not surprisingly, these measures led to widespread resentment and sporadic uprisings."

In February 1956, after a Tibetan attack on a Chinese garrison in the eastern town of Lithang, in today's Sichuan Province, Chinese troops surrounded the monastery, where the Khampa freedom fighters had retreated. After a sixty-four-day siege, the Chinese killed several thousand Tibetans during an aerial bombardment of an ancient monastery. Any success that the freedom fighters had against the Chinese—and the Khampas repeatedly cut the road to China in 1956—was paid for with terrible retribution. Such events vindicated the Dalai Lama in his view that to resist through violence would only lead to the death of his people. When, appalled at the course of events, he sent letters to Mao reminding him of the promises that had been made about autonomy, they went unanswered even as the violence spread toward Central Tibet.

Starting in 1957, CIA plans bore fruit. Between 1957 and 1961, eight small teams of guerrillas were airdropped back into Tibet, and a few weapons were parachuted to them as well. But this effort ended in tragedy, since most of the fighters, even those who managed to link up with Tibetans on the ground, either were soon killed or they committed suicide with their CIA-supplied cyanide capsules. These few CIA-trained guerrillas were not sufficient to help the widespread bands of freedom fighters achieve victory, but they were enough to convince the Chinese that the rebel fighters were under the direction of foreign imperialists—although this was never the case. In addition, the CIA's covert actions made the Dalai Lama's attempt to reach an accommodation with the Chinese more difficult. Washington was involved in a classic cold war denial operation, whose purpose was to hurt the Communists by denying them a victory, not to help the Tibetans. If the Tibetan agents supplied the United States with useful intelligence, so much the better.

"The U.S. support for Tibet in the 1950s," the Dalai Lama told me, "was not out of moral principle or sympathy but because of its worldwide anti-Communist policies." American support was, as he wrote in his autobiography, "a reflection of their anti-Communist polices rather than genuine support for the restoration of Tibetan independence."

Despite the growing rebellion against Chinese rule, Beijing allowed the Dalai Lama to travel to India in 1956 for a celebration of the 2,500th birth anniversary of the Buddha. By then, the Dalai Lama was convinced that he was attempting the impossible inside Tibet. In India, he had a chance to reconsider his course of actions. He met with his elder brothers, who were already living in exile. Both urged him to remain in India.

The Dalai Lama appealed directly to the Indian prime minister, Jawaharlal Nehru, explaining that his efforts at cooperation with the Chinese had been unsuccessful. Nehru, who was determined to prove that the grand new socialist, anticolonial alliance between China and India would work despite "antiprogressive" forces in the West, was implacable. He told the Dalai Lama to go back to Tibet and work with the Chinese on the basis of the Seventeen-Point Agreement. At the acme of his career, Nehru was not about to let a young Tibetan derail one of the cornerstones of the new Asia that would arise from the collapse of European colonialism. He spoke directly with the Chinese leadership, explaining that the Dalai Lama felt that Beijing was not holding up its end of the bargain. The Dalai Lama received assurances from Chairman Mao, through Nehru, saying that the

Socialist reforms that had caused so much trouble in eastern Tibet would not be enacted in Tibet for fifty years. Mao promised to Tibet, or that part of it now within the TAR, what was later granted to Hong Kong: one country, two systems. Though the Dalai Lama had no faith in these promises, he returned to Lhasa in April 1957, compelled—as Tibetan history and culture say that a manifestation of Chenrizi must be—to try to defend his people.

On his return to Tibet, he saw that the situation there was just short of chaos. Neither he nor the Chinese could prevent the people of Tibet from rebelling against the occupation. While, for centuries, Buddhist ideals have been strong in Tibet, it is a mistake to think of all Tibetans as unwilling to fight to defend their country, or that all Tibetans believed in nonviolence as the only way to oppose the invasion. The Thirteenth Dalai Lama had left clear instructions on the subject: "Use peaceful means where they are appropriate, but where they are not appropriate do not hesitate to resort to more forceful means." The primary problem faced by the freedom fighters, as the Thirteenth had foreseen, was that Tibet had no army and no weapons because, for fifteen years before the 1950 invasion, the Tibetan regency failed to provide them.

In the 1950s and 1960s, tens of thousands of Tibetans, as the writer Jamyang Norbu says, "took up arms to fight for the freedom of their country," and many thousands died for that cause. Though most of the armed encounters between the PLA and the freedom fighters in 1957 were still in eastern Tibet, fighting had begun to spread westward to the areas around Lhasa. As soon as the Dalai Lama returned from India, the Chinese increased their pressure for cooperation. China forced him to revoke the citizenship of his brothers (safe in exile) as well as of others who openly supported the rebellion. The Chinese even went so far as ordering the Dalai Lama to mobilize the tiny fragments of the Tibetan army against the rebels. The spiritual leader refused, saying that if he did so, the soldiers would all desert to the rebels. China mobilized 150,000 troops in Kham and Amdo to suppress the fighters there, and the resulting clashes sent a wave of refugees into Lhasa.

In 1958, Communists assumed control of Tibetan regions in Kham and Amdo. Many of the nomads of Amdo revolted. Some areas were reported virtually empty of men: they either had been killed or imprisoned or had fled. The largest monastery in Amdo was forced to close. Of its three thousand monks, two thousand were arrested. In many other areas of Amdo, the monasteries were "depopulated and looted of their valuable metals and artifacts and then physically destroyed." The lumber and stones were used to construct barracks for arriving PLA troops or Chinese settlers. This wave of revolt, invasion, and conquest radicalized tens of thousands of Tibetans and sent even greater numbers of refugees toward Lhasa.

As the anti-Chinese uprising spread, pushing ever closer to Lhasa, the Dalai Lama prepared for his final exams for his doctorate in Buddhist studies. From a young age he had memorized the five classical Buddhist texts that all Gelug monks must study and then had learned to use logic to debate the fine points of the texts. Now, over a period of several months, he went to the large monasteries around Lhasa where older graduates barraged him with questions on the texts. It was an intense period of study and examination for him.

By the spring of 1959, events in Tibet had reached a tipping point. Large tracts of southern Tibet were controlled by the freedom fighters, who called themselves the Chushi Gangdruk, a name referring to the four river gorges and six mountain ranges that bisect the rugged land of Kham, where the anti-Chinese revolt was born. China had driven most of the Chushi Gangdruk fighters out of Kham; by 1959, they had retreated to a region just south of Lhasa called Lhoka.

In Lhasa, a senior Chinese general invited the Dalai Lama to visit his headquarters to see a performance of a play. The Chinese issued special instructions that the Dalai Lama should come without his armed guards.

The population of the city had doubled that spring. The capital was swarming with refugees, camped on the outskirts of town, telling horror stories of the fighting they had fled from in Kham and Amdo. Lhasa was swirling with rumors, and the strange invitation from the Chinese to the Dalai Lama spread like wildfire. On March 10, 1959, thousands of Tibetans thronged the Norbulingka at dawn. By noon, thirty thousand people had gathered. They declared that they would not allow the Dalai Lama's procession to leave the walled summer palace. The crowd, furious at what it called the government's collaboration with the Chinese, beat up some officials, those seen as collaborators, who tried to enter the Norbulingka. One official was killed.

"I think in 1959 on the tenth of March, the whole history *(of Tibet)* returned," the Dalai Lama said. "That day, the people stopped my journey to the Chinese army camp. The people prevented me from dealing with the Chinese by popular expression, and in the meantime, they declared the independence of Tibet. So it broke down. Just before noon, the lord chamberlain Mr. Phala came to see me to report something. We went on the top roof of the Norbulingka. It was a sunny day, and the sun was shining very brightly. We could hear a lot of the noise from the public. After some discussion, I said this day could be a real turning point, but still at that time we did not know what would happen and had no plan to escape. Then the seventeenth of March, seven days later, I escaped. Before that decision was made, I felt a lot of fear, a lot of anxiety, but after the decision was made, I had no regrets. Whatever comes hence will come. No going back, now go ahead. One small act."

By March 17, the crisis in front of the Norbulingka had been brewing for a week. The people blocked roads into Lhasa to prevent Chinese reinforcements. The public held a conference at which the people officially repudiated the Seventeen-Point Agreement and declared the independence of Tibet. The Chinese in Lhasa were furious at what they saw as a CIA-aided revolt. In fact, the rage, which the Dalai Lama had tried to contain for nine years, had boiled over. During these events, the Dalai Lama repeatedly asked Tibet's State Oracle whether he should remain or flee to India. Each time, the Oracle had gone into a trance and said he should stay. Then on the seventeenth, two Chinese mortar shells exploded in the Norbulingka compound, not far from the Dalai Lama's house. When the Dalai Lama again consulted the Oracle, the answer had changed: the spiritual leader should flee Lhasa at once. His departure was kept secret except from a few popular leaders. It was decided that he could take almost nothing with him. Only his family members and his closest tutors would accompany him. The only way the Dalai Lama could escape from the Norbulingka was in disguise, so he donned the uniform of a Tibetan army trooper. When the time came, the commander of the troops at the Norbulingka left the walled compound with a few troops on patrol. The crowds that had gathered to protect the Dalai Lama allowed them to depart without noticing that the twenty-three-year-old Dalai Lama of Tibet was with them, sneaking first through the crowd and then past the nearby Chinese patrols.

"I needed to be very careful," he told me. "We came so near the Chinese that we could hear them. That was dangerous and frightening."

His small party, traveling under cover of night, evaded the Chinese and met up with members of the resistance, who formed an armed escort as the Dalai Lama fled south into liberated territory. The next week he made an official proclamation, saying that China had forced him to accept the Seventeen-Point Agreement under duress and that he now abrogated it. He also announced the formation of an independent Tibetan government.

As he fled south deeper into resistance-held territory, toward India, he received reports about events in Lhasa. Two days after he left the Norbulingka, the crowd agitating for independence gathered there and was attacked by PLA troops with machine guns, while the Norbulingka and the Potala were shelled. According to Chinese sources, the PLA killed 86,000 Tibetans. Beijing said the troops crushed a revolt fueled by foreign forces and led by the "feudal" elite.

"We just escaped Lhasa," the Dalai Lama said, "and were going to stay in southern Tibet and hoped there would be some negotiation or talk with the Chinese. That was our original plan and then as soon as we received information about the Chinese bombardment, we just decided to cross the border. Then when we received reports about what was happening in Lhasa, that was very painful. I felt a lot of pain because of the destruction. Then when I was near the Indian border, I saw an airplane come and that was mysterious and frightening. We did not know if it was a Chinese, Indian, or American plane. Or from Shambhala," he laughed. "So that night we were facing the danger of what will happen when the airplane comes back. That night we went to sleep without untying our bags. Then the next day we left in the early morning, looking at the sky, scared, but nothing happened."

"These were the moments when you were in danger or felt scared. Were there any more?" I asked.

"On the border," the Dalai Lama said, "I had to leave some men and officials and they had to go back. They were willing to face the Chinese, but their future was very uncertain, and that was very sad. At the same time, I was also very sick with dysentery, and I was very weak. By then we heard more through the radio about the bombardment in Lhasa and all the other things, and I felt very sad. That was the saddest moment."

The Dalai Lama was now on the Indian border, Lhasa was in revolt, and the Chinese were starting a wave of repression throughout the country. Chushi Gangdruk and the Tibetan patriots fighting the Chinese were not up to the task. They were all soon defeated, and during the next few years the last vestiges of armed resistance retreated into secret bases along Nepal's northern border, where, with CIA support, they made the occasional raid into Tibet until about 1971. The Dalai Lama's attempt to work with the Chinese ended, and Beijing crushed an armed rebellion in Tibet.

"When we approached the border," the Dalai Lama said, "we were not even sure whether or not the Indians would allow us in. If not, we decided to go into Bhutan. So we sent two officials to the border and at the Indian border they heard that India was ready to receive me. They had received instructions from Delhi, and they were ready to receive the Dalai Lama."

The Dalai Lama crossed into India with a party of eighty and was escorted by an Indian government liaison officer to the town of Bomdila, where the Dalai Lama remained in seclusion as he recovered from his bout of dysentery. The liaison officer also gave the Dalai Lama a telegram from Prime Minister Nehru, which welcomed the young refugee and offered "the necessary facilities" to him, his family, and his entourage. But there were limits to this hospitality.

"Our worry was the government of India's attitude," the Dalai Lama said. "One immediate sort of anxiety was to meet some *(Tibetan government)* officials who had stayed in Kalimpong when I returned to Tibet in 1956. And there were my brothers in India, Gyalo Thondup was there, and we were very much anxious to meet them. But then the Indian government did not allow Gyalo to meet with us."

By 1959, New Delhi knew that the Dalai Lama's elder brother Gyalo Thondup worked with the CIA to aid the rebels in Tibet, though no one knew how paltry that assistance was. The Indian government wanted

China to understand that New Delhi had nothing to do with these covert operations, and in fact it did not at that time, though the situation changed after China invaded India in 1963. When the Dalai Lama mentioned that the Indians would not allow him to meet with his brother, I offered, "Because, by then, Gyalo Thondup already had contact with the CIA."

"That is right," the Dalai Lama acknowledged. "Then at the last moment, Gyalo came to meet me. I was anxious to see him."

As soon as he arrived, India pressured the Dalai Lama about a number of things—in particular, his first press statement. "At that time many people were anxious or concerned about what I would say. And then Pandit Nehru and the government of India decided to send special experts from somewhere," the Dalai Lama said. "And he suggested that this was not the right moment to make some decisions. Nehru said I should first establish what happened. He said, 'You should be clear and then after you reach Mussoorie, then you can make a major policy statement.'"

The Dalai Lama's escape was one of the biggest news stories of 1959, establishing him as a world figure. Nor was Beijing silent about the event. The New China News agency said the reports were false, stipulating that the Dalai Lama had, in fact, been abducted by rebels and was speaking under duress. The "rebellion" had been organized by "a reactionary upper-strata clique" and was crushed with the aid of "patriotic Tibetan monks and laymen, the People's Liberation Army." What is more, "The Tibetan people," NCN said, "are patriotic, support the Central People's Government, ardently love the PLA, and oppose the imperialists and traitors."

After the Dalai Lama settled in the hill town of Mussoorie, in accommodations provided by the Indian government, he issued a second statement to the press. "Chinese propaganda burst and said our statement was false," the Dalai Lama explained, "so the government of India officer told me that we should have another statement, with my name. The statement made in Mussoorie is my view and not India's." He gave a weary sigh. "So that is the beginning of politics."

In April 1959, as the Dalai Lama took stock of his situation, he met with Nehru, who visited him in Mussoorie. During their meeting, the Dalai Lama explained what he planned to do next.

The twenty-four-year-old Dalai Lama told the sixty-year-old Nehru, "I am determined to win independence for Tibet, but the immediate requirement is to put a stop to the bloodshed." The prime minister, who had come to power because of a political campaign, led by Mahatma Gandhi and founded on nonviolence and civil disobedience, was outraged.

"That is not possible!" Nehru shouted. "You say you want independence and in the same breath you say you do not want bloodshed. Impossible!"

Thirty years later, in 1989, the Dalai Lama received the Nobel Peace Prize. Since 1959, he has devoted his life to the ideal of nonviolence. Although his goal would slowly change from independence for Tibet to genuine autonomy within China, his devotion to nonviolence has remained unwavering.

13

SINCE 1959

In the 1980s, I interviewed poor peasants in a remote area of Tibet without Chinese officials present. I spent a week in a village, living in the headman's house. He was the local Communist Party boss and had all the party posters and certificates on his mud walls to prove it. Despite the fact that power lines went past the village, smoke from his dung fire had blackened his posters. He had once been a landless peasant working the fields of the local noble. Now he and a dozen other farmers lived in the noble's old mansion, while the former aristocrat lives in exile in India.

The Chinese Communist Party collectivized the aristocrat's stony fields, in the 1960s, and all the villagers worked the land together. When he laughed about that experiment, the headman had few visible teeth. "We shared everything, and there was nothing for anyone. We starved some years, and that had never happened under the nobles."

During the 1980s, Deng Xiaoping's reforms overturned Mao's forced collectivization, and the peasants divided the communal acreage among themselves, working their own fields. As state-run crony capitalism and a massive investment of foreign capital brought wealth to China, roads were built even to this remote village and power lines supplied the new PLA base near town. The Communist revolution had come and gone while the peasants of Tibet were farming the same fields and still barely getting by.

The headman I stayed with (whose name and location I am disguising to protect his identity) took me on a tour of the village. There were still no schools (though some villages nearby had them), and he sadly showed me how the once vast monastery nearby had been destroyed by Chinese and Tibetan students during the Cultural Revolution.

As we roamed over the fields of rubble from the temples, the old man stopped to pick a small flower and offered it to the empty niche where a Buddha had once stood in a wall that had been half demolished by dynamite. "No one wants to work for the old nobles for free again," he said, "but everyone wants the Chinese to leave and for the Dalai Lama to return. We pray for that every day. If you are ever able to speak the truth for us, please speak it. We cannot. The old nobles were harsh, and we do not want that back. But from what we hear, the Dalai Lama has said the old system would not return—that we will have democracy when he returns. The new nobles are all Chinese, and they are even harsher than the old ones. We are just insects, and the Chinese crush us." Fifty years of Chinese liberation has failed to extinguish the flame of Tibetan patriotism. The average Tibetans have learned not to revolt, not to protest, not to speak; they have learned how to survive day to day.

While I was in this village, Chinese Communist Party members drove out from Lhasa on an inspection tour. When they arrived, they stepped delicately out of their Toyota Land Cruiser. They looked clean and eager to stay that way. The rough farmers of Tibet, with their calloused hands, hard as their rocky fields, surrounded the Chinese. With broad smiles, they helped the Chinese put on silk robes, like those Tibet's nobles had worn. They bowed low to help the Chinese climb up on docile yaks, which a woman brought up. One old man, in a faithful imitation of days past, bent down and formed a stirrup with his hands so that one fat Chinese man could crush the peasant's fingers and mount the yak. The peasant laughed loudly at the pain, making the visitor from Lhasa feel comfortable. The Chinese donned the long turquoise earring that Tibetan aristocrats once wore, with the matching silk hats with long red fringes. The peasants laughed loudly and professed their undying comradeship. Once the Chinese were properly attired and aboard the obedient female yaks, the Chinese took photographs of one another, dressed in the kind of garments that Tibet's nobles, before 1950, had donned for festivals.

Once the photography was over, my friend the village headman helped the Chinese off the yaks, and the entire party retired into a beautiful tent the farmers had erected. As the headman popped a bottle of beer and bent low to serve his new masters, he managed to glance up at me and winked.

The spirit of Tibet was still alive, and his smile, his honesty, and his jaunty attitude—despite the despair and humiliation he had lived through—were the only evidence I needed to see that. So long as Tibetans plant barley in stony fields, knowing they have a laughable chance of seeing a crop; so long as nomads herd their yaks on high pastures where snow squalls rage in July—just so long as that, the heart springs of Tibet will flow freely despite all external obstructions. This may be why China today is working to end all of that.

The Dalai Lama's transformation from a twenty-four-year-old refugee fleeing for his life over the Himalayas with Chinese troops in hot pursuit to a universally lauded globe-trotting elder statesman is a product of the remarkable and tragic journey the Tibetan nation has made since 1959.

When the Dalai Lama fled to India, most of his countrymen had no choice except to remain in Tibet. Escape attempts were perilous because of attacks by the PLA. In some cases, fewer than 10 percent of a party that set off from eastern Tibet, on a four-month trek to India, arrived there alive. Despite such odds, 80,000 emigrants survived their trans-Himalayan treks to India in the years just after the Chinese defeated the Tibetan Rebellion of 1959. Today there are an estimated 135,000 Tibetans living in exile. Perhaps 20 percent of all Tibetan refugees in India arrived between 1986 and 1996. Even now, 2,500 Tibetans a year make perilous winter journeys across the Himalayas to escape. It remains the longest, most difficult escape route in the world. Every year a few of the refugees die en route, while a few survivors lose limbs to frostbite. Refugees caught attempting to escape are regularly jailed and tortured.

In 1959, as the Dalai Lama arrived, renounced the Seventeen-Point Agreement, and established a government in exile, New Delhi housed the first 30,000 bedraggled refugees in makeshift tented camps along the Himalayan border with Tibet. The government donated basic amenities and offered work on road construction gangs when it was available. Conditions were rough. The refugees, who arrived in handspun woolen robes, had to toil in India's tropical heat and monsoon rains, exposed for the first time to a deadly tropical stew of viruses and bacteria. During the first year, there were high mortality rates among the young and the elderly. Few of the arriving refugees spoke English or Hindi, or had ever seen a train. The Indian government and the newly formed exile government, called the Central Tibetan Administration (CTA), sought to improve conditions for the refugees. In 1960, New Delhi donated agricultural land, in south India, where refugees started farms and constructed self-sufficient communities. Private charities devoted to aiding Tibetan refugees sprang up in Canada, Switzerland, France, England, Norway, the United States, and many other countries around the world.

During the 1960s and 1970s, thirty-five Tibetan resettlement camps were established in India, ten in Nepal, and seven in Bhutan. At each camp, Tibetans built schools, handicraft centers to generate income, vegetable plots, and medical clinics. Refugees in Nepal set up carpet-weaving shops; by the 1990s, their efforts had proven so successful that the industry became one of Nepal's largest sources of foreign exchange. Some Tibetans who became Nepali citizens grew so wealthy that they could afford to send their children to college in the United States and Europe. Over the years some refugees took foreign citizenship in Nepal and India, while small numbers of Tibetans migrated (with the help of charities) to Switzerland, Canada, and the United States, where they eventually took citizenship. The vast majority of refugees remain in India; they are legally stateless and must travel on Indian-issued identity certificates.

As the exiles strove to ensure the survival of Tibetan Buddhism, they reestablished, in India, some of the best-known monasteries, such as Drepung, Sera, and Ganden. These monasteries provided a place for refugee monks to transfer their wisdom to the younger generation, born in exile. Today there are Tibetan monasteries, libraries, schools, herbal medical clinics, and other exile-created cultural institutes all over Nepal and India.

Tibetan refugees began to pay a voluntary tax to support the work of the exile government, which wrote a constitution. Every five years Tibetans elect representatives to govern the affairs of the exiled nation. The old noble families who surrounded the Dalai Lama when he first came into exile are slowly being pushed aside, and democratic voices rising from the exiles find fault with their governing bodies. Yet a strange thing has happened to this exile community. Some of the Buddhist teachers who journeyed with the emigrants began to teach Buddhism not to Tibetans but to Westerners. Europeans and Americans met Tibetan monks in Nepal and India in the 1960s and 1970s, took meditation courses, and found much to study and admire. During the 1970s and into the next decade, charismatic elderly Tibetan teachers worked with a tiny but ever-growing cadre of converts to found the first Tibetan Buddhist centers in France, Britain, Italy, Germany, Spain, Australia, the United States, Greece, Canada, and elsewhere. In addition, the field of Tibetan studies has emerged in universities around the world, and translators have made Buddhist texts from Tibet's spiritual treasure house accessible to millions. Though sometimes wildly misunderstood, the remote nation's religious ideas found global resonance. Today books by Tibetan teachers, such as the Dalai Lama's *The Art of Happiness* and Sogyal Rinpoche's *The Tibetan Book of Living and Dying*, are best sellers read by mainstream audiences as well as Buddhists. For the first time in its history, Buddhism has been firmly established on six continents, and Tibetan exiles have played a large part in this phenomenon.

By the early twenty-first century, conditions in the West that may have caused a surge of interest in Buddhism—disillusionment with a manic devotion to prosperity—arose in Asia. After middle-class prosperity arrived in Taiwan, young people established two hundred Tibetan Buddhist centers there. Younger Chinese in Taiwan have shown an affinity for Tibetan Buddhism rivaling that shown among members of the Manchu court two centuries ago. Even in China there is a small but growing interest in Buddhism as taught by Tibetan masters. A few Chinese (often from wealthier, more-educated circles) are now eager to study the religion. Today there are persistent rumors that some of the highest members of the Chinese Communist Party are devout Buddhists. Such Chinese are traveling to Tibet, where, in some monasteries, they have become a noticeable, welcomed minority. Surely, this movement causes a tendril of fear to shoot through the heart of China's leaders. Could China's relations with Tibet ever return to their original religious, nonpolitical foundation? It is not by accident that translation headsets for Chinese are available during the Dalai Lama's teachings in America, or that he frequently gives teachings for Chinese Buddhists outside China.

Many Tibetans, the Dalai Lama included, are amazed at the global interest in Tibetan Buddhism. For centuries in Tibet, nationalism was secondary to religion; the ruling elite strove to prevent contact with the outside world for fear that foreign ideas, or any hint of modernism, might damage the country's Buddhist culture. Ironically, Tibetans lost their country, and Buddhism was nearly eradicated there, in large part because Lhasa failed to modernize quickly enough; on the other hand, it was the destruction of Tibet that caused Tibetan Buddhism to spread around the world.

Since 1959, Tibetans who remained in their homeland have followed a course opposite that of their exiled brethren. As Tibetan Buddhism spread throughout the world, China attempted to exterminate the philosophy in Tibet. While communities in exile developed self-governing bodies, Beijing forcibly collectivized all means of production in Tibet. As the idea of Tibet grew in the West, China has tried to erase the nation's past, present, and future.

After the Dalai Lama fled in 1959, Tibetans lived at first under the direct rule of the People's Liberation Army, and then power shifted slowly back to the CCP's local administration, the Preparatory Committee for the Autonomous Region of Tibet (PCART). Choekyi Gyaltsen, the Tenth Panchen Lama, remained as the highest-ranking religious leader. He served as acting chairman of PCART, but he was no more able to restrain the Chinese than the Dalai Lama had been. Leftists in the CCP insisted that Tibetans experience the full power of Communism. Soon after the Dalai Lama's departure, Chinese media reported urgent demands from the "serfs" for collectivization, which Mao had promised would not happen for fifty years.

The Tibetan historian Tsering Shakya, whose family fled the occupied state in 1967, points out that "the Tibetans were not mere passive agents who were totally manipulated by the Chinese cadres: the Communists' promise of modernity, progress and economic and social justice did indeed entice many Tibetans to work for the new society." Reading those words, I could not help but recall the Fourteenth Dalai Lama's respect for the ideals of Communism. Apparently, he was not the only Tibetan who felt that way.

During the first stage of collectivization, the land seized from the wealthy was redistributed equitably. Shakya says that initially "the land reform was genuinely liked by the Tibetan peasantry." However, in the next stage on the path to absolute Communism, the CCP stripped ownership of land and animals from individuals and gave it to communes or collectives. In many cases, the PLA forcibly established the communes. Communist theory says communal ownership of the means of production will increase production and the living standards of workers, yet, as has been the case in every experiment with forced collectivization, food rations declined instead of increasing. By then the Communist Party cadre in Tibet had destroyed the old economic system. Private stores, private sources of credit, production of food, and traders all had been forced out of business or taken over by the Communist Party. After a decade of intermittent famines, punctuated by chronic food shortages, even the poorest former serf realized that the egalitarian ideals of Communism were a sham. According to the Dalai Lama's exile government, the CTA, about 342,000 Tibetans starved to death. It was obvious that Tibetans were, as Shakya says, "mere recipients of commands," while the Chinese exercised all the power. Chinese outnumbered Tibetans at the national level of Tibet's administration, the old Tibetan elite having been replaced with a Chinese one.

The promise of religious freedom for Tibetans proved equally false, as Beijing destroyed more than six thousand monasteries and temples between 1950 and 1980. By the end of the 1970s, a total of eight monasteries were still operating in Tibet, with fewer than one thousand monks in all. The other monasteries had been destroyed or converted to nonreligious use. Monasteries had often been centers of learning in which artists, writers, and doctors were trained. To decimate the monasteries was to strike at the heart of Tibetan culture.

Though some of the monasteries were demolished during aerial bombardments and military attacks in eastern Tibet during the invasion of 1949–1951 and incursions in 1958 and 1959, most survived until the 1960s. Under the watchful eyes of young Red Guards, both Tibetan and

Chinese, the surviving monasteries were systematically dismantled during the now infamous Cultural Revolution. Mao's philosophical battle cry
for this campaign was "Create the new by smashing the old." While China
destroyed "old" Tibet, a "new" China emerged with timber and construction material, recycled from the sacked monasteries, to build barracks for
the PLA troops or Chinese administrators in Lhasa.

Occasionally the Tibetans were able to convince the Red Guards that
the people's labor invested in the giant monastic buildings should not be lost.
The CCP allowed some temples to be kept as grain storehouses, or party
headquarters (after the monks were thrown out). In some places, this ruse
even protected ancient murals inside. Images of the Buddha were rarely so
lucky. It was easy to destroy statues made of adobe, even with pickaxes, and
those that were ignored would simply melt in the rain after roofs were ripped
off the temples. If made of copper, statues were sometimes smashed and
left in a heap at the site. Statues made of gold, silver, or bronze were carted
out of the temples, thrown into trucks, and shipped to China. One foundry
near Beijing alone melted more than six hundred tons of Buddhist statues.
For Tibetans, the merit in these statues and their sacred presence, like the
deities of earth and sky, protected their land. That the spiritual accumula-
tion of the ages could be melted, that the concept of cherishing such images
could become a crime, shattered ingrained cultural values. Some of the worst
horrors of the Cultural Revolution are seen in the tearful eyes of middle-
age Tibetans today, when they explain how, as children, they were forced
to dismantle the temples they had built and worshipped in. Many still feel
guilty and can never forgive themselves.

In the chaos of destruction, Tibetans sometimes pushed an ancient
Indian bronze Buddha beneath the rubble to hide it, or saved an ancient
text. In some cases, like the Potala, edicts from Beijing protected an entire
building and all its contents, but such mercy was rare. The first foreign
tourists to Tibet in 1985 found rooms in dozens of temples, all over the
country, stacked to the ceiling with hundreds of copper statues, which had
been smashed during the Cultural Revolution. By then, Tibetans were
cheerfully beating them back into shape if possible, and returning them
to the monasteries, though the majority of Tibet's cultural patrimony was
gone forever.

During the Cultural Revolution, Red Guards treated monks and nuns even more ferociously than they did the buildings and statues. Since Buddhist vows forbid monks and nuns to work or to marry, Maoists saw clerics as sterile parasites on the working class. The party ordered them to work and to marry. Since monasteries often owned most of the arable fields, land redistribution erased the monasteries' source of rental incomes. The Chinese scholar Zhang Yianlu asserts that there were 114,000 nuns and monks in Central Tibet (or in today's TAR, where only a third of all Tibetans live) in 1958, but that by 1960 the number dropped to 18,000.

The aristocrats who tried to work with the Chinese in 1951 were, like the monks, among the first victims of the Cultural Revolution. It is perhaps not an accident that China eliminated these traditional elites just after they had outlived their practical usefulness. When China first invaded Tibet, collaboration from the monastic and aristocratic elite, or at least their acquiescence, was essential. By the 1960s, high-ranking monks and the aristocrats had nothing more to offer, and the party singled them out for public class-struggle sessions during the Cultural Revolution. As the former elites were paraded through the streets with dunce hats on, "victims of the aristocrats" in the "old society" gathered to hurl accusations at the aristocrats or monastic chiefs, and to beat and torture them. Survivors went to prison.

Red Guards in Lhasa and then Beijing subjected even the Panchen Lama to a public struggle session. After 1959, the Panchen Lama tried to work with the Chinese but grew disillusioned with the cost of China's liberation and made the mistake, in 1962, of writing a secret catalogue of the CCP's errors in Tibet, called the Seventy Thousand Character Petition. He was twenty-four years old when he finished his petition and submitted it to the CCP, thinking the party wanted to reform itself. Two years later, in 1964, he was subjected to struggle sessions in Lhasa. In 1966 he went through even worse public sessions in Beijing and then he disappeared, for the next twelve years. He would be forty years old when the CCP released him from prison, in 1978, but today the Seventy Thousand Character Petition is the only insider's account of what the CCP did to Tibet.

The Dalai Lama's exile government, the CTA, estimates that 92,000 Tibetans who were subjected to struggle sessions died or committed suicide. It also estimates that 173,000 Tibetans died in prison, or in Reform Through Labor camps (China's dreaded prison camp, or *Laogai* system, which is still active), from overwork, torture, or malnutrition. This class warfare, so Maoist theory said, was part of the cathartic price of destroying injustice and creating equality, but in the process it also destroyed Tibetan culture.

During the Cultural Revolution, the Chinese leadership skillfully encouraged the Tibetans to attack their country's traditional social and religious system. In China, on the other hand, while the people destroyed ancient art and temples as symbols of the old society, Mao focused much of the public fury on the power elite within the Communist Party itself. Indeed, for Mao, the Cultural Revolution was in great part a tool to oust the Rightists, or "Capitalist Roaders," hiding within the party—a tool to eliminate those who threatened his authority. He urged the people to reform the Communist Party itself.

In Tibet, however, the CCP discouraged the people from attacking the party itself, when possible, since it was Chinese. The Cultural Revolution in Lhasa was not just a political campaign; it became a vehicle for cultural genocide, a means for the Chinese to terrorize the Tibetans into assimilation. This peculiarity of the Cultural Revolution had, as Tsering Shakya has pointed out, a "devastating effect on Tibetan culture."

Tibetans were given no choice but to abandon their ethnic attire and wear the drab green uniforms that all Chinese wore. They were required to cut their hair short and to coat the rainbow-painted windows of Lhasa with a drab olive green. After China forced the people to help destroy the temples and monasteries, they were then shuttled into communes where they were subjected to close supervision and were urged to report on one another to curry favor. The coercive power of the state controlled every aspect of life, and propaganda broadcasts echoed from loudspeakers in every commune. Just as earlier imperial occupiers had demanded that the Chinese wear Manchu clothes and haircuts, on pain of death, Tibetans were terrorized into submission. Before he vanished into prison, the Panchen Lama wrote specifically about this issue, in his Seventy Thousand Character Petition. "Once a nationality's language, costume, customs and other important characteristics have disappeared, then the nationality itself has disappeared too—that is to say, it has turned into another nationality." The Chinese had learned such lessons throughout their history, when foreign invaders subjugated them. Now it was Beijing's turn to have the upper hand.

A thousand years of artifacts of Tibetan civilization—paintings, books, murals, architecture, textiles, statues—was destroyed during the Cultural Revolution, and a generation of devout Buddhists had to profane themselves by dismantling their nation's artistic and relgious heritage. Even Tibet's most sacred statues, like those in the Jokhang, founded by Songzen Gampo a millennium earlier, were demolished. The language, too, had transmuted; under Chinese tutelage, newly minted words littered Tibetan speech to express new ideas. Now ethnic Chinese became Han Chinese so that their neighbors of ethnic minority origin could become Tibetan Chinese. Names were transcribed into Chinese characters, which, when pronounced, became Chinese. Higher education was available to Tibetans, if at all, only in Chinese-speaking classrooms. Thousands of young Tibetans were taken from their parents and shipped to boarding schools deep in the interior of China: by the time they returned, many spoke only Chinese.

Chinese today claim that the Cultural Revolution damaged both Chinese and Tibetan alike. This is true, but it misses the heart of the matter. As Tsering Shakya writes, Red Guards "felt that Tibet and Tibetans needed to be revolutionized and saw themselves as advanced revolutionaries who had come to the aid of the backward students in this retarded region." There is little difference between this attitude and that of the Chinese toward Inner Asian nomads a thousand years ago. Even today, the poorest Chinese taxi driver plying the streets of Lhasa shares this underlying chauvinism. In the eyes of the Chinese, their nation sacrificed much to help educate their benighted neighbors, and the Cultural Revolution in Tibet was a temporary aberration, not an expression of arrogance. After Deng Xiaoping's reforms began, in the late 1970s, China has grown much wealthier, because the party allowed the return of certain forms of capitalism. Some of the resulting wealth, invested in Lhasa, has even helped

Tibetans. Yet it is the desire to root out Tibetan nationalism that primarily motivates Beijing's investments in Tibet. The Chinese intellectual Wang Lixiong wrote in 1999:

> The current line of thinking on ruling Tibet is to speed up the pace of Tibetan modernization to win public opinion and break down religious control, and to use steadily rising living standards to undermine the influence of the Tibetan separatists.

Ma Lihua, a Chinese scholar who has lived and traveled in Tibet for decades and written sixteen books on the country, makes the government's case:

> We are helping Tibetans catch up with the west. . . . It is not "Hanification" [i.e., Sinification] but globalization. I'm not saying this because I simply accept government propaganda, but because I have seen the improvements in Tibet with my own eyes. The west should be more objective, but it's not.

According to Wang Lixiong, economic development in Lhasa has, to a degree, undermined religious fervor among certain classes. But he bemoans that "the space left by traditional religion is being filled up by another quasi-religion of modern society: nationalism. . . . The facts show that the most secularized urban Tibetan youth are characterized by the strongest . . . nationalist sentiment."

The Dalai Lama's Central Tibetan Administration, after a village-by-village accounting, estimates that actions of the Chinese state killed 1.2 million Tibetans between 1950 and 1980, a figure the Chinese reject out of hand. The British writer Patrick French, in his recent book *Tibet, Tibet,* disputes the Tibetan figure, controversially asserting the death toll was certainly no more than 500,000.

What is beyond dispute is that during the Chinese invasion and the ensuing Cultural Revolution, Tibetans of all classes paid a terrible price, a price the Thirteenth Dalai Lama had predicted in the 1930s, for not working together to defend their nation:

The Monasteries will be looted and destroyed, and the monks and nuns killed or chased away. The great works of the noble Dharma kings of old will be undone, and all of our cultural and spiritual institutions persecuted, destroyed and forgotten. . . . We will become like slaves to our conquerors . . . and the days and nights will pass slowly and with great suffering and terror.

Many Tibetans have begun to understand that the destruction of their country was not inevitable. Unfortunately the elite who inherited the authority of the Thirteenth Dalai Lama was so convinced of the unquestioned truth of its belief system that it saw no reason to study the world as it really is. Such fatal hubris is one of the most powerful lessons that history has to teach us.

After Mao's death, in 1976, Deng Xiaoping's capitalist counterrevolution swept across China. Communities redivided collectivized farmlands among the tillers. No explanation was offered as to why three million Chinese landlords were murdered in the 1950s as the price for a communalization that was now abandoned as a failed policy. The fruits of private ownership were quickly obvious. Within a few years, Chinese agriculture provided more meat, eggs and dairy products, and other foods than it ever had under Communism. With this economic pragmatism came a hint of political reform, and Tibetans slowly benefited from both.

The Tibetan elite who had survived the prison camps, including the Panchen Lama, were released starting in 1977. Two years later the party freed more Tibetans, and Chinese newspapers appealed to Tibetan exiles to "return home to participate in socialist construction." Few immigrants took up the offer.

Religion, banned for more than a decade, was slowly revived. During the 1980s, the surviving temples were reconsecrated, and a vast program of reconstruction began. China claims to have invested $65 million between 1980 and 1994 to rebuild some of the monasteries it had destroyed, though Tibetans say the vast majority of the investment required has come from devout Tibetans. Monks returned to monasteries across Tibet and monastic education resumed, though a strict limit on the number of monks was imposed, as was attendance at "patriotic education" sessions. China does not assert this control delicately. I have seen plainclothed Chinese with handguns visible, tucked into their pants, living at isolated monasteries; they, too, attend the education sessions and have no other job except to watch the monks. Despite such efforts, or perhaps because of them, the monasteries became flash points of Tibetan patriotism.

As the reforms of Deng Xiaoping swept across China, tens of thousands of Tibetans appeared in public in Lhasa chanting mantras and prostrating before temples. Rainbow-colored prayer flags sprouted on the roofs of homes across the land, where, before, each house flew only the red flag of China. If Tibetans lived once in a country split, in part, by religion and factionalism, religion is today the root of patriotic nationalism that binds them all.

As some capitalism and some civil liberties returned to China, the people of Tibet were also granted some private freedoms, so long as the party line was adhered to in public. The drab Mao suits vanished and Tibetan clothes and hairstyles returned. For those who had lived through the previous thirty years, these reforms, though small, were welcome. Still, Tibet had one of the lowest literacy rates in China in the 1990s, and one in three children received no education and no health care. Even so, Tibetans slowly began to produce as many goods and services as they had before China first invaded.

As reforms brought change to Tibetans' private lives, the freeze on talks between the Dalai Lama and Beijing showed signs of thawing. In December 1978, Deng Xiaoping, the architect of the revolution sweeping China, quietly initiated meetings with the Dalai Lama's representatives, the first since 1959. Gyalo Thondup, the Dalai Lama's elder brother, traveled to Beijing, where Deng Xiaoping informed him in a face-to-face session that besides independence everything was open to discussion. After working with the CIA in the 1960s and 1970s, Gyalo Thondup decided that Tibet's fate lay within China, and some observers feel he may have given Deng Xiaoping the impression that his brother was ready to give up independence for real autonomy. The Dalai Lama himself made statements, between 1978 and 1980, in which he said that the happiness of the Tibetan people, not the status of the Dalai Lama, was the core of the issue and that he was willing to begin a dialogue with China on resolving the issue. In December 1978, as these steps began, Deng Xiaoping reaffirmed, to an AP reporter, China's basic stand. "The Dalai Lama may come back, but only as a Chinese citizen," Deng Xiaoping said. "We have but one demand—patriotism." As a confidence-building gesture, Deng Xiaoping permitted exiled Tibetans to send fact-finding teams to Tibet. These missions—which were actually delegations sent by the Dalai Lama and the CTA, though China did not want to view the undertaking that way—included important officials of the Tibetan exile government, as well as members of the Dalai Lama's family.

Despite stern warnings from the Chinese Communist Party and Tibetan Autonomous Region (TAR) officials that the exiles should be ignored, large crowds of Tibetans in Lhasa and everywhere the teams went mobbed the exiles and gave them a hysterical welcome. Chinese leaders were stunned that decades of propaganda and class warfare had failed to destroy Tibetan nationalism. As a Chinese official present at the Lhasa welcome for the exiles said, "The efforts of the last 20 years have been wasted in a single day."

In May 1980, just before a second tour by exiles, the CCP's general secretary, Hu Yaobang, went to Tibet to investigate. The poverty in Tibet shocked Hu; he said that China's efforts in Tibet reminded him of colonialism. He admitted that not only were Tibetans poor but that in some areas they were poorer now than before 1950. Proposing legitimate reform, Hu asked that the Chinese in Tibet learn Tibetan and that their numbers be reduced. Hu essentially tried to carry out the reforms that the Panchen Lama had proposed in 1962. With real autonomy in Tibet, there could have been grounds for a negotiated settlement. Tibetans and Chinese continued to talk.

The negotiations soon revealed a fundamental problem. The Tibetans insisted that the issue to be negotiated was a political solution for all of Tibet, including the eastern parts of the nation, Amdo and Kham, which China had incorporated into its provinces and where as many as two thirds of all Tibetans lived. However, Beijing wanted to talk about the Dalai Lama's personal status, not about Tibet's status or China's policies in

Tibet. The Chinese were eager for the Dalai Lama to return to Beijing and live there, where he would have ceremonial duties. Chinese sources say the "lion-mouthed" aspirations of the Tibetans stunned the negotiators, while the Dalai Lama could hardly agree to a settlement in which most Tibetans would remain outside the borders of an autonomous region. After 1984, the dialogue stalled and fell apart.

Ultimately, the Dalai Lama asked the international community to exert pressure on the Chinese to negotiate in good faith. In June 1987 the U.S. House of Representatives accused Beijing of having "invaded and occupied Tibet" in 1950. In September of the same year, the Dalai Lama personally urged the Human Rights Caucus of Congress to help him restart negotiations with the Chinese. Standing in the Capitol surrounded by members of Congress, the Dalai Lama said:

> The real issue . . . is China's illegal occupation of Tibet. . . . The Chinese authorities have attempted to confuse the issue by claiming that Tibet has always been a part of China. This is untrue. Tibet was a fully independent state when the People's Liberation Army invaded the country in 1949/50. . . . As China's military occupation of Tibet continues, the world should remember that though Tibetans have lost their freedom, under international law Tibet today is still an independent state under illegal occupation.

Despite this history, the Dalai Lama sought a negotiated settlement with the Chinese and offered a five-point peace plan in hopes that it would bring the parties back to the table. He proposed that China agree to respect the human rights of Tibetans, release all political prisoners, and respect the nation's environment; that talks should begin in earnest on a means to end the transfer of Chinese people into Tibet, and that Tibet eventually become a demilitarized zone of peace.

The Chinese responded to the peace plan by saying that "the status of Tibet" was "a question which simply does not exist." Beijing specifically denounced the plan as nothing but "the continued preaching of 'the independence of Tibet.'" In Lhasa, popular anger at China's vehement criticism of the Dalai Lama and his proposal erupted into street demonstrations in favor of independence. About two hundred protesters were beaten and arrested and at least six were shot dead during months of protests. Jail terms for some demonstrators were severe, up to nineteen years. The U.S. Senate responded in October by accepting the Tibet resolution passed earlier by the House, while adding language that condemned China's violent repression of peaceful protesters. Protests in Tibet continued regularly, during which several more Tibetans were killed. The Panchen Lama and Nagwang Jigme Ngapo, both living in China, condemned the protesters and Ngapo spoke against "any move aimed at splitting the motherland."

In June 1988, during an address at the European Parliament at Strasbourg, France, the Dalai Lama officially stated for the first time that although Tibetans wanted independence, and even though history showed they had long enjoyed it, he was willing to negotiate with China over real autonomy for Tibet. He spoke about a self-governing entity, "in association with the People's Republic of China," in which the Chinese government would remain responsible for Tibet's foreign policy and defense. With protests in Tibet and a tide of international attention focused on the Dalai Lama, Beijing initially agreed to meet with His Holiness at a place of his choosing. When the Dalai Lama responded with a concrete proposal for such talks, however, the process stalled. Ultimately the Chinese rejected the Strasbourg proposal, because, they said, the Dalai Lama had not "relinquished the concept of the 'independence of Tibet.'"

As protests continued into late 1988, the Panchen Lama was sent to Lhasa to quell the disturbances. During a speech in Shigatse on January 17, 1989, he dramatically called for the Dalai Lama to be allowed to work with him in Tibet: "It is necessary for both the Dalai Lama and Panchen [Lama] to confer. . . . I alone cannot make a decision." Just two days later he made another important announcement: "Since liberation, there has certainly been development, but the price paid for this development has been greater than the gains." These statements attracted worldwide media coverage and showed that the Panchen Lama was not, in his heart, the collaborator many had thought. Five days later, the fifty-year-old was dead, under mysterious circumstances—allegedly felled by a heart attack.

During the late 1980s, the liberal faction of the Chinese Communist Party that supported Hu Yaobang and his call for reforms was driven out of power in both China and Tibet. As the liberals and the hard-liners fought for control of the CCP, a then-unknown rising star, Hu Jintao, was appointed as party secretary of the TAR and arrived in Lhasa in January 1989. The general secretary of the CCP, Zhao Ziyang, a liberal, instructed Hu Jintao to treat the Tibetans softly, despite the protests. Yet only two months after his appointment, Hu Jintao ignored the directions and worked with the military to shift tens of thousands of troops into Tibet. For two years, the Tibetans had challenged Chinese control, and while resisters had been killed, there had not been the hard-line crackdown that prior events in Tibet would have suggested. The CCP's "liberals" had not reacted as harshly, and the demonstrators continued to return to the streets. On March 7, 1989, after two days of protests during which troops killed seventy Tibetans, Hu Jintao, acting with Beijing, declared the imposition of martial law. During the next eighteen months, all dissent was crushed, and there has been no large-scale resistance since. Hu Jintao gained credibility with the hard-liners by ignoring the liberals and cracking down so harshly. It was a prescient move that would contribute to his election as president of the People's Republic of China, in 2003.

The decline of the liberal faction of the CCP that began in Lhasa in March 1989 accelerated after Hu Yaobang's death in April, though he had been removed from party power five years earlier. Reformers took to the streets in Beijing to memorialize the achievements of Hu Yaobang, and their numbers ultimately grew to the size of the crowds that filled Tiananmen Square. In June, when the hard-liners massacred hundreds in Tiananmen, they also killed the reformist movement within the CCP. Tibet had become a litmus test for liberals and conservatives in Beijing. As the hard-liners gained control, China turned its back on dialogue with the Dalai Lama. Hu Jintao helped to install 170,000 PLA troopers and 30,000 People's Armed Police in Lhasa alone. Hu Yaobang's liberal policies were blamed for the explosion of nationalism in Tibet, and now hard-liners quashed talk of negotiations. At the same time, Tibetans in exile expressed their opposition to the Dalai Lama's willingness to renounce independence as the price of negotiations.

On December 10, 1989, in his acceptance speech for the sixty-ninth Nobel Peace Prize, the Dalai Lama said,

> The suffering of our people during the past forty years of occupation is well documented. Ours has been a long struggle. We know our cause is just. Because violence can only breed more violence and suffering, our struggle must remain nonviolent and free of hatred. We are trying to end the suffering of our people, not inflict suffering upon others.

The following day, during his Nobel lecture, the Dalai Lama told his listeners that

> I speak not with a feeling of anger or hatred toward those who are responsible for the immense suffering of our people and the destruction of our land, homes and culture. They, too, are human beings who struggle to find happiness and deserve our compassion. I speak to inform you of the sad situation in my country today and of the aspirations of my people, because in our struggle for freedom, truth is the only weapon we possess.

From about the time of the Strasbourg proposal, in mid-1988, and the Dalai Lama's acceptance of the Nobel Peace Prize, a year and a half later, we can date the start of the modern struggle for Tibet. During the most recent chapter, the Dalai Lama has said repeatedly that despite Tibet's history as an independent country, he is willing to accept true autonomy within China. Beijing has repeatedly rebuffed this offer, insisting that the Dalai Lama is intent on complete independence, or the splitting apart of China itself.

Since the early 1980s, an ever-increasing number of Chinese have been encouraged by their government to move to Tibet, which is, today, being overwhelmed by a wave of migrants. As it is, Chinese make up more than half the population of Lhasa. Many of these immigrant workers appear to be lured by government subsidies and generally profess a dislike of Tibet's harsh terrain and weather. Without the subsidies, in fact, many would not stay. During the 1990s, China embarked on a vast infrastructure program in Lhasa, designed to make the city livable by Chinese standards. According to Beijing, the economic migrants are only temporary workers who have come to help Tibetans, and all of them will leave, eventually. The Dalai Lama has expressed his concern that China is searching for a demographic "final solution" to its Tibet problem.

In the first years of the twenty-first century, as China's economic bubble continues to swell, the government is rushing to complete the first railroad line from China to Lhasa. The train was completed ahead of schedule in 2006, at a cost of $3 billion. As soon as daily trains are running into Lhasa, Tibet will face the ultimate test. Can the Chinese be induced to live in Tibet, year-round, in numbers that could subsume Tibetan identity? Chinese migration to Inner Mongolia has already taken a similar path.

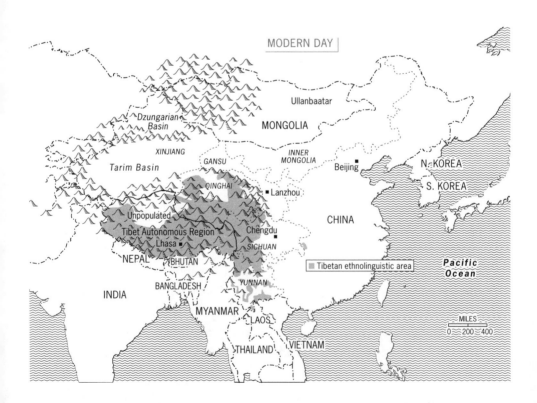

One Chinese writer, looking pragmatically at Tibet and wondering why China fights so doggedly to hold it, explains China's underlying motivations. Wang Lixiong thinks that the reason China's leaders promote the retention of Tibet as "a righteous national cause" is that they are frightened of the facts of geography. The provinces of Amdo and Kham, which the Dalai Lama insists must be part of any Tibetan autonomous region if he is to work with the Chinese, are perched on a two-mile plateau just above some of China's most heavily populated provinces. Which Chinese leader could agree to return territory that is only one hundred kilometers from Chengdu, capital of Sichuan Province? Besides national security, Wang says the issue is about resources:

> While the Han Chinese make up 93 per cent of the Chinese population, minority ethnic regions make up 60 per cent of Chinese territory, 89.6 per cent of our grasslands, 37 per cent of our forests, 49.7 per cent of our timber resources, and over 50 per cent of our water conservancy resources. . . . China's grim population explosion, spatial crowding, and resource shortage are the basic limiting factors as to why China cannot solve our minority ethnic group problem in the Soviet breakup model.

Wang also concedes that "China's establishment of sovereignty over Tibet hinges not on a military victory, but rather essentially on the ability of the Han Chinese to go there and stay there. . . . Of course, the current situation is that it is only the military stationed in Tibet that keeps the separatists from shaking Chinese sovereignty." The train to Lhasa, the migration of Chinese to Tibet, the modernization of the nation: none of these projects is being undertaken for the benefit of the Tibetans.

Yet China's leaders, at least for public consumption, veer away from realpolitik discussions. Instead, they preach a vision of Tibetan history. In 1997, speaking at the White House with President Clinton and Hillary Clinton in the Lincoln Bedroom, President Jiang Zemin recited the first line of the Gettysburg Address; later he pounded the table as he insisted that Tibetans had been "victims of feudalism," as if Tibetan sins explained China's colonization. In an interview with the *Washington Post* only a few days earlier, Jiang Zemin said, "Lincoln was a remarkable leader, particularly in liberating the slaves in America. When it comes to slavery in China, most of China got rid of slavery long ago, except in Tibet, where it was not until the Dalai Lama left that we eliminated serfdom." Jiang seemed genuinely puzzled that the United States does not support China's effort in Tibet: "The impression I get is that you [Americans] are undoubtedly opposed to slavery, yet you support the Dalai Lama."

Speaking at Harvard, Jiang Zemin stuck to China's preconditions for any talks with the Dalai Lama. The Dalai Lama "must publicly state that Tibet is an inalienable part of China and must publicly state that he will give up the goal of Tibet independence and stop all activities aimed at splitting the motherland." The Dalai Lama has been very clear: "While it is the overwhelming desire of the Tibetan people to regain their national independence, I have over the years repeatedly and publicly stated that I am willing to enter into negotiations and work from an agenda that does not include independence."

After invasion, revolution, terror, death camps, and economic revival, the root of the struggle between Tibet and China remains mired in history.

Even among the rich Tibetans who work with the Chinese to control their nation, patriotism has never died, though nearly all Tibetans are smart enough to keep such feelings private. However, there are young Tibetans born after the Cultural Revolution who have not yet learned this lesson. They show up in Lhasa, often from remote villages. Usually they are young Buddhist nuns or monks. Many Americans and Europeans have a fundamental misunderstanding of freedom of speech, so they find it hard to understand what these young men and women do once they arrive in the capital. They walk out in a public square and shout out words that they know will guarantee them an existence in a living hell.

"Free Tibet!"

"China should leave Tibet!"

"Long live the Dalai Lama!"

In 1994, when the Buddhist nun Pasang Lhamo shouted, "Free Tibet!" on a street in Lhasa, she was just seventeen years old. A year later, the nun Chuying Kunsang was only nineteen when she made the same fateful decision. Both of these young women served five years in jail in Lhasa's infamous Drapchi Prison, where political prisoners are held.

After their release, both nuns escaped to the West. When I interviewed them in 2003 in Chicago, both told me they had been tortured in prison. The reason? They refused to lie about Sino-Tibetan history.

"We were given flyers in prison with China's version of Tibetan history," Chuying said. "They told the details of how Songzen Gampo married the Chinese Princess Gyasa [Wencheng in Chinese]," during the Tang Dynasty, a thousand years ago—a period in history when even Tibetans who support China's occupation, like Ngawang Jigme Ngapo, say that Tibet was an independent country. In fact, the Chinese government officially maintains that "China's rule over Tibet" began only during the thirteenth century. "After we read the flyers they provided us with," Chuying said, "we were told to write our opinions about Tibetan history.

"I agreed that Gyasa came as a bride to Tibet," she continued, "but I explained that this did not prove that Tibet was part of China at that time. After I turned in my written response, there was an assembly, and they called out my name. Then one guard said to me, in front of all the other prisoners, 'You ignorant fool. How dare you disagree with history!' Then they took me away from the group. Then they tortured me."

"Did this happen only once?" I asked.

"No," Chuying said. "This happened three or four times a year." She had months to think about changing her answer. And then they came and asked the question, again.

"What were they doing?" I inquired.

"They wanted to brainwash me about history, and they used torture to do it," Chuying said with a smile. Then she looked at her fingers, bitten to the quick, as her answer was translated for me.

"Was it always Chinese who did this?" I asked.

"I do not speak Chinese," Chuying said, "so all the experts who lectured me about history were Tibetans."

"Were they all guards from the prison?" I asked.

"Generally they were from the prison system," she said, still looking away from me. "But once, in 1996 I think, they brought a female professor from

Tibet University, in Lhasa, to lecture us. Just once. The session, as usual, was about politics and history. Normally these sessions were held just for the political prisoners, but when the Tibetan professor came, they called all of the prisoners to hear her. She told us how the nobles before 1959 had tortured the serfs of Tibet and how the Chinese had liberated us and brought an end to that."

Chuying scratched her nose with one of her bitten nails and stopped speaking. There were no tears, but she could not look up. Pasang Lhamo, who is now twenty-six, continued for her friend. "We did not know one another in prison. We could not speak then and were not in the same cell. But I remember this, too. Yes, she was a professor from Tibet University. She seemed about fifty and sort of chubby. She was a professor who would be able to educate us about Tibet." Tibet University is the only institution China opens up to any Western academic who wants to study in Tibet. Universities around the world cooperate with it, and many have funded its work.

"Did you ask her any questions?" I inquired.

Pasang smiled at my ignorance. "We were not to ask questions or raise doubts. It was not like that. These 'Reform Through Education' sessions went on for perhaps five days. We were always being told we would be well-educated and well-adjusted citizens when we left, if we would only try to learn and quit being so ignorant."

Chuying found the strength to continue. "After these sessions we were told to write our response. To tell them what we had learned. And then to sign it with our name and ward and block number."

"Did you both tell the truth, again?" I asked, hoping they had learned to lie. Instead, they both nodded their heads yes.

"And so you were both tortured again, after the Tibetan professor came to speak," I said.

The two women nodded their heads, though by now both were looking at their bitten nails. Pasang said, "The guards who tortured us and talked to us were always Tibetan, because we do not understand Chinese. They interrogated us and tortured us in a small room."

Chuying slowly wiped a tear from her eye and then said in a calm voice, "Yes, they tortured us again after she left and then they said the same thing, again. 'You are ignorant country fools. You are a splittist trying to destroy the motherland!' "

"What did they do?" I wanted to know.

"My written response paper was on the desk," Chuying said, "and I was made to kneel on the cement floor in front of the interrogator. 'You are a stray dog of the Dalai Lama!' they shouted. Then when I would not say what they wanted, they put electric cattle prods on my hands, on my behind, on my lips, on my cheeks."

We stopped speaking and drank hot Tibetan tea. It was early spring. The mixture of butter, milk, salt, and tea coming from the blender smelled the same as when it wafts out of a wooden churn inside a nomad's tent on the Tibetan Plateau. It was disorienting. After we had all drunk, I asked, "Were they trying to change your mind? Was that the purpose of what they were doing?"

Chuying looked at me with infinite patience, smiled sweetly, and said, "Yes, that was the basic idea. After these sessions they wanted us to say Tibet had always been part of China and that I was a fool to think otherwise. We never broke. We never agreed with them. The system is set up to reward people who are reformed, who admit their mistake. All of us accepted that death was part of the risk we were taking for our ideas and swore, even so, not to break."

A cool spring breeze came in through the window. So many centuries of history blew through the room; so many dead people were with us.

In May 1998, two years after they were tortured for refusing to lie about history, Chuying and Pasang watched as guards beat fellow prisoners to death. A few dozen prisoners in a group of about one thousand at a flag-raising ceremony in a courtyard shouted, "Free Tibet!" In the ensuing days and months, guards killed ten of the protesters, including five young nuns, whom they beat to death. China originally arrested these nuns for the same crime as Chuying and Pasang had been accused of. They stood up in a public place and shouted, "Free Tibet!"

The Tibetan poet Woeser, in her poem "Secret Tibet," writes eloquently about torture in modern Tibet.

When I think of it, what do they have to do with me?
Palden Gyatso, imprisoned for thirty-three years;
Ngawang Sangdrol, locked up since she was twelve;
then the newly-freed Phuntsok Nyidron
and Lobsang Tenzin, imprisoned somewhere.
I don't know them, really haven't even seen their photos.

I only saw on the web, in front of an old lama,
shackles, sharp knives, cattle prods with multiple functions.
Loose skin, bony cheeks, furrowed wrinkles,
a recognizable handsomeness from his youth,
a beauty that doesn't belong to the mundane.
Becoming a monk early in life,
the Buddha's spirit glows in his face.

October, outside Beijing, chilly wind of autumn, a changed world.
I was reading the biography I downloaded in Lhasa,
seeing the sentient beings of the Snowland crushed
by iron hoofs from the outside. Palden Gyatso in a quiet voice:
"I spent most of my life in prisons
built by Chinese in my country."
And through another voice,
one can "recognize the forgiving words."

When I began working on this book and I saw how fiercely Chinese and
Tibetans disagree about their history, presenting both sides seemed an impossible task. The Dalai Lama, who has lived with this issue his whole life
and who is such a great believer in the victory of truth and logic, told me
that, ultimately, "the only solution is to publicly set up some special commission, a joint commission, invite some Chinese historians, invite some
Western scholars and Tibetans and independents, and let them study the
history and the legal situation and let them decide." Unfortunately, even
discreet queries about interviewing Chinese experts in the People's Republic on the subject of Tibet went nowhere. I was told that those who

studied Tibet in China would be endangering their freedom if they had any conversations with me. Thus this book relies on Chinese publications to present Beijing's viewpoint on Tibet.

Even arranging interviews with historians and political scientists in the West proved to be a challenge. When I contacted experts and told them that I was writing a concise history of Tibet and that I was interviewing the Dalai Lama for my book, many refused to cooperate. Speaking off the record, a respected historian laughed at me and said, "Look, we have to get visas to work in China and everyone knows the Chinese are sensitive about this history." China's power to influence the dialogue is immense.

Do American historians shape their writing according to Chinese sensitivities? Dr. Perry Link, a professor of East Asian studies at Princeton University, was banned from traveling in China because of his work on *The Tiananmen Papers*.

"I know this is sensitive," I told Link. "But do you believe that some U.S. historians fudge historic facts—or refuse to talk about these facts—to avoid irritating the Chinese government, though they know the facts of history do not support China's stance that 'history proves' Tibet has always been part of China?"

"You are right. That is a sensitive question," Link replied, "and, on the whole, I think there is some truth in what you say. If you use the term 'political scientist' in your question, instead of historian, then yes, I'd go further; there is no doubt about it."

Political scientists and former government officials who develop U.S. policy toward China and Tibet, no matter which political party is in power, tread carefully around Beijing sensitivities. Their careers depend on visas and on access to archives and to China's leaders. They learn that use of the revolving door between government offices and well-paying jobs at think tanks and universities requires them to speak about China, and incidentally its history with Tibet, within parameters set by Beijing. Such high-level facilitators, who are often called on to explain China to television viewers, exist in every country that trades with China: in the United States, Australia, Japan, South America, Africa, and throughout Europe.

In an aptly entitled article, "Anaconda in the Chandelier," Link explains the pressure brought to bear on such professionals to censor themselves.

Attending a grand reception, those who feed on China's prosperity and strength are, metaphorically, ignoring the constrictor entwined in the elaborate light fixture above. Everyone in the room adjusts subtly to the powerful creature, hanging over their heads, that no one wants to talk about. The smallest clink of crystal is interpreted very carefully.

Link put it in polite terms before we ended our conversation. "The banning of scholars to travel to China has a chilling effect on all other scholars who know about it." Those who are in the coal mine and see the dead canary are learning to be silent. Or is it worse than that?

The central committee of the Chinese Communist Party, in a classified report on Tibet—leaked and translated in 1993—stressed that one of the main targets for its "external propaganda" was "high-level people abroad." Party functionaries were urged to "use people from abroad to carry out the propaganda on Tibet for us, because propaganda created by foreigners is more powerful" than propaganda produced by Chinese.

My last session with the Dalai Lama took place on a rainy day during the monsoon. I arrived early and heard him coming in out of the rain, shaking off his umbrella and clomping his flip-flops loudly to knock off the mud. As soon as he sat down, I asked him to summarize the history we had discussed, to speculate on the future, and, most of all, to do so concisely, please.

The Dalai Lama laughed. "A few-thousand-year history. It is difficult to say. Tibet is a part of the world, so it's similar to other countries. But then the Tibetan case is unique because there is connection to a mysterious level of sorts. Actually there is very much connection. Sometimes more happy. Sometimes more suffering. But then I think I can also say, in spite of many drawbacks, that the Tibetan spirit is still strong and the Tibetan nation quite tough."

"What is your prediction for the future?" I asked.

"I believe truth has its own strength and we must retain our faith in truth," he answered, returning to a theme he referred to during one of our first interviews. "Of course guns have their own unique strength. But the strength or force of a gun is short or temporary. Temporarily it is decisive, but in the long run it is weak. The power of truth stands up. Truth always remains unchangeable. Then there is another manifestation of these two. The power of guns is often not compatible with truth and very much depends on untruths or lies. So with guns, there are usually lies and destruction. When governments keep so many state secrets, this is a sign of weakness, despite military strength. If a government is compelled to keep secrets from its own people, this is a weakness. Also in China, the government has kept too many secrets from its own people. This is not good. Tibetans do not have guns, but we are very strong. We have suffered a lot. We have been victimized but still *(tell)* the truth. There is no lie, no effort to hide our mistakes. We are open. Anybody is welcome to look at what we are doing. We are trying to be open, and this is a manifestation of the truth and this is real strength. That is why I feel that, for the future, there is hope and it is positive."

"Some people might not see the situation you face so positively," I said.

"If you look at the Tibet situation locally," he replied, "then it seems hopeless, desperate, and it seems that our time is running out. But in reality the Tibetan problem is not hopeless at all, not like problems from a civil war. Our problem is that we had a conflict with a new guest with a gun who came without proper invitation. But things change. The Tibet issue is very much linked to the situation within China proper. China, no matter how organized, is part of the world, *(and)* change is part of the world. In the last fifteen to twenty years, China has changed dramatically, and this change will continue. The totalitarian system has changed and has lost its ideology, and politicians seem primarily concerned with power. Sometimes I feel that I am a more genuine Communist than them.

"The existence of a totalitarian government requires military force," the Dalai Lama continued firmly. "If it does not have any proper sort of aim or ideology, just power, such a system is unhealthy and is bound to change. Because of different technologies like the Internet, it is impossible for any government to keep so many secrets or secrecy, and this makes change inevitable. Therefore, change is already taking place, and the time for totalitarianism is running out. On the Tibetan side, the spirit is strong, and support from the outside world is increasing. I feel from a wider perspective there is very much hope."

"What is your advice to Tibetans as they face the future?" I asked.

"We need more effort by everyone," he said. "I am telling Tibetans and our supporters that in the last forty years, our motto or slogan has been hope for the best but prepare for the worst. In the early 1960s, we hoped that we would return to Tibet in a few years. But in the meantime, we prepared for it to take a longer time, perhaps a few generations. We knew that if that were to be the case, our way of life and culture must be preserved. Today, hope for the best means that we must engage the Chinese government. We hope that we will reach some mutually agreeable solution, and we should work sincerely toward that: leave no stone unturned. Many governments support that. That is good. We must make real effort. Many Tibetans support that, which is very good. In the meantime, we must also prepare for the worst. If our genuine efforts to find a negotiated solution fail, we must be prepared. We have to think that fifty years have passed. Whether you call it liberation, invasion, or colonization, fifty years have passed. Perhaps fifty years remain. That means that my life would end before those fifty years. In twenty to thirty years my life will end. So there could be a time without the Dalai Lama."

The Dalai Lama has repeatedly said that if there is no resolution with China before his death, the next manifestation of Chenrizi will be found outside Tibet, an event by no means unheard of, since the Fourth Dalai Lama was a Mongolian.

Discussing such comments, I asked, "And what would happen with China if you were to pass away before the issue is resolved?"

"At such a moment . . ." the Dalai Lama began and then paused. He looked away and then back at me. "The Chinese today, they describe the issue in terms of a dialogue with the Dalai Lama. So when the time comes, when there is no Dalai Lama, then this very sort of idea would have no basis. So this is a mistake. Many times I have made it clear that the issue with China is not about the Dalai Lama or the institution of the Dalai Lama. Nor is it the issue, as the Chinese often claim, of the elder generation, the elite who exploited the people. It is not the interests of this group that is the issue. It is the interest of the six million Tibetans alive today. That is the issue. I always make it clear. We have to continue to make this clear. Otherwise, many leaders and governments think that the only problem is the Dalai Lama. They sometimes still seem to think that the main issue is the return of the Dalai Lama."

"You mean Western governments want you to make a gesture?" I suggested.

The Dalai Lama blinked his eyes shut for a long moment and then continued, with evident restraint. "They say that the Dalai Lama should make some friendly gesture or positive statement toward China. Two, three years ago in Paris, the French government had that sort of feeling. I told them if the problem is just my problem, if the problem is just about the Dalai Lama, then yes, it is very easy. I can make a beautiful statement and the Chinese government will welcome it and next week I will be in Beijing." He wagged his head in exasperation.

"But that is not the issue, is it?" I asked.

He shook his head in agreement. "But this is not the case—unless the Chinese government realizes that the real problem is the resentment and the deep dissatisfaction of six million Tibetans toward China caused by the treatment they have been subjected to in the past. Only when China realizes that, and is ready to address that, then that is the time when I return to Tibet. Then I can help both sides."

"And what would the Dalai Lama's position be in Tibet if such a time were to come soon?" I asked.

"I have decided," he said, "that I will no longer be head of the Tibetan government as soon as we return to Tibet and there is a certain degree of freedom. That I have decided. Also the Dalai Lama and all monks should not be, I feel, involved in party politics. Monks should be above politics. That is what I suggest. Even the ordinary monks had better avoid politics. They should even avoid voting, because then people will ask what way you are voting."

"You are saying," I observed, "after what you have seen in your life, and after you have traveled all over the world, that now you believe, assuming Tibetans will govern themselves in Tibet, there should be a separation of church and state?"

"Yes," he said with great conviction. "Institutions of religion and institutions of politics should be separated. I think even in ancient times."

Laughing, I said, "But we cannot change the past. Are you saying that, definitely, now it is time for a change?"

"Yes," he replied without hesitation.

"And what is the task before the exiled Tibetans in the meantime?" I wondered.

The Dalai Lama explained, at length, that exiled Tibetans must prepare themselves, through education and training, to create effective development plans, based on the needs of Tibetans, while at the same time logically pointing out the specific errors of Chinese administration in Lhasa. "It is our moral responsibility to make plans and send them to the Chinese, whether they implement them or not. Just to protest that the Chinese should go away—this is empty. This is the negative way, not proper. The positive way is to push China by our own effort and study. This is our own side."

"If that is what the Tibetans should be doing, what do you see foreigners doing?" I asked.

"Our supporters have to explain the truth about the past and present situation of Tibet and its people. Only if people, especially the Chinese people and their government, understand the nature of the Tibetan issue, and how it came about, can we find a mutually acceptable solution. So according to this, we have to find some solution. As I said, at the moment some may still think it is just the Dalai Lama, the problem of the Dalai Lama's return. But I think this is nonsense. It is the Tibetan people, with a long, rich past and culture—it is the distinctiveness of our community that must be recognized. When the Dalai Lama is no longer there, the Tibetan people and their history will still be there."

"So are you saying that a growing international awareness of Tibetan history and of the nature of the issue is important now?" I inquired.

"Yes, certainly," he said, and in the same breath, "but let me be clear: I am not seeking independence. I am seeking some sort of genuine self-rule. And why am I asking for some sort of unique or special case for Tibet? It is because of the nature of our issue. It is because of our history and culture."

"Because historically Tibet was independent," I noted.

"If our history and especially our cultural distinctness are not understood, then the need for a special solution, for genuine autonomy that satisfies the Tibetan people, will also not be understood. If we were like the Cantonese, then there would be no problem: but we are not Cantonese, we are Tibetan."

"You cannot change this fact," I said.

"Whether the Chinese accept or not, what is true is true. Reality is reality. I cannot change the historical or cultural reality and I cannot lie."

The Dalai Lama paused, looking at me carefully. "If the Chinese government put a condition on me *(that I)* should accept that Tibet has historically always been an inalienable part of China—if I say yes, history will not change because of that, history will always remain as history. The historical status of Tibet is not a matter for political decision. It is a matter for the historians to determine. As to the future status of Tibet, this is something one can determine through a political process. That is something I wish to discuss with the Chinese for the benefit of the Tibetan people, for their future welfare and also for the benefit of the Chinese people."

"And so how will you proceed?" I asked.

"I believe that we must focus talks with China on the future. We each have our own understanding and interpretations of history. We should not force our interpretation on others. We should leave history to the historians, not the politicians. I am a Buddhist monk. I cannot tell a lie, because this monk's tongue is not for lying."

"You are relying on the power of truth itself," I replied.

"My basic belief is that the power of truth, although it may be weak at times, does not change as time goes by. The power of the gun is immediate and strong, very powerful and very decisive, but as time goes by, it easily becomes weak. Truth is weak but steady, weak but eternal and sometimes increasing slowly. The Tibetan case is exactly like that."

"You don't want to conflict with Chinese leaders," I said.

"Definitely not," he agreed. "We need to develop the same understanding, have the same meaning. Of course, we know and recognize that Tibetans have close ties with many of the peoples who today form part of the People's Republic of China, such as the Mongolians, the Uighurs, the Manchu, and the Han. They are our brothers and sisters. We have influenced each other's culture and developed spiritual bonds in the past. Even political ties. There are times that we shared a common history. That is difficult to translate into modern international legal terms, especially since international law is itself based mainly on Western concepts, not Asian ones!"

"You are not ready to say Tibet is not part of the People's Republic of China either," I said.

"No, I have not done that, and I think we need to face the current reality," the Dalai Lama responded.

"And in the future?"

"If we can come to a settlement with China," the Dalai Lama said, "that is good for both sides, for both peoples. I have clearly said this can be done within the framework of the Chinese constitution: with Tibet as a part of the People's Republic. This is what I am seeking. But if the Chinese do not want to agree to a genuine autonomy for Tibetans, for all Tibetans, if they do not understand our distinctiveness and our need to govern ourselves and protect and practice our culture then of course the right of the Tibetans is always there."

"Is it hard to start a dialogue if China demands such difficult conditions?"

"I strongly believe that the only way forward is through dialogue," the Dalai Lama said, "through mutual respect and genuine understanding. History is history, the past is the past. It should not stand in the way of dialogue nor of an agreement for a better future. I am looking forward."

A secretary suddenly pointed at the clock. It was time to go. The Dalai Lama had another appointment. I was sad to be leaving him, knowing I might not ever sit down with him again. I asked him to write a few words for me to focus on as I wrote this book. He sat for several minutes patiently thinking and then carefully wrote out these lines:

If it is reasonable action
which is by nature beneficial to truth and justice,
then by abandoning procrastination and discouragement
the more you encounter obstruction
the more you should strengthen your courage and make effort.
That is the conduct of a wise and good person.

Tibetan Shakya Bhikshu, Dalai Lama,
Tenzin Gyatso, July 22, 2000

At the door, as we said good-bye, he took my hand and said one last thing. "I think you have gained knowledge about Tibet and even about some mysterious things."

14

EPILOGUE

In the nine years since my first interview with His Holiness the Fourteenth Dalai Lama for this book, the situation in Tibet has continued to evolve. The Dalai Lama's representatives have resumed their dialogue with China. The two sides have met, about once a year, every year since 2002, most recently in February 2006. The Central Tibetan Administration's chief elected official, Kalon Tripa Samdhong Rinpoche, says that the dialogue can pave the way for real negotiations. A less optimistic take is that there has been no visible progress as of late. In the February 2006 press release put out by the Dalai Lama's special envoy, who heads the delegations to China, Lodi Gyari sums up the situation: "Today there is a better and deeper understanding of each other's position and the fundamental differences that continue to exist. . . . This round of discussion also made it clear that there is a major difference even in the approach in addressing the issue. However we remain committed to the dialogue process and are hopeful that progress will be possible by continuing the engagement." Lodi Gyari went on to say that the Chinese government "made clear its interest in continuing the present process and the firm belief that the obstacles can be overcome through more discussions and engagements."

In May 2006 Lhakpa Phuntsog, the head of the China Tibetology Research Center in Beijing, held a rare meeting with Western journalists and gave a glimpse of how Beijing sees these talks. He said that the Dalai Lama was "demanding" that all of historical Tibet—the Tibetan Plateau, large parts of which have been incorporated into several Chinese provinces—be joined together and that the entire area should be given real autonomy.

"These two demands do not match the history of Tibet," Phuntsog said, insisting, "The Dalai Lama's demands have set up great obstacles." Despite this, the talks are continuing and the Dalai Lama has even suggested that perhaps he should make a spiritual pilgrimage, just as the Thirteenth Dalai Lama did, to the Bodhisattva Manjushri's sacred mountain in China, Wutaishan. Such a trip would be a breakthrough for the dialogue with China. The Dalai Lama has reiterated in the press several times that the Tibetans "are not seeking separation," while insisting that indeed Tibet needs "meaningful autonomy" within China. Once again it seems Sino-Tibetan talks have run head on into the two sides' different interpretations of their shared history.

The current dialogue began as China's president Hu Jintao began his final march to power through the ranks of the Communist Party. Some analysts say that Hu is ready for a compromise, which would bring the Dalai Lama back from his exile, and many foreign governments have publicly urged Beijing to negotiate with the Dalai Lama without preconditions. China's release, in 2003, of several Tibetan political prisoners a few years before the completion of their terms might indicate that Hu is serious about dialogue. At the same time, at least one Tibetan political prisoner, Tenzin Delek Rinpoche, was sentenced to death after he was convicted, in a show trial, of several bombings. The signals from Hu are therefore mixed. After the Dalai Lama recognized the Eleventh Panchen Lama, he and his family were detained; they have been held under house arrest, in an undisclosed location, since the boy was six years old—making him the youngest political prisoner in the world. The Chinese Communist Party has responded to this situation exactly as the Manchu emperor did, in 1720, when he tried to install a fake Seventh Dalai Lama. The party, which proclaims atheism as the state religion, chose a young Tibetan and certified him as the "true" reincarnation of the Tenth Panchen Lama. Even as China continues its halting dialogue with the Dalai Lama's representatives, it has forced monks at the Panchen Lama's monastery to swear allegiance to the government-imposed candidate (only the Dalai Lama can certify a Panchen Lama) or face expulsion. Such signals have led many foreign observers to doubt the sincerity of Hu's commitment to a negotiated settlement. They insist that China's eagerness to hold a controversy-free Olympics in 2008 is leading the country to hold talks simply to keep Tibetan protesters off the streets and attention away from Tibet. In fact, Kalon Tripa Samdhong Rinpoche, in a controversial move, has asked Tibetans and their supporters not to demonstrate when China's leaders travel abroad. Such steps are supposed to create a positive atmosphere for the ongoing dialogue.

Watching these events unfold I could not help but recall one criticism the Dalai Lama had made of his predecessor. Speaking of how the Thirteenth Dalai Lama did not push forward with his modernization program forcefully, after he encountered public resistance, the Dalai Lama said, "He saw the necessity of change. . . . He should have taken his reasons to the public and they would have understood." This may explain why the Fourteenth Dalai Lama takes every opportunity to explain the current dialogue with the Chinese to his supporters, so carefully and frequently.

One analyst believes that a hard-line faction inside Beijing's power circles is using the Sino-Tibetan dialogue to prove to a more liberal faction that a negotiated settlement is impossible—and, as well, to curry favor with the foreign governments who have pressed Beijing to start a dialogue with the Dalai Lama. In the opinion of these hard-liners, the Tibet issue will cease to exist on the death of the Fourteenth Dalai Lama; meanwhile, they are encouraging the transmigration of Chinese to Tibet. Completion of the first direct train line to Lhasa in 2006 should certainly make that easier.

The Dalai Lama's representatives have expressed hope that a dialogue can lead to earnest negotiations, even though China's representatives, at least publicly, have denied that a dialogue is even taking place. Clearly, much is being considered in private, and both the exiled Tibetans and Beijing are withholding details.

Many in the exile Tibetan community have been vocal in their criticism of the dialogue and of what some see as the Dalai Lama's offer to surrender independence in exchange for real autonomy. Attitudes about whether to struggle for autonomy or to hold out, no matter the cost, for independence are changing. In the words of Jamyang Norbu, a writer who believes Tibetans must struggle for independence:

It did not help matters that the Dalai Lama himself . . . offered to surrender Tibetan independence for a measure of autonomy. The world of Tibet activism was thrown into disarray. . . . The Tibetan government-in-exile itself became directionless and attempted to reorient their objectives around . . . everything but the previous goal of Tibetan independence.

Internet chat rooms in which young exiles gather around an electronic hearth seethe with doubt about the Dalai Lama's nonviolent approach, frustrated that the world ignores Tibet's plight.

So many people in this world are fighting for their rights and their country. . . . There are a lot of killings and some people blow themselves up to prove their point. And the world political leaders condemn them. Everybody says violence is not the answer. So what about us Tibetans, we believe in nonviolence. But I don't see any world politicians supporting our cause.

In fact, there is support among political leaders the world over for the approach the Dalai Lama has taken and this is amply shown by the respect he is accorded wherever he travels. Young Tibetans in exile are frustrated that despite such support, despite popular sympathy and support for Tibet abroad, conditions for the people inside Tibet do not seem to change. The level of frustration continues to grow.

In 1998 an elderly Tibetan, Thubten Ngodup, set himself on fire during a protest in New Delhi to draw world attention to the cause of independence. He died several days later. More recently, in 2004, three Tibetans in their thirties, members of the Tibetan Youth Congress, which has repeatedly questioned the effectiveness of the Dalai Lama's commitment to nonviolence as the only form of protest, conducted a thirty-two- day fast in front of the United Nations in New York. They demanded, among other things, that China simply tell the world where the Eleventh Panchen Lama is being held and that the UN address at least the basic human rights of Tibetans. The secretary-general of the UN, Kofi Annan, refused to meet with the hunger strikers because of China's sensitivity about even the appearance of interference in what it claims to be its internal affairs. The situation was defused when a face-saving, behind-the-scenes compromise was worked out and UN Assistant Secretary-General Carolyn McAskie met with the hunger strikers.

In a letter to the *International Herald Tribune*, the hunger strikers wrote:

> We have undertaken this hunger strike as the most serious nonviolent means we have to display the depth of both our frustration and our resolve. We look at the world around us caught in an endless cycle of violence, fear and anger. Those who resort to violent means, taking innocent lives and sowing chaos, receive the attention of the media and the world community. The U.N. calls for world peace, and yet it ignores and silences a people who have steadfastly waged their struggle through nonviolent means.

One of the hunger strikers, Dolma Choephel, was quoted as saying, "You probably didn't know about us because we don't believe in drawing attention to ourselves by killing people with bombs."

According to the president of the New York–New Jersey chapter of the Tibetan Youth Congress, "When hunger strikers are ready to take their own lives, you cannot rule out the possibility that Tibetans could also become suicide bombers in the future if neglected by the UN for a very long time."

The Dalai Lama, who is aware of the frustration among Tibetans in exile, especially the young, has said publicly that he risks alienating his supporters by sticking to the path of nonviolence to which he is firmly committed. If he cannot deliver a negotiated settlement in his lifetime, he knows, the youngest exiles may well turn to violence to assert their demand for complete independence, after he dies. Some Chinese intellectuals argue (and some of the leaders in Beijing agree) that in the Dalai Lama, Beijing has a golden opportunity to negotiate a nonviolent end to the conflict and that Chinese leaders who are simply waiting for the Dalai Lama to pass from the scene are foolish. He has the power to speak for all Tibetans.

The Dalai Lama, who was born in 1935, continues to travel the globe where he and the Tibetan cause enjoy tremendous support and often meets with foreign leaders, who invariably urge China to enter into sincere negotiations with the Dalai Lama on the protection of human rights in Tibet and some real form of autonomy for the Tibetan people. They are careful to express themselves in a way that does not challenge China's claim to sovereignty over Tibet. Although no government on earth recognizes Tibet as an independent state, many urge China to protect the linguistic, cultural, and religious rights of the Tibetan people.

Several times a year, China denounces some foreign political leader who dares to meet with the Dalai Lama, charging them with encouraging activities that might "split the Chinese motherland." China threatens that it will cancel business contracts, or that the countries who receive the Dalai Lama will suffer in an unspecified way. Beijing continues to insist that "the issue of Tibet is neither a religious issue nor an issue of human rights but rather a matter of principle concerning China's sovereignty and territorial integrity."

As China continues to expand its power and influence, Tibet—and its history with China—will become of far greater importance than it has in the past. Beijing's treatment of Tibetans will become a litmus test by which other nations can decide how much they can trust China. If China is willing to distort facts, as it has with regard to Tibet, what other questionable methods would China's rulers find acceptable?

In the mid-1990s, China was a major exporter of oil. Ten years later, it is the world's second largest importer. China's rise to greatness depends on importing foreign oil from the Middle East and eventually from the developing fields in international waters in the South China Sea. Many observers are worried that China may take action to enforce its territorial claims in the South China seabed. Does history prove that islands just a few miles off the coast of the Philippines and Vietnam are now part of China, too? To what extent is China willing to go to assert its vision of that history? If China believes that to continue a 10 percent annual growth it must exploit oil in the South China seabed, is Beijing willing to enforce its vision of history there as it has done in Tibet?

Every country has minorities and is judged by the way it treats them. Even if we ignore fifteen hundred years of history and were to accept the argument that Tibetans are Chinese citizens of Tibetan ethnic descent, we must still wonder why China rejects all foreign criticism of its treatment of them. China rebuffs all such criticism of its policies in Tibet—including the arbitrary detention, torture, and extrajudicial execution of Tibetans—as unwarranted interference in China's internal affairs, despite the acceptance by the UN and its members that human rights in any state are a legitimate concern of the international community. In January 2006, a special court in Spain was authorized to investigate charges of genocide against Tibetans. In June, as proceedings began, the Chinese Foreign Ministry said the charge that more than one million Tibetans have been killed or gone missing since 1950 was "slanderous and fabricated." It will be interesting to see how this tribunal rules—the same court that convicted Chile's dictator Augusto Pinochet.

China's major foreign policy goal is to convince the global community that the nation's rise to greatness in the twenty-first century will be achieved only through peaceful means. Beijing insists that the rule of law (not the methods used by the Chinese Communist Party in Tibet) will govern China's future and its relations with other states. The nation wants to convince the world community that it will play by internationally accepted rules and that it can be trusted to live up to its agreements. The world is eager to believe China because of its untapped economic possibilities. In the long run, however, China's treatment of Tibet, not the number of high-rises in Shanghai, may be the real test of Beijing's nature.

In the near term, the 2008 summer Olympics in China will be watched as an indicator of where China is headed. Sun Weide, a spokesman for the Olympics organizing committee in Beijing, has tried to debunk any concerns China's history might arouse among those warning of an impending China threat.

"If you know our history, it's not our nature," Weide said. "The more you know about our history, the more correct understanding you will have about today's China." Today, China would like to convince the world that history proves it cannot be a threat to world peace. How should we view this conclusion in light of China's history with Tibet?

What stands out after studying Tibetan history is that China is still searching for a way to join the world community on equal footing—not as a superior or inferior nation. Such equality has no basis in ancient imperial victories or defeats, nor can China's imperial history define a modern nation or its borders. Only when China shakes off its attempts to rationalize its borders with this ancient history, when it respects the human rights and the religious and cultural freedoms of the Tibetan people, can the ongoing search for a modern China bear the fruit which the Chinese people and their well wishers sincerely dream of.

As I edited this book for the last time, a letter from His Holiness the Dalai Lama arrived. It seemed appropriate, at the end of our long conversation, to give him the final word.

THE DALAI LAMA

Dear Tom,

For nine years you have worked hard to put the many hours of conversations we had into a book which will allow people to better understand the history of Tibet. It is important to understand the past as we are trying to find solutions for the future. Our own perception of our history as Tibetans of course shapes our identity and our needs today. Others may have a different perception, and they will therefore approach problems from the point of view of their understanding. So there are different interpretations of the same things, and those interpretations are quite important, because they may help us understand why Tibetans and Chinese see things differently. At the same time we must focus on the present and the future. We may disagree on the past, but we should work constructively to improve the present and to reach an agreement on the way to move forward, together, in the future in the interest of the Tibetans and the Chinese.

As you know we are today engaged in serious dialogue with the Chinese government. So it is important to pause and consider what this means as the final pages of this book are being prepared.

For many years we have been calling on the Chinese government to enter into a dialogue with us and to work with us to jointly resolve the differences between us, and many concerned individuals, institutions and governments have supported our efforts. I have always believed that a solution to the question of Tibet that can bring an end to the suffering of our people can be achieved only through dialogue and the development of genuine understanding between Tibetans and Chinese. Neither side can achieve anything by imposing its will on the other. Rather, each side must understand the situation and genuine needs of the other and act accordingly. We are all the same human beings with the same needs and fears. So let us understand each other on a human-to-human level. We must not let politics or even history stand in the way of true human understanding and the satisfaction of human needs.

So from this point of view, if we live together as brothers and sisters, as a family, it is better for the Tibetans and also for the Chinese themselves. But family members cannot bully each other; otherwise, those who feel hurt will want to leave the family: so here this is why understanding each other and each other's needs is so important. Only this kind of human understanding can form the basis for a genuine coming together that will benefit all of us.

There have been a series of meetings between my envoys and senior Chinese government officials since direct contact was reestablished in 2002 after a gap of nearly ten years. This is a good sign. The process of resolving our differences will require great effort, patience and flexibility on both sides. Most of all, we need to develop trust in each other.

For such a trust to exist, we must all do our utmost to create the right atmosphere. You cannot convince the other of your good intentions if at the same time you take actions that could hurt them. Now this is very difficult, unless both sides equally make an effort. It is difficult to convince Tibetans and their supporters to show restraint in opposing Chinese policies in Tibet so long as the human rights of Tibetans are being violated inside Tibet. The opposite is also true. So the Chinese government must see to it that all abuses and policies by their officials at both national and local levels that cause harm to Tibetans, at both national and local levels, are stopped and Tibetans and their supporters must stop actions that cause embarrassment and harm to the Chinese government and the Chinese people.

On our side, we are fully committed to the current process of dialogue, and we will continue to do what is necessary to intensify our discussions and to move forward toward a mutually beneficial solution. I have explained many times that I believe a solution must be found within the framework of the constitution of the People's Republic of China. This is our firm policy. What we expect from the Chinese leadership is to display maximum flexibility in accommodating the needs for genuine autonomy of the entire Tibetan people within that framework. I am convinced that if we can achieve this kind of self-government, which makes it possible for us to develop our own culture and way of life and to manage our own environment, this will only strengthen the PRC as a whole and the unity among the various nationalities within the PRC. I think this kind of readjustment is possible within the framework of the PRC constitution. Obviously, there may be a need for mechanisms that protect and further clarify some of the rights enshrined in the constitution.

Recognition and respect for each other's needs does not drive people apart, but allows them to become closer. We must accentuate our common interests, our common dependence on the environment we live in, and our common future. But human beings can only be persuaded to do this once their distinctiveness is recognized and respected by the other. This is not unique to Tibetans: it is true everywhere in the world where peoples and minorities struggle for recognition of their distinct identities and cultures before they voluntarily and happily unite with others to reap the benefits of living in a larger family, within one state.

Tibetans have much in common with their Chinese brothers and sisters, as of course we do with our Mongol and Uighur neighbors. So whereas we are firm on our objective to achieve genuine autonomy, I encourage Tibetans to acknowledge also our commonalities.

I am well aware that the process of dialogue and negotiations that we have embarked upon with the Chinese government will take time. On our part we will work hard to make it succeed. We hope the Chinese government will equally demonstrate its commitment and faith in this process by making visible changes in its policies toward Tibetans. Tibetans must have patience and work together with our many supporters in different parts of the world to ensure that this process succeeds. Let us try our utmost, and future generations will have no reason to say we did not make full use of the opportunity that now exists, and which we helped to create, in order to heal the wounds of the past and move toward a better future.

I hope that we succeed in turning a new leaf in the story of Tibet. We may not be able to change the past, so I would gladly leave history to the historians to analyze and interpret in shades of gray— for it is never as black and white as we often portray it. But it is our responsibility, and my responsibility as Dalai Lama and as a Buddhist monk, to do our utmost to shape the future for the good of all sentient beings, not least for the well-being of Tibetans for whom I bear a special responsibility.

Tenzin Gyatso
The Fourteenth Dalai Lama of Tibet

BIBLIOGRAPHY

Ahmad, Zahiruddin, trans. *A History of Tibet,* by the Fifth Dalai Lama of Tibet (Nag-Dban-Blo-Bzan-Rgya-Mtsho). Bloomington: Research Institute of Inner Asian Studies, 1995. Vol. 7 of Indiana University Oriental Series, Denis Sinor, ed.

————. *Sino-Tibetan Relations in the Seventeenth Century.* Serie Orientale Roma 40. Istituto Italiano per il Medio ed Estremo Oriente, 1970.

Amitai-Preiss, Reuven, and David O. Morgan, eds. *The Mongul Empire and Its Legacy.* Leiden, Boston, Koln: Brill, 1999.

Barrett, T. H. *Qubilai Qa'an and the Historians: Some Remarks on the Position of the Great Khan in Premodern Chinese Historiography.* In *The Mongol Empire and Its Legacy,* ed. Reuven Amitai-Preiss and David O. Morgan. Leiden, Boston, Koln: Brill, 1999.

Bawden, Charles R. *The Modern History of Mongolia.* London: Kegan Paul, 2002.

Beckwith, Christopher I. *The Tibetan Empire in Central Asia.* Princeton, N.J.: Princeton University Press, 1987.

Bell, Sir Charles. *Portrait of a Dalai Lama: The Life and Times of the Great Thirteenth.* Delhi: Book Faith India, 1998. Reprint.

Bernstein, Richard, and Ross H. Monro. *The Coming Conflict with China.* New York: Vintage, 1998.

Bierlein, J. F. *Parallel Myths.* New York: Ballantine, 1994.

Bira, Sh. *Qubilai Qa'an and 'Phags-pa bLa-ma.* In *The Mongol Empire and Its Legacy,* ed. Reuven Amitai-Preiss and David O. Morgan. Leiden, Boston, Koln: Brill, 1999.

Chang, Garma C. C. *The Hundred Thousand Songs of Milarepa*. Boston: Shambala, 1999.

Chang, Gordon R. *The Coming Collapse of China*. New York: Random House, 2001.

Clarke, John. *A History of Ironworking in Tibet: Centers of Production, Styles, and Techniques*. In *Warriors of the Himalayas: Rediscovering the Arms and Armor of Tibet*, by Donald J. LaRocca. New York: Metropolitan Museum of Art, 2006.

Conze, Edward, et al. *Buddhist Texts Through the Ages*. New York: Harper Torchbooks, 1964.

Cotterell, Arthur. *China: A History*. London: Pimlico, 1990.

Craig, Mary. *Kundun: A Biography of the Family of the Dalai Lama*. Washington, D.C.: Counterpoint, 1997.

Craven, Roy C. *Indian Art: A Concise History*. London: Thames and Hudson, 1987.

Cummings, Bruce. *Korea's Place in the Sun*. New York: Norton, 1998.

Dibble, Charles. *The Chinese in Thailand, Against the Background of Chinese Thai Relations*. 1961. Ann Arbor: University Microfilms International, 1985.

Epstein, Israel. *Tibet Transformed*. Beijing: New World Press, 1983.

Fairbank, John King, and Merle Goldman. *China: A New History*. Cambridge, Mass., and London: Belknap–Harvard University Press, 1999.

Fleming, Peter. *Bayonets to Lhasa*. Oxford and Hong Kong: Oxford University Press, 1984.

Ford, Robert. *Captured in Tibet*. Oxford: Oxford University Press, 1990.

Goldstein, Melyvn. *A History of Modern Tibet, 1913–1951: The Demise of the Lamaist State*. Berkeley: University of California Press, 1989; New Delhi: Munshiram Manoharilal Publishers, 1993.

————. *Nomads of Western Tibet: The Survival of a Way of Life*. Hong Kong: Odyssey, 1990.

————. *The Snow Lion and the Dragon: China, Tibet and the Dalai Lama*. Berkeley: University of California Press, 1997.

Goleman, Daniel. *Destructive Emotions: A Scientific Dialogue with the Dalai Lama*. New York: Bantam, 2003.

Grant, Michael. *Hecataeus and Herodotus: The Ancient Historians*. New York: Barnes and Noble Books, 1994. 18–35.

Grousset, René. *The Empire of the Steppes: A History of Central Asia*. New Brunswick, N.J.: Rutgers University Press, 2000.

Grunfeld, A. Tom. *The Making of Modern Tibet*. New York: Sharpe, 1996.

Gup, Ted. *The Book of Honor: Covert Lives and Classified Deaths at the CIA*. New York: Doubleday, 2000.

Gyatso, Tenzin (Fourteenth Dalai Lama). *Freedom in Exile: The Autobiography of the Dalai Lama of Tibet*. London: Hodder and Stoughton, 1990.

————. *The Spirit of Tibet: Universal Heritage. Selected Speeches and Writings of His Holiness the Dalai Lama XIV*, ed. A. A. Shiromany. New Delhi: Allied Publishers, 1995.

Hager, John Winthrop. *Crisis and Prosperity in Sung China*. Tucson: University of Arizona Press, 1975.

Harmatta, Janos, et al. *History of Civilizations of Central Asia*. Vol. 2, *The Development of Sedentary and Nomadic Civilizations: 700 BC to AD 250*. Delhi: Motilal Barnasidass, 1999.

Harrer, Heinrich. *Lost Lhasa: Heinrich Harrer's Tibet*. New York: Harry N. Abrams, 1992.

————. *Seven Years in Tibet*. New York: Flamingo, 1997.

Hearder, Harry. *Italy: A Short History*. Cambridge, UK, and New York: Cambridge University Press, 1990.

Hidehiro, Okada. *China as a Successor State to the Mongol Empire*. In *The Mongol Empire and Its Legacy*, ed. Reuven Amitai-Preiss and David O. Morgan. Leiden, Boston, Koln: Brill, 1999.

Hopkirk, Peter. *Setting the East Ablaze*. London: John Murray, 1984.

Kahn, Paul. *Secret History of the Mongols: The Origins of Chinghis Khan*. San Francisco: North Point Press, 1984.

Knaus, Kenneth. *Orphans of the Cold War: America and the Tibetan Struggle for Survival*. Washington, D.C.: Public Affairs Press, 2000.

Kuleshov, Nikolai S. *Russia's Tibet File*, ed. Alexander Berzin and John Bray. Dharamsala: Library of Tibetan Works and Archives, 1996.

Laird, Thomas. *Into Tibet: The CIA's First Atomic Spy and His Secret Expedition to Lhasa*. New York: Grove Press, 2002.

Landon, Kenneth. *The Chinese in Thailand*. New York: Russell & Russell, 1973.

LaRocca, Donald J. *Warriors of the Himalayas: Rediscovering the Arms and Armor of Tibet*. New York: Metropolitan Museum of Art, 2006.

Lattimore, Owen. *Inner Asian Frontiers of China*. Hong Kong: Oxford University Press, 1992.

Lhalungpa, Lobsang. *The Life of Milarepa*, trans. Lhalungpa. New York: Dutton, 1977.

Linduff, K. M. "The Chinese Imperial City of Chang'an." In *Art Past/Art Present* by D. Wilkins, B. Schultz, and K. Linduff, 4th ed. New York, 2000.

Miller, Merle. *Plain Speaking: An Oral Biography of Harry S. Truman*. New York: Berkley Publishing, 1974.

Misra, V. N. *Prehistoric Human Colonization of India*. Indian Academy of Sciences, vol. 26, no. 4, Supplement, Nov. 2001.

Nazaroff, Paul. *Hunted Through Central Asia: On the Run from Lenin's Secret Police*. Oxford: Oxford University Press, 1993.

Norbu, Jamyang. *Warriors of Tibet: The Story of Aten and the Khampas' Fight for the Freedom of Their Country*. London: Wisdom Publications, 1986.

Norbu, Namkhai. *Journey Among the Tibetan Nomads: An Account of a Remote Civilization*. Dharamsala: Library of Tibetan Works and Archives, 1997.

O'Flaherty, Wendy Doniger. *Hindu Myths: A Sourcebook*. London: Penguin Books, 1975.

Pan, Yihong. *Son of Heaven and Heavenly Qaghan: Sui-Tang China and Its Neighbors*. Bellingham: Center for East Asian Studies, Western Washington University, 1997.

Petech, Luciano. *Tibetan Relations with Sung China and with the Mongols*. In *China Among Equals: The Middle Kingdom and Its Neighbors, 10th–14th Centuries*, ed. Morris Rossabi. Berkeley: University of California Press, 1983.

Purcell, Victor. *The Chinese in South East Asia*. London: Oxford University Press, 1965.

Reeves, Thomas C. *The Life and Times of Joe McCarthy: A Biography*. New York: Stein and Day, 1982.

Rockhill, W. W. *The Dalai Lamas of Lhasa and Their Relations with the Manchu Emperors of China, 1644–1908*. Dharamsala: Library of Tibetan Works and Archives, 1998. Reprint.

Rossabi, Morris, ed. *China Among Equals: The Middle Kingdom and Its Neighbors, 10th–14th Centuries*. Berkeley: University of California Press, 1983.

Schaller, Michael. *The United States and China in the Twentieth Century*. New York: Oxford University Press, 1979.

Schell, Orville. *Virtual Tibet: Searching for Shangri-La from the Himalayas to Hollywood*. New York: Metropolitan Books, 2000.

Shakabpa, Tsepon W. D. *Tibet: A Political History*. New Haven: Yale University Press, 1967.

Shakya, Tsering. *The Dragon in the Land of Snows: A History of Modern Tibet Since 1947*. London: Pimlico, 1999.

Short, Phillip. *Mao: A Life*. London: Hodder and Stoughton, 1999.

Skinner, G. William. *Chinese Society in Thailand*. Ithaca, N.Y.: Cornell University Press, 1962.

Smith, Warren W. *Tibetan Nation: A History of Tibetan Nationalism and Sino-Tibetan Relations*. Boulder, Colo.: Westview Press, 1996.

Snellgrove, David, and Hugh Richardson. *A Cultural History of Tibet*. Boulder, Colo.: Prajna Press, 1980.

Snow, Edgar. *Red Star over China*. New York: Grove Press, 1978.

Soucek, Svat. *A History of Inner Asia*. Cambridge: Cambridge University Press, 2001.

Spence, Jonathan. *The Search for Modern China*. New York: Norton, 1990.

Stein, R. A. *Tibetan Civilization*. London: Faber and Faber, 1962.

Strober, Deborah, and Gerald Strober. *His Holiness the Dalai Lama: The Oral Biography*. New York: John Wiley, 2005.

Thomas, Lowell, Jr. *Out of This World: Across the Himalayas to Forbidden Tibet*. New York: Greystone Press, 1950.

Tsu, Lao. *Tao Te Ching*, trans Gia-Fu Feng and Jane English. New York: Vintage Books, 1989.

Tucci, Guiseppi. *Tibetan Painted Scrolls*. Rome: La Libreia dello Stato, 1949.

Tuchman, Barbara W. *Stillwell and the American Experience in China, 1911–1945*. New York: Macmillan, 1970.

Tung, Rosemary Jones. *A Portrait of Lost Tibet: Photographs by Ilya Tolstoy and Brooke Dolan*. Ithaca, N.Y.: Snow Lion Publications, 1980.

Van Walt van Praag, Michael C. *The Status of Tibet: History, Rights, and Prospects in International Law*. London: Wisdom Publications, 1987.

Viraphol, Sarasin. *Tribute and Profit: Sino-Siamese Trade, 1652–1853*. Harvard East Asian Monographs, 1977.

Vitalai, Roberto. *Early Temples of Central Tibet*. London: Serindia, 1989.

Ya, Hanzhang. *The Biographies of the Dalai Lamas*. Beijing: Foreign Language Press, 1991.

Wu, Harry, with George Vecsey. *Troublemaker: One Man's Crusade Against China's Cruelty*. London: Chatto & Windus, 1996.

Wyatt, David. *Short History of Thailand*. New Haven, Conn.: Yale University Press, 1986.

Academic Periodicals

"Current Trends in Tibetan Political Imprisonment." tibetinfo.net, Feb. 6, 2004.

Dhondup, K. "The Regents Reting and Tagdra." *Lungta*, no. 7 (Aug. 1993).

Ewing, Thomas. "Ch'ing Policies in Outer Mongolia 1900–1911." *Modern Asia Studies*, vol. 14, no. 1 (1980).

Fairbank, J. K., and S. Y. Teng. "On the Ch'ing Tributary System." *Harvard Journal of Asiatic Studies*, vol. 6 (June 1941).

"Hu Jintao: Reformer or Conformist?" A Report by Free Tibet Campaign into Hu Jintao's relationship with Tibet, at freetibet.org.

Link, Perry. "Anaconda in the Chandelier." *New York Review of Books*, Apr. 11, 2002.

Lixiong, Wang. "The People's Republic of China's 21st Century Underbelly." *Beijing Zhanlue Yu Guanli* (Jan. 2, 1999). Trans. by BBC Monitoring service. http://www.columbia.edu/itc/ealac/barnett/pdfs/link14-wang-lixiong.pdf.

Mullin, Glenn, trans. "Last Political Testament of the 13th Dalai Lama." *Lungta*, no. 7 (Aug. 1993).

Okada Hidehiro. "The Third Dalai Lama and Altan Khan of the Tumed." Tibetan Studies, Proceedings of the 5th Seminar of the International Association for Tibetan Studies, Narita 1989, vol. 2, pp. 643–52. 1992.

Prasenjit, Duara, "De-Constructing the Chinese Nation." *Australian Journal of Chinese Affairs* (July 1991).

Rawski, Evelyn. "Presidential Address: Reenvisioning the Qing: The Significance of the Qing Period in Chinese History." *Journal of Asian Studies,* vol. 55, no. 4 (Nov. 1996). 829–50.

Thurman, Robert. "Sino-Tibetan Relations: Prospects for the Future." *Potamac Conference* (Oct 5–6, 1992).

Tkacik, John, Joseph Fewsmith, and Maryanne Kivlehan. "Who's Hu? Assessing China's Heir Apparent, Hu Jintao." Heritage Foundation, Web site.

Newspapers and Magazines

Almond, Elliott. "Spotlight Will Reveal China's Contradictions." *Mercury News,* Feb. 28, 2006.

Bradsher, Keith. "Newest Export Out of China: Inflation Fears." *New York Times,* Apr. 16, 2004.

Cheung, Ray. "Beijing Helping Tibetans Catch Up with the West, Says Author." *South China Morning Post,* Jan. 28, 2004.

————. "China Leader Asks for Understanding." AP, Oct. 19, 1997.

Collinson, Stephen. "Time Is Running Out, Dalai Lama Tells Clinton." *AFP,* June 20, 2000.

Cordon, Sandra. "Canada Shouldn't Flirt with Separatist Dalai Lama: Chinese Embassy." *Canadian Press,* Apr. 14, 2004.

Dalai Lama. "Critical Reflections—Human Rights and the Future of Tibet." *Harvard International Review,* Special Feature—Human Rights. Winter 1994–95

————. "Dalai Lama Admits His Death Would Set Back Tibetan Movement." *AFP,* Oct. 11, 2000.

French, Howard. "Billions of Trees Planted, and Nary a Dent in the Desert." *New York Times,* Apr. 11, 2004.

Graham, Ron. "There's Something Happening Here." *Globe and Mail* (Toronto), May 8, 2004.

"Hillary Clinton Talks About Tibet In Her Memoir." Review of Hillary Clinton's book, by International Campaign for Tibet. http://www.tibet.ca/wtnarchive/2003/6/25_2.html.

Holland, Lorien. "Jiang Shrugs Off Protests but Acknowledges 'Mistakes.'" *AFP*, Nov. 3, 1997.

Jamyang, Tenzin. "Waning Health, Gaining Strength." *Tibet News,* May 1, 2004.

Norbu, Jamyang, "Hopelessly Hopeful." *Tibetan Review,* Jan. 13, 2004. http://www.phayul.com/news/article.aspx?c=4&t=1&id=5837.

————. "The Incredible Weariness of Hope." http://www.tibet.ca/wtn archive/2003/10/1_1.html.

————. "Non-Violence and Non-Action." http://www.timesoftibet.com/artman /publish/article_1431.shtml.

————. "The Myth of China's Modernization of Tibet and the Tibetan Language, Part V." http://www.tibetwrites.org/articles/jampyang_norbu/jamyang_norbu16.html.

"Our Struggle Is for the Six Million Tibetans…" *AFP,* Oct. 11, 2000, *Dalai Lama admits his death would set back Tibetan movement.*

Sun, Lena H. "China Rebuilds Its Image in Tibet's Monasteries." *Washington Post,* Sept. 12, 1994.

Wade, Nicholas. "A Prolific Genghis Khan, It Seems, Helped People, the World." *New York Times,* Feb. 11, 2003.

Web Sites

For any news story about Tibet in recent years, including ones cited in this book, search here first: http://www.tibet.ca/en/wtnarchive/.

92,000 Tibetans died because of Struggle Sessions: Estimate from the CTA, see: http://www.tibet.com/WhitePaper/white5.html.

173,000 Tibetans died in prison, CTA estimate see: http://www.tibet.com/WhitePaper/white5.html.

The Dalai Lama speaking to Human Rights Caucus U.S. Congress, 1987: http://www.tibetjustice.org/materials/tibet/tibet3.html.

The Dalai Lama in a speech to the U.S. Congress, April 18, 1991: http://www.tibet.com/DL/rotunda.html.

Strasbourg Proposal (1988): http://www.tibetjustice.org/materials/tibet/tibet4.html.

HHDL Nobel Peace Prize Acceptance Speech: http://www.nobel.se/peace/laureates/1989/lama-acceptance.html.

http://www.nobel.se/peace/laureates/1989/lama-lecture.html.

Statement by Chuye Kunsang published in Tibetan Centre for Human Rights and Democracy January–June 2000 Half-Yearly Report: http://www.tchrd.org/hrupdate/2000/hr200004.html.

Tripa Samdhong Rinpoche says that the current Sino-Tibetan dialogue is a means: http://www.tibet.net/tibbul/2004/0102/doc2.html.

Eleventh Panchen Lama arrested, detained since age of six: http://www.tibetjustice.org/reports/children/epilogue/.

Life of Tsongkhapa: http://www.tsongkhapa.org.

Obituary of Bomi Rinpoche (1918–2002), TIN News Update, November, 29, 2002: http://www.tibetinfo.co.uk/news-updates/2002/2911.htm.

Historical Path of Mongolia's Statehood and Independence by the President of Mongolia, a speech delivered in July, 1996: http://drlee.org/mongolia/article02.html.

More on Mongolia: http://drlee.org/mongolia/article03.html.

200 Tibetan Centers in Taiwan: http://www.taipeitimes.com/News/archives/1999/11/15/0000010765.

Chinese monks in Tibet, in Tibetan monasteries. At Sertar, for example: http://www.tibet.ca/en/wtnarchive/2004/3/10_8.html.

Fifty-two major and minor Tibetan settlements in India (35), Nepal (10), and Bhutan (7): http://www.tibet.net/home/eng/settlements/.

Buryatia: http://gov.buryatia.ru:8081/obur/history/index.html.

Robbie Barnett's Introduction to the Panchen Lama's Seventy Thousand Character Petition at: http://www.tibetinfo.net/pl-preface.htm.

Panchen Lama's 70,000 Character Petition at: http://www.tibetinfo.net/pl-preface.htm.

"Once a nationality's language . . ." from the Seventy Thousand Character Petition by the Panchen Lama, as cited by Professor Dawa Norbu in his Historical Intro-duction of the text: http://www.tibetinfo.net/pl-intro.htm.

Tibet Justice Center's Chronology of Tibetan History: http://www.tibetjustice.org/reports/chron.html.

Excerpt from 1906 Convention Between Great Britain and China Respecting Tibet: http://www.tibetjustice.org/materials/treaties/treaties11.html.

1909 Convention Between Great Britain and Thibet: http://www.tibetjustice.org/materials/treaties/treaties10.html.

Taking the Kalachakra Initiation: http://www.berzinarchives.com/e-books/kalachakra_initiation/kalachakra_initiation_2.html.

Songs of Tsangyang Gyatso (the Sixth Dalai Lama), translated by Simon Wickham-Smith: http://www.qamutiik.net/6dlmgu-gluindex.

Tenzing Sonam and Ritu Sarin on their Web site, Shadow Circus: http://www.naatanet.org/shadowcircus/chu.html.

Sun Yat-sen, "The policy of the Manchus has been one of . . . unyielding tyranny China and the Manchus..." by Herbert A. Giles published 1912, chapter 12: http://www.worldwideschool.org/library/books/hst/asian/ChinaandtheManchus/chap12.html.

The Value of the Pound 1750–1998: available from www.parliament.uk/commons/lib/research/rp99/rp99–020.pdf.

Prajnaparamita, Madhyamaka, Pramana, Abhidharma, Vinaya. *Overview of the Gelug Monastic Education System*, Tsenzhab Serkong Rinpoche II. Translated and compiled by Alexander Berzin: http://www.berzinarchives.com/history_buddhism/overview_gelug_monastic_education.html.

Fourteenth Dalai Lama's gold Patek Philippe watch: http://www.brilliantbooks.co.uk/ourWork_client.asp? ClientID=1&PageID=4 http://www.tibet.com/DL/rotunda.html.

June 2000 meeting with President Bill Clinton: http://hongkong.usconsulate.gov/uscn/wh/2000/062001.htm. White House press secretary on Clinton–Dalai Lama meeting.

"The efforts of the last 20 years have been wasted in a single day": http://www.tibet.ca/en/wtnarchive/1995/1/20_1.html.

Chinese Government Views on Tibet

Patriotism: Quotes by Deng from AP reporter Stille, Deng Xiaoping, then vice chairman of the CPC Central Committee: http://www.tibet.ca/en/wtnarchive/1999/7/26_3.html.

Chinese sources on serfdom as justifications for the invasion: http://www
.swans.com/library/art9/mparen01.html.
http://www.nickyee.com/ponder/tibet.html.
http://english.peopledaily.com.cn/features/Tibetpaper/tb1.html.

Chinese government sources say that 95 percent of Tibetans were serfs or
slaves: http://english.peopledaily.com.cn/features/Tibetpaper/tb1
.html http://www.tibetinfor.com.cn/english/services/library/serialise/
h_status/his_04.htm.

Wang Jiawei and Nyima Gyaincain, *The Historical Status of China's Tibet*,
China Intercontinental Press: http://www.tibet-china.org/historical
_status/ english/content.html.

Beijing Lama Temple: http://ulink.ourfamily.com/city/cityguides/beijing
.htm#harmony.

Chinese leaders and government publications assert that Tibet was part of
the Manchu Empire and thus part of China—and the tribute missions are
cited as proof of this: for example, see: http://www.china-un.ch/eng/
premade/60544/TibetFAQ2.htm.

A critique/attack on the Dali Lama's position in the latest round of Sino-
Tibetan dialogue, as of 2006, and a presentation of China's views on where
this dialogue is now: *What Is Dalai Lama's "Middle Way."* Dated July
26, 2006; author "Yedor." Since it is in *China Daily* it reflects the views of
China's leaders. http://www.chinadaily.com.cn/china/2006-07/26/
content_649545.htm.

NOTES

Foreword

x   no universally accepted transliteration standard for Tibetan: Although this is obvious from the fact that academic texts on Tibet seem to use one of a variety of systems, the point is noted by the historian Christopher I. Beckwith, *The Tibetan Empire in Central Asia*, p. 218.

xi   Interview with Pasang Lhamo and Chuying Kunsang: By Thomas Laird, in Chicago, through a translator, in April 2003.

Introduction

4   do not have this control: Daniel Goleman, *Destructive Emotions*, pp. 15–26. Also see research about "Lama Oser" online.

6   so reverential that they cannot contradict him: Deborah Strober and Gerald S. Strober, *His Holiness the Dalai Lama*. See the passage by the Tibetan historian Tsering Shakya in which he writes, "as a Tibetan you are so reverential that it is not an interview. . . . I could not contradict him. . . . There were many questions I wanted to ask but in his presence just couldn't ask."

7   The Western academics just pick one viewpoint: In fact, he spoke specifically of the work of Melvyn Goldstein.

7   unlike Tibetans, I needed to challenge the Dalai Lama: Strober and Strober. See the Tsering Shakya passage cited earlier.

8   "inalienable part of Chinese territory": *AFP*, Nov. 3, 2005.

Chapter One

10   In one of several Hindu creation myths: Rg Veda (10.90) as cited by Wendy Doniger O'Flaherty, *Hindu Myths*, pp. 27–28.

10   A Chinese myth tells of warring mythical emperors: J. F. Bierlein, *Parallel Myths*.

11   first heard this myth : He was born July 6, 1935; begins trek to Lhasa from Eastern Tibet in August 1939; arrives Lhasa, October 8, 1939; enthroned as spiritual and temporal leader of Tibet, in his minority, on Feb. 22, 1940. Thus he was four and a half when enthroned. Data are from Tibet Justice Center chronology on Web and from conversations with the Dalai Lama.

11   "It is said that the flesh eating red-faced race": Zahiruddin Ahmad (trans.), *A History of Tibet,* by the Fifth Dalai Lama of Tibet.

12   Buddha lay on his deathbed in northern India: http://icg.harvard.edu/ ~eabs114/handouts/BuddhasDates.pdf. This site describes the historical debate over the date of the Buddha's death. Tibetans have asserted, since the fourteenth century, that the Buddha died in 881 B.C. The Theravada tradition (in Sri Lanka, Thailand, Burma, Myanmar) maintains that the Buddha died in 544. Until recently, however, academic scholars in Asia and the West said—and dismissed without discussion both the Tibetan and Theravadan dates—that the Buddha died between 487 and 483. Newer scholarship has begun to move from that monolithic position to discuss the possibility that the Buddha died sometime between 399 and 368. At the other end of the spectrum, some Hindu scholars posit that the Buddha died about 1807. See http://www.stephen-knapp.com/ reestablishing_the_date_of_buddha.htm. For the purposes of this book, I have stuck with the standard date used in accepted sources—483 B.C.

12   "unprotected by your words": Ahmad, *History.*

12   "The kingdom of snows in the north": Ibid.

13   repeated their creation myth: The Dalai Lama and many scholars assume that the creation myth emerged from the pre-Buddhist period, long before Songzen Gampo, and that Buddhist ideas were later grafted onto an existing myth, through a process of accretion.

13   "As far as the appearance of human beings": Ahmad, *History.*

13   examined a photograph of a mural: He was looking at photographs, from the Hall of Political Success, that were painted in 1957, in the Dalai Lama's summer home within the Norbulingka gardens in Lhasa.

14   V. N. Misra has shown: V. N. Misra, *Prehistoric Human Colonization of India.*

15   "It seems that the first Tibetans": The direction of migration of the first humans into Tibet remains a topic of research. R. A. Stein, in his work from the 1960s, suggests that the first migrants were from the east and moved westward.

15   Exactly when Tibetans developed a culture: Beckwith, pp. 3–9.

15   The first Chinese references to proto-Tibetans: Beckwith, pp. 5–6.

15   the metaphors Lao Tsu used: Lao Tsu, *Tao Te Ching*, p. 89.

15   "A great country": Ibid., p. 61.

16   "Why is the sea king": Ibid., stanza 66.

16   "Be the valley": Ibid., stanza 28.

16   "The highest good": Ibid., stanza 8.

16   "Land so high": This version of the poem is from David Snellgrove and Hugh Richardson, *A Cultural History of Tibet*, but see alternative translation in Stein, p. 42.

17   Shang Shung kingdom: spelled *Zhang Zhung* by some authors and *Zan Zun* by Christopher Beckwith.

17   The *mar yig* script is mentioned in *Opening the Door to Bon*, by Latri Khenpo Geshe Nyima Dakpa Rinpoche, Snow Lion Publications, 2006.

17   Ladakh: Indian province in the Himalayas, along the Tibetan border, whose population is nearly 100 percent ethnic Tibetan.

17   Tibetan Plateau: The plateau is 965,000 square miles (2.5 million square kilometers), according to *Wikipedia* and the Central Tibetan Administration.

17   the size of the European Union: As of the latest enlargement of the European Union, in 2004, it is 1,535,103 square miles (3,976,952 square kilometers), whereas the Tibetan Plateau is 965,000 square miles (2.5 million square kilometers). Thus the plateau is roughly 60 percent of the EU's size, or about 40 percent smaller than the EU. EU data from *Wikipedia*.

18   Chinese provinces of Qinghai, Gansu, Sichuan, and Yunnan: See paper and map by Wang Lixiong, "The People's Republic of China's 21st Century Underbelly."

18   one third of the Tibetan population lives inside the TAR: according to the Dalai Lama's exile government. See http://www.tibet.net/.

18   entire population was only six million in 1990: Lixiong does an excellent job of contrasting the Dalai Lama's vision of Tibet, as the entire Tibetan Plateau, with China's vision of Tibet, as only the TAR.

18   much larger number of Chinese in Tibet: http://www.tibet.net/en/tibet/glance.html.

18   Tibetan people coalesced: Stein says: "It is its civilization that unifies Tibet. In doing so it overlays a wide assortment of elements, as we know already in connection with sub-climates, plant life and dwelling sites, dialects and customs. Much the same is true of ethnic make-up. Different racial types live side by side or coalesce. The predominant strain in most

cases is Mongoloid, but many travelers have been struck by the prevalence of what they describe as a 'Red Indian' type (in Kongpo). Others have noted a European, Hellenic or Caucasian element. . . . The explanation really is that different populations have occupied various parts of Tibet in the course of history. . . . The origins of the Tibetans is still a mystery" (p. 27). According to Beckwith, information about where the Tibetans came from, and to which other peoples they are related, is "lost in the mists of time" (p. 8).

22   "between Tibetan myth and modern science": Although the Dalai Lama has not read Hecataeus and Herodotus, the foremost Greek historians, his pursuit of a middle way between science and faith is similar to the method adopted by the first Western historians, thousands of years ago. Hecataeus examined the myths, rather than just repeat them, as ancient bards before him had, in search of a more objective truth. Yet both of these earlier historians remained believers in divine intervention in human affairs. Listening to the Dalai Lama millennia after these historians, as he sought his "middle way," I was struck to see how persistent this thread is within human history. See, for example, Michael Grant, *Hecataeus and Herodotus*, pp. 18–35.

Chapter Two

27   mythology gave way to history: The period begins in the sixth century. See Stern, p. 45; Yihong Pan, *Son of Heaven and Heavenly Qaghan*, p. 231; Beckwith.

27   flarerd across the Tibetan Plateau: The historical narrative in this chapter is based on a close reading of Tsepon Shakabpa, *Tibet: A Political History;* Stein; Snellgrove and Richardson; Yihong; Beckwith.

27   After unifying the entire plateau: Beckwith, p. 20.

28   Tsangpo: "Gtsanpo," in Beckwith , p. 13.

28   he was poisoned and died: Beckwith, pp. 14–16.

28   Songzen Gampo ascended: the most trusted sources disagree on the exact year. Compare dates in Snellgrove and Richardson with those in Shakabpa and in Beckwith. These books all agree on what happened, and the difference in chronology is never more than a decade. Robert Thurman, in a personal communication, suggests that the date may have been as early as 598 but acknowledges that the date remains uncertain.

28   Songzen Gampo: At the suggestion of Robert Thurman, Laird uses Songzen Gampo as the transliteration, although the emperor is also known as Srong-

brtsan-sgam-po (Snellgrove and Richardson) or Sron btsan sgampo (Beckwith). In using various systems of transliteration, Laird always seeks to make this book readable. Songtsen-gampo is another commonly used transliteration. The Chinese translated the old Tibetan word *btsangpo* as *T'ien tʒu,* or "Son of Heaven," the title for Chinese emperors. See Beckwith, p. 14, FN 10. The Dalai Lama referred to him as emperor, not king, during interviews. Furthermore, Songzen Gampo was a king of kings, making him an emperor in contemporary usage.

30   poison his father: Snellgrove and Richardson; Beckwith.

30   Never will we be faithless: Oath of Allegiance, revised for spelling and for the use of "Emperor" rather than "King," and edited for brevity, by Laird; based on the translation by Snellgrove and Richardson (p. 27), from the Tibetan Chronicles found at Tun-huang.

30   Sadmakar: "Sad mar kar" in Beckwith, p. 20.

30   Sui Dynasty fell, and the Tang emerged: See Yihong, p. 132.

31   most serious foreign threat: See Beckwith; Yihong.

32   internally fractured Tang was never able to defeat: Beckwith, pp. 37–38, 244, 353.

32   Great Wall was the line of stalemate: This train of thought is influenced by Owen Lattimore, *Inner Asian Frontiers of China.* Though later scholars have found fault with Lattimore, his concepts are helpful in framing these issues.

32   nomadic tribes that threatened the Tang: The information in this paragraph paraphrases the spectacular research and analysis by Yihong, pp. 231–35. Others contributing to my understanding of this crucial subject include Beckwith and Stein.

33   Tibet would compete with China: Ibid.

33   nomadic group they call the Aza: See Beckwith; Shakabpa; Stein; Snellgrove and Richardson.

33   prompted a Tibetan diplomatic mission: The first missions took place in 608.

34   Emperor Taizong: as transliterated by Yihong, p. 237. Beckwith, p. 20, has Tai-sung.

34   he would lead fifty thousand troops to kill the emperor: Yihong, p. 237.

34   looted the Chinese town of Sung Chou: Beckwith, p. 23.

34   face-saving pretense: Beckwith, p. 23

34   Both sides say the other came to their court: Yihong, p. 238.

34   Gar Tongzen: See Stein, p. 59.

34   five thousand ounces of gold: Beckwith, p. 24.

34   Princess Wencheng: Princess Jincheng, in Yihong, p. 247; in Tibetan, the name is Princess Gyasa.

35   Chinese Web sites: For "outstanding contributions to the unification of the Chinese nation," see http://www.members.tripod.com/~journeyeast/wenzheng.html.

35   "civilizational [sic] center of East Asia": See http://www.members.tripod.com/~journeyeast/wenzheng.html.

35   "Princess Wencheng was touched": http://www.members.tripod.com/~journeyeast/wenzheng.html.

36   "The men and horses all wear chain mail armor": See Stein.

36   no evidence that China was the source of Tibet's iron technology . . . Sasanian dynasty . . . eighth century, the production of iron . . . quite mature: Clarke in LaRocca, p. 21.

36   Thomi-sambhota: Alternative transliterations include Thonmi, Tonmi, and Togmey. In this instance I have used the system created by Thupten Jinpa and the the Library of Tibetan Classics series.

36   may have gone to Khotan: See Introduction to the History of the *Five Tibetan Traditions of Buddhism and Bon*, by Dr. Alexander Berzin, at http://www.berzinarchives.com/history_buddhism/introduction_history_5_traditions_buddhism_bon.html: "Thus, he sent his minister, Togmey-sambhota, to obtain the alphabet from Khotan—not from India, as is often explained in the traditional Tibetan histories. Khotan was a Buddhist kingdom north of Western Tibet in Central Asia. The route to Khotan that the minister took passed through Kashmir. When he arrived there, he discovered that the master he was going to meet in Khotan happened to be in Kashmir at the time. This is how the story evolved that the Tibetan writing system came from Kashmir. Orthographic analysis reveals that the Tibetan alphabet actually follows features distinctive only to the Khotanese script."

36   where Indian scripts were also used: Apparently Bon sources also claim a possible origin of the script in Central Asia or Iran. See http://www.ancientscripts.com/tibetan.html or http://en.wikipedia.org/wiki/Tibetan_script.

36   the main impetus for the invention of this script was to facilitate the translation of Buddhist texts . . . rulers of the Yarlung dynasty needed a means to administer their far-flung empire: Jamyang Norbu, "The Myth of China's Modernization of Tibet and the Tibetan Language Part V." http:

//www.tibetwrites.org/articles/jamyang_norbu/jamyang_
norbu16.html

37   "all of Tibet for the first time": The Dalai Lamai means that the entire
Tibetan Plateau was under Tibetan rule, though, for the Chinese, the
Tibetan Autonomous Region occupies only a fraction of the plateau,
which is divided between the TAR and the Chinese provinces of Gansu,
Qinghai, Sichuan, and Yunnan.

38   a horrible fate at the hands of his emperor: This traditional account
(which may have conflated Gar Tongzen with someone else who plotted against Songzen Gampo) seems to be contradicted by historians. For
example, Beckwith, pp. 26–27, suggests that Gar Tongzen took control of the army, after Songzen Gampo died, and was regent for twenty
years.

38   "created some dissension": The Dalai Lama said, "Then, you see,
Lonpo Garwa Tongzen, one minister, went to China to get the princess. I have great sympathy for this person because his eyes were taken
out by Songzen Gampo, because he created some dissension with others. He served him well and then created problems. This story is very
strange. One reincarnated lama in Drepung Monastery. The Thirteenth
Dalai Lama one regent. Demo Rinpoche was a reincarnate of Garwa
Tongzen, this minister who had his eyes taken out. My junior tutor in
1954–55, I can't remember, he made a pilgrimage to India, when he was
in Kumbu area, near Lhari. He spent his first night there and then spent
the night in one small monastery. There he found many old handwritten scriptures. And he was very fond of these. One of these scriptures
mentioned some prediction that the reincarnation of Avalokiteshvara,
the name Thupten (the Thirteenth Dalai Lama) will come that is Thirteenth. That reincarnation of Avalokiteshvara will strike Garwa
Tongzen. Because the regent's servant created some problem, the Thirteenth Dalai Lama felt compelled to dismiss this regent and then later
because of some of the monks of the regent's monastery in Ten-gye-
ling, they collaborated with the Chinese in 1910, when the Thirteenth
went to India. Later, when he returned, that monastery was closed. So
this prediction was fulfilled. My tutor was really surprised. This confirmed that this lama was the reincarnation of Garwa Tongzen.

TL: So you believe that these people have continued to reincarnate?

DL: Yes, some have reincarnated again, some have not. I don't know.
At least Garwa Tongzen people recognize.

39 a slaughterhouse for pigs: From interviews with monks, in Lhasa, by Laird.

39 fewer than one thousand monks: Estimate of the Dalai Lama's exile government, cited by Warren Smith, *Tibetan Nation*, p. 561.

39 restoration began in the Jokhang: Smith, p. 577.

40 Red Guards attacked the Jokhang in 1966: Smith, pp. 542–43.

40 died at the age of thirty-seven: From Beckwith, p. 26; Yihong says he died in 649 (pp. 238–39); Snellgrove and Richardson give 649 as well (p. 288).

Chapter Three

42 refused to offer military assistance to Tibet: Some readers will consider this too harsh an assessment, since there were attempts to give military aid and to organize a fair vote at the UN. The Dalai Lama said that he felt betrayed by the paltry support and that he had no choice but to talk with Mao. The lack of foreign support in 1950 was one of the reasons he did not go into Indian exile then.

42 Dalai Lama saw no alternative: See Tenzin Gyatso, *Freedom in Exile*, p. 128. He explained to India's prime minister, Nehru, how "unprepared we were to meet an enemy and of how hard I had tried to accommodate the Chinese as soon as I was aware that no one in the outside world was prepared to acknowledge our rightful claim to independence."

42 "There was no choice": Ibid.

44 Tang dynastic histories: Reference to the Jiu Tang Shu ("the Old Tang History"), written in 945, and the Xin Tang Shu ("the New Tang History"), finished in 1060. Scholars who have studied them, and the Arab, Tibetan, and Turkish records that complement them, seem in universal agreement about the broad strokes of the events in this chapter. See especially Beckwith, Yihong.

44 one of the first planned cities: See http://www.pitt.edu/~asian/week-10/week-10.html; K. M. Linduff, "The Chinese Imperial City of Chang'an," in *Art Past/Art Present*, by D. Wilkins, B. Schultz, and K. Linduff, 4th ed. (New York, 2000).

45 China's isolation ended in 128 B.C.: See Arthur Cotterell, *China: A History*, p. 108.

45 Hadrian: Hearder, *Italy: A Short History*, p. 33.

45 Terrified overcompensation: See Yihong.

45 maggots and slaves: See Yihong.

45   "the only legitimate ruler": Yihong, p. 5.

46   died within a few months: About the death of Taizong, see Beckwith, p. 227.

46   succeeding Chinese emperor, Kao-Tsung, attacked Tibet: Beckwith, p. 227; Yihong.

46   concluded six written treaties: Beckwith; Yihong; Shakabpa.

46   five empires fought for supremacy: Beckwith; Yihong; Shakabpa; Snellgrove and Richardson.

46   Tibet controlled the entire Tarim Basin: Beckwith, p. 43. It is the largest depression, or basin, on earth, largely covered by the Taklamakan Desert. The Dzungarian Basin, farther north, is named after the Dzungar Mongols, who dominated the area in the seventeenth century. Today both basins are in the Chinese province of Xinjiang. The area has been occupied by the Chinese only since the twentieth century—much in the way Tibet has been occupied. The Tang Chinese did occupy the Tarim Basin, for a few decades at a time, just as did their competitors, the Turkic princes, the Arabs, and the Tibetans.

46   Tibetans controlled the Silk Road for two periods: Beckwith.

46   occupied most of western China: Beckwith, p. 244. Tibet controlled all routes leading from China to the West, and deprived China of tributary treasure, horses, taxes, and one third of Tang territory. In this and the preceding paragraphs, I am summarizing this vast sweep of history from detailed histories—Beckwith; Yihong; Cotterell. Yihong and Beckwith rely almost entirely on primary classical sources for their works; Cotterell, on secondary sources for his popular work. Stein, and Snellgrove and Richardson, also contributed to my understanding of this period, as did Shakabpa; John King Fairbank and Merle Goldman, in *China: A New History;* Svat Soucek, *A History of Inner Asia;* and René Grousset, *The Empire of the Steppes*—all of whom used primary sources. In fact, no single work summarizes this period briefly. Tibet's history falls between the cracks. A great deal of academic research on this period has been done since Stein and Richardson and Snellgrove wrote their narratives.

47   allied and vassal kingdoms: Yihong and Beckwith, both citing Tang Dynastic histories.

48   hid the news . . . sacked: Yihong, pp. 324–25.

48   Borders on map and map data: http://depts.washington.edu/chinaciv/1xartang.htm. Also, drawing on Pan, Beckwit, and others.

48   pay Tibet fifty thousand bolts of silk a year in tribute: From Shakabpa, translating the Shol Doring inscription.

48   Daizong recovered his capital, and the Tibetans' usurper, one of the emperor's sons, was soon dead: Yihong; Shakabpa; Beckwith.

49   "different things to the two sides": Yihong.

49   it finally signed a written treaty with Tibet: Yihong.

50   Trisong Detsen: Khri sron lde brtsan in Beckwith, p. 229.

50   "rites due to a subject": Tang Shu, as cited by Michael C. van Walt van Praag, *The Status of Tibet*, p. 119. This interpretation of the Tang Shu is shared by Beckwith; Yihong, Stein; and Snellgrove and Richardson. Chinese writers do not challenge this; they simply do not discuss it.

50   spreading the blood from animals: Beckwith; Yihong.

50   "The great king of Tibet . . . witnesses": See van Walt van Praag, p. 287.

51   Indian masters defeated the Chinese masters in two-year public debate: Tibetans traditionally have asserted that the debate lasted two years. Scholarly opinion knows nothing about the duration of the debate. However, one Indian master involved in the debate wrote three books about it, so it must have taken some time. From Robert Thurman, private communication.

52   *khata:* Ceremonial scarves are still offered to the Dalai Lama or other lamas—who return the scarf to the person who has offered it, or give another *khata* in exchange. A *khata* touched by the Dalai Lama is believed to have been blessed by him; a scarf that has been on a statue is believed to have been blessed by the Buddha or Bodhisattva represented by the statue.

53   Santaraksita: Alternatively transliterated as Shantirakshita. Santarakshita, in Snellgrove and Richardson, p. 78; Shakabpa, p. 36.

53   "were so resentful and displeased": Shakabpa, p. 36.

55   one who has power to control physical reality: *Thu-nue Dhenpa*, one who possesses miraculous power.

56   *Vinaya:* See Alexander Berzin's site: http://www.berzinarchives.com.

56   "So at Samye . . . practitioners": The Dalai Lama said that "the Tantric practitioners were there after Padmasambhava came and left. How long I don't know, and I don't think it matters. I think each carried his special or unique responsibility continuously."

56   Kamalasila debated the Chinese for two years: In a private communication, Robert Thurman wrote, "Tibetan oral tradition would have it be two years. Scholarly opinion knows nothing much about duration. Cer-

tainly Kamalasila wrote three books about it so it must have taken quite some time."

Chapter Four

62   Muni Tsenpo: The exact dates of his reign are debated—797 to 804 or 797 to 799.

62   "to reduce the great disparity between the rich and the poor": Shakabpa, p. 46.

64   comparable to the skimpy sources: Beckwith, pp. 223, 228–29.

64   battles with both the Arabs and the Chinese: Beckwith, p. 163.

64   Lang Darma: Glang-dar-ma.

64   Tride Songzen died in 815: Beckwith, pp. 228–29.

64   anti-Buddhist and a hothead: From Shakabpa and from interviews with the Dalai Lama.

65   two anti-Buddhist ministers: Be Gyaltore and Be Taknachen; see Shakabpa, p. 51.

68   "force monks to become hunters, to marry, or to become soldiers": Shakabpa, p. 51.

69   Buddhist persecution in China: Yihong.

69   to read an inscription on a stone pillar: Shakabpa, p. 52.

72   that was to last over three hundred years: The regionalism and factionalism that emerged after Lang Darma have probably defined Tibet in the millennia since then. Tibet was not reunited again until the Mongols.

Chapter Five

73   Buddhist monks returned: Stein; Snellgrove and Richardson; Shakabpa; Melvyn Goldstein.

73   As the Dalai Lama said: Luciano Petech, one of the finest Western historians of Tibet, concurs. He wrote, "The texts dealing with this period are exclusively religious, being written by monks for monks," in "Tibetan Relations with Sung China and with the Mongols."

73   Nyingma, Sakya, Kagyu: I have not discussed the origins and history of Bon, not because it is not a major school in Tibet but because it was one of the subjects the Dalai Lama and I could not discuss in the limited amount of time we had together. I hope that adherents of Bon will not take this editorial decision, which was entirely mine, in a negative way.

74   "robber Monks": Stein, p. 71.

75   maintained *Vinaya*. In contrast: Snellgrove and Richardson, p. 115.

76   "very secretly some of the masters practiced Tantra": The Dalai Lama also told me: "See, when they passed away, among their possessions they would find Vajra and Bell, which is used only in Tantrayana. So then the disciples would know that their masters practiced Tantrayana but this was done in strict secrecy."

76   Nyingma: Transliteration as used on Nyingma.com, the official Web site of the Nyingma order, today led by Penor Rinpoche. For the Ancient Ones, see Nyingma.com and Snellgrove and Richardson. Alternative translation is offered by Alexander Berzin as the "old tradition."

76   a distinct school of its own: Thupten Jinpa, in a private communication, wrote: "To suggest that there was a school called Nyingma prior to Kadam is difficult. Atisha's reformed movement did not take issue with a particular school or a tradition; rather it took issue with certain interpretations of dharma, especially with regard to the Vajrayana teachings. To say that Atisha attacked Nyingma school is incorrect."

77   Drom Tonpa founded the first order: Shakabpa, p. 60. For this transliteration I have relied on Alexander Berzin. See http://www.berzinarchives .com/history_buddhism/introduction_history_5_traditions_ buddhism _bon.html.

78   Lha Lama Yeshe Od: This was his name as a monk; his first name as king was Tsenpo Khore. See Shakabpa; Stein; Snellgrove and Richardson.

78   descendant of Songzen Gampo from the sons of Lang Darma: Shakabpa, p. 53.

78   famous translators: Rinchen Zangpo and Lekpe Sherab; see Shakabpa, p. 56.

78   greatest Indian Buddhist master of the day: Snellgrove and Richardson, p. 129.

78   city of Vikramashila: Shakabpa, p. 56.

79   Lama Yeshe Od refused: Ibid., p. 57.

79   who ruled the many rival principalities . . . invited Atisha: Ibid., p. 59.

80   Thus emerged the Kadam order: Ibid., p. 60. For this transliteration I have relied on Berzin.

81   so widely written about: Amazon.com lists more than 400 books about Tantra, including *Blazing Splendor: The Memoirs of Tulku Urgyen Rinpoche*, by Tulku Urgyen Rinpoche; *Introduction to Tantra: The Transformation of Desire*, by Lama Yeshe, Jonathan Landaw, and Philip Glass; *The Six Yogas of Naropa: Tsongkhapa's Commentary*, by Glenn H. Mullin;

Buddhist Masters of Enchantment: The Lives and Legends of the Mahasiddhas, by Keith Dowman and Robert Beer; *Tantra in Tibet,* by the Dalai Lama, Tsong-Ka-Pa, and Jeffrey Hopkins.

There are also hundreds of books claiming to be about Tantra whose titles announce, Ecstatic Sex! and so on. As in ancient Tibet, many modern writers seem to be more interested in popularizing and distorting Tantric teachings than in propagating the practices that have been passed down through true lineages. Tantra remains a widely misunderstood, and easily exploited, concept.

81   some Nyingma and Kagyu teachers still follow a literal path: Nyingma and Kagyu are not the only orders that still practice sexual Tantra.

82   Buddhist teachers used talk about Tantra as a means to seduce students: In the United States, Tibetan Buddhist teachers have been involved in legal disputes resulting from this matter. For Tibetans, discussion of sexual yoga remains controversial.

82   Buddhists in Tibet who disparaged *Vinaya* practice as relevant only to the beginner's path: This phrase is a direct quotation from Thupten Jinpa, who reviewed this book in manuscript form, in an attempt to bring more nuance to the text. While I am grateful for his assistance, I bear sole responsibility for any unfounded generalizations that remain.

82   to expose his naked buttocks: Garma C. C. Chang, *The Hundred Thousand Songs of Milarepa,* p. 495.

83   *thangkha:* These scroll paintings are made to be rolled up and transported, and then unrolled and hung on a wall, or a tent pole, for viewing. They reflect the mobile nature of Tibetan society.

83   "These were very beautiful paintings of the lives of Tilopa":
      TL: The paintings that you spoke of Milarepa, Marpa—did they remain in the Potala or did they go with you?
      DL: Still in the Potala. Actually, those *thangkhas,* there are many sets of them and they started from the Fifth Dalai Lama. Some of the paintings were according to the Fifth Dalai Lama's vision. . . . There was a special house for *thangkhas* inside the Potala in the eastern block. I do not have clear information if they are there or not.

83   the fathers of the Kagyu lineage: The line is founded on the "Whispered," or secret, yogic instructions, transmitted in an unbroken oral chain from Tilopa through Milarepa, to Gampopa and thus on through the teachers of the Kagyu sect in Tibet, to teachers today.

84   "Above all, remember our misfortune . . . ": Lobsang Lhalungpa, *The Life of Milarepa*, p. 24.

84   "Imagine what my happiness . . . ": Ibid., p. 28.

84   "She may be right . . . ": Ibid., p. 29.

85   unburied bones in the moonlight: Ibid., p. 102.

85   "he was so mean to Milarepa": Lhalungpa provides a number of examples, including these: "He hurled me to the ground on my face, and everything went black. He threw me on my back and I saw stars" (p. 58); he came out and slapped me again and again" (p. 56).

85   would first have to atone: Lhalungpa, p. 70.

90   must rely on meaning, not words: Paraphrase of Stein, p. 168.

90   Dzogchen . . . Chan . . . Zen: Stein, p. 73.

91   little central administration: See Introduction to the History of the *Five Tibetan Traditions of Buddhism and Bon*, at http://www.berzinarchives.com.

91   Gelug order would not emerge: Thupten Jinpa wrote, in a private communication: "Gelug emerged in the early fifteenth century after the founding of Ganden Monastery by Tsongkhapa, while Kadam evolved as a school in the eleventh century with the founding of Radreng Monastery by Drontönpa. I would in fact argue that Kadam is really the first school; only after its emergence and its critique of many of the old Tantras [did the] Nyingma evolve as a school on the basis of those [who] continued to hold deep allegiance to the earlier translation [of the] Tantras."

91   Drogmi: Spelled Brogmi in Snellgrove and Richardson, p. 132; Drogmi in Stein.

91   Drogmi is famous for acquiring a teaching: It was named lam-'bras,' the path and fruit of action; see Stein, p. 73.

91   Grass hut . . . enshrined: Snellgrove and Richardson, pp. 135–36.

92   between 20 and 30 percent of the population: This figure is hotly debated.

92   "So half were rubbish": The word *rubbish* is used frequently in Indian English and is not pejorative. Here it means that the monks were not real or genuine, because they did not follow their vows.

93   feuds and wars between the orders centered on politics and economics rather than on any religious differences: Stein, p. 146.

93   highwaymen . . . hospices: Ibid., p. 147.

94   It came as a shock: Snellgrove and Richardson, p. 144.

96   Dusum Khyenpa: He was actually of the Karma Kagyu sect—a suborder of the Kagyu.

96   Dusum Khyenpa: The spelling is slightly modified from the form in Goldstein, *A History of Modern Tibet*, p. 7.

96   "In a world where religious sects constantly competed": Ibid.

97   "helped to keep the Kagyu tradition alive": The Dalai Lama is actually speaking of a suborder of the Kagyu, the Kamtsang Kagyu.

99   head of the Buddha glimmering four stories above: This giant image is of "The Coming Buddha," Maitreya, who, Mahayana Buddhists believe, is the next Buddha, who will be born in a Western land.

Chapter Six

104   their leader Genghis Khan: Grousset; Soucek.

104   paid tribute, or . . . exterminated: Grousset, pp. 189–256.

104   The illiterate Genghis Khan: There are several alternative transliterations for this name today; the most common in academic publications is Chinggis Khan.

104   Eternal Blue Heaven: An epitaph for the highest, to whom all Mongols prayed: Paul Kahn, *Secret History of the Mongols*, p. 150.

104   divine right to rule the world: Soucek, p. 105. See also Kahn's translation, pp. 150–63.

104   The best life for a man . . . rape their women: My paraphrase of Rashid ad-Din in d'Ohsson, *Histoire des Mongols*, I, p. 404; Grousset, p. 249, and *National Geographic*, Dec. 1996, p. 24. Grousset quotes it thus: "to cut my enemies to pieces, drive them before me, seize their possessions, witness the tears of those dear to them and embrace their wives and daughters." *National Geographic* renders the passage as "Man's greatest good fortune is to chase and defeat his enemy, seize his total possessions, leave his married women weeping and wailing, ride his gelding, use the bodies of his women."

105   Recent genetic evidence: Nicolas Wade, "A Prolific Genghis Khan, It Seems, Helped People the World."

105   butchered, be it man, woman, or child: Grousset, p. 228. God gave him the world and resistance was punishable by death; so was lying, theft, adultery, and sodomy. Skilled artisans were sometimes spared: they were enslaved and sent back to work in Mongolia. Archaeologists who excavate cities abandoned as ruins since Genghis have found a thick layer of bones on top.

105   "Genghis then gathered his spoils from the . . . camp": Kahn, p. 66. The spelling of *Genghis* has been changed to conform to the transliteration standard used in this book.

105   Extermination awaited those: Grousset, p. 249.

105   The state remained disunited: Petech, p. 173.

105   competing nobles: Ibid.

106   "Chinese government publications," I said, "insist that Tibet became part of China: Wang Jiawei and Nyima Gyaincain, *The Historical Status of China's Tibet.*

106   "present the government's viewpoint": Ibid.

106   One key assumption: The Yuan Dynasty became a Chinese state—in fact, there seems to be a broad consensus among scholars outside China that this is a false claim. See Fairbank and Goldman; Smith; Goldstein, *A History of Modern Tibet;* Soucek; Grousset. Also see papers in *China Among Equals,* edited by Morris Rossabi, particularly Petech. Laird interviewed several unnamed professors who laughed at the conceit; one said that Genghis Khan would be very surprised to hear that he has become a Chinese. Several viewed this spin as pure propaganda. On the other hand, numerous prominent professors in the United States refused to be interviewed on this subject, apparently fearing controversy with China. It is clear that the Mongol state that ruled China slowly adopted many Chinese cultural norms. To what degree did this make the Mongol rule of China a Chinese one? That is debated. What is undebated is that the Mongol rule in China was ended by a Chinese-led revolt and the Mongols were chased out of China, back to their home in what is now Mongolia. Ultimately Chinese rejected Mongol rule as alien. None of this history, no matter how it is viewed, offers any "evidence" that Tibet was part of China at this time. The Mongol state also slowly adopted some aspects of Tibetan culture. Did that make it a Tibetan state?

106   "The Yuan Dynasty": I have accepted Wang Jiawei and Nyima Gyaincain's work as an expression of the PRC's official position on Tibet. Since it is on the Tibet-China Web site and the book was published in China, this is a logical assumption. See http://www.tibet-china.org.

107   this blind spot . . . was absorbed into a larger non-Chinese political unit: This perspective has been noted by many non-Chinese historians. For example, see T. H. Barrett, *Qubilai Qa'an and the Historians.* "This, incidentally, illustrates one of the most remarkable features of Chinese writing on the Mongol empire: its total failure to comprehend that China had been absorbed into a larger political unit. The automatic assumption, even with scholars as alert and as critical as the Great Ch'ing historian Chao I (1727–1814), is that the Mongols extended the Chinese empire. I am not

sure that this assumption could have been questioned under Manchu rule, or even (given the nature of the Chinese claim on much of the Western portion of the territory of the People's Republic) today, but, be that as it may, this ability to conceive of Mongol China as an age of Chinese glory may explain why some of Liang's contemporaries make even more positive statements about Qubilai."

107 Temujin . . . survived a youth of extreme poverty: Kahn, pp. 20–67; Soucek, p. 104.

107 "Killers, both of you!": Kahn, p. 21.

108 probably means "oceanic" or "world-embracing": Soucek, p. 104.

108 Between 1207 and 1215: Soucek, p. 104, gives 1206; Fairbank and Goldman, pp. 112–27, give 1207, 1215. Beijing insists that the Jurchen and Tangut kingdoms were Chinese states, since they ruled what is now north China; however, because both empires extracted tribute from the Song Dynasty and were ruled by non-Chinese-speaking people, this revisionist interpretation is, at the least, disingenuous. Holding to this belief may indicate that this argument is part of the framework for modern China's justification of the occupation of Inner Mongolia, Sinkiang, and Tibet.

Jurchen and Tangut extracted tribute from the Chinese and did not speak Chinese as their native tongues; see Yihong, pp. 356–61; Fairbank and Goldman, pp. 112–27; Soucek, pp. 77–113.

108 Xinjiang: There is controversy about this word. The Uighur, who were 95 percent of the population of the area before 1950, prefer the term East Turkistan. Many Uighurs consider themselves non-Chinese, but more than half of the population of this oil- and mineral-rich region is now Chinese. Chinese consider the use of East Turkistan (rather than Xinjiang) and discussion of the Uighur's position to be anti-Chinese. See http://www.uygur.org/.

108 Qocho: The Qocho borders may have extended beyond those of Xinjiang, as may the Tangut and Jurchen borders.

108 Uighur: Natives of East Turkistan seem to prefer the transliteration "Uyghur," but I have followed what seems to be the more common usage in English (and as in Beckwith). See Jonathan Spence, *The Search for Modern China*.

108 Indo-European natives: Soucek, pp. 77–82.

108 1206 A.D. Map: http://depts.washington.edu/chinaciv/1xarsong.htm. Also, drawing on Cambridge History of China, and consultation with several Chinese history experts who prefer to remain unnamed.

109   transliterated Mongolian into their script: Soucek, p. 81.

109   The Tangut were: Yihong, p. 357; Fairbank and Goldman; Soucek, p. 104.

109   From 1044 onward: Fairbank and Goldman, p. 114.

109   Jurchen (or Jin) Empire: For history, see Grousset, p. 136. The most important part of the Jin Empire was the northeastern corner of the north China plain—including what is now Beijing—which China lost in 936. Only when the Ming Dynasty rose to power in 1368, after the Mongols, did the Chinese regain this territory.

109   the territory within the Jin Empire had been lost to non-Chinese-speaking nomads: See Yihong; Fairbank and Goldman; Soucek.

109   siphon off the wealth of China's sedentary farmers: See introduction, Reuven Amitai-Preiss and David O. Morgan *The Mongol Empire and Its Legacy*: "The Mongols were more successful than any of their Inner Asian predecessors in siphoning off the surplus of the surrounding sedentary states" (p. 1).

110   Did not become Chinese: Jurchen is the example cited by Fairbank and Goldman (p. 117), but they make the same case with the Tangut, whom they call the Xixia.

110   Mongols attacked the Jurchen in 1211: Grousset, p. 228.

110   ninety walled cities . . . to rubble: Fairbank and Goldman, p. 121.

110   Chinese and non-Chinese not joined. In fact the Chinese under non-Chinese rule hated the aliens but they were forced to keep silent about that. This was known as "outer acceptance inner hatred": alien rule of north China, aliens never seen as Chinese: Fairbank and Goldman, pp. 112–19.

110   what could not be avoided had to be rationalized: Fairbank and Goldman, p. 118.

110   rice fields of Song China were a quagmire: Fairbank and Goldman, pp. 112–24.

110   He spent the rest of his life conquering: Genghis never bothered to conquer most of China. See Fairbank and Goldman; Grousset; Soucek.

111   Prince Godan: Petech uses the transliteration KÖDEN (p. 181). Shakabpa uses Godan.

111   he ordered every Tangut to be slaughtered: Grousset, pp. 247–48.

111   sent a small army into Tibet: Petech, p. 181.

111   "I, the most powerful . . . to bring you here": Shakabpa, p. 62.

112   Sakya Pandita left Tibet: The description of Sakya Pandita's journey to meet Prince Godan is based on Shakabpa, p. 63, who has based his account

on what he calls the *Gdung-rab*, or *The History of the Sakya;* see his bibliography of Tibetan sources, p. 336.

112   stop throwing . . . into river: Shakabpa, p. 63.

112   Mongols saw Chinese farmers as pests: Grousset, p. 251.

112   Mongols were convinced that they could make more money . . . than by eliminating them: Ibid.

112   After Sakya Pandita saw the power of the Mongols firsthand: Shakabpa, pp. 61–72; Petech, pp. 173–94. Where there is conflict between these two sources, Petech is given precedence.

112   he sent a final letter to his homeland: Petech, p. 182.

112   "The Prince has told me . . . to my nephew": Shakabpa, translating Tibetan sources of the period, pp. 63–64.

113   they wanted an influential monk: Petech, p. 181.

114   two Mongol princes invaded Tibet: Ibid., p. 182

114   Phagpa remained . . . accustomed to Mongol ways: Ibid., p. 185.

114   to receive instruction in Buddhism: Ibid., p. 184.

114   became chief of the Mongol world: Fairbank and Goldman, p. 121.

114   imperial preceptor: Petech translates *Kuo-shih* as "national preceptor" (p. 184).

114   "I wish to present you the gift of my Doctrine": Academician Sh. Bira, in Reuven Amitai-Preiss and David O. Morgan, p. 244.

115   *White History*. "The cornerstone of": Ibid., p. 246.

115   Tibetan linguistic skills; Tibetan lexicon for translating Buddhist texts: Jamyang Norbu, *The Myth of China's Modernization of Tibet and the Tibetan Language,* at http://www.tibetwrites.org/articles/jamyang_norbu/jamyang_norbu16.html

115   a universal script . . . unification of the empire: Ibid., citing work of Morris Rossabi.

116   Phagpa's alphabet used for 110 years: http://tech2.npm.gov.tw/khan/english/ss/i2l.htm.

116   Phagpa's script for forcefully imposed: Norbu, *The Myth of China's Modernization.*

116   Modern Korean script an adaptation of Phagpa: Ibid., citing work by linguistician Roy Andrew Miller.

116   Tibetan temples, monks . . . in Iran: Petech, p. 183.

116   Mongol historian believes that Kublai . . . such protection: Academician Sh. Bira, in Reuven Amitai-Preiss and David O. Morgan, pp. 240–49.

116   Forbidden City in Beijing, begun by Kublai Khan . . . as a sanctuary for Mongol culture: Richard Hooker, of Washington State University, writes, "The Forbidden City of Kublai Khan, then, was in many ways a protected sanctuary of Mongolian culture. This aloofness from the Chinese exemplified by the Forbidden City was carried over into almost every other aspect of Mongolian rule. Although they adopted some aspects of Chinese culture, the Mongols pretty much refused to learn the Chinese language." See http://www.wsu.edu/.

117   "mandala appeared in the sky": Dalai Lama, citing Tibetan texts.

118   Kublai agreed to prostrate to his spiritual teacher: Shakabpa, p. 64.

119   Kublai agreed to seek Phagpa's consent before making decisions regarding Tibet: Ibid.

119   a tool to obtain political influence in Tibet: Petech, p. 194.

119   establish Mongol sovereignty over Central Tibet: Ibid., pp. 179 and 185.

119   incorporated the old eastern provinces . . . sent troops to subdue Amdo: Ibid., p. 185.

120   return to Tibet . . . and the Tibetan chiefs came to pay homage: Shakabpa, p. 67.

120   ways that were acceptable to Tibet and that reflected its native culture: Petech, p. 185. Also see Shakabpa, pp. 64–71.

120   Kublai sent a small army . . . to crush any resistance: Petech p. 186.

120   the Mongols had established their domination of Tibet: Ibid., pp. 186–94.

120   Beijing, Kublai's new capital: Ibid.

120   myriarchies: Ibid., p. 187.

120   ten thousand Tibetans killed: Ibid., p. 189; most administrators were Tibetan; see Petech pp. 186–94.

121   exterminated millions of farmers in north China: Grousset; Soucek.

121   Mongols depopulated north China . . . slaves to farm the land: Fairbank and Goldman, p. 122.

122   "Phagpa sent one letter back to Tibet": To Kunga Gyeltsen, as cited earlier.

Chapter Seven

124   Tsongkha . . . Tsongkhapa: These transliterations and many other details about the life of Tsongkhapa can be found here: http://www.tibet.com/Buddhism/gelug.html.

124   born there in 1357: Date is from Snellgrove and Richardson. Tsongkhapa arrived in Central Tibet in 1372 to study; Goldstein, *The Snow Lion*, p. 5.

124   one hundred of the most respected teachers: See biography at http://
       www.tsongkhapa.org.

124   from all of Tibet's schools of Buddhism: Ibid.

125   fused into the New Kadam order: "In the meantime, he elaborated a bit
       more on the study of the Tantric tradition. So we call the teachings of
       both Atisha and Tsongkhapa the Kadampa tradition, and then slowly
       this becomes the New Kadampa and then finally it is known as the
       Gelugpa."

126   Bomi Rinpoche: "Death of a Controversial Lama," obituary of Bomi
       Rinpoche (1918–2002), TIN News Update, Nov. 29, 2002. http://
       www.tibetinfo.co.uk.

126   inappropriate for a monk . . . to discuss those lives in public. . . . "Let them
       talk about this after I am dead!": There are parts of this interview that he
       requested be made public only after his death.

126   "human soul": Buddhists do not believe in a human soul, so these words
       are used as metaphors for a complicated reality that is not discussed here.

127   Lama Umapa Po Dorje: This is one transliteration; however, at
       Tsongkap.org, the spelling Lama Umapa Pawo Dorje is used.

127   about thirty: from Tsongkhapa.org.

128   "how will we save these people?": The Dalai Lama is discussing an event
       that is also discussed online. At Tsongkhapa.org, see the biography, in
       the section entitled "Becomes the disciple of Manjushri."

131   they receive gifts of much greater value in return: Chinese government
       sources confirm this: http://www.tibetinfor.com.cn/english/services/
       library/serialise/h_status/his_04.htm. See also Chapter 3.

131   trade missions were "tribute missions": Western historians who have stud-
       ied the Ming records dismiss this idea; Petech, last page of his chapter in
       China Among Equals.

131   a vassal to the Ming Dynasty: Tibet was not part of the Ming Dynasty;
       see maps in Spence, p. 19.

131   one of his closest disciples: He sent his cook, Jamchen Choje Shakya
       Yeshe; see Stein p. 80.

133   founded . . . Ganden: Goldstein; Snellgrove and Richardson; Stein.

133   Gendundrup . . . First Dalai Lama: The name is sometimes transliterated
       as Gedun Trupa (1391–1474); van Walt van Praag, p. 8.

135   Mongols maintained . . . remained with the Tibetan viceroy and with
       the monasteries and nobles: Snellgrove and Richardson, p. 288; Stein,
       pp. 78–79.

135   death of Phagpa, in 1280: Snellgrove and Richardson, p. 288.

136   Gyaltsen, revolted against Sakya hegemony from about 1352: See Shakabpa, pp. 73–90.

136   In 1358, the Mongols . . . accepted Gyaltsen as their viceroy: Ibid.

136   After he had killed: Ibid.

136   he showed the Mongols that he was not their vassal . . . essentially freed Tibet: Shakabpa, p. 82.

136   China and Tibet . . . at different times: "The political issue here that modern Tibetans and Chinese argue about"; see http://www.tibetanyouth congress.org/publication/history%20Part1.html.

136   Gyaltsen died 1364: Shakabpa, pp. 73–90.

136   Modern Chinese historians dispute . . . that Tibet was a part of the Ming Dynasty: The Phamo Drupa regime, led by Qamqu Gyaincain and his children, was never independent from the central government, whether in the late period of the Yuan Dynasty or the early period of the Ming Dynasty. It remained a local political power subject to rule by the central government. See http://www.tibetinfor.com.cn/english/services/library/serialise/h_status/his_04.htm.

137   honorary titles from Ming: Stein, p. 79.

137   Phamo Drupa: summary guided by Shakabpa and Petech.

137   Kagyupa were eager to check the growing strength of the Gelugpa: It was primarily the Karmapa Kagyu who were at war with the Gelugpa. They are a distinct suborder of the Kagyu.

137   1400 A.D. map: http://depts.washington.edu/chinaciv/1xarming.htm. Also see Spence.

138   war was common: Stein, p. 81.

138   were not about differences in philosophy but about wealth and control: Stein; Snellgrove and Richardson.

138   By 1565, the princes of Tsang Province . . . become the kings of Tibet: Snellgrove and Richardson, their chronology, p. 288. For the Gelugpa under attack by Kagyu and the kings of Tibet, see Stein, p. 81.

139   Chokhor-gyal, in 1509: Shakabpa, p. 91.

139   went to a sacred lake named Lhamo Latso: Ibid., pp. 192–93.

139   Third Dalai Lama . . . who presided during the funeral rites: Ibid., p. 92.

139   was advanced and attractive: Charles R. Bawden, *The Modern History of Mongolia*, p. 28.

140   last Mongol emperor of China, Toghan Temur: Grousset, p. 502. Soucek, p. 167, has the transliteration Toghon Temur.

140   assassinated the grandson of Toghan: Grousset, p. 503. His name was Toquz Temur.

140   Mongol princes to reclaim their autonomy: Ibid. They reclaimed it from the heirs of Genghis—clearly, all Mongol banners were free of the Chinese.

140   Mongols . . . unity was rarely achieved: Bawden, pp. 20–50. Also see "Historical Path of Mongolia's Statehood and Independence," by the president of Mongolia, a speech delivered in July 1996, available at: http://drlee.org/mongolia/article02.html.

140   no sense of nationhood: Bawden says of this period that there was "fatal disunity" and that it "lacked all sense of nationhood" (p. 24).

140   Mongols had reverted to their faith in shamans: Bawden, pp. 20–30.

140   tribes were divided roughly into two camps, the eastern and western Mongols: Laird is simplifying a very complicated stretch of history. Those interested in Mongolia might turn to Bawden for a good introduction, or consult Soucek or Grousset.

141   Tumet: The spelling is as in Bawden, p. 25. Tumed is an alternative spelling, also frequently seen—for example, in Grousset and in Smith.

141   Oriat: Sometimes spelled Orad. The Oriat were sometimes called the Kalmuck Mongols; see Grousset, pp. 506–07. At a later period the tribe was also called the Zunghar or the Dzungar.

141   Torghuud, Khoyid: See Morris Rossabi, at http://drlee.org/mongolia/article03.html.

141   Ming emperor Ying-tsung: Grousset, p. 507.

141   Oriat hegemony . . . not broken until Karakorum about 1550: Bawden, p. 24. Soucek says the conquest of the Oriat took place in 1552 (p. 169).

141   Altan was the most prominent prince: Bawden, p. 25.

141   his reign, from 1543 to 1583: Grousset p. 510.

141   Altan was famous during his youth . . . Great Wall: Okada Hidehiro, *China as a Successor State to the Mongol Empire*; Bawden.

141   In 1550, he set fire to the suburbs of Beijing: Grousset p. 511.

142   Koko Khotan: Bawden, p. 25; Smith, p. 106.

142   He made peace with Ming China in 1571: *The Third Dalai Lama and Altan Khan of the Tumed*, Okada Hidehiro. Made peace with Chinese, opened border markets: Smith, p. 106.

142   Life of Altan Khan to 1573: Bawden, pp. 29–40.

142   felt that appeasement . . . might work: Smith, p. 106.

142   Altan forced the Ming to treat him as an equal: Bawden sites Mongol documents. According to the Japanese historian Okada Hidehiro, Altan

feared that Mongolian culture would be eroded by the peace with China and therefore he turned to Tibetan Buddhism as a bulwark. Beijung, denying this view, says that Mongolia was part of China in 1571 and that Altan was a loyal citizen. "When Althan Khan, the 17th-generation offspring of Genghis Khan, placed himself under the rule of the Ming Dynasty, he was granted the official Ming title of Prince Shunyi in 1571." See http://www.tibetinfor.com.cn/english/services/library/serialise/h_status/his_04.htm. The attacks on van Walt van Praag and on Shakabpa, who contradict this view, are at the same site.

142   A nephew of Altan's . . . think of higher things: Bawden, p. 29.

142   "in the western land of snows": Ibid.

142   Altan invited the Third Dalai Lamai: Smith, p. 106. While Tibetans believe that Altan was converted to Buddhism in 1578 by the Third, Mongol historians record a different account. In 1573, Altan captured four Tibetan monks (Bawden, p. 28) in a raid. Mongols believe that one of these monks converted Altan to Buddhism. Tibetans make no mention of this early conversion and say he was converted by the Third.

142   June 1578: Okada Hidehiro, "The Third Dalai Lama and Altan Khan of the Tumed," Tibetan Studies, Proceedings of the 5th Seminar of the International Association for Tibetan Studies, Narita 1989, vol. 2, pp. 643–52, 1992.

142   "oceanic virtue": Smith, p. 106.

142   "the wonderful Vajradhara, good splendid meritorious ocean": Hidehiro, "The Third Dalai Lama and Altan Khan of the Tumed."

143   "Even now I am Tenzin Gyatso": "The First Dalai Lama did not take this name, but from the second on, this is always there. Normally there is a popular saying in Tibetan: 'Someone with the name of Tenzin, someone with the name of Ocean.'"

143   Tibetans believe that the Third Dalai Lama converted Altan: Mongol sources disagree, saying that he was converted three years earlier, by other Tibetan monks, but the Mongols still value the meeting with the Dalai Lama, because of the many important events that followed—the burning of Altan's totems, for example. See Bawden, pp. 20–50.

143   financed the printing and translation: Ibid., p. 36.

143   Altan allowed the Third Dalai Lama to burn . . . shamanic totems: Smith, p. 106, Shakabpa, p. 95; Bawden, p. 32.

143   ordered all his subjects to burn their totems: Bawden p. 33; Shakabpa, p. 95.

143 banned blood sacrifices: Bawden, p. 33.

143 monks were . . . gave the nobility: Ibid., p. 32.

143 Some shamanic practice survived: Ibid., p. 33.

144 princes converted, the people followed: cujus regio ejus religio, Bawden, p. 32.

144 at Koko Khotan: Shakabpa, p. 94; Bawden, p. 27; Smith, p. 106.

144 site of these teachings became blessed ground . . . there: Shakabpa, pp. 91, 95.

144 silver and gold for use in Mongolia: Bawden, p. 36.

144 Within fifty years, nearly all Mongolians were Buddhists: Western Mongols converted more slowly, only in the 1620s. For details on the conversion of Mongolia to Buddhism, see Stein; Snellgrove and Richardson; Bawden; Shakabpa. Only a few Mongols became followers of Buddhist orders other than the Gelug.

144 Dalai Lama could be a tool to help . . . keep the Mongols at bay: Shakabpa, p. 95. Also see Bawden; Smith; Stein.

145 predestined . . . connections: Okada Hidehiro says, "It was the time for opening the door on his work in that direction," in the biography of the Third Dalai Lama as written by the Fifth Dalai Lama, translation by Okada.

145 "The khan and I have the signs that": Ibid.

145 The Third Dalai Lama publicly proclaimed he was a reincarnation of the priest Phagpa and that Altan was . . . Kublai Khan: Bawden, p. 30.

145 Karma Kagyu in particular, though all the older sects were aligned against the Gelugpa.

146 Third Dalai Lama died . . . in Mongolia: Shakabpa, p. 96; interview with the Dalai Lama.

146 Chinese authorities . . . attacks: Shakabpa, p. 95.

146 visit the Chinese capital, but he declined because of a prior commitment: Ibid., p. 96.

146 was only 250 miles from Beijing: He was at or near Hohhot, the modern capital of the province of Inner Mongolia.

146 requested that the Dalai Lama grant them their titles . . . great impact: Ahmad, *Sino-Tibetan Relations in the Seventeenth Century*, p. 146.

146 In 1580 the Third Dalai Lama founded the monastery of Lithang in Kham: Shakabpa, p. 96.

146 Third Dalai Lama accepted an invitation back to Mongolia: Sources conflict as to whether this invitation came from the son of Altan Khan

or from Ligdan Khan, the nominal emperor of the Mongols. See Bawden, pp. 30–31; Shakabpa, p. 95.

147   all were convinced that he was the reincarnation of Sonam Gyatso: Bawden, p. 31; Shakabpa, p. 96.

147   Fourth Dalai Lama . . . left Mongolia in 1601: Shakabpa, p. 97.

147   the Gelugpa gained the interested support of the Mongols: Snellgrove and Richardson: "By this piece of diplomacy the Gelugpa Order gained conclusively the interested support of the Mongol ruling family . . . which was bound to involve foreign influence in Tibetan affairs sooner or later."

148   The eastern Mongolian cavalrymen who followed him to Lhasa stayed: Shakabpa, p. 98.

148   perceived slight: Ibid., p. 98.

148   one of the princely defenders of the Kagyu: He was Karm Tensung Wangpo, chief of the Tsang; see Ibid., p. 98.

149   in 1617 . . . died: Shakabpa, p. 99; Smith, p. 107.

149   that he was poisoned: Snellgrove and Richardson, p. 193.

Chapter Eight

152   Ngawang Lozsang Gyatso . . . born in 1617: Shakabpa, p. 101.

152   The Fifth reforged a mountaintop: There were some buildings already on the Potala, from the time of Songzen Gampo, when he began construction, according to many sources.

153   In 1619 . . . was the reincarnation of the Fourth Dalai Lama: Shakabpa, p. 101.

153   some returned in 1619: Ibid., p. 100.

153   In 1620 . . . as a monk: Ibid., pp. 101–02.

154   some Gelug monasteries were forcibly converted: Ibid., p. 100. Also see Goldstein.

155   Tsogtu Taji: Bawden, pp. 41–46.

155   eastern Mongols . . . allied themselves with king of Tsang: Bawden p. 46.

155   1653 A.D. map: following descriptions and maps in Spence, Cambridge history of China, and also drawing on some data here: http://depts.washington.edu/chinaciv/1xaryuan.htm.

155   Sonam Rapten: He is sometimes called Sonam Chospel, especially by Shakabpa, but the Dalai Lama used the form "Sonam Rapten."

159   Sonam Rapten . . . good use should be made of him: Shakabpa, p. 106.

159   "I am supposed to be a lama . . . predicament": Quotation is from the Fifth

Dalai Lama's autobiography, as translated and cited by Shakabpa, p. 106.

159   "tune of the flute . . . arrow": Shakabpa, quoting the Fifth Dalai Lama, p. 107.

159   Gushri . . . Tibetan fighters: As described by Shakabpa, pp. 105–11, who based his account on Tibetan records that he cites.

159   Gushri fought against eastern Mongols: Bawden, p. 46.

160   Gushri often put the Tibetan princes to death: Snellgrove and Richardson, p. 194; Smith, p. 107; Shakabpa, p. 107; Bawden, pp. 41–46; Soucek, pp. 169–70; Grousset, p. 523.

160   ignored the Dalai Lama's advice: Shakabpa, p. 108.

160   The historic synopsis of Gushri's military activities in Tibet and Sonam Rapten's involvement is based on Ibid., pp. 107–10.

160   The Fifth was "so disturbed": As cited by Shakabpa, p. 110.

161   Gushri and Sonam often jointly led armies: Ibid., p. 112.

161   Indian and Nepalese kings: Ibid.

163   In 1644 . . . conquered Beijing . . . Ming pretenders: Spence, pp. 32–39.

163   eastern Mongols . . . surrendered to the Manchu by 1636: Bawden, p. 47.

163   Two years later the Manchu conquered Korea: Also sons of the Korean king were held hostage. Spence, p. 31. However, ultimately Korea did not become part of the empire but became a tributary or vassal state—it established diplomatic relations with the Manchu within the only norm accepted at the time. The original Manchu invasion of Korea was aimed mainly to force the Koreans to shift their allegiance from the Ming to the Manchu—which took place before the Ming were conquered. From the seventeenth century until 1881 Korea sent missions to the Manchu court, four times a year, and sought Manchu approval for the investiture of each new king. This was similar to some aspects of the Manchu relations with Thailand and Tibet. Such relations were seen, by some Chinese and Manchu, as making Korea (and Thailand and Tibet) part of "China"—whereas Koreans (and Thais and Tibetans) saw these relations differently. See Cummings, *Korea's Place in the Sun*.

163   The Khalkha tribes of the eastern Mongols . . . independent: The Khalkha did not become Manchu subjects until 1688; see Ahmad, *A History of Tibet*, p. 151. However, the Chahar, Tumet, and other eastern Mongols, in what is today Inner Mongolia, were subdued in the 1630s and 1640s, before the Manchu took Beijing. See Bawden, pp. 41–46.

164   "clear or pure": Spence, p. 31.

164   they had unified the nomadic tribes: The Manchu relations with different tribes and nations had different meanings in each case. Korea did not become part of the Manchu empire, whereas the Mongol banners seem to have submitted to the emperor in a variety of ways. The word "unified" is used to broad-brush many types of relations with the Manchu. Naturally, none of these relations had anything to do with China; they were relationships between the Manchu (who also ruled China) and the various people the Manchu controlled, or had influence over, in a variety of ways.

164   the Manchu were never more than 2 percent of the population of the dynasty: http://www.ibiblio.org/chinesehistory/contents/c11sa02.html.

164   Intermarriage between the Manchu and the Chinese was forbidden: Spence.

164   After the conquest, the Manchu subdued the rest of the eastern Mongols: Bawden, pp. 40–70; Ahmad, *A History of Tibet*, pp. 144–66.

164   "almost creating an empire": Bawden.

165   forced monks . . . to convert: These accounts are mentioned by Tibetan sources of the day and cited by Tibet's first modern historian, Tsepon Shakabpa, in *Tibet: A Political History* (p. 113).

165   "some insist that there were forced conversions": "Gushri Khan gave supreme authority over all of Tibet to the Fifth Dalai Lama and appointing the chief steward . . . as regent. The main rival of the yellow hat sect, the Karma Kagyu, bore the brunt of this defeat and were actively persecuted by the Gelugpa government. Much of their wealth and property was confiscated and many of the monasteries were forcibly converted to the Gelugpa sect." Goldstein, *The Snow Lion*.

166   Rimey: Transliteration as used by Alexander Berzin; http://www.berzinarchives.com.

167   "someone who is always thinking about politics": The historian that the Dalai Lama used as an example was Melvyn Goldstein.

168   He has no ordinary thirst for power: Laird is not the only observer who has noted the Dalai Lama's curious lack of interest in political power. See the article "There's Something Happening Here," by Ron Graham.

169   "convert China, Tibet and Mongolia" to Buddhism: Ahmad, *A History of Tibet*, p. 167.

169   "one of the many rulers in Tibet, Mongolia and [now] Manchuria, who were [the Dalai Lama's] Worshippers, Patrons and Protectors": Ahmad, *A History of Tibet*, p. 159.

170   subdue the Mongols who still threatened their conquest of China: Ahmad,

A History of Tibet, pp. 166–89; Goldstein, *The Snow Lion,* pp. 9–14; Shakabpa, pp. 112–18; Smith pp. 107–13.

170   the Manchur emperor . . . China: Ahmad, *A History of Tibet,* pp. 166–70; Shakabpa, pp. 113–15.

170   Shunzhi, the first emperor to rule . . . China: Spence, pp. 10–50.

170   Emperor Hong Taji: It was during the reign of Hong Taji, eighth son of Nurahachi, that the Jurchen people seem to have changed their name to Manchu and the name of the dynasty from Jin to Qing. Nurahachi and Hong Taji were primarily responsible for conquering the Ming and establishing the Manchu as the rulers not just of China but of Korea and large areas the Ming had never ruled. See Spence, pp. 10–50.

170   *"all the Tibetans and Mongols obeyed the words of the Lamas":* Italics added. Quotation from Shunzhi is from Ahmad, *A History of Tibet,* p. 169. Ahmad transliterates the names of the two emperors as "T'ai Tsung" and "Shun Chih." For consistency and readability, I have relied on Spence's transliteration.

170   "We would like to go outside the border": Ahmad, *A History of Tibet,* p. 169.

171   "If the Emperor meets him in person": Ibid.

171   "Lord Paramount of the whole world": Ibid.

171   Shunzhi sent a letter . . . Great Wall: Ibid., p. 170.

171   "Venus has dared to challenge": Ibid., p. 171.

171   "Being outside the frontier": Ibid.

172   "a sign that I was the legal King": Ibid., p. 175.

173   "The Emperor descended from his Throne": Ibid., p. 176.

173   "A person of royal lineage . . . hospitable": Ibid.

173   the essentially religious character: This is a direct quote from Ahmad, characterizing the visit. Ibid., p. 180.

174   "Mongols obeyed the words of the Lamas" : Ibid.

174   "with all the ceremony . . . to question" : William Woodville Rockhill.

174   upward flight: See Snellgrove and Richardson on this aspect of the Potala.

175   "If only this survived . . . culture": Ibid., p. 200.

176   Lhasa is lucky to have ten inches of rain a year: Web sources say that average rainfall in Lhasa varies from 230 to 570 millimeters. Average rainfall in India is 110 centimeters.

178   "pull down the Chinese flag": Tashi Tsering, a Tibetan farmer in his late thirties, was later said to have been tortured and killed after his failed attempt to set off explosives strapped to his body. He first tried to pull down

the flag, but when officers rushed him and beat him, they prevented him from setting off the explosives. See http://www.tibet.ca/wtnarchive/1999/10/9_1.html.

180   corvée labor: By modern definitions, corvée labor is close to slave labor, as the laborers are not paid for their work and are commanded to appear, on pain of punishment. In Tibet those subject to corvée labor could pay someone to take their place. Corvée labor was also imposed on the people of Mongolia and China by the Manchu emperors. To this day, corvée labor exists in Nepal and India.

180   Desi Sangye Gyatso . . . appointed him in 1679: Shakabpa, p. 122.

181   he was the son of the Fifth: Ibid., p. 125.

181   first instance in which they used that system to find the head of state: Snellgrove and Richardson, p. 204.

182   In 1682, when the Fifth died: Shakabpa, p. 123.

182   the Desi hid his death: Though there is debate whether instructions were given from the Fifth to do so, the incident is accepted belief among Tibetans. See *Songs of the Sixth Dalai Lama*, K. Dhondup, Library of Tibetan Works and Archives, 1981, p. 12.

182   three-year-old boy . . . in 1685: Shakabpa, p. 128.

182   "lead a frivolous life": Ibid., p. 129.

182   The summary of the life of the Sixth Dalai Lama is based on interviews with His Holiness the Dalai Lama and Shakabpa, pp. 128–29.

182   "When I'm meditating . . . I become a Buddha": See *Songs of Tsangyang Gyatso*, translated by Simon Wickham-Smith, "based upon the critical edition prepared by Per K. Sørensen."

183   "Is this girl not born of a mother? . . . tree's blossom": Ibid.

184   Kangxi's powers . . . lost its independence: Under Kangxi's rule, the Manchu penetrated Tibet for the first time, in 1720; see Spence, pp. 67–69.

Chapter Nine

185   the Qoshot of the western Mongols, who were still based around the Dzungarian Basin: Bawden, pp. 40–55; Stein, p. 85; Goldstein, *The Snow Lion*, pp. 9–15; Petech, pp. 8–50; Grousset.

186   The Fifth Dalai Lama's Desi, and even the Fifth himself, had long-standing ties to the Dzungars: Bawden, p. 52.

186   stampeded the Khalkha into the arms of the Manchu: Ibid., pp. 52, 76.

187   Lhazang's queen was in love with the Desi: Robert Thurman, private communication.

189   seized the Sixth Dalai Lama, and brought him to Drepung: Petech, p. 16.

191   He then agreed for Tibet to become a protectorate of Manchu: Goldstein, *The Snow Lion*, p. 12.

191   this figure, called an Amban, was the first: Petech, pp. 19–21.

192   In 1717 the Dzungars . . . failed to capture the child: Ibid., 19–55.

192   Dzungar invasion of Lhasa, 1717: Bawden; Goldstein, *The Snow Lion;* Smith; van Walt van Praag; Soucek; Spence; Petech.

193   1720 A.D. map: Drawing on data in Spence, Shakabpa, Richardson.

194   ill-defined Manchu protectorate status: The exact date this begins is unclear. The first Amban arrived in 1709, but he may have been just an ambassador, since he had no troops. Some historians date the start of the protectorate from about 1720, others from about 1750.

195   1792 A.D. map: Drawing on data in Spence, Shakabpa, Richardson.

195   next time the Manchu would not come to help them : Goldstein, *The Snow Lion.*

196   the regents ruled Tibet for 160 years under nebulous Manchu protection: The period was 1751–1912; Petech, p. 260. See also Stein; Smith; Snellgrove and Richardson.

200   Lama Temple: The only temple in Beijing to have its own subway stop, the Harmony and Peace Palace Lamasery, or Yonghegong, is the most handsome and impressive Buddhist temple in the city. The Lama Temple was originally the residence of Prince Yongzheng, who later became emperor. His mansion was converted into a temple in 1744 after he ascended the throne. . . . Today, the Lama Temple is home to about seventy lamas, who are actually from Mongolia, even though it is a "Tibetan Lama Temple." See http://tour-beijing.com/sightseeing/showsight.php?sight_id=11.

201   replica of the Potala built at the Manchu summer palace, in Jehol: Spence, p. 100.

201   The Manchu emperors promoted cultural and ethnic differences, between Manchu and Chinese, to prevent the absorption of the Manchu into the numerically larger Chinese population: Spence, p. 41; Fairbank and Goldman, p. 148.

201   banned all intermarriage . . . with the subject Chinese peoples: Bawden, p. 77.

201   maintain their ethnic purity: Fairbank and Goldman, p. 148.

201   the Manchu encouraged Mongol princes . . . to intermarry with the Manchu: Bawden, p. 77.

201   Manchu defended their ethnic identity . . . to rule their subjects: Fairbank and Goldman, p. 146.

201   Qing ("Pure"): Ibid., p. 144.

201   bureaucratic machinery was absorbed: Spence, p. 40

202   completed the conquest of what is now Mongolia, between 1688 and 1691: Bawden, pp. 55–85.

202   "The celestial Court reigns over the whole world . . . one family": G. William Skinner, *Chinese Society in Thailand*, pp. 23–25.

202   were forced . . . to signify their status as subjects: http://en.wikipedia.org/wiki/History_of_China#Qing_Dynasty.

202   pigtails . . . were a sign of shame for centuries: See Mao Tse-tung on this subject, in *Red Star over China*, by Edgar Snow.

204   "Concur with the Dalai Lama": Fairbank clearly supports the Dalai Lama's interpretation: "For the purpose of analysis, it may be pointed out (1) that the tributary system was a natural outgrowth of the cultural preeminence of the early Chinese; (2) that it came to be used by the rulers of China for political ends of self defense; (3) that in practice it had a very fundamental and important commercial basis. And (4) that it served as the medium for Chinese international relations and diplomacy. It was, in short, a scheme of things entire, and deserves attention as one historical solution to problems of world organization" (J. K. Fairbank and S. Y. Teng, "On the Ch'ing Tributary System"). Perry Link and William Kirby discussed this issue in a private communication with me and agreed that tribute relations between Manchu and bordering states did not, in modern times, make states in the same territory part of China.

204   Thai kings accepted the Manchu emperors as their "suzerain": Thais were the first to do this; Sarasin Viraphol, *Tribute and Profit*, p. 30.

204   tributary missions were in fact trade missions: Fairbank and Teng. See also Fairbank and Goldman.

204   Thai kings sent a tribute mission to China to ask for a title: "Taksin was finally permitted to send a tribute mission to Peking in 1777, but not until 1781, after the completion of wars with Burma and Cambodia, was he able to attain full recognition as King of Siam" (Skinner, p. 23). This view is widely accepted; see Viraphol; Charles Dibble, *The Chinese in Thailand*; Victor Purcell, *The Chinese in South East Asia*; David Wyatt.

204   to enhance their political standing: See Skinner, pp. 5–6, 23; Dibble; Purcell; Wyatt; Viraphol.

205   provides no rationale for modern China to claim that these nations were part of China: Private communication with William Kirby, Perry Link, and Mark Selden; reading of works by Fairbank and others.

205   government leaders and publications . . . part of China today: For example, see http://www.china-un.ch/eng/premade/60544/TibetFAQ2 .htm.

206   At the start of the Manchu Empire's conquest of Mongolia, in 1688, the Chinese could not enter Mongolia: Bawden.

206   By 1850, the Chinese had set up shops in every Mongol encampment: Ibid.

206   Mongol wealth was on the hoof: Ibid.

206   Chinese merchants in Canton . . . that the Manchu forbade: "If . . . our suggestion is correct, that embassies grew more frequent in the early nineteenth century in order to facilitate a generally expanded trade in the then tributary system had indeed fallen upon evil days and was being prostituted by the tributaries and no doubt by Chinese merchants as well" (Fairbank and Teng).

207   Since the Mongol nation was destroyed, to a large degree, by the Manchu's imposition of high taxes . . . Chinese moneylenders: Bawden.

207   from the men who had governed Tibet during the Manchu period: The Dalai Lama cites Ngapo. "Never paid. The head of the Tibetan delegation, Mr. Ngapo, of course signed the seven-point agreement and after that the Tibetans considered him as pro-Chinese, but as one of my delegation he visited there and we at least in central Tibet under Tibetan jurisdiction never paid taxes to any Chinese government including Manchu. Ngapo made this clear."

208   five hundred Chinese families in all of Central Tibet: Lixiong, "The People's Republic of China's 21st Century Underbelly," pp. 21–33.

208   a corruption of the . . . corvée system for colonial purposes by a vast wave of Chinese: Bawden.

209   "The Thai historian": Viraphol.

Chapter Ten

211   Thupten Gyatso, the Thirteenth Dalai Lama, was born on May 27, 1876, in the southeastern village of Thakpo Langdun: Shakabpa, p. 193.

211   "I studied a number of histories about the Thirteenth Dalai Lama": My summary is based on the account in Shakabpa.

211   went first to the vision lake, Lhamo Latso: Shakabpa, pp. 192–93.

212   "He had not, during his youth . . . of the world": Sir Charles Bell, *Portrait of the Dalai Lama*, p. 121.

212   Phurchok Jampa Gyatso: This spelling is as given by Thupten Jinpa. Another scholar I consulted said this tutor's name was Phuchog Sangpo Rinpoche or Lobsang Tsultrin Jhampa Gyasto.

213   in 120 years: The Eighth Dalai Lama, born in 1758, died about 1804; he lived to about forty-eight. The Ninth through the Twelfth all died before they were twenty.

213   British viceroy in India: The Thirteenth's meeting with the viceroy is recounted in Bell, p. 95.

214   Summary of life of Thirteenth Dalai Lama: Shakabpa, pp. 192–277. See also Nicolai S. Kuleshov, *Russia's Tibet File;* Smith; Goldstein, *The Snow Lion.*

214   in 1895, predatory . . . ring the Manchu Empire and Tibet: *The Water-Bird and Other Years: A History of the 13th Dalai Lama and After* (New Delhi: Rangwang, 1986).

214   the imperialist Japanese forces . . . Ryukyu Islands: Spence, pp. 220, 221.

214   The Japanese colonization of Korea: Though earlier Western historians gave credence to the Japanese idea that Japan had a modernizing role in Korea, Bruce Cummings demonstrates the callous nature of the colonization of Korea by Japan.

214   In 1880, despite . . . Hanoi and Haiphong: Ibid.

214   French sank an enemy fleet . . . Chinese sailors: Ibid., pp. 221, 222.

214   Russians . . . silver to the Manchu: Thomas Ewing, "Ch'ing Policies in Outer Mongolia," pp. 145–57.

214   watched European colonialists . . . newspapers: Ibid.

215   a Chinese state from which all other races would be expelled: Ibid.; see also Evelyn Rawski, "Presidential Address."

215   "Powerful foes encroached": http://www.worldwideschool.org/library/ books/hst/asian/ChinaandtheManchus/chap12.html.

215   Chinese nationalism is a creation of the twentieth century: Rawski.

215   Chinese saw the Manchu tributary states as rightfully Chinese: Ewing.

215   seize on the "solution" of colonizing the borderlands of Mongolia and Tibet, which the Manchu had until then prevented the Chinese from settling: Any who doubt the sweeping nature of this assertion might want to read Ewing; Duara Prasenjit, *De-constructing the Chinese Nation*; and Rawski.

216   "This is like the young sparrow . . . tigers": Ewing.

216   The vultures circling the Manchu Empire and Tibet drew closer: Kuleshov, p. 2.

216   In 1890, the British . . . Manchu China: Shakabpa, p. 202; Kuleshov, pp. xii, 2.

216   series of armed skirmishes: They occurred in 1888 (Goldstein, *The Snow Lion*, p. 22).

216   dried dung: personal communication from Dr. Michael van Walt van Praag.

216   had an agreement . . . discussion with the British: Peter Fleming, *Bayonets to Lhasa*, p. 45

216   Dalai Lama had no interest in establishing relations with London: Goldstein, *The Snow Lion*, p. 23

218   Chensalingka: Spelling is as in Shakabpa.

219   he sent cuttings from Tibetan roses as a gift to the Russian czar: Kuleshov.

221   Dorjiev was a Mongol Buddhist monk: See Kuleshov; Berzin's Web site.

221   Buryatia was invaded and then colonized by European Russians starting in 1666: http://gov.buryatia.ru:8081/obur/history/index.html.

221   For information about Dorjiev, his relations with the Thirteenth, and his foreign policy ideas, see Kuleshov; berzinarchives.com. Also see Tibet Justice Center's chronology, at tibetjustice.org/reports/chron.html.

221   he no longer bothered to consult the Manchu emperor's representatives about his appointment of officials in Tibet: Goldstein, *The Snow Lion*, p. 21.

221   told the young ruler he would need a new patron: Kuleshov, p. 2.

222   "The necessity of seeking the patronage . . . preference": From the Russian Foreign Policy Archive, as cited by Kuleshov, pp. 2, 130. More about the Manchu from interviews with the Dalai Lama:

   Turning back to the Manchu, I asked the Dalai Lama, "What about the Dalai Lama's relations with the Amban, in Lhasa, the representative of the emperor?" "Before the British invasion, relations with the Manchu Amban in Lhasa were very bad," the Dalai Lama said. "Actually very bad. He showed no sign of respect toward the Dalai Lama. That is clear. I don't know why it was so. But there were problems, and there was one Amban who was a late riser and an opium addict."

222   Once the decision . . . trip to Russia a secret: Kuleshov, citing Russian Foreign Office Archives.

223   Curzon decided it was "necessary to preserve the status quo in Tibet": Kuleshov.

223   the press report was a complete fabrication: Fleming.

223   By November 1902, Curzon was determined to send an army into Tibet: tibetjustice.org/reports/chron.html.

223   British soldiers . . . armed with an early version of a machine gun: British forces in Tibet had several Maxim guns, named after Hiram Maxim,

the maker. See Fleming, pp. 151–52; http://www.firstworldwar.com/weaponry/machineguns.htm.

224 "I hope I shall never" and "I got so sick": Fleming, p. 151.

225 Thirteenth Dalai Lama was twenty-eight years old when he rode into an exile: Bell, p. 63.

225 Ulaanbaatar: Bell says the Thirteenth went to Urrga, which is modern Ulaanbaatar.

225 "some misunderstanding with one Mongol priest": The Thirteenth Dalai Lama and the Huhuktu found Ulaanbaatar too small for two high lamas, according to the Fourteenth.

226 English-occupied Tibet: For Melvyn Goldstein, Britain's 1904 invasion of Tibet "set in motion a host of conflicting and uncontrolled forces that have dominated Tibetan history up to the present day" (*A History of Modern Tibet*, p. 45).

226 the Manchu made no move to absorb Tibet as a province: Goldstein, *The Snow Lion*, p. 14

226 Tibet also maintained its legal and administrative systems, with its own officials: Ibid., p. 20. The Dalai Lama confirms that officials told him the same thing.

226 Qianlong knew that the Dalai Lama . . . supposed to govern Tibet: Goldstein, Ibid., p. 21, quoting from Hanzhang Ya, *The Biographies of the Dalai Lamas* (Beijing: Foreign Language Press, 1991).

226 The Taiping Rebellion: "costing 30 million lives—50 times the death toll of the U.S. Civil War"; see http://www.washtimes.com/upi-breaking/20030725–110656-5354r.htm. Nearly half of the country was under the control of the Taiping Tianguo (Heavenly Kingdom of Great Peace), between approximately 1853 and 1865. Twenty to thirty million people were killed on both sides. See http://members.tripod.com/~american_almanac/taiping.htm. *The Guinness Book of World Records* lists the rebellion as the deadliest human conflict ever.

226 Tibet fought two wars: Goldstein *The Snow Lion*, p. 21.

226 Manchu's ability to intervene in Tibetan affairs had vanished: Ibid.

227 Tibetan officials left in charge by the Thirteenth Dalai Lama capitulated: Goldstein, *The Snow Lion*, p. 24.

227 Convention Between Great Britain and Thibet: http://www.tibetjustice.org/materials/treaties/treaties10.html, citing van Walt van Praag's *Status of Tibet*.

227   agreed not to conduct relations with foreign states: Goldstein, *A History of Modern Tibet*, p. 45.

227   Tibet became its protectorate: It was, as Warren Smith has written, the establishment "of a British protectorate over Tibet, without any of the responsibilities usually associated with such an arrangement" (p. 159).

227   "protection from the dangers": Goldstein, *A History of Modern Tibet*, p. 47, citing Bell.

227   Manchu's second-to-last head of state: Spence, p. 217.

228   attempted to limit the power of the monasteries: Smith, p. 169; Goldstein, *A History of Modern Tibet*, p. 47.

228   land grant to French Catholic priests: Goldstein, *A History of Modern Tibet*, p. 46.

228   two French priests: Smith, p. 159.

228   "advance of civilization": Ibid., p. 170.

228   monks . . . were executed; Lhasa was ordered to pay taxes to the Manchu . . . and to adopt Chinese surnames; colonization was promoted: Smith, pp. 170, 171; Goldstein, *A History of Modern Tibet*, p. 47.

228   proclamation . . . colonialists: Smith, p. 171.

228   "The native Rulers have been abolished forever . . . clothe her" : Proclamation was issued by Chao Erh-feng, commissioner in charge of the Yunnan-Szechuan frontier, calling for settlers for the new District of Batang, Feb. 7, 1906; Parliamentary Papers, cd. 5240 (1910), 109, as cited by Smith, p. 171.

228   colonizing efforts in Mongolia, Inner Mongolia, and Manchuria: Ewing, p. 152.

228   Manchu emperors had always protected the Mongols and Tibetans as distinct races: Ibid.

229   "The Government of Great Britain engages . . . of Tibet": excerpt from the 1906 Convention Between Great Britain and China Respecting Tibet; http://www.tibetjustice.org/materials/treaties/treaties11.html, courtesy van Walt van Praag.

230   Through its treaties with the Manchu and Russia, Britain . . . that the Qing had never had: Both Goldstein (*A History of Modern Tibet*) and Smith support this interpretation.

230   Under Western legal precedent, the status of a state cannot be changed unless it is a party to the agreement: Van Walt van Praag clearly presents the evidence for this conclusion in *The Status of Tibet*.

231   The Russians would not help: Goldstein, *A History of Modern Tibet*, p. 48, *The Snow Lion*, pp. 26–27; Smith, pp. 164, 165; Bell, p. 69.

231   Dalai Lama went to Beijing . . . so he could return safely: Goldstein, *The Snow Lion*, p. 27.

231   pointed out . . . he would go to Beijing in his own time: Rockville's conversation with the Dalai Lama is cited by Smith, p. 167

232   Thirteenth finally arrived at the capital: The chronology has been established by multiple sources; see http://www.tibetjustice.org/reports/chron.html.

232   "I went . . . help each other": Bell, p. 77.

232   stripped the Thirteenth of temporal authority, and no one thought he could recover it: Bell, p. 76.

232   Thirteenth refused . . . bend to one knee, or genuflect: Bell, p. 73; Goldstein, *A History of Modern Tibet*, p. 49.

232   Dalai Lama . . . assurances about the continuation of his rule in Tibet: Ibid., p. 51.

232   "loyal and submissive vice-regent": Goldstein, *The Snow Lion*, p. 27.

233   Chao Erh-feng: Spelling as in Goldstein, *A History of Modern Tibet*, p. 51.

233   ordered to continue the assimilation of Tibet: Smith says, "The Ching court in an edict of 9 March 1908 announced an ambitious program of military advances, administrative reorganization, colonization and civilization of the natives of the Tibetan frontier" (p. 172).

233   the Butcher: Shakabpa, p. 226; Smith, pp. 170–80.

234   "We are very anxious . . . Chinese troops" : Goldstein quoting the Dalai Lama's letter to British Indian officials, 1996, p. 28 (see *A History of Modern Tibet*, p. 51).

234   not a single country . . . to establish administrative control over Tibet, something no Chinese or Manchu government had ever accomplished: Goldstein, *A History of Modern Tibet*, p. 28.

234   the Dalai Lama reached India safely: Bell.

235   "At first sight . . . to his own country": Ibid.

235   "give China practically complete control over Tibet . . . Bhutan": Ibid., pp. 98–99.

235   "It was not long before . . . to China": Ibid., p. 99.

235   "would not intervene between Tibet and China": Ibid., pp. 100–01.

236   Bell met the Dalai Lama about fifty times: Ibid., p. 103.

236   covert attempts to approach Czar Nicholas: Ibid., p. 117.

236   "Tibet down through the centuries . . . tell you this": Ibid., p. 118.

236   He knew of Tibet's sack . . . Manchu distorted this history: Ibid.

237   under Bell's guidance . . . Britain governed even all of vast India . . . British troops: Ibid., pp. 120–21. Bell says that the Dalai Lama's chief ministers, who had fled with him, were impressed by Britain's treatment of the princely states. The way they were "being made safe by the British power from external aggression, and granted freedom by the same power in their internal administration," was "ideal." They sighed and said, "That is how we should like Tibet to be." The princely states in India were tiny, however, and Britain had no intention of defending a country as large as Tibet.

237   zoo; "a gurgle of laughter": Bell, p. 95.

238   The Manchu raised questions about the exact border with India: Bell.

239   "I don't want any titles from the Chinese . . . about us": This assertion by the Fourteenth is supported by Bell and others.

240   "The policy of the Manchus has been one of . . . final victory": Cited by Herbert A. Giles, published 1912, Chapter 12. http://www .worldwideschool.org/library/books/hst/asian/ChinaandtheManchus/ chap12.html.

241   "The Han flag raised": Edgar Snow, quoting Mao, in *Red Star over China*, p. 127.

241   by hiding their ethnic identity: Duara Prasenjit, *De-constructing the Chinese Nation*, p. 23.

241   are no longer willing to consider "Manchu" or "Qing" as synonymous with "China": Rawski did not acknowledge this claim: "The Republic of China claimed to have inherited the rights to rule the empire built by the Manchus from the last (*Manchu*) emperor when he abdicated in 1912, but neither the Mongols nor the Tibetans acknowledged them" (Hidehiro Okada, *China as a Successor State to the Mongol Empire*).

243   Chinese monks who fought for the Tibetans . . . for the Chinese: Shakabpa, p. 240.

243   pro-Chinese Tibetan officials. Tibetan forces . . . returned to Lhasa: Ibid.

244   Lungshar: Tsipon Lungshar Dorje Tsegyal: See Goldstein, *A History of Modern Tibet*, pp. 156–65.

244   ambassador-at-large: Ibid.

245   "one Japanese man came to teach the Tibetan army . . . different places": Yasujiro Yajima spent six years in Lhasa. See Shakabpa, p. 250.

247   remove the tax-free estates of some of the monks and noble lords: Goldstein, *A History of Modern Tibet;* Smith.

247   controlled 185 estates with 20,000 serfs . . . animals: Goldstein, *A History*

of Modern Tibet, p. 34, citing Tom Grunfeld. Grunfeld, in private communication and in his works, has said that such numbers are only rough estimates and that reliable figures are impossible to ascertain. These statistics are probably indicative, however.

247   estates fed the monks when they performed religious services: Ibid., p. 35.

247   Any new tax: Goldstein, *A History of Modern Tibet;* Smith; Shakabpa.

247   Monks may have been up to 30 percent of the population: Estimates are a subject of heated debate even today. These estimates are rough but are generally indicative. The Dalai Lama says that there were too many monks and that their numbers negatively affected the population's ability to reproduce; worse, he says, a majority were not true, or *Vinaya*-following, monks.

247   Lungshar began to force . . . to pay increased taxes: Goldstein, *A History of Modern Tibet*, p. 162.

247   Lungshar increased the size of the army, and pay for the troops: Ibid., p. 163.

248   Panchen Lama . . . moved into the Norbulingka: Smith, p. 177.

249   Chinese were happy . . . China to reign over them: Ibid., pp. 216–25; Goldstein, *A History of Modern Tibet*.

249   "Tibet lost its best chance . . . to survive in the modern world": In fact, as I spoke I quoted some of what Goldstein has written to the Dalai Lama: "Overnight Tibet lost its best chance to create a modern polity capable of coordinating international support for its independent status and defending its national territory."

250   *Nye-droen:* The lord chamberlain, translation of title, and name of the official (Thubten Lekmon) supplied by HHDL to Laird, private communication, 2006.

258   Dalai Lama died, on December 17, 1933: Goldstein, *A History of Modern Tibet*, p. 141.

258   at the age of fifty-eight: Snellgrove and Richardson, chronology, p. 289.

258   "political bandits": Shakabpa, p. 276.

259   botched the job: Goldstein, *A History of Modern Tibet*, pp. 186–212.

Chapter Eleven

261   He was born Lhamo Dhondup on July 6, 1935: For birth date, see Gyatso, *Freedom in Exile*, p. 3. That work transliterates the name as Lhamo Dhondup; Mary Craig, in *Kundun,* uses the form Lhamo Dhondup. I am following the guidance of Thupten Jinpa.

261 eighty sheep . . . hens: Gyatso, *Freedom in Exile*, p. 6.

261 Dekyi Tsering: Spelling as in Craig, p. xx, family tree of the Dalai Lama.

261 was back in the fields: Ibid., p. 56. It is not clear if she returned to work that same day or within a few days.

261 not far from manure piles and suckling calves: Ibid., p. 57.

261 Choekyong Tsering: Ibid., p. xx, family tree of the Dalai Lama.

261 improved . . . rainbow: Ibid., pp. 54–58; Gyatso, *Freedom in Exile*, pp. 3–10.

262 Xining: Also sometimes written as Siling.

262 two of the seventeen households were Chinese: Craig, p. 54.

263 Reting Rinpoche . . . was selected as regent: The date was January 24, 1934; see Goldstein, *A History of Modern Tibet*, p. 189.

263 Conversions from Chinese silver dollars (cited in British pounds) to modern U.S. values are precise, and the same means was used here as earlier; Guildhall, City of London, referencing parliamentary sources.

264 condolence mission . . . handed out vast sums . . . to Reting Rinpoche: Goldstein, *A History of Modern Tibet*, p. 229; also Gyalo Thondup, interview.

264 For details of Tibetan, British, Russian, and Chinese views of Tibetan status, see Smith, p. 228. The rest of the discussion is informed, to a large degree, by my readings of Smith and Goldstein—as is all the politics in this chapter—and of NARA original documents for the period.

264 gave nearly every monk in Lhasa two Chinese silver dollars: Hugh Richardson, as cited by Goldstein, *A History of Modern Tibet*, p. 224; also Smith, p. 232.

264 insisted . . . introduction of Chinese influence: Smith, p. 229.

264 restricted arms purchases from India and began to disband the Tibetan army: Ibid., p. 241.

264 radio operator to remain in Lhasa: Smith; Goldstein, *A History of Modern Tibet*.

264 "In order to cement the relations . . . in Lhasa": Goldstein, *A History of Modern Tibet*, p. 145, citing *China Weekly Review* of Dec. 15, 1934.

264 by opening relations with China on the Nationalists' terms: Smith, p. 240.

264 withered away: Interviews with Gyalo Thondup and with the Dalai Lama. Smith, p. 241.

265 Palden Lhamo had promised the First Dalai Lama: Craig, p. 13.

265 omens given by Reting Rinpoche: See Gyatso, *Freedom in Exile*, p. 12; Goldstein, *A History of Modern Tibet*, p. 313; Craig, pp. 54–65. The Dalai Lama also spoke about this in interviews with Laird.

265   Panchen Lama had been stuck in Jyekundo: The date was Feb. 1937; see Goldstein, *A History of Modern Tibet*, p. 316.

265   Ketsang Rinpoche, spelling as in Gyatso, *Freedom in Exile*, p. 12. Ketsang transliteration in Goldstein, p. 317, but Kewtsang in Autobiography, p. 13.

266   "I want that": Goldstein, *A History of Modern Tibet*, p. 317.

266   "If you know who I am . . ." quote attributed to Ketsang Rinpoche: Goldstein, *A History of Modern Tibet*, p. 317.

266   "Sera Lama, Sera Lama": Gyatso, *Freedom in Exile*, p. 13.

266   boy kept holding the rosary . . . to go with the group: Goldstein, *A History of Modern Tibet*, p. 317.

266   discarded the fakes: The recognition of the Dalai Lama in Taktser is discussed in Gyatso, *Freedom in Exile*, pp. 3–16; Goldstein, *A History of Modern Tibet*, pp. 317–19; Craig, pp. 54–66.

266   dozen other boys tested: Goldstein, *A History of Modern Tibet*, p. 320.

267    $2.5 million today: Conversions done at the following Web sites: http://www.eh.net/ehresources/howmuch/poundq.php; to convert 1936 pounds to pounds of 2003, http://www.xe.com/ucc/convert.cgi. The author thanks Peter Ross and the principal reference librarian at Guildhall, London, for their assistance, via Internet, at Search.Guildhall @corpoflondon.gov.uk.

267   pilgrims paid Ma Pu-fang: Gyatso, *Freedom in Exile*, pp. 3–16; Goldstein, *A History of Modern Tibet*, pp. 317–19; Craig, pp. 54–66.

268   Lhamo Dhondup "dissolved in tears . . . all three in tears": Thubten Jigme Norbu, quoted by Craig, p. 60.

268   July 21, 1939: Goldstein, *A History of Modern Tibet*, p. 324.

269   announced . . . Dalai Lama: Ibid.

269   October 8, 1939 . . . to Lhasa: Ibid.

270   two dozen men were needed to carry it: Gyatso, *Freedom in Exile*, p. 2. Description of palanquin is from documentary films.

270   Uyab Podrang: I use a transliteration recommended by Jakob Winkler, private communication, 2003. The Wylie transliteration is U yab Pho brang.

272   Jampel Ngawang Lobsang Yeshe Tenzin Gyatso: Gyatso, *Freedom in Exile*, p. 19.

272   Kundun: Personal communication from Tenzin Choegyal, the Dalai Lama's youngest brother.

273   his first regent was notoriously corrupt: Gyatso, *Freedom in Exile*, p. 18; Goldstein, *A History of Modern Tibet*, pp. 325–65.

273   The standards the Thirteenth Dalai Lama had imposed . . . all eroded: Interview with the Dalai Lama; Goldstein, *A History of Modern Tibet*, p. 365.

273   army particularly suffered . . . purchases were restricted: Smith, p. 241; Goldstein, *A History of Modern Tibet;* interview with the Dalai Lama.

273   Reting Rinpoche accepted presents from the Chinese government: Smith, p. 240.

273   For a summary of Reting Rinpoche's corruption, see Gyatso, *Freedom in Exile*, p. 18; Goldstein, *A History of Modern Tibet*, pp. 325–65.

273   Taktra Rinpoche: spelled Tathag Rinpoche in Gyatso, *Freedom in Exile*, p. 19; I have chosen the form used by Goldstein, *A History of Modern Tibet*, p. 369.

273   take his first vows as a monk, in 1942: Craig, p. 79.

273   For why Reting resigned, see Goldstein, *A History of Modern Tibet*, pp. 325–65. I also interviewed the Dalai Lama on the subject.

275   Ponpo: His full name was Lobsang Jinpa; the Dalai Lama also spoke with Craig about Ponpo, p. 99.

275   Ponpo had a large brown mole . . . sucked at it for comfort: Ibid.

280   "But before Heinrich, there was an electrician . . .": There was an English engineer hired to install the new General Electric generators for the Lhasa hydroelectric project, about 1949. Apparently this is whom the Dalai Lama is referring to. He had one assistant, a White Russian by the name of Nedbailoff. Both are mentioned in Thomas Laird, *Into Tibet*, and Heinrich Harrer, *Seven Years in Tibet*.

281   five great Indian Buddhist classics: *Prajnaparamita, Madhyamaka, Pramana, Abhidharma, Vinaya*. See Tsenzhab Serkong Rinpoche II, *Overview of the Gelug Monastic Education System*, translated and compiled by Alexander Berzin, at http://www.berzinarchives.com.

281   *Geshe* degree: Geshe Lharampa (dGe-bshes Lha-ram-pa); see Tsenzhab Serkong Rinpoche II and http://www.berzinarchives.com.

281   A respected monk has concisely outlined: Ibid.

281   *Last Testament:* Glenn H. Mullin's translation is in *Lungta*, no. 7, Aug. 1993, pp. 8–10.

285   K. Dhondup: "The Regents Reting and Tagdra," in *Lungta*, p. 11.

286   he took a more anti-Chinese stance than Reting Rinpoche: Smith, p. 243.

286   The power struggle came to a head when Taktra Rinpoche: Summary of

Civil War of 1947, Reting Taktra war; see Goldstein, *A History of Modern Tibet*, pp. 464–521; Smith, pp. 231–63; K. Dhondup, "The Regents Reting and Tagdra."

286   Taktra moved first . . . in April 1947: Goldstein, *A History of Modern Tibet*, p. 473.

287   "one handwritten letter by Reting Rinpoche": The Dalai Lama said that Chikhyap Khyempo brought him a bunch of letters, including the one with a direct order from Reting to kill Taktra. I believe this is the first time that the Dalai Lama has said bluntly that Reting ordered the murder of Taktra.

287   Gyalo Thondup . . . was poisoned: Interview with Laird.

287   by enemies he made during tense conflicts: Goldstein, *A History of Modern Tibet*.

288   In 1946 he . . . study in China: Interview with Laird; also see Craig, p. 119. In the argument about allowing Gyalo Thondup to go to China, he is supported by Reting Rinpoche; interview with GT by Laird.

288   From the 1950s until today: Gyalo Thondup: Reliable sources assert that on some occasions the initiative for some of these contacts came from Gyalo Thondup. They also say that Gyalo Thondup has not always acted in a capacity as emissary of His Holiness the Dalai Lama during his travels and talks with various governments, and that Gyalo Thondup has not been the only emissary of His Holiness.

288   Gyalo Thondup ate his meals . . . 1949: Interview with GT.

291   fifteen hundred Americans who lost their lives flying the Hump: This estimate is from Chinese government sources on the Internet.

291   the leader of one Chinese road team . . . was killed: Goldstein, *A History of Modern Tibet*; Smith.

292   For a summary of events leading up to the Tolstoy and Dolan OSS mission to Lhasa in 1943, see Goldstein, *A History of Modern Tibet*, pp. 391–97; Smith. I also interviewed the Dalai Lama on the subject.

292   Chinese suzerainty, not sovereignty, over Tibet, insisting on Tibet's full autonomy in matters of defense, foreign affairs, currency: Thanks to M. Van Walt van Praag for pointing out some of the nuance here.

293   Surkhang Dzasa: Name spelled as in Goldstein, *A History of Modern Tibet*, p. 395.

293   "Tibet owed her independence . . .": Surkhang, speaking to Tolstoy and Dolan; ibid.

293   the nation had great sympathy for the freedom of small, oppressed countries everywhere: Ibid., p. 393.

293   so as not to challenge Nationalist Chinese claims: Ibid.; Smith; and read-
      ing of original files at the National Archives in Silver Springs, Maryland.

294   gold Patek Philippe watch: http://www.brilliantbooks.co.uk/ourWork
      _client.asp?ClientID=1&PageID=4 and http://www.tibet.com/DL/
      rotunda.html.

295   Americans believed that with funding and training by the United States,
      the Nationalist armies . . . could defeat the Communists: This interpre-
      tation of Sino-American history is extensively discussed and supported
      in Laird, *Into Tibet.*

296   Almost half of . . . made in America: Apr. 21, 1999, e-mail from Profes-
      sor Ellis Joffe.

296   Mao drove up to the podium in a U.S. jeep: Newsreel footage and news
      photos show this.

296   except for brief moments, Britain and the United States essentially refused
      to recognize Tibet as an independent state: During various treaty nego-
      tiations Britain occasionally seemed to call Tibet independent—at least
      independent enough to assign territory to Britain's Indian colony with-
      out Chinese approval. The United States toyed with the idea of recog-
      nizing Tibet, but Taiwan's objections made that a politically untenable
      stance during the McCarthy period.

297   Tibetans tried to send a delegation to the United Nations in 1949 . . .
      membership: As cited by Smith, pp. 267–69.

297   Both countries . . . invasion: Regarding efforts to prevent the Tibetans
      from applying for UN membership, see records at the National Archives:
      RG 59—General records of the Department of State, Entry 1305. Box
      11, NND 897209, Records relating to South Asia, 1947–59, Lot file No.
      57 D 373 & Lot File No 57 D 421. Subject Files of the Officer in Charge
      of India-Nepal-Ceylon-Pakistan-Afghanistan Affairs 1944–1956. Dec. 28,
      1949. See also Department of State, Memorandum of Conversation, Sub-
      ject: "US Government's Reply to the Tibetan Appeal for Assistance in
      Obtaining Membership in UN"; Smith; Goldstein, *A History of Modern
      Tibet.*

298   Republicans were sniping at Truman, claiming that he had "lost China,"
      the president . . . publicly: See Laird, *Into Tibet*, citing extensive documen-
      tation on this at NARA; Kenneth Knaus, *Orphans of the Cold War*, p. 40.

298   also knew that with Chiang's veto in the UN, China could prevent Tibet
      from joining the organization if it applied: National Archives files, in
      Laird, *Into Tibet*, pp. 128, 129, 140.

298   without being seen as unpatriotic: Smith; Laird, *Into Tibet*.

299   Douglas S. Mackiernan: See Laird, *Into Tibet*.

300   June 2000 meeting with President Bill Clinton: http://hongkong .usconsulate.gov/uscn/wh/2000/062001.htm; White House press secretary on Clinton–Dalai Lama meeting.

301   On October 7, 1950 . . . had invaded: The details of this complex event are thoroughly documented in three complementary books—Shakya, pp. 41–45; Smith, pp. 272–80; Goldstein, *A History of Modern Tibet*, pp. 690–97. Goldstein records that the first troops crossed into Tibet on October 5, but the generally accepted date is October 7. Many of the details are debated even now. There are conflicting accounts, for example, about whether the Kashag had its picnic, and heard of the invasion on October 7, or whether it heard of the events only on October 15.

301   forty thousand troops had made an incursion: Shakya, p. 43.

301   "Shit on their picnic!": Shakya, p. 44; Goldstein, *A History of Modern Tibet*, p. 692.

301   By October 19, five thousand Tibetans had been "liquidated": Shakya, p. 45. It is not clear if the term "liquidated" means that all these Tibetans were killed.

302   "the most gloomy, cruel, and uncultured in the history of mankind": Stephen Collinson, "Time Is Running Out."

303   "between China and Tibet as between neighbors . . . had with China" and "The armed invasion . . . Chinese aggression": Text of the cablegram from Kashag (Kalimpong), Nov. 11, 1950, UN Doc. A/1549; in *Tibet in the United Nations* (New Delhi: Bureau of His Holiness the Dalai Lama), as cited in Smith, p. 283, FN 66.

304   "as a matter of fact . . . China does not have and has not had 'sovereignty' over Tibet": Smith, p. 291, citing "Memorandum on the Legal Status of Tibet," Dec. 5, 1950, National Archives, 793b.00/11–2250.

304   London was concerned . . . claim over Hong Kong: Laird, *Into Tibet*, p. 266; Shakya, p. 58.

304   The United States and Europe let newly liberated India take the lead with Tibet in the UN: This political review is based on Smith; Shakya; Goldstein, *A History of Modern Tibet* and *The Snow Lion*; and primary research in State Department files at NARA.

305   Mao and the Chinese Communist Party controlled the actions of its troops: Smith; Shakya; Goldstein, *A History of Modern Tibet* and *The Snow Lion*.

305   surrendered . . . governor in eastern Tibet, Ngawang Jigme Ngapo: Smith, pp. 279, 288.

305   "like blind men" whose eyes had now, after their education, been opened: "The Graces of Mao Are Higher Than Heaven," cited by Smith p. 288, FN 79.

306   Faced with the complete lack of international support, those around the Dalai Lama, now living in exile at Yatung, felt that they had no choice but to enter into negotiations with the CCP: Smith; Shakya; Goldstein, *A History of Modern Tibet* and *The Snow Lion*.

306   One of the negotiators was Ngawang Jigme Ngapo: Smith, pp. 279, 288. See also Shakya and Goldstein.

307   referred to as the Seventeen-Point Agreement: See Smith, p. 297.

307   "Do you want a peaceful liberation or a liberation by force?": Smith, p. 295, citing the eyewitness Puntsok Tashi, brother-in-law of the Dalai Lama.

307   "other nations also . . . of China": Smith, p. 296, citing Puntsok Tashi.

309   In July 1951 . . . General Chiang Chin-wu: Gyatso, *Freedom in Exile*, p. 72.

Chapter Twelve

315   first Chinese troops arrive in Lhasa in October 1951: Gyatso, *Freedom in Exile*, p. 78.

315   price doubled and government storehouses emptied: Ibid; interviews with the Dalai Lama.

316   Tibetan government, though under duress to cooperate outwardly with the Chinese, were ready to rebel: http://www.tibetjustice.org/reports/chron.html.

316   Relations between the Dalai Lama's officials and those of the PLA and the CCP deteriorated: See Gyatso, *Freedom in Exile*, pp. 82–120.

316   "Yes, I use these words today . . . popular later": The Dalai Lama commonly uses the words *serf* and *feudal* to describe Tibet prior to 1959. See Potomac Conference, Oct. 5–6, 1992, *Sino-Tibetan Relations: Prospects for the Future*, in which Robert Thurman said: "For example, the use of the term 'feudalism' which everyone uncritically throws around, including the Dalai Lama who says, 'Yeah, we were feudal.'" The Dalai Lama's use of these words as shorthand should in no way be misconstrued to imply that the Nyamthag were treated exactly like serfs in Europe or elsewhere during the medieval period. Nor does it mean

that the severe social problems in Tibet were any excuse for foreign invasion.

317   Chinese government source argues that . . . 95 percent of the population, owned no land: http://english.peopledaily.com.cn/features/Tibetpaper/tb1.html.

317   Chinese source says that 60 percent of all Tibetans were landowning peasants who paid taxes: *Concerning the Question of Tibet* (Beijing: Foreign Languages Press, 1959), pp. 213, 215, as cited by A. Tom Grunfeld, *The Making of Modern Tibet*, p. 14.

317   reliable documentation about the number of Tibetans who were serfs does not exist: Grunfeld, interviewed by Laird.

318   reflect Beijing's need to justify its invasion more than it does the history of Tibet: http://www.swans.com/library/art9/mparen01.html; http://www.nickyee.com/ponder/tibet.html; http://english.peopledaily.com.cn/features/Tibetpaper/tb1.html.

318   Grunfeld gives some credence to Chinese claims . . . that 60 percent of the population were serfs: Grunfeld, p. 14.

318   make gross generalizations: It is not even clear when the serf system started. Tibetan sources from the time of Songzen Gampo, for example, describe peasants who bought and sold their land, even though they were vassals of their local lord. The right to buy and sell land is not a right that serfs in feudal Europe, or Russia, had. Laird has interviewed former serfs in Tibetan areas of Nepal, freed only in the 1960s; their descriptions of how the local lords, in Mustang, owned the land and the serfs' houses, and controlled every aspect of the serfs' lives, were disturbing.

Wading through the morass of conflicting descriptions—many motivated more by a desire to support or oppose China's invasion than to objectively describe traditional Tibet—it is clear that no objective cross-cultural criteria exist that would allow us to say with confidence that most Tibetans were serfs or that Tibet was a feudal society. For example do the words "most Tibetans" apply to the people of Kham and Amdo? Then the statement is certainly false. When using such words as general descriptions it should be recalled that they do not fully define the socioeconomic reality of traditional Tibet. None of this is intended to downplay the injustices that serfs lived under in some areas of Tibet.

318   Beijing worked with Tibetan nobles . . . to preserve aristocratic rights: See text of the Seventeen-Point Agreement.

318   Travelers who passed through both China and Tibet: In interviews with Laird, Frank Bessac and Vasili Zvansov said the Tibetans were rich compared to Chinese peasants, and missionary travelers in Kham said the same.

319   "The Tibetan local government . . . motherland": http://www.stanford.edu/~geeyuen/struggle.html.

320   CIA formulated plans to airlift Tibetan freedom fighters out of Asia: Knaus; Shakya; Jamyang Norbu, *Warriors of Tibet*.

321   he would have opposed the plans if he had known about them: Dalai Lama, in conversation with Laird.

321   Only through dialogue with the Chinese . . . could he protect his people: The Thirteenth Dalai Lama said that violent resistance to invasion was acceptable. Tibetan Buddhism has always argued that it is morally defensible to murder a murderer, if doing so will prevent the killings of hundreds of people. The Fourteenth Dalai Lama, as young man, seems to have opposed military resistance as futile in the face of the PLA's overwhelming superiority.

321   the death of twenty million to forty million people: Phillip Short, *Mao: A Life*. Other books have given even higher estimates.

323   "His rule brought about the deaths . . . in history": See Short.

323   was sixty-one years old in 1954: He was born on Dec. 26, 1893.

323   the highest crop yields in the world . . . steel produced was useless: Howard French, "Billions of Trees Planted, and Nary a Dent in the Desert."

325   returned to Lhasa in June 1955: Gyatso, *Freedom in Exile*, p. 113; Tibet Justice Center, Web site chronology, gives June 29, 1955.

326   "Of course my mind is more scientific and I love science and technology": Edited out, as extraneous to the narrative thread: "So there are many occasions when I discuss that the late Panchen Lama was more orthodox and my mind was more flexible, because I had much more knowledge about technology and the Western world because of these war tutorial books. The Panchen Lama was really isolated and had much less opportunity."

330   Eastern Tibetans . . . Beijing had manipulated them: Jamyang Norbu in "Hopelessly Hopeful," in *Tibetan Review*.

330   "collectivization, measures to settle the nomads . . . sporadic uprisings": Tenzing Sonam and Ritu Sarin on their Web site, http://www.naatanet.org/shadowcircus/chu.html.

330   monastery . . . aerial bombardment: See chronology at tibetjustice.org/ reports/chron.html; see also Gyatso, *Freedom in Exile*, p. 121.

330   Between 1957 and 1961, eight small teams of guerrillas: See Knaus; http: //www.naatanet.org/shadowcircus/bg1.html; and the wonderful documentary by Sonam and Sarin.

331   they were enough to convince the Chinese that the rebel fighters were under the direction of foreign imperialists: As Gyalo Thondup says, "Just enough to make the Chinese really angry" (GT interview with Laird).

331   If the Tibetan agents supplied the United States with useful intelligence: There are many similarities between CIA support for Tibetans in the 1950s and the CIA officer Douglas Mackiernan's agents in Sinkiang. Mackiernan's agents thought the United States would support their fight for independence. Washington could use these agents to obtain helpful intelligence, though ultimately the nation did not assist the freedom fighters of Sinkiang. See Laird, *Into Tibet*. Mackiernan's status as a CIA officer working under State Department cover was maintained by the CIA until June 2006, when the CIA finally agreed to recognize, at least within the "CIA Family," that Mackiernan was indeed a CIA officer under cover. Declassification of the CIA's immense Mackiernan files has still not been approved.

331   "a reflection of their anti-Communist policies": Gyatso, *Freedom in Exile*, p. 211.

331   He told the Dalai Lama to go back to Tibet: Ibid., p. 129.

332   he returned to Lhasa in April 1957: See chronology at tibetjustice.org/ reports/chron.html; Gyatso, *Freedom in Exile*, p. 134.

332   it is a mistake to think of all Tibetans as unwilling to fight to defend their country: See the work of Jamyang Norbu—in particular, see his article "Non-Violence and Non-Action."

332   "Use peaceful means . . . to more forceful means": Thirteenth Dalai Lama, *Last Political Testament, Lungta*, no. 7, Aug. 1993, pp. 8–10.

332   "took up arms to fight for the freedom of their country": Jamyang Norbu, "Non-Violence and Non-Action."

332   Chinese . . . as ordering the Dalai Lama to mobilize the tiny fragments of the Tibetan army against the rebels: Gyatso, *Freedom in Exile*, p. 140.

332   mobilized 150,000 troops in Kham and Amdo: Ibid., p. 137.

333   "depopulated and looted of their valuable metals . . . physically destroyed": Smith, p. 442, citing interviews.

333   The lumber and stones were used to construct barracks: Ibid.

333   On March 10, 1959 . . . was killed: Smith; Shakya; Goldstein; interviews with the Dalai Lama.

335   According to Chinese sources, the PLA killed 86,000 Tibetans: Smith cites documents.

336   with CIA support, they made the occasional raid into Tibet until about 1971: Knaus; Shakya; Smith; and interviews by Laird with survivors, such as Baba Yeshi.

336   "the necessary facilities": Gyatso, *Freedom in Exile*, p. 158.

337   "a reactionary upper-strata clique" and "patriotic Tibetan monks and laymen": from New China News agency, cited by Gyatso, *Freedom in Exile*, p. 160.

337   "The Tibetan people . . . ardently love the PLA, and oppose the imperialists and traitors": Chinese views of the events of 1959 have not changed much since 1959. Speaking in 2001, Raidi, deputy secretary of the Tibet Autonomous Regional CPC, said:

> In 1959, Tibet's ruling group, with the Dalai Lama as its head, started a rebellion under the control of Western hostile forces. They escaped to foreign countries and vainly attempted to seek Tibet's independence for more than 40 years. During the past 40 years, the Dalai clique has always tried to infiltrate into, and instigate troubles within, Tibet, under the cover of religion and vainly attempted to split the country, seeking "Tibet independence." The danger of their activities of instigation and sabotage is still quite big. Besides, due to the intervention of Western hostile forces, there are a few of their accomplices in Tibet. However, the overwhelming majority of Tibetan people recognize that they are Chinese. Those who practice "Tibet independence" inside the autonomous region are only a small number.
>
> Tibet has been an inseparable territory of China since ancient time, and there is no such problem as "Tibet independence." However, for some 100 years, imperialists invaded China and continuously tried to split China, and vainly attempted to separate Tibet from China. Hong Kong *Ta Kung Pao* (Internet version), in Chinese, Aug. 2001.

338   "I am determined to win independence for Tibet": Gyatso, *Freedom in Exile*, p. 161.

338   "You say you want independence. . . . Impossible!": Ibid.

Chapter Thirteen

341   In some cases, fewer than 10 percent of a party arrived there alive: Smith, p. 451, citing International Commission of Jurists, 1960, p. 227.

341   an estimated 135,000 Tibetans living in exile: http://www.tibet.com/exileglance.html.

341   Perhaps 20 percent of all Tibetan refugees in India . . . 1996: Maura Moynihan, testimony before the Senate Foreign Relations Committee hearing on Tibet, May 13, 1997; http://www.tibet.ca/en/wtnarchive/1997/5/20_3.html.

341   Even now, 2,500 Tibetans a year . . . to escape: News reports and figures are from the UN High Commissioner for Refugees.

342   resettlement camps were established: http://www.tibet.net/home/eng/settlements/.

342   they are legally stateless . . . Indian-issued identity certificates: http://www.tibet.com/exileglance.html.

343   Buddhism has been firmly established on six continents: The number of Buddhist centers in the U.S. more than doubled from 1994 to 2004, and there are nearly a million converted American Buddhists and another three or four million immigrant Buddhists. Canada has seen similar growth. In Germany the number of Buddhist centers has grown from fewer than forty to more than five hundred in the past few decades. In Britain the number quintupled between 1979 and 2000. It is a similar story in France, Italy, Australia, and around the world. While some centers are small, others are based in old châteaux or converted Christian monasteries. It is suspected, though difficult to prove, that one of the four Tibetans sects, alone, owns an estimated half a billion dollars in real estate, outside of Tibet, all donated by devout European and American Buddhists.

343   two hundred Tibetan Buddhist centers in Taiwan: http://www.taipeitimes.com/News/archives/1999/11/15/0000010765.

343   Such Chinese are traveling to Tibet . . . welcomed minority: At Sertar, for example, see http://www.tibet.ca/en/wtnarchive/2004/3/10_8.html.

344   Tibetans lived at first under the direct rule of the People's Liberation Army: Smith, p. 452.

344   the Tibetans . . . new society: Shakya, p. 305.

345   "the land reform was genuinely liked by the Tibetan peasantry": Ibid., p. 309.

345   the PLA forcibly established the communes: Smith, p. 551.

345   food rations declined instead of increasing: In fact, the amount of grain

reaching Tibetans after 1960 was lower than it had been before. Smith says, "Tibetans received less since the majority of agricultural produce was confiscated by the Chinese" (p. 473; see also pp. 552, 553). Shakya says virtually the same thing.

345   destroyed the old economic system: Shakya, p. 313.

345   Private stores . . . forced out of business: Smith, p. 473.

345   famines . . . and chronic food shortages: Ibid., p. 552. Starvation occurred in 1959–62 and 1968–73.

345   egalitarian ideals of Communism were a sham: Shakya, pp. 310, 306–13.

345   about 342,000 Tibetans starved to death: CTA estimate ; see http://www.tibet.com/WhitePaper/white5.html.

345   destroyed more than six thousand monasteries and temples : Dalai Lama, in a speech to Congress, April 18, 1991; http://www.tibet.com/DL/rotunda.html.

345   eight monasteries . . . with fewer than one thousand monks: Smith, p. 561, citing Ch'ing Jun, "Socioeconomic Changes and Riots in Lhasa."

345   Red Guards, both Chinese and Tibetan . . . Cultural Revolution: Smith, Shakya, and other historians concur that Tibetans were heavily involved, though, of course, under duress.

346   "Create the new by smashing the old": Shakya, p. 317.

346   recycled from the sacked monasteries, to build barracks for the PLA troops or Chinese administrators in Lhasa: Smith.

346   One foundry near Beijing alone melted more than six hundred tons of Buddhist statues: Ibid., p. 475, FN 71.

346   tearful eyes of middle-age Tibetans . . . forced to dismantle the temples . . . still feel guilty: Lena H. Sun, "China Rebuilds Its Image in Tibet's Monasteries," writes: "At the time, I didn't really think about it because we were young," said Doje, now forty-four, his eyes welling up with tears. "Now as I get older, I feel bad. I have regrets." Laird has also carried out interviews in Tibet on this subject with several subjects who prefer to remain anonymous.

347   monks and nuns were ordered . . . to work and to marry: Shakya, pp. 320–21.

347   there were 114,000 nuns and monks in Central Tibet . . . dropped to 18,000: Smith, p. 474, FN 70, citing *Population Change in Tibet*, by Zhang Yianlu (Beijing: Tibetan Studies Publishing House of China, 1989), p. 28.

347   The aristocrats who tried to work with the Chinese in 1951 were, like the

monks, among the first victims of the Cultural Revolution. . . . paraded through the streets with dunce hats on: Shakya, pp. 322, 325.

347   Panchen Lama to a public struggle sessions . . . released him from prison: See Robbie Barnett's introduction to the Seventy Thousand Character Petition, at: http://www.tibetinfo.net/pl-preface.htm.

347   estimates that 92,000 Tibetans . . . died or committed suicide: Estimate from the CTA; see http://www.tibet.com/WhitePaper/white5.html.

348   also estimates that 173,000 Tibetans died in prison: Ibid.

348   Chinese skillfully encouraged the Tibetans to attack . . . religious system: Tibetans were "primarily tools of Chinese Red Guard leaders." See Smith, p. 548.

348   "devastating effect on Tibetan culture": Shakya, p. 321.

348   to abandon their ethnic attire . . . to cut their hair short: Smith, p. 545.

348   "Once a nationality's language . . . nationality": from the Seventy Thousand Character Petition by the Panchen Lama, as cited by Professor Dawa Norbu in his historical introduction to the text; http://www.tibetinfo.net/pl-intro.htm.

349   the language, too, had transmuted under Chinese tutelage: Smith, p. 563.

350   "The current line of thinking on ruling Tibet . . . separatists": Lixiong, "The People' Republic of China's 21st Century Underbelly," pp. 21–33; at http://www.columbia.edu/itc/ealac/barnett/.

350   "We are helping Tibetans catch up with the west. . . . It is not 'Hanification.'": Ray Cheung, "Beijing Helping Tibetans Catch Up with the West, Says Author"; online at World Tibet News.

350   economic development in Lhasa has . . . "the space . . . nationalist sentiment": Lixiong, pp. 21–33.

350   killed 1.2 million Tibetans between 1950 and 1980: See http://www.tibet.com/WhitePaper/white5.html.

350   asserting the death toll was certainly no more than 500,000: French, *Tibet, Tibet,* at http://www.nationalreview.com/derbyshire/derbyshire091603.asp.

351   "The Monasteries will be looted . . . and terror": Thirteenth Dalai Lama, *Last Political Testament,* in *Lungta,* no. 7, Aug. 1993, pp. 8–10.

351   The Tibetan elite . . . were released . . . appealed to Tibetans . . . "to return home to participate in socialist construction": Smith, p. 564.

351   China claims to have invested $65 million between 1980 and 1994: Lena H. Sun.

352 lowest literacy rates in China in the 1990s, and one in three children received no education: Ibid.

352 In December 1978, Deng Xiaoping . . . met with Gyalo Thondup: GT interview with Laird; also see Smith, p. 565.

352 GT decided that Tibet's fate lay within China: GT Interview with Laird; also see Smith, p. 575, FN 36.

353 In December 1978 . . . "We have but one demand—patriotism": From AP reporter Stille. See http://www.tibet.ca/en/wtnarchive/1999/7/26_3.html.

353 "The efforts of the last 20 years have been wasted in a single day": http://www.tibet.ca/en/wtnarchive/1995/1/20_1.html.

353 CCP's general secretary, Hu Yaobang, went to Tibet: Smith, p. 568; the date was May 1980.

353 poverty in Tibet shocked Hu . . . were poorer now than before 1950: Smith, p. 568, citing Jigme Ngapo and Hu's speech in Lhasa.

353 The negotiations . . . of all Tibetans lived: From interviews with GT and the Dalai Lama, and based on a reading of Goldstein; Smith; and Shakya.

354 "lion-mouthed": Lixiong, "The People's Republic of China's 21st Century Underbelly," p. 5.

354 U.S. House of Representatives accused Beijing of having "invaded and occupied Tibet": Smith, p. 598.

354 "The real issue . . . state under illegal occupation": The Dalai Lama, speaking to Human Rights Caucus, 1987; http://www.tibetjustice.org.

355 About two hundred protesters were beaten and arrested and at least six were shot dead: Smith, pp. 602, 603.

355 "any move aimed at splitting the motherland": Ibid., p. 608.

355 In June 1988 . . . over real autonomy for Tibet: See http://www.tibetjustice.org; also see Smith, pp. 608, 615.

355 Ultimately, the Chinese rejected . . . "relinquished the concept of the 'independence of Tibet'": cited by Smith, p. 615.

355 [Panchen Lama said,] "Since liberation . . . than these gains": http://www.tibetinfo.net/pl-preface.htm. A variant of this quotation appears at http://www.kotan.org/tibet/10th_panchen_lama.html. And Smith uses this version: "the price paid by Tibet for its development over the last thirty years has been higher than the gains" (p. 61).

355 the Panchen Lama was not, in his heart, the collaborator: http://www.tibetinfo.net/pl-preface.htm.

356   rising star, Hu Jintao, was appointed as party secretary of the TAR and arrived in Lhasa in January 1989: John Tkacik, "A Biographical Look at Vice President Hu Jintao," http://www.heritage.org.

356   Zhao Ziyang, a liberal . . . instructed Hu Jintao to treat the Tibetans softly: Zhao asked Hu Jintao to "overcome the hard with the soft" in Tibet. See Tkacik.

356   Hu Jintao ignored the directions . . . troops into Tibet: Two sources concur that Hu Jintao rejected the liberals and established his hard-line credentials by helping bring martial law to Tibet in the spring of 1989. One is a report by the ICT ("Hu Jintao: Reformer or Conformist?" A report by Free Tibet Campaign into Hu Jintao's relationship with Tibet, at http://www.freetibet.org/press/HuJintao.pdf), and the other is presented by the Heritage Foundation in the piece by Tkacik.

356   Hu Jintao gained credibility with the hard-liners: Ibid.

356   Hu Jintao helped to install 170,000 PLA troopers: John Tkacik, Joseph Fewsmith, and Maryanne Kivlehan, "Who's Hu? Assessing China's Heir Apparent, Hu Jintao." Heritage Lecture 739, Apr. 19, 2002. FN 21 says that "the *South China Morning Post* reported on March 8, 1989, that the central government had deployed 170,000 troops (17 divisions of the PLA) to Lhasa." See http://www.heritage.org.

357   "The suffering of our people . . . upon others": Dalai Lama's Nobel Peace Prize acceptance speech is at http://www.nobel.se/peace/laureates/1989/lama-acceptance.html. "I speak not with a feeling of anger or hatred . . . we possess" is at the same site.

357   Chinese economic migrants are only temporary . . . and all of them will leave: Jiang Zemin to President Bill Clinton, during Clinton's Beijing visit.

358   China's economic bubble: Morgan Stanley's China economist Andy Xie, as quoted in Keith Bradsher, "Newest Export Out of China: Inflation Fears."

358   Modern-day map: China's external and internal borders as shown in modern maps from PRC. Not all provinces are shown, for lack of space. Tibetan-ethnolinguistic area, following Wang Lixiong, in *New Left Review*.

359   "a righteous national cause": Lixiong, "21st Century Underbelly," pp. 21–33.

359   "While the Han Chinese make up 93 per cent . . . breakup model": Ibid.

359   "victims of feudalism": Jiang Zemin, as quoted by Hillary Clinton, *Washington Post*, Oct. 19, 1997, at http://www.tibet.ca/wtnarchive/2003/6/25_2.html.

360   Jiang Zemin said, "Lincoln was a remarkable leader . . . liberating the slaves in America": "Excerpts of an Interview with Jiang Zemin," *Washington Post*, Oct. 19, 1997.

360   "must publicly . . . motherland": Lorien Holland, "Jiang Shrugs Off Protests but Acknowledges 'Mistakes.'"

360   "While it is the overwhelming desire of the Tibetan people . . . include independence": "Critical Reflections—Human Rights and the Future of Tibet," by the Dalai Lama, *Harvard International Review*, Winter 1994–95.

361   Interview with Pasang Lhamo and Chuying Kunsang, conducted by Thomas Laird in Chicago, through a translator, in April 2003. Chuying Kunsang's name has been variously transliterated as Chuye, Dhoeying, Choeying. See statement by Chuye Kunsang, published in *Half-Yearly Report*, Tibetan Center for Human Rights and Democracy, Jan.–June 2000; *Miami Herald*, Mar. 7, 2003; Amnesty International, Feb. 20, 2002.

363   five young nuns, whom they beat to death: They died on June 7, 1998. Their names are Tsultrim Zangmo (age 25), Tashi Lhamo (24), Khedron (or Kundol) Yonten (28), Drugkyi Pema (21), and Lobsang Wangmo (31); Amnesty International, 2002.

364   "Secret Tibet" by Woeser: The first three stanzas translated by Susan Chen, Jane Perkins, Bhuchung D. Sonam, Tseten Gya, Phuntsok Wangchk, Sangje Kyap, and Tenzin Tsundue, at Dharamsala on January 18, 2005. http://www.tibetwrites.org/articles/woeser/woeser.html

364   I was told that those who studied Tibet in China would be endangering their freedom if they had any conversations with me: My attempts to arrange for interviews with Chinese experts on Tibet were conducted through intermediaries who must remain anonymous, for fear of causing trouble for those in China.

365   "Look, we have to get visas . . . about this history": A prominent historian speaking on condition of anonymity.

365   Political scientists and former government officials who shape U.S. policy toward China and Tibet: Neither Perry Link nor I is the first to see a revolving door where those shaping U.S. foreign policy seem to go on to lobby for the corporations in both Washington and Beijing. Jamyang Norbu, for example, writes about this in "The Incredible Weariness of Hope."

366   "because propaganda . . . more powerful": *The Conference on the Work of External Propaganda on the Question of Tibet*, classified government document, smuggled abroad, translated, and made available by Kelsang D. Aukatsang, International Campaign for Tibet, Nov. 16, 1993.

Epilogue

373   chief elected official, Kalon Tripa Samdhong Rinpoche, says that the dialogue can . . . real: http://www.tibet.net/tibbul/2004/0102/doc2.html.

373   "This round of discussion . . . dialogue process: Statement by special envoy Lodi Gyari, head of the delegation sent by His Holiness the Dalai Lama to China, at http://www.phayul.com/news.

373   Lhakpa Phuntsog, "These two demands do not match": Laba Pincuo, in the Chinese transliteration, as used in the Reuters news report, datelined, Beijing, May 26, 2006.

374   Eleventh Panchen Lama . . . since the boy was six years old: http://www.tibetjustice.org/reports/children/epilogue/.

375   One analyst: A senior analyst of the Tibet situation, speaking on condition of anonymity.

376   "It did not help matters that the Dalai Lama himself . . . Tibetan independence": Jamyang Norbu, "The Incredible Weariness of Hope," at http://www.tibet.ca/wtnarchive/2003/10/1_1.html.

376   "So many people in this world . . . supporting our cause": From an Internet chat room frequented by Tibetans.

376   In 1998 an elderly Tibetan, Thubten Ngodup, set himself on fire: Norbu, "Incredible Weariness of Hope." The site says, "To draw world attention to the cause of Tibetan independence this former monk and ex-paratrooper doused his body with gasoline and set himself on fire."

377   "We have undertaken this hunger strike . . . through nonviolent means": "An Open Letter to Kofi Annan from Three Tibetans on Hunger Strike," *International Herald Tribune*, Apr. 29, 2004, at http://www.tibet.ca/en/wtnarchive/2004/4/28–2_1.html.

377   "You probably didn't know . . . with bombs": *New York Post*, Apr. 14, 2004.

377   "When hunger strikers are ready to take their own lives . . . very long time": Tenzin Jamyang, "Waning Health, Gaining Strength."

378   Beijing continues to insist that "the issue of Tibet is . . . integrity": Sandra Cordon, "Canada Shouldn't Flirt with Separatist Dalai Lama."

379   a special court in Spain . . . genocide against Tibet: Lisa Abend and Geoff Pingree, in *Christian Science Monitor*, Mar. 2, 2006.

379   "If you know our history . . . today's China": Elliott Almond, "Spotlight Will Reveal China's Contradictions."

379   search for a modern China: I have benefited from study of *The Search for Modern China*, by Jonathan Spence. This passage particularly benefits from Mr. Spence's thoughts as expressed on page xx, as well as the work of Okada Hidehiro, Luciano Petech, Yihong Pan, and others.

INDEX